I0815459

Words of Faith

A VOCABULARY OF PAUL THE APOSTLE

BRENDAN BYRNE, SJ

Paulist Press
New York / Mahwah, NJ

Scripture translations in this text are by the author unless noted otherwise.

Material taken from *Paul and the Economy of Salvation* by Brendan Byrne, copyright © 2021. Used by permission of Baker Academic, a division of Baker Publishing Group.

Cover image of Byzantine icon; Paul the Apostle by Asia/commons.wikimedia.org
Cover design by Sharyn Banks
Book design by Lynn Else

Library of Congress Cataloging-in-Publication Data
Names: Byrne, Brendan (Brendan J.) author.
Title: Words of faith : a vocabulary of Paul the Apostle / Brendan Byrne, SJ.
Description: New York ; Mahwah, NJ : Paulist Press, [2023] | Includes index. | Summary: "A glossary of theological themes that appear in the letters attributed to St. Paul"— Provided by publisher.
Identifiers: LCCN 2023006186 (print) | LCCN 2023006187 (ebook) | ISBN 9780809106691 (cloth) | ISBN 9781587688560 (ebook)
Subjects: LCSH: Christianity—Dictionaries. | Bible. Epistles of Paul.
Classification: LCC BR95 .B97 2023 (print) | LCC BR95 (ebook) | DDC 230.003—dc23/eng/20230629
LC record available at https://lccn.loc.gov/2023006186
LC ebook record available at https://lccn.loc.gov/2023006187

ISBN 978-0-8091-0669-1 (cloth)
ISBN 978-1-58768-856-0 (e-book)

Published by Paulist Press
997 Macarthur Boulevard
Mahwah, New Jersey 07430
www.paulistpress.com

Printed and bound in the
United States of America

CONTENTS

PREFACE

This work is the product of over four decades of teaching, research, and writing focused on the letters of the apostle Paul. As such, it basically represents my own views of his theology as distilled from the letters.

Needless to point out, the secondary literature on Paul is immense and continues to pour out in an unending stream. Almost everything one says about Paul is likely to be controversial in some respect. As it is impossible in a work of this kind to engage with scholarly discussion at any length, I have set out my own understanding drawn from reading of the texts, while indicating areas where significant alternative views are also held. The case for many of the positions that I hold is largely set out in my recent monograph, *Paul and the Economy of Salvation: Reading from the Perspective of the Last Judgment* (Grand Rapids, MI: Baker Academic, 2021). I am grateful to the publishers for permission to make use of material from this study in the present work. Although the reading section appended to each entry has itself needed to be selective, I trust that it provides a range of views on the topic discussed. I have chosen to include in this section only works in English, resisting the temptation to include works in other languages, especially German. I trust that the immense contribution of German scholarship, past and present, to the interpretation of Paul will be represented by works that are available in translation and that it will also come through my own interpretation of Paul, which is greatly indebted to it.

As a "vocabulary," this work addresses words (in English translation) Paul actually uses rather than "topics" determined from the categories of later Christian theology. There are, however, some exceptions to this rule—as, for example, in the case of "Ethics," "Eucharist," and "Sexuality." Moreover, the significance of apocalyptic and eschatology in his thought makes it imperative, I believe, to offer a separate discussion of these two intimately connected topics. I have set the entries for these two topics at the head of the work in the hope that readers will regard a consideration of them as a necessary prelude to the consultation of any subsequent entry.

In line with most recent critical interpretation of Paul, I have chosen to treat separately and primarily occurrences of words in the seven undisputed letters (Romans, 1 and 2 Corinthians, Galatians, Philippians, 1 Thessalonians, and Philemon). This means regarding Ephesians and Colossians as "deutero-Pauline" and the remaining Pauline letters (2 Thessalonians, 1 and 2 Timothy, and Titus) as "post-Pauline." While acknowledging that many specialists in the field, for good reasons, retain belief in the Pauline authorship of Colossians, and, to a lesser degree, Ephesians, I believe that to treat these letters separately is a "cleaner" way to proceed. In so doing, I in no way wish to communicate a sense of these two letters as in any way "inferior" in the depth or richness of their theology. In some areas, for example, "Church," "Mystery," and "Principalities and Powers," their contribution has to be discussed in equal or greater measure than that of the undisputed seven. This is rarely the case in regard to the post-Pauline letters and, while separate treatment is required in some cases, elsewhere their contribution can simply be indicated in the major discussion by references headed "see also" and so on.

Needless to say, many passages in the letters are significant for the discussion of more than one topic. To avoid unnecessary repetition where this is the case, I have, in many cases, instructed the reader to "see" entries that provide the most substantial discussion of the topic in question. I trust that reader will not be inconvenienced by this stratagem designed to keep the total work down to a manageable size.

This project was originally intended to be part of a series consisting of works of much smaller size. I am indebted to Paulist Press, particularly its Editorial Director Paul McMahon, for allowing me to go ahead with a work on the much larger scale that the scope and theological richness of Paul's vocabulary appeared to require.

I came to appreciate the editorial skills of the Reverend Dr. Ronald D. Witherup, PSS, when composing my contribution ("Matthew") to the *Paulist Biblical Commentary* (2018). I was accordingly delighted that Ron, despite his high responsibilities as Sulpician superior general and multiple other commitments, graciously accepted the invitation of Paulist Press to act in a similar capacity for the present volume. Ron's keen editorial eye, his wide theological learning, his comprehensive knowledge of Paul and current Pauline scholarship, have saved me from many a pitfall and greatly enhanced the quality of the work. In the editorial connection, I must also acknowledge the assistance of Dr. José Enrique Aguilar Chiu of St. Joseph's Seminary in Dunwoodie, New York, and many others at Paulist Press, who have helped bring this project to a successful conclusion.

"Whatever was written in former days was written for our instruction, so that by steadfastness and by the encouragement of the Scriptures we might have hope" (Rom 15:4 NRSV).

Brendan Byrne, SJ
Jesuit Theological College
University of Divinity (Melbourne)
May 1, 2022

ABBREVIATIONS

ABD	*Anchor Bible Dictionary*. Edited by D. N. Freedman. 6 vols. New York: Doubleday, 1992.
ABR	*Australian Biblical Review*
Barclay, *Gift*	Barclay, John M. G. *Paul and the Gift*. Grand Rapids: Eerdmans, 2016.
Barclay, *Obeying the Truth*	Barclay, J. M. G. *Obeying the Truth: Paul's Ethics in Galatians*. Minneapolis: Fortress, 1988; repr. Vancouver, BC: Regent College Publishing, 2005.
Barrett, *Freedom*	Barrett, C. K. *Freedom and Obligation: A Study of the Epistle to the Galatians*. Philadelphia: Westminster, 1985.
BDAG	*Greek-English Lexicon of the New Testament and Other Early Christian Literature*. Edited by F. W. Danker, W. Bauer, W. F. Arndt, and F. W. Gingrich. 3rd ed. Chicago: University of Chicago Press, 2000.
Becker, *Paul*	Becker, Jürgen. *Paul: Apostle to the Gentiles*. Louisville: Westminster/John Knox, 1993.
Beker, *Paul the Apostle*	Beker, H. Christiaan. *Paul the Apostle: The Triumph of God in Life and Thought*. Philadelphia: Fortress, 1980.
Bib	*Biblica*
BJRL	*Bulletin of the John Rylands Library*
Byrne, "Glory"	Byrne, Brendan. "'Glory' as Apostolic Credibility in 2 Corinthians 2:14–4:18," *ABR* 66 (2018): 13–30.
Byrne, "Jerusalems"	Byrne, Brendan. "Jerusalems Above and Below: A Critique of J. L. Martyn's Interpretation of the Hagar-Sarah Allegory in Gal 4:21—5:1," *NTS* 60 (2014): 215–31.
Byrne, "Living Out"	Byrne, Brendan. "Living Out the Righteousness of God: The Contribution of Rom 6:1—8:13 to an

	Understanding of Paul's Ethical Presuppositions," *CBQ* 43 (1981): 557–81.
Byrne, *PES*	Byrne, Brendan. *Paul and the Economy of Salvation: Reading from the Perspective of the Last Judgment*. Grand Rapids: Baker Academic, 2021.
Byrne, *Romans*	Byrne, Brendan. *Romans*. Sacra Pagina 6. Collegeville, MN: Glazier, 1996.
Byrne, *"Sons of God"*	Byrne, Brendan. *"Sons of God"—"Seed of Abraham": A Study of the Idea of the Sonship of God of All Christians in Paul against the Jewish Background*. AnBib 83. Rome: Biblical Institute Press, 1979.
Bultmann, *Theology*	Bultmann, Rudolf. *Theology of the New Testament*. Translated by Kendrick Grobel. 2 vols. London: SCM, 1952–1955.
Campbell, *Deliverance*	Campbell, Douglas A. *The Deliverance of God: An Apocalyptic Rereading of Justification in Paul*. Grand Rapids: Eerdmans, 2009.
CBQ	*Catholic Biblical Quarterly*
CurBR	*Currents in Biblical Research*
DPL	*Dictionary of Paul and His Letters*. Edited by Gerald F. Hawthorne and Ralph P. Martin. Downers Grove, IL: Intervarsity, 1993.
DRev	*Downside Review*
Dunn, *Beginning*	Dunn, James D. G. *Beginning from Jerusalem*. Grand Rapids: Eerdmans, 2009.
Dunn, *Romans 1–8*	Dunn, James D. G. *Romans 1–8*. WBC 38A: Dallas: Word, 1988.
Dunn, *Romans 9–16*	Dunn, James D. G. *Romans 9–16*. WBC 38B: Dallas: Word, 1988.
Dunn, *Theology*	Dunn, James D. G. *A Theology of Paul the Apostle*. Grand Rapids: Eerdmans, 1998.
Dunn, *CCP*	*The Cambridge Companion to Paul*. Edited by James D. G. Dunn. Cambridge: Cambridge University Press, 2003.
EBR	*Encyclopedia of the Bible and Its Reception*. Edited by Hans-Josef Klauck, et al. Berlin: de Gruyter, 2009–.

ECB	*Eerdmans Commentary on the Bible*. Edited by James D. G. Dunn and J. W. Rogerson. Grand Rapids: Eerdmans, 2003.
EDNT	*Exegetical Dictionary of the New Testament*. Edited by Horst Balz and Gerhard Schneider. 3 vols. Grand Rapids: Eerdmans, 1990–93.
Fee, *1 Corinthians*	Fee, Gordon D. *The First Epistle to the Corinthians*. NICNT; rev. ed. Grand Rapids: Eerdmans, 2014.
Fee, *God's Empowering Presence*	Fee, Gordon D. *God's Empowering Presence: The Holy Spirit in the Letters of Paul*. Peabody, MA: Hendrickson, 1994.
Fee, *Pauline Christology*	Fee, Gordon D. *Pauline Christology: An Exegetical-Theological Study*. Peabody, MA: Hendrickson, 2007.
Fitzmyer, *1 Corinthians*	Fitzmyer, Joseph A. *First Corinthians*. AB 32. New Haven and London: Yale University Press, 2008.
Fitzmyer, *Romans*	Fitzmyer, Joseph A. *Romans*. AB 33. New York: Doubleday, 1993.
Gaventa, *Apocalyptic Paul*	*Apocalyptic Paul: Cosmos and Anthropos in Romans 5–8*. Edited by Beverly Roberts Gaventa. Waco, TX: Baylor University Press, 2013.
Gorman, *Apostle*	Gorman, Michael J. *Apostle of the Crucified Lord: A Theological Introduction to Paul and His Letters*. 2nd ed. Grand Rapids: Eerdmans, 2017.
Harris, *2 Corinthians*	Harris, Murray J. *The Second Epistle to the Corinthians: A Commentary on the Greek Text*. NIGTC. Grand Rapids: Eerdmans, 2005.
Hays, *Echoes*	Hays, Richard B. *Echoes of Scripture in the Letters of Paul*. New Haven: Yale University Press, 1989.
HBD	*HarperCollins Bible Dictionary*. Edited by Mark Alan Powell et al. 3rd ed. New York: HarperOne, 2011.
Holloway, *Philippians*	Holloway, Paul A. *Philippians: A Commentary*. Edited by Adela Yarbro Collins. Minneapolis: Fortress, 2017.
Horrell, *Introduction*	Horrell, David G. *An Introduction to the Study of Paul*. 3rd ed. London: T&T Clark, 2015.

HTR	*Harvard Theological Review*
Hurtado, *Lord Jesus Christ*	Hurtado, Larry W. *Lord Jesus Christ: Devotion to Jesus in Earliest Christianity*. Grand Rapids: Eerdmans, 2003.
Int	*Interpretation*
JBL	*Journal of Biblical Literature*
Jewett, *Anthropological Terms*	Jewett, Robert. *Paul's Anthropological Terms*. Leiden: Brill, 1971.
JRE	*Journal of Religious Ethics*
JSNT	*Journal for the Study of the New Testament*
JTS	*Journal of Theological Studies*
Käsemann, *Essays*	Käsemann, Ernst. *Essays on New Testament Themes*. London: SCM, 1964.
Käsemann, *Perspectives*	Käsemann, Ernst. *Perspectives on Paul*. Philadelphia: Fortress, 1971.
Lincoln, *Ephesians*	Lincoln, Andrew T. *Ephesians*. WBC 42; Nashville: Nelson, 1990.
Lincoln, "Colossians"	Lincoln, Andrew T. "The Letter to the Colossians," *NIB* 11:551–669.
LSJ	Liddell, Henry George, Robert Scott, and Henry Stuart Jones. *A Greek-English Lexicon*. 9th ed., with revised supplement. Oxford: Clarendon, 1996.
Matera, *GSG*	Matera, Frank J. *God's Saving Grace: A Pauline Theology*. Grand Rapids: Eerdmans, 2012.
Moo, *Romans*	Moo, Douglas J. *The Epistle to the Romans*. NICNT. Grand Rapids: Eerdmans, 1996.
MSJ	*The Master's Seminary Journal*
NIB	*The New Interpreter's Bible*. Edited by Leander E. Keck. 12 vols. Nashville: Abingdon, 1994–2004.
NIDB	*New Interpreter's Dictionary of the Bible*. Edited by Katherine Doob Sakenfeld. 5 vols. Nashville: Abingdon, 2006–2009.
NTS	*New Testament Studies*

OEBT	*The Oxford Encyclopedia of the Bible and Theology*. Edited by Samuel E. Ballantine. 2 vols. Oxford: Oxford University Press, 2015.
OED	*The New Shorter Oxford English Dictionary*. Edited by Lesley Brown. 2 vols. Oxford: Clarendon, 1993.
PBC	*Paulist Biblical Commentary*. Edited by José Enrique Aguilar Chiu et al. Mahwah, NJ: Paulist Press, 2018.
PRSt	*Perspectives in Religious Studies*
Rainbow, *Way of Salvation*	Rainbow, Paul A. *The Way of Salvation: The Role of Christian Obedience in Justification*. Milton Keynes: Paternoster, 2005; repr. Eugene, OR: Wipf & Stock, 2012.
Sampley, *Paul*	*Paul in the Greco-Roman World*. Edited by J. Paul Sampley. 2 vols. 2nd ed. London: Bloomsbury T&T Clark, 2016.
Sanders, *Paul*	Sanders, E. P. *Paul: The Apostle's Life, Letters, and Thought*. Minneapolis: Fortress, 2018.
Schnelle, *Apostle Paul*	Schnelle, Udo. *Apostle Paul: His Life and Theology*. Translated by M. Eugene Boring. Grand Rapids: Baker Academic, 2005.
ScrB	*Scripture Bulletin*
SJT	*Scottish Journal of Theology*
Stacey, *Pauline View of Man*	Stacey, W. David. *The Pauline View of Man*. London: Macmillan, 1956.
TBT	*The Bible Today*
TDNT	*Theological Dictionary of the New Testament*. Edited by Gerhard Kittel and Gerhard Friedrich. 10 vols. Grand Rapids: Eerdmans, 1964–76.
TS	*Theological Studies*
Thiselton, *1 Corinthians*	Thiselton, Anthony C. *The First Epistle to the Corinthians*. NIGTC. Grand Rapids: Eerdmans, 2000.
WBC	*Word Biblical Commentary*
Wells, *Grace and Agency*	Wells, Kyle B. *Grace and Agency in Paul and Second Temple Judaism: Interpreting the Transformation of the Heart*. NovTSup 157. Leiden: Brill, 2015.

Westerholm, *Justification*	Westerholm, Stephen. *Justification Reconsidered: Rethinking a Pauline Theme*. Grand Rapids: Eerdmans, 2013.
Westerholm, *Paul*	Westerholm, Stephen, ed. *The Blackwell Companion to Paul*. Oxford: Wiley–Blackwell, 2011.
Westerholm, *Perspectives*	Westerholm, Stephen. *Perspectives Old and New on Paul: The "Lutheran" Paul and His Critics*. Grand Rapids: Eerdmans, 2004.
Wolter, *Paul*	Wolter, Michael. *Paul: An Outline of His Theology*. Translated by Robert L. Brawley. Waco, TX: Baylor University Press, 2011.
Wright, *PFG*	Wright, N. T. *Paul and the Faithfulness of God*. 2 vols. *Christian Origins and the Question of God* 4. Minneapolis: Fortress, 2013.
Wright, "Romans"	Wright, N. T. "The Letter to the Romans," *NIB* 10:303–770.
ZNW	*Zeitschrift für die neutestamentliche Wissenschaft*

READ ME FIRST

Apocalyptic and Eschatology

APOCALYPTIC

For well over a century and increasingly in recent decades, it has been recognized that the conceptual background to Paul's theology is that of Jewish apocalypticism. Strictly speaking, as the derivation of the term from the Greek suggests, what makes a text apocalyptic is the presentation of its contents as something received by "revelation." (The Greek word *apokalypsis* literally means "uncovering" or "unveiling" and hence "revelation.") A spiritually privileged person—a prophet or seer—through dreams or interviews with angels or through being taken on a heavenly tour receives information regarding the future or an interpretation of the present from a divine point of view. The written communication of revelation received in this way results in the literary genre "apocalypse," of which the most familiar examples would be the biblical Book of Daniel and the Book of Revelation ("the Apocalypse") that concludes the canonical New Testament.

The description "apocalyptic," however, is applied to works beyond those strictly derived from revelation in the form described above. It refers to various expressions of thinking, imagining, analyzing, and hoping to be found in the Book of Daniel and many documents of postbiblical early Judaism, including the Dead Sea Scrolls, and the New Testament, beginning with Paul. Rather than giving a definition that covers all aspects of apocalyptic in a synthetic way, it is more helpful to list features that are typical of the literature as a whole.

1. The doctrine of the **Two Ages**. The **present** age has fallen irreversibly into a sinful state of corruption and alienation from God. As such, it will soon be brought to an end by God, who will intervene and institute a great **judgment**, in which the present evil age will be condemned and destroyed in an exercise of divine **wrath**,

while the faithful righteous will be vindicated ("justified") and enjoy forever a **new** age under the triumphant rule of God.

2. **Dualism**. There is not only a radical discontinuity between the present and the new age but also a contest between the forces of good and evil. Great pessimism prevails regarding human capacity for good. All hope rests on the intervention of God.
3. **Cosmic** scale. While often having Palestine or Jerusalem as a focal point, the coming transformation will take place on a universal scale, involving not only the entire earth and humanity as such but also heaven and the underworld.
4. **Individual responsibility**. The fate of people is not determined by their belonging to communal entities (e.g., Israel); rather, each individual will be accountable on their own to God.
5. The moral degeneration of the present age is attributed to the malign influence of **Satan** and other **evil spiritual powers**.
6. **Determinism**. All has been predetermined by God according to a plan that is unfolding in fixed periods, knowledge of which, while hidden from all eternity, is the subject of revelation to privileged recipients.
7. In most apocalyptic scenarios, a **Mediator** or **Savior** figure will be the instrument of the divine intervention, although there is great variety in the way such a figure is presented: for example, a superior angel (e.g., Michael); transcendent Son of Man as eschatological judge; Davidic Messiah; and so on.
8. Discourse of an apocalyptic nature is marked by **vivid** and **extreme imagery** depicting upheavals and calamities on a cosmic scale—earthquakes, stars falling from heaven, moon turning into blood, and so on.
9. **Resurrection**: following the Book of Daniel (see 12:2), many texts of an apocalyptic nature feature the general resurrection of the dead as a measure bringing those who have died before the judgment seat of God to receive their reward: good or ill, as the case may be.

Apocalyptic discourse tends to arise in communities under extreme social and religious pressure, especially in situations of persecution, where the faithful, despairing of human resources, feel they can look to God alone for salvation. The apocalyptic movement is the successor of prophecy in ancient Israel. But whereas the prophets foretold calamities and pointed to hopes that would emerge on a this-worldly historical scale—for example, from foreign nations and rulers—apocalyptic speculation ranges beyond the terrestrial to embrace the whole of reality: heavenly, earthly, and infernal. Perhaps its most characteristic feature is the expectation of an imminent great judgment.

Virtually all of these features appear in some form in the theology of Paul. However, the distinctive nature of the divine intervention in Christ demanded of Paul a radical reinterpretation of the apocalyptic expectation that, as a devout Pharisee, he brought to his faith in Messiah Jesus, especially a total revisioning in the area of eschatology (see ESCHATOLOGY).

Reading

D. E. Aune, *DPL*, 25–35; Beker, *Paul the Apostle*, 135–81; Byrne, *PES*, 9–34; "Apocalyptic as God's Eschatological Activity in Paul's Theology," in *Paul and the Apocalyptic Imagination*, ed. B. C. Blackwell, J. K. Goodrich, and J. Maston (Minneapolis: Fortress, 2016), 45–63; Campbell, *Deliverance*, 188–92; J. J. Collins, *The Apocalyptic Imagination: An Introduction to Jewish Apocalyptic Literature*, 3rd ed. (Grand Rapids: Eerdmans, 2016); J. Davies, *Apocalyptic Paul: Retrospect and Prospect* (Eugene, OR: Wipf & Stock, 2022); M. de Boer, "Paul and Apocalyptic Eschatology," in *The Origins of Apocalypticism in Judaism and Christianity*, ed. J. J. Collins (vol. 1 of *The Encyclopedia of Apocalypticism* [New York: Continuum, 1999]), 345–83; P. D. Hanson, "Apocalypse, Genre; Apocalypticism," in *IDBSup* 27–34; *The Dawn of Apocalyptic: The Historical and Sociological Roots of Jewish Apocalyptic Eschatology*, rev. ed. (Philadelphia: Fortress, 1979); J. L. Martyn, "Apocalyptic Antinomies," in *Theological Issues in the Letters of Paul* (Nashville: Abingdon, 1997), 111–23; *Galatians*, AB 33A (New York: Doubleday, 1997), 35–41, 97–105; D. S. Russell, *The Method and Message of Jewish Apocalyptic: 200 BC–AD 100* (London: SCM, 1964).

ESCHATOLOGY

Eschatology derives from the Greek term *eschatos*, which means "last." It attempts to indicate or describe the final acts or events to take place in the cosmic drama: the end of the (present) world or at least its radical transformation. Concepts such as the resurrection of the dead, the final judgment, and post-earthly rewards (positive or negative) are eschatological because they belong to an era beyond the limit of present human existence.

The apocalyptic worldview, since it foresees a more or less imminent intervention of God, is in most of its manifestations thoroughly eschatological. At its heart is the radical division between the present age and the age to come, separated by the divine intervention and the judgment.

Paul's Eschatology: The Overlap of the Ages

Paul's eschatological understanding had to undergo a decisive transformation following his encounter with the once-crucified and now risen Messiah on the Damascus road (Gal 1:15–16). Coming to faith in Christ meant accepting that the divine intervention had already taken place in the sending of the Son (Rom 8:3–4; Gal 4:4–5), in the saving effects his death on a cross, and in his vindication in being raised from the dead (Rom 4:25; 5:10). God had in effect initiated the last judgment, condemning human sin, while at the same time graciously offering justification, reconciliation, and renewed relationship with human beings simply on the basis of faith (Rom 3:21–26). God had sent the Holy Spirit, the power of the new age, into the hearts of believers as a guarantee of the new relationship with God and the hope of full salvation that it held out (Rom 5:5; 8:4–11, 15–16, 23; Gal 3:2–5, 14; 4:6–7).

All this meant the breaking down of the neat division between the present (evil) age and the age to come according to conventional apocalyptic understanding. There is now an "interpenetration" or, better, a situation of "overlap" between the ages hitherto unforeseen. God's intervention in Christ has created a "space" of time when believers, as attested by the Spirit (Rom 5:5), enjoy the relationship with God characteristic of the new age—the new creation, in effect (2 Cor 5:17; Gal 6:15)—while bodily still tied to the conditions of the present, with its characteristic trials of weakness, suffering, and death. The full sharing of the risen life of Christ, and hence the full measure of salvation, must await the resurrection of the body. The distinct ethical challenge that ensues is that in their present life in the body believers must live the values of the new creation in the prevailing conditions of the old. Though still physically "in" the flesh, they have to live, not "according" to the flesh—Paul's term for the conditions of the present era—but "according to the Spirit" (Rom 8:4–13; Gal 5:16–26).

A great deal of Paul's pastoral advice and admonition addresses this situation of living in the "overlap of the ages" time that is the present lot of believers. Though already justified (Rom 5:1) and in this sense already passed through the judgment, believers, empowered by the Spirit, must live out the righteousness that has been graciously gifted to them in Christ. They remain in this sense accountable at a reckoning yet to come (Rom 14:10b–12; 2 Cor 5:10; see also 1 Cor 3:13–15; 4:4–5), although in Romans 8:31–39, Paul evokes the final judgment more as an assurance of hope stemming from God's love than in any sense as a threat.

The Day of the Lord

Nonetheless, Paul's entire interaction with the communities to which his letters are addressed takes place under the horizon of the looming "day of the Lord" (1 Cor 1:8; 5:5; 2 Cor 1:14; Phil 1:10; 2:16; 1 Thess 5:2; see 2 Thess 2:2; 2 Tim 1:18; 4:8). To calm anxiety in Thessalonica over the fate of believers who have already died, Paul offers a description of the scenario he envisages on that day (1 Thess 4:13–18). The picture is filled out in 1 Corinthians 15 with less attention to heavenly phenomena and more to the transformation of human existence when Christ completes his messianic role with the conquest of death and subjection of the universe to the rule of God (15:23–28, 35–57; see 2 Cor 5:1–5).

The Eschatology of the Deutero-Pauline Letters

The tension between aspects of the divine saving plan that believers already experience and those still outstanding remains in the deutero-Pauline letters, although the focus is far more on the present than the future. God's decisive intervention in Christ has broken the grip of the powers of darkness and transferred believers into the kingdom of the beloved Son (Col 1:13). Where in Romans believers' participation in the resurrection of Christ is cast into the future (6:5, 8), in Colossians 2:12–13 they are already raised with him. Indeed, albeit in a hidden way, they already share the life of the exalted Christ in heaven (3:1–3). Nonetheless, there is a revelation of their glory still to come (v. 4), which in continuity with texts such as Romans 8:18–19 suggests that bodily resurrection, although not explicitly mentioned, remains an expectation. Moreover, in a negative vein, the writer speaks of the wrath that is coming on those who are disobedient (Col 3:6) and also, positively, of the inheritance that will be the reward of faithful service (v. 24). Such allusions indicate that a fading of the eschatological hope is far from complete.

The move toward a more realized eschatology is further advanced in Ephesians. Christ's subjection of the authorities and powers that is still a work in progress according to 1 Corinthians 15:24–28 has already been accomplished (Eph 1:20–23). The divine plan to bring all things to unity in Christ (1:10), especially the overcoming of the division between Jews and Gentiles, is already manifest in the church (2:14–18; 3:6, 10). As in Colossians, believers have been raised with Christ and sit with him in heaven (2:5–6). Yes, the church still has to grow to the full stature of its Head (Christ) (4:12–13, 24) and believers have received the Holy Spirit as a seal for "the day of redemption" (v. 30). Yet, aside from that brief allusion to a liberation still to come, there is no mention of the coming of Christ or final judgment

The Eschatology of the Post-Pauline Letters

The post-Pauline letters situate the present existence of believers between the two "appearances" of Christ: the first (2 Tim 1:10; Titus 2:11; 3:4) and the second (1 Tim 6:14; 2 Tim 4:1; Titus 2:13). All are called so to live as to be worthy, at the coming of Christ, to take hold of the (eternal) life that "really is life" (1 Tim 6:19; see 4:8–10; 6:12; 2 Tim 1:10; Titus 3:7). Eschatology is a particular concern of the author of 2 Thessalonians who is at pains to counter any suggestion that the day of the Lord has already taken place. That cannot occur until a malevolent force, "the lawless one," who is currently being restrained, is revealed (2:3, 7). Then, the Lord Jesus, will destroy him with the breath of his mouth (v. 8).

Reading

D. E. Aune, "Eschatology (Early Christian)," *ABD* 2:594–609, esp. 602–3; Beker, *Paul the Apostle*, 135–81; B. Byrne, "Eschatologies of Resurrection and Destruction: the Ethical Significance of Paul's Dispute with the Corinthians," *DRev* 104/ No. 357 (October 1986): 288–98; *PES*, 3, 9–16, 130–31, 177–78, 211–24, 234–39, 241–45; Dunn, *Theology*, 461–72, 407–98; Horrell, *Introduction*, 95–100; L. J. Kreitzer, *DPL*, 253–69; A. T. Lincoln, *Paradise Now and Not Yet: Studies in the Role of the Heavenly Dimension in Paul's Thought with Special Reference to His Eschatology* (Cambridge: Cambridge University Press, 1981); Schnelle, *Apostle Paul*, 577–97; B. Witherington, *Jesus, Paul, and the End of the World* (Downers Grove, IL: Intervarsity, 1992); Wolter, *Paul*, 177–220.

A

ABRAHAM

As shown by extensive arguments from Scripture in Romans and Galatians, the patriarch Abraham is a truly significant biblical figure for Paul (Rom 4:1–25; 9:6–9; Gal 3:1–29; 4:21–31; see also Rom 11:1; 2 Cor 11:22). The significance stems from the patriarch's prominence in the Jewish tradition within which Paul was conducting his polemical arguments in Romans and Galatians. Abraham is not merely the ancestor of the Jewish nation. He has a truly representative role in the sense that the stance he took before God, the choices he made, and the promises that he received remain paradigmatic and determinative for his descendants and for the nation as a whole. One cannot "define" Israel, without "defining" Abraham and what it means to be his descendants and hence heirs to the promises he received concerning the messianic age (see 2 Cor 1:20).

In the biblical and postbiblical Jewish tradition, Abraham features above all as a figure of obedience and trust. His fulfillment of the circumcision command (Gen 17:9–14, 23–27) was taken to be an anticipatory fulfillment of the Mosaic law (Sir 44:19–20). In this respect Abraham modeled the kind of torah obedience seen to be necessary if one was to be pronounced righteous ("justified) at the last judgment and so gain salvation.

Abraham in Romans

Paul had to counter this tradition in order to establish and sustain the truth of the gospel according to which the eschatological righteousness was not to be gained through practice of the torah ("works of the law" [Rom 3:20; Gal 2:16]) but rather through an obedience of faith (Rom 1:5; see 16:26). This meant claiming Abraham primarily as a person of faith and as a receiver of the promise concerning the messianic age solely on that basis. The scriptural passage that served well in this task was Genesis 15. Following Abraham's complaint that he continued childless, lacking an heir in the direct line (vv. 2–3), God promised that he would have a son and a vast progeny (vv. 4–5). Abraham put his trust in this promise: "Abraham believed the Lord, and the Lord reckoned it to him as righteousness" (v. 6; cited Rom 4:3; Gal 3:6). The gold in this sentence for Paul was its linkage of faith and being reckoned righteous by God aside from any mention of obedience. Moreover, the same chapter 15 of Genesis features a second divine promise: to bestow on his descendants (literally, "seed" [*sperma*]) the land, in vast extent, on which he presently lived (15:18–21). This second ("land") promise (see also

12:7; 13:15; 17:8; 24:7) had undergone considerable development in the postbiblical Jewish tradition to include, beyond Canaan, the entire world, and then, in a transcendent sense, all the blessings of the messianic age (see PROMISE).

To be in line to receive these blessings—to "inherit the earth" in this sense (Rom 4:13)—one had to be "seed" (a descendant) of Abraham, the proto-father of Israel. The question then concerns the basis on which one could claim to be an heir in this sense. In the Jewish tradition, the inheritance came through natural descent; Abraham was "our father according to the flesh" (Rom 4:1). But Paul exploited further texts of Genesis, such as 17:4–5, where God promised Abraham that he was to be the "father of many nations" (see Rom 4:17), and also 12:3 and 18:18, which spoke of all the nations being "blessed in him" (see Gal 3:8). Since the Greek word for "nations," *ethnē*, serves equally for "Gentiles," Paul could argue from these references that Abraham was not only "father" of Jews but, in a distinctive way, also "father" of Gentiles. He was father of Gentiles precisely through putting his faith in God and finding justification when he himself was "ungodly," that is, in a "Gentile" position before God (Rom 4:5). His fatherhood, then, was a fatherhood of faith in a God who justifies the ungodly, and it was in virtue of such faith that he received the promise for himself and for all who would become his "descendants" by following him in faith. In this way, Paul wrested the fatherhood of Abraham away from fleshly descent (v. 1) to establish its consisting primarily in faith, thereby opening up justification and the inheritance of the promise to people of faith, both Jewish and Gentile, away from restriction to those who pursue the way of the torah (Rom 4:11b–12; Gal 3:6–9).

In Romans 4:17–25, Paul establishes a further parity between Abraham and his believing progeny as he explores what belief in the first ("son") promise (Gen 15:5) entailed. Granted his advanced age, the reproductive capacity of his body was "as good as dead," as was also the womb of his wife, Sarah (Rom 4:19). Belief in the promise that he would have a son meant believing in a God "who gives life to the dead and calls into existence the things that do not exist" (v. 17b). Christian faith matches this belief in the sense that at its center stands belief in the God who raised Jesus Christ from the dead (v. 24). Moreover, just as Abraham put his faith in a divine promise that would be fulfilled only when his son was born, his believing necessarily involved an aspect of hope (vv. 20–21). Christian faith likewise involves an element of hope in that, while focused directly on the resurrection of Christ (Rom 4:24; 10:9; 1 Thess 4:14), it involves hope that the God who raised Christ from the dead will also raise the mortal bodies of believers (Rom 8:11; see also 1 Cor 15:1–22; 2 Cor 4:13–14). In this sense Abraham is as much a paradigm for believers in respect to hope as in respect to faith.

Paul further exploits this "promise" aspect of Abraham's faith as he takes up the issue of Israel's continuing resistance to the gospel in Romans 9:6–9. The birth of Isaac consequent to a promise enables Paul to detach the line of salvation from a strictly "fleshly" (i.e., ethnic) line of descent to allow God to operate with sovereign freedom, independent of human right or merit (vv. 10–23).

Abraham in Galatians

In Galatians 3:6–9, as in Romans 4, Paul appeals to Genesis 15:6 to redefine Abraham as a figure of faith. He then decisively privileges the covenant (*diathēkē*) God made with Abraham (see Gen 15:7–21) over against the Sinai covenant that introduced obedience to law (see Exod 24:3–8). In Galatians 3:15–18, Paul uses the image of a human will (*diathēkē*) to make clear that the Sinai covenant, coming some four hundred years later, could not displace or introduce new conditions (namely, obedience to the Mosaic law) into the prior covenant focused on a single descendant, namely Christ (v. 16). Through faith and baptism believers enter "into" Christ and so become in him heirs of the promise God made to Abraham (vv. 27–29). In this sense Paul draws a straight line between Abraham and Christ, including believers in a covenant that would come into force in the messianic age, whereas the Sinai covenant is a temporary dispensation introduced not to provide justification but to call out human sin (vv. 19, 22; see 2 Cor 3:6–18). The Abrahamic covenant is a dispensation of freedom, in contrast to the Sinai covenant, which is one of slavery (Gal 4:21–5:1). In a sense, Paul extradites Abraham from his original context, making him a paradigm of true response to God in the messianic age. He even speaks of Abraham's having received a "pre-evangelization" in this respect (Gal 3:8).

BLESSING; CIRCUMCISION; COVENANT; FAITH; GENTILES; ISRAEL; LOVE; PROMISE

Reading

Beker, *Paul the Apostle*, 47–52, 100–102; Byrne, "Jerusalems," 215–31; *PES*, 103–5, 178–81; *Romans*, 141–43, 144–62; N. L. Calvert, *DPL*, 1–8; S. J. Gathercole, *Where Is Boasting? Early Jewish Soteriology and Paul's Response in Romans 1–5* (Grand Rapids, Cambridge: Eerdmans, 2002), 233–51; Moo, *Romans* 255–57; Schnelle, *Apostle Paul*, 286–88, 292–94, 323–26; Wright, *PFG*, 783–95.

ADAM

Explicit references to Adam in the letters of Paul are few: Romans 5:14; 1 Corinthians 15:22, 45 (see 1 Tim 2:13–14). This paucity belies the significance of the ancestor of the human race in Pauline theology. In Romans 5:12–21, Paul sets up an extended comparison/contrast between Christ and a figure he refers to over and over as "one man." Writing to a community he has not himself founded or instructed, he simply presumes when he begins the passage that his Roman audience will immediately recognize that "one man" as Adam. Writing in 1 Corinthians 15:22 to a community he has founded, he simply asserts, "As in Adam all die…," presuming that this statement needs no further explanation because he is alluding to an accepted tenet. Because these Adamic statements are made so much in passing, they testify to the existence in early Christian communities of a tradition about Adam as the instigator of a legacy of sin and death in the human race.

A tradition concerning Adam as instigator of death has its parallels in several documents of the postbiblical Jewish tradition (4 Ezra 3:7; 2 Bar 17:2–3; 23:4; 48:42–43; LAB 13:8; Apoc Mos 14:2–3; CD III, 20; 1QS IV, 23; 4Q171 III, 1). Less evident is the sense of Adam as responsible for the transmission of sin (but see 4 Ezra 3:21–22). While some of these documents postdate the writings of Paul, it is likely that in setting up Adam as a foil to Christ he was drawing on a preexisting Jewish tradition.

Adam in Romans 5:12–21

In the reiterated comparison/contrast in Romans 5:12–21, Adam and Christ are similar in that both are individual figures who had an influence of universal significance on others. In every other respect they are dissimilar. Where Adam instigated a legacy of sin leading to death, Christ has instigated a legacy of righteousness, leading to life. In neither case is the influence automatic. The final relative clause in Romans 5:12d ("for this reason that all sinned" [*eph' hō pantes hēmarton*]) indicates human ratification of the legacy of sin received from the ancestor, a ratification that Paul believes to have been factually universal (besides Rom 5:12d, see also 3:23; 11:32a; Gal 3:22a). Likewise, on the positive side, although Christ died for all, human beings do not benefit from his death without entering into his legacy through faith and baptism, and living out the gift of righteousness they have thereby received (Rom 5:17; see 8:4–13; Gal 5:5–6). Over and over again, however (Rom 5:16, 17, 18, 19, 20b, 21), Paul makes the case for hope on the basis that the gift of grace and righteousness available in Christ is so much more powerful than the legacy of sin and death inherited from Adam.

In 1 Corinthians 15, in the face of those who say there is no resurrection of the dead (v. 12), Paul argues that belief in the resurrection of Christ (the fundamental tenet of Christian faith: vv. 3–11) so necessarily implies belief in the resurrection of the dead that the denial of the latter inevitably means denial of the former, and hence the collapse of all benefit from the saving work of Christ (vv. 13–19). Christ has been raised as "the first fruits" of those who have died, the "harvest" image implying the eventual raising of the rest (v. 20):

> [21] For since death came through a human being, so also through a human being has come the resurrection of the dead; [22] for as all die in the Adam, so also in the Christ all will be made alive. (author's translation)

The references with the definite article in verse 22 argue for a corporate sense in both cases. As Adam embodies all humanity in a solidarity of death, Christ embodies a human solidarity destined through faith and baptism to share in his risen life (see also Rom 6:3–11; 1 Cor 12:12–13; Gal 3:27–28).

Later (1 Cor 15:35–49), attempting to explain the possibility of the resurrection body, Paul writes in the same antithetic mode:

> [44b] If there is a physical body, there is also a spiritual body. [45] Thus it is written, "*The first man, Adam, became a living being*" (Gen 2:7); the last Adam became a life-giving spirit.... [47] The first man was from

> the earth, a man of dust; the second man is from heaven. [48] As was the man of dust, so are those who are of the dust; and as is the man of heaven, so are those who are of heaven. [49] Just as we have borne the image of the man of dust, we will also bear the image of the man of heaven. (NRSV, italics added)

Paul quotes Genesis 2:7 to stress that Adam, being a "man of dust," could only transmit mortal life to those begotten "in his image" (see Gen 5:3), whereas the risen Christ, as "last Adam" (*ho eschatos Adam*), became in his resurrection (see Rom 1:4) "*life-giving* Spirit" (*pneuma zōopoioun*), and so a transmitter of resurrection life. As in our human mortality we have borne the image of the first Adam, so we shall bear the likeness of the risen Christ, the "man of heaven" (v. 49).

Adam as Paradigm Sinner

Paul obviously believed that Adam existed historically as the first human being. However, the protopatriarch is significant not only as an instigator of a regime of sin in humanity but also as a paradigm of human sinning in the face of an explicit command of God. In Romans 7:7–12, Paul describes what he believes to be Israel's fatal confrontation with the Mosaic law at Sinai in a first-person singular account that appears to evoke Adam's similarly fatal encounter with the prohibition against eating the fruit of a particular tree. The law introduced the possibility of defying the express will of God in a way that harked back to the prohibition in Genesis 2:16–17; 3:2–3, 11. Hence Paul could present Israel as placed in an "Adamic" situation in this sense.

Adam and the Fall of Creation

In the apocalyptic sequence in Romans 8:19–21 a further allusion to the "Fall" narrative in Genesis 3 describes the eager longing of "creation" (the non-human remainder of creation; see CREATION) for liberation on the basis that its subjection to "futility" was not something for which it was responsible; the subjection came about "because of the subduer" (*dia ton hypotaxanta* [Rom 8:20]). While a majority of interpreters find in "the subduer" a reference to God—since it was in fact God who cursed the earth (see Gen 3:17–19)—there are good grounds for seeing a reference, in a causal sense (see *dia ton hypotaxanta*), to Adam and his sin. The antithesis here is not between creation and God but between creation and human beings. In the first creation account (Gen 1:1—2:3), God commands the original human pair to "subdue" the remainder of creation (Gen 1:26, 28), a motif expressed poetically in Ps 8:6–8. Paul cites or alludes to this psalm in reference to the messianic rule of the exalted Christ (1 Cor 15:27; Phil 3:21; see also Eph 1:22).

Many interpreters also see Christ played off against Adam in the hymnic text appearing in Philippians 2:6–11. Christ did not, as Adam disobediently did, "snatch" (*ouk harpagmon hēgēsato* [v. 6]) "likeness to God" (Gen 3:5, 22) but obediently submitted to death, even that of a cross (Phil 2:7–8; see Rom 5:19). Whereupon God exalted him and bestowed on him the lordship of the universe originally intended for Adam (vv. 9–11; see Gen 1:26, 28). Such allusions suggest that Paul saw the messianic rule of Christ in the new creation (2 Cor 5:17; Gal 6:15) as a successful replaying of the role that Adam muffed in the old. Adam plays a significant role in Pauline Christology and soteriology to highlight, by contrast and comparison, what Paul wants to say about Christ.

CHRIST; CREATION; DEATH; LIFE; RESURRECTION; SIN

Reading

Byrne, *PFS*, 135–40, 148–51, 185–89, 199–203, 220–22; *Romans*, 174–82; M. C. de Boer, "Paul's Mythologizing Program in Romans 5–8," in Gaventa, *Apocalyptic Paul*, 1–20; J. D. G. Dunn, *Christology in the Making: A New Testament Inquiry into the Origins of the Doctrine of the Incarnation*, 2nd ed. (London: SCM, 1989), xix, 98–128; *EBR* 1:306–11; *OEBT* 1:4–11; *Theology*, 200–204; Fee, *Pauline Christology*, 513–23; L. J. Kreitzer, *DPL*, 9–15; Matera, *GSG*, 75–78; N. A. Meyer, *Adam's Dust and Adam's Glory in the Hodayoth and in the Letters of Paul Rethinking Anthropogony and Theology* (Leiden: Brill, 2016), 95–236; P. Perkins, "Adam and Christ in the Pauline Epistles," in *Celebrating Paul*, ed. P. Spitaler (Washington, DC: Catholic Biblical Association of America, 2011), 128–51; R. Scroggs, *The Last Adam* (Oxford: Blackwell, 1966); Wright, "Romans," 512, 524–25; *PFG*, 2:745, 762, 769, 783–95, 889–95, 908.

ADOPTION

In the Greek-speaking world of Paul's day, the term *huiothesia* (Rom 8:15, 23; 9:4; Gal 4:5; see also Eph 1:5) referred to adoption, a widespread socio-legal custom of social advancement in the Greco-Roman world whereby a person was taken into the family of a prominent or wealthy citizen to enjoy the rights and privileges of natural heirs. The practice secured the continuance of the family and its fortune in situations of childlessness or lack of worthy descendants in the natural line. The most famous instance in antiquity is seen in Julius Caesar's adoption of his niece's son Octavian (later Augustus) by naming him his heir.

The term never appears in the Septuagint (LXX) and in fact the practice, while not unknown, was not prevalent in the Jewish world. The question, then, is whether Paul's use of *huiothesia* represents a case of reaching out beyond his own Jewish background to employ an image from the wider cultural milieu. Other things being equal, it is reasonable to conclude that the Greek-speaking audience of the letters would hear and understand *huiothesia* as referring to the Greco-Roman practice with which they were familiar.

Israel's Filial Relationship to God

In Romans 9:4, however, Paul lists *huiothesia* as the first of six privileges of Israel (the others being "the glory," "the covenants," "the law-giving," "the worship," and "the promises"), all of which are rooted in the Old Testament tradition. Understood in the sense of adoptive sonship, *huiothesia* goes along with the widespread biblical designation of Israel and the Israelites as God's "son" (Exod 4:22–23; Hos 11:1), "sons (and daughters) of God," "children of God" (Deut 14:1; 32:5–6, 19–20; Isa 1:2–4; 30:9; 63:8; Hos 1:10 [MT and LXX 2:1]; Wis 12:7, 21; 16:10, 21, 26; 18:13; 19:6; Sir 36:17). The motif denotes a privilege reserved to Israel as God's people, enjoying a closeness to the divinity shared by no other nation. In the postbiblical apocalyptic tradition, divine filiation came to be associated particularly with the eschatological Israel, God's people destined to "inherit" the promises of salvation. Since Israel's theology could not countenance any suggestion of a physical "begetting" of the nation by God, "adoption" would be a satisfactory designation of the process by which Israel attained the filial status.

Some (e.g., J. M. Scott) have understood the throne oracle in 2 Samuel 7:14 as an instance of divine adoption of the Davidic king, a privilege extended to the people as a whole as the promise to the king was assumed into the overall covenantal understanding of Israel's relationship to God and acquired messianic resonance in the years leading up to the Christian era. Granted, however, the widespread designation of Israel (and Israelites) as "son," "child," "children" of God in both the biblical and postbiblical literature, the throne oracle in 2 Samuel 7:14 may provide too slender a base from which to derive the filial privilege. It is preferable to see Paul's usage of *huiothesia* in continuity with the broader tradition of Israel's filial status in respect to God.

Believers as Sons (and Daughters) of God

In Galatians, Paul sets the status of being sons and daughters of God alongside the freedom from the law that believers enjoy as a consequence of justification. Baptized "into Christ," they are already "sons (and daughters) of God" (3:26–28) and, as such, "heirs" destined to inherit the eschatological blessings contained in the promise to Abraham (v. 29). Paul contrasts the current filial status of believers with the "slavery" under the law and under the "elemental spirits" (*stoicheia*) of both Jews and Gentiles respectively. In that former situation, like an heir not yet arrived at maturity, "we" were in a situation of subjection akin to slavery (4:1–3). But the sending of the Son has brought about both freedom from the law and the gift of "sonship"/"adoption" (*huiothesia*) (vv. 4–5). As attestation of this new status God has sent the Spirit into the hearts of believers, making them cry out, "*Abba*, Father" (v. 6). They are no longer slaves but rather "sons (and daughters)" (v. 6), and, as such, heirs through the disposition of God (v. 7).

In Romans, Paul introduces the motif of divine filiation at a point where he is arguing that the replacement of the law by the Spirit as a consequence of the sending of the Son (Rom 7:14—8:4) has made possible a living out of the righteousness required for the gaining of "(eternal) life" (8:5–11). Those who are "led" by the Spirit in this way are (already) "sons (and daughters) of God" (v. 14). As in Galatians 4:6–7, Paul points to the gift of the Spirit, as witness to the enjoyment of this status: a Spirit not of slavery, inspiring fear, but of "sonship"/"adoption" (*huiothesia*), again impelling the "*Abba*" cry to God (8:15–16). As in Galatians, the filial status also holds out the promise of inheritance (v. 17a), but here with the added proviso of sharing, as "co-heirs," Christ's suffering in order to share his glory (v. 17bc).

The suffering that believers, along with the remainder of creation, endure at the present time (vv. 18–22) means that the filial status they currently enjoy is hidden. It will be revealed (vv. 18, 19), as that of Christ was revealed (see Rom 1:4), when they fully share his risen existence. Meanwhile, along with creation (v. 22), believers "groan" awaiting the public revelation of their filial status (*huiothesia*) when their bodies are redeemed in resurrection (v. 23). All this is part of the inexorable unfolding of the predetermined design of God that the elect should share in the "image" way of being of the Son, thereby rendering him the "Firstborn" among a multitude of "brothers (and sisters)" (v. 29).

In dealing with the issue of the current failure of Israel to respond to the gospel—an issue exacerbated by the positive response on the part of many Gentiles—Paul reworks the privilege of divine filiation (Rom 9:4) from the aspect of the sovereign freedom of God. In a complex scriptural argument, he first establishes that the filial privilege (*tekna theou* [vv. 7–8]) does not derive from "fleshly" (natural) descent from Abraham, nor is it dependent in any way on human meriting; it rests entirely on God's free choice and decision (9:6–18). Finally, he blends Hosea 1:10 with Hosea 2:23 to argue that it was always the divine intention to extend to the Gentiles (originally "not my people" [Rom 9:25b]) the eschatological privilege of divine filiation (*klēthēsontai huioi theou zōntos* [v. 26]).

Aside from these extensive appearances in Roman and Galatians, a more ethical note attaches to the motif in Paul's passing expression of hope (Phil 2:15), couched in language echoing Moses's sermon in Deut 32:1–43, that the Philippians will be "blameless and innocent children of God" (*tekna theou*; see Deut 32:5). In what may be a fragment of an earlier text appearing in 2 Corinthians 6:14—7:1, the assurance of protection in terms of divine filiation originally addressed to the ruler alone in the Davidic throne oracle 2 Samuel 7:14 is extended to the entire community: "you shall be my sons and daughters" (6:18).

In the deutero-Pauline material, the motif appears only in the opening thanksgiving blessing in Ephesians, where, echoing Romans 8:29, the author recalls the pretemporal design of God that the elect should share the "sonship"/"adoption" (*huiothesia*) of Christ (Eph 1:5).

Recent studies in this area of Pauline theology (see references to Burke, Heim, Hodge below) have reasserted the case for the more likely provenance of *huiothesia* from the Greco-Roman practice of adoption, which itself has aspects congenial to Paul's theology, such as the fatherhood of God, election, inheritance, and so on. The fact, however, that Paul contrasts *huiothesia* with slavery (Gal 4:1–4), which is an enduring status, and also that he can speak of believers as "awaiting" *huiothesia* even though they are already God's sons (and daughters), albeit in a hidden way (Rom 8:19–23), argues against seeing the term narrowly tied to the act of adoption in the Greco-Roman sense. Rather than opting strictly for one background over against the other, it may be best to see Paul's usage of *huiothesia* as a case of early inculturation where the biblical background read in the light of Christ was enriched by the understanding stemming from the wider cultural milieu.

FREEDOM; ISRAEL; LIFE; REVELATION, REVEAL; SLAVERY; SON OF GOD

Reading

T. Burke, *Adopted into God's Family: Exploring a Pauline Metaphor* (Downers Grove, IL: Intervarsity, 2006); Byrne, *ABD* 6:156–59; *Romans*, 249–50, 252; *"Sons of God,"* 8–70, 79–195, 213–26; E. M. Heim, *Adoption in Galatians and Romans: Contemporary Metaphor Theories and the Pauline* huiothesia *Metaphors* (Leiden; Boston: Brill, 2017); C. J. Hodge, *If Sons, Then Heirs: A Study of Kinship and Ethnicity in the Letters of Paul* (Oxford: Oxford University Press, 2007); J. M. Scott, *Adoption as Sons of God: An Exegetical Investigation into the Background of HUIOTHESIA in the Pauline Corpus* (Tübingen: J. C. B. Mohr, 1992), 3–57; "Adoption, Sonship," *DPL*, 15–18; J. C. Walters, "Paul, Adoption, and Inheritance," in Sampley, *Paul*, 1:33–67; J. L. White, *The Apostle of God and the Promise of Abraham* (Peabody, MA: Hendrickson, 1999), 176–91.

ANGEL

The Greek word *angelos* behind the English "angel" basically means "messenger" or "announcer." The LXX translates the Hebrew *malak* with *angelos* in this sense with reference to human messengers but more frequently to refer to emissaries from the divine sphere. Angels also constitute a heavenly court around God; they mediate that transcendent world to human beings and act as God's instruments, performing in the world various tasks of accompaniment, protection, and at times chastisement (see Job 1:6; 2:1). Belief in angels intensified in the later biblical and then postbiblical period, especially in works of an apocalyptic nature, where the angelic world is seen to be divided into spiritual powers on the side of God and evil powers resistant to the divine rule and human welfare.

As a Pharisee, Paul would have inherited a belief in angels, a distinctive tenet of that movement. The comparatively few references to angels in his letters, however, testifies to no great enthusiasm on his part in their regard. They seem to have connections with spiritual forces otherwise designated as "rulers" (Rom 8:38; see 1 Cor 2:8) or "powers" (see Rom 8:38; 1 Cor 15:24) that Christ has either to subdue or do away with in order to reclaim the world for God and the new creation.

A significant clue to Paul's view of angels is provided by the statement in Galatians 3:19d that the law, in contrast to the promises directly spoken by God to Abraham, was "ministered through angels at the hands of a mediator (Moses)" (*diatageis di' angelōn en cheiri mesitou*). This brief remark does not give much away but it suggests that Paul regarded angels as "the police" of the old dispensation ruled by the law, on the watch for any infringements of its edicts. This would explain the listing of "angels" (along with "rulers" [*archai*]) among the various powers that will not succeed in separating believers from the love of God at the great judgment (Rom 8:38–39a). With God already "acquitting" (*dikaiōn*) (v. 33b) and the risen Lord interceding (v. 34), who or which of these would dare to bring accusation against God's elect (v. 33a)? The obscure injunction, with reference to the necessity for a woman to be veiled when praying in the assembly (1 Cor 11:2–16) on the grounds that she should "have power on her head because of the angels" (*exousian echein epi tēs kephalēs dia tous angelous* [v. 10]) has been variously explained. If the reference is not to the thought of angelic susceptibility to feminine beauty (see Gen 6:1–4), the idea of angelic watchfulness over the order of creation (see 1 Cor 11:7–9) may again be in mind (see WOMAN). A similar suggestion of the presence of angels in worship may be implied in Paul's reference to charismatic utterance as "speaking in tongues of human beings and angels" in 1 Corinthians 13:1. However, the low ranking he accords to such a gift (see 12:10) and its disparagement here in comparison with love again suggests scant enthusiasm for angels.

This impression is not dispelled by Paul's insistence early in Galatians (1:8) that "if we or an angel from heaven" were to preach a gospel contrary to that already preached to the community, they should be accursed ("anathema"). His later observation that the Galatians received him "as an angel of God, as Christ Jesus" (4:14) sounds more positive, but it is possible that "angel" has its basic sense of "messenger" in both cases.

In a few cases, a negative rating is clear, as when Paul pictures Satan as an angel able "to disguise himself as an angel of light" (2 Cor 11:14) and attributes his own suffering from a "thorn in the flesh" as the work of an "angel of Satan" (12:7). In 1 Corinthians 4:8–9, Paul ironically contrasts the situation of the Corinthians, whose over-realized eschatology suggests arrival at the fullness of salvation, with that of the suffering apostles. When he describes the latter ("we"), placed last like captives in a triumphal procession destined for death, as "a spectacle to angels and human beings" (1 Cor 4:9), it is not clear whether he thinks of the angels in question as benign or hostile spectators of the suffering. Their association here with human beings, who clearly belong to the present, passing world, does suggest that they belong to the age now being wound up in Christ. If, as Paul later remarks, believers are to judge angels (1 Cor 6:3), some at least of the angels in question must be headed for condemnation.

Angels in the Later Pauline Letters

In Colossians 2:18, the worship of angels—or perhaps joining in worship conducted by angels—appears as one feature of the religiosity that poses a threat to the all-sufficiency of Christ as mediator between God and human beings. Elsewhere, in the more traditional sense of angels as a heavenly court (1 Tim 5:21), they are a feature of the eschatological scenario at the coming of Christ. The "call of the archangel" (*en phōnē archangelou*) and the blast of the trumpet, will signal his arrival from heaven and the resurrection of the dead (1 Thess 4:16; see 2 Thess 1:7). In the hymnic fragment quoted in 1 Timothy 3:16, setting out a series of contrasts between Christ's earthly and post-resurrection existence, the phrase "seen by angels" (*ōphthē angelois*), would seem to refer to the acknowledgment by angelic powers of the vindication and lordship of Christ, along the lines of the hymn in Philippians 2:9–11.

LAW; LORD; PRINCIPALITIES AND POWERS; RULERS; WOMAN

Reading

S.-T. Bonino, *Angels and Demons: A Catholic Introduction* (Washington, DC: Catholic University of America Press, 2016), 41–45; W. Carr, *Angels and Principalities: The Background, Meaning and Development of the Pauline Phrase* hai archai kai hai exousiai (Cambridge: Cambridge University Press, 1981), 5–123; Dunn, *Theology*, 104–110; R. E. Moses, *Practices of Power: Revisiting the Principalities and Powers in the Pauline Letters* (Minneapolis: Fortress, 2014); D. G. Reid, *DPL*, 20–23; Schnelle, *Apostle Paul*, 300–301, 326–33; W. Wink, *Naming the Powers: The Language of Power in the New Testament* (Philadelphia: Fortress, 1984), 22–35.

ANGER (*see* Wrath)

APOCALYPTIC (*see* READ ME FIRST)

APOSTLE

"Apostle" is Paul's favored self-designation, the title by which, for the most part, he introduces himself at the start of his letters (Rom 1:1; 1 Cor 1:1; 2 Cor 1:1; Gal 1:1; see also Eph 1:1; Col 1:1; 1 Tim 1:1; 2 Tim 1:1; Titus 1:1). In itself, the Greek term *apostolos* refers to one sent by another on a particular mission (see Phil 2:25 [Epaphroditus]; 2 Cor 8:23). Use of the term in this sense is rare outside early Christianity. It is likely that the strong missionary impulse attending the Christian movement led early believers to imbue the term with fresh significance. Paul's characteristic usage of *apostolos* reflects this early tradition where the term designates a respected class of believers sent to preach the gospel and found communities ("churches") as envoys of the risen Lord.

It is important to distinguish Paul's use of the term *apostolos* from the twelve close disciples of Jesus designated as *apostoloi* in the gospels (Matt 10:2; Mark 3:14; 6:30; Luke 6:13; 9:10; 17:5; 22:14; 24:10; see also Acts 1:2, 26). The list of resurrection witnesses in 1 Corinthians 15:5–7 lists "the Twelve" (v. 5) as a category distinct from "the apostles" (v. 7), although obviously there was overlap between the two categories in some cases. For Paul (contrast Acts 1:21–22), recognition as an apostle did not require having been a disciple of Jesus in his historical life. In fact, defending his apostleship in 2 Corinthians, Paul seems to explicitly reject such a qualification: "Even though we once knew Christ according to the flesh, we no longer know him in that way. If anyone is in Christ, there is a new creation" (2 Cor 5:16bc–17a). For Paul, two conditions in particular attached to apostleship: to have "seen" the risen Lord and to have been commissioned by him to preach the gospel and found churches: "Am I not an apostle? Have I not seen the Lord? Are you not my work in the Lord?...You are the seal of my apostleship in the Lord" (1 Cor 9:1–2; see 15:8).

Introducing himself as apostle at the beginning of his letters, Paul expressly relates his tenure of this role to the will of God (1 Cor 1:1; 2 Cor 1:1; Gal 1:1; see also Eph 1:1; Col 1:1; 1 Tim 1:1; 2 Tim 1:1). His calling specifically to be apostle to the Gentiles he relates to his vision of the risen Lord (Gal 1:16; see Rom 1:5; 11:13; 15:15–21), although some regard this attribution as retrospective rather than strictly historical. Stemming directly from God, his apostolic calling and field of mission (the Gentile world) is totally independent of human authority (Gal 1:11–12), although recognized by the leading apostles (Cephas [Peter], James, and John; see 2:6–9). It is the source of his authority not only to found churches but to offer subsequent guidance and correction as required. In virtue of the gift and overall responsibility he has for the Gentile churches (Rom 1:13–15; 15:14–21), he can write "rather boldly" (15:15) in this vein to the believing community in Rome that he himself has not founded.

Paul has absolutely no need for letters of credence from apostles in Jerusalem or elsewhere to establish his authority (2 Cor 3:1–3). His apostolic credentials stem from the existence of the communities that he has formed through the proclamation of the gospel (1 Cor 9:2; 15:10; 2 Cor 1:14; 3:2–3; Phil 1:3–6; 1 Thess 1:2–10) and also from the conformity of his life to the pattern of the suffering, death, and resurrection of Christ (1 Cor 4:9–13; 2 Cor 4:7–18; 6:3–10; 11:21–33; 12:7–10, 12; 13:4; Phil 3:10–11). Because of the lateness of his calling by the risen Lord, Paul can indeed think of himself as "the least of the apostles, unworthy to be called an apostle because he had persecuted the church" (1 Cor 15:9). However, when challenged, he reckons himself in no way inferior to those who either claim themselves or are reckoned to be "super-apostles" (2 Cor 11:5; see 1 Cor 9:2).

While secure, though not unchallenged, in his own apostolic calling, Paul acknowledged that others had been called to be apostles before him (1 Cor 15:7–8; Gal 1:19; 2:9). In Romans 16:7, he sends greeting to two individuals, Andronicus and Junia, acknowledging their seniority to him as believers ("in Christ before me") and remarking that they are "prominent among the apostles" (*episēmoi en tois apostolois*). If, as is now recognized to be the case, the name Junia belongs to a woman, this would indicate that at least one woman was included among those recognized as apostles. It is possible, however, to read Paul's praise of the couple in the sense of being "held in high repute *among* the apostles" but this is less likely.

In the Pauline churches, the apostles rank highest among all the roles gifted by the Spirit for the preservation and building up of the community, the "body of Christ" (1 Cor 12:28). In the deutero-Pauline letter to the Ephesians, the role of apostle is similarly ranked but portrayed as foundational rather than current as an office in the church (2:20; 3:5; 4:11). The apostles constituted a foundation for the church in the sense that to them, especially Paul, the mystery of God's plan has been revealed (see 3:3–7).

CALL; GENTILES; GIFT(S) OF THE SPIRIT; GOSPEL; RESURRECTION; SUFFERING

Reading

F. H. Agnew, "The Origin of the NT Apostle-Concept: A Review of Research," *JBL* 105 (1986): 75–96; P. W. Barnett, *DPL*, 45–51; Becker, *Paul*, 69–81; Beker, *Paul the Apostle*, 3–10; Byrne, *Romans*, 38–39, 41–42; Dunn, *Beginning*, 530–41; *Theology*, 571–80; Fitzmyer, *Romans*, 231–32; Gorman, *Apostle*, 68–91; Lincoln, *Ephesians*, lxii–lxiii, 153–54, 178–80; Matera, *GSG*, 19–26, 41–46; Sanders, *Paul*, 99–111; Schnelle, *Apostle Paul*, 88–90, 158–59, 245–48; J. H. Schütz, *Paul and the Anatomy of Apostolic Authority* (Cambridge: Cambridge University Press; repr. with Introduction by W. A. Meeks, Louisville: Westminster John Knox, 2007), 22–53; Thiselton, *1 Corinthians*, 666–73.

AUTHORITY

As expressed by the Greek term *exousia* (and the corresponding impersonal expression *exestin*), "authority" appears in Paul in two rather distinct ways: (1) indicating the capacity or right to have or do something and (2) referring to beings that have power or authority, whether in the human or in the transcendent sphere.

1. *Exousia* as Right or Capacity

In Romans 9:21, Paul illustrates the divine freedom to dispose over human beings in accordance with the divine will through the image of a potter who has similar right (*exousia*) over the clay that he is shaping. As pertaining to human beings this meaning of *exousia* features prominently in two sequences in 1 Corinthians where Paul discusses appropriate use of freedom. In 1 Corinthians 6:12, beginning a sequence dealing with the dignity and responsibility of life in the body (6:12—7:40), he twice quotes what appears to be a statement of Christian freedom cited by the Corinthians, "All things are lawful for me" (*panta moi exestin*) (vv. 12a, 12c). Each time Paul adds a correction: first with "But not all things are beneficial" (v. 12b), then with "But I will not be dominated by anything" (*all' ouk egō exousiasthēsomai hypo tinos*) (v. 12d). The correction introduces the sense that an acting out of freedom in some circumstances can lead to a subtle erosion of freedom more deeply understood. This principle comes to a head in a long response, 1 Corinthians 8:1—11:1, dealing with the issue of eating meat sacrificed to idols. Paul points out that, other things being equal, the knowledge that idols have no reality (8:4–6) gives believers the freedom to eat such meat. But if the exercise of such freedom should scandalize a brother or sister who, weak in faith, does not have such knowledge, then a deeper exercise of freedom, stemming from love (see v. 1), requires refraining from such food, lest "your very freedom [*hē exousia hymōn autē*] in this regard might become a stumbling block to the weak" (v. 9). To illustrate this principle, Paul appeals at some length (9:1–27) to his own practice. As an apostle (vv. 1–2), he has the right (*exousia*) to be supported by the communities he has founded, and to travel with a wife (vv. 3–12a, 13–14). So as not to place a burden on them or any obstruction to the gospel, however, he has chosen to forgo this right (*ouk echrēsametha tē exousia tautē* [v. 12b]; see also v. 18). Toward the end, he reiterates his correction of the Corinthians' slogan, "All things are lawful" (*panta exestin* [10:23a]), insisting that the exercise of freedom in such matters must always yield to the higher requirement to act in a way that builds up the community and leads to the salvation of all (10:24—11:1). An echo of this principle appears in 2 Thessalonians 3:9.

The term *exousia* appears in the related sense of having control over something or over other persons. In the matter of refraining from marriage in view of the imminent passing of the present age (1 Cor 7:25–38), Paul advises that an unmarried man, if his passions are strong, should go ahead and marry his fiancée, if such is his wish (v. 36). If, however, he has his own desire under control (*exousian echei peri tou idiou thelēmatos*), he will do well to refrain from marriage (vv. 37–38). Likewise, as an apostle, Paul is not ashamed to "boast...of the authority [*peri tēs exousias*] that the Lord has given (him) for the building up" of the community (2 Cor 10:8; see also 13:10).

A highly anomalous instance of *exousia* appears in Paul's instruction concerning how women should appear when praying or prophesying in the assembly (1 Cor 11:2–16). He argues that a woman ought to have "authority on her head [*exousian echein epi tēs kephalēs*] because of the angels" (v. 10). It is not clear whether the "authority" is something that woman herself exercises or is something to which she is subject (an otherwise unattested usage of *exousia*). On what is meant by "having the head uncovered" (vv. 4–7, 13), see WOMAN.

2. *Exousia* as Authority

Paul employs *exousia* in regard to those who exercise authority as earthly rulers in the instruction he gives regarding the payment of taxes in Romans 13:1–7 (see also Titus 3:1). He rests the specific requirement regarding taxes (vv. 6–7) on the principle that all authority (*exousia*) derives from God (v. 1b) and therefore, resisting the governing authorities (*exousiais hyperexousais*) is tantamount to resisting God (v. 2). His confidence that the authorities are a terror only to evildoers, not the good, seems unrealistic in the context of Rome under Nero. However, for reasons that are not entirely clear, Paul felt constrained to reassert the traditional view that God's authority lies behind that of earthly rulers.

For the use of "authority" (*exousia*) with reference to transcendent powers of a spiritual or angelic nature (1 Cor 15:24; Eph 1:21; 3:10; 6:12; Col 1:16; 2:10, 15), see PRINCIPALITIES AND POWERS.

APOSTLE; FREEDOM; IDOLATRY; PRINCIPALITIES AND POWERS; WOMAN

Reading

I. Broer, *EDNT* 2:9–12; Byrne, *Romans*, 384–93; Dunn, *Theology*, 104–10, 571–80; M. D. Hooker, "Authority on Her Head," *NTS* 10 (1963–64): 410–16; R. A. Horsley, "Consciousness and Freedom among the Corinthians: 1 Corinthians 8–10," *CBQ* 40 (1978): 574–89; J. Murphy-O'Connor, "Corinthian Slogans in 1 Cor 6:12–20," *CBQ* 40 (1978): 391–96; D. G. Reid, *DPL*, 746–52; W. Wink, *Naming the Powers: The Language of Power in the New Testament* (Philadelphia: Fortress, 1984).

B

BAPTISM, BAPTIZE

The practice of baptism as an initiatory rite seems to go back to the very origins of the Christian community, predating the conversion of Paul. While purificatory immersions were practiced by Jewish groups such as the Pharisees and the Qumran community, Christian practice seems to owe more to that of John the Baptist, who offered baptism as a one-off conversion rite in preparation for the onset of the rule of God. Post-Easter, it became the principal initiatory rite into the community of the Messiah, Jesus.

The paucity of references to baptism in Paul's letters is not an indication of its significance in his theology. Baptism gives physical and social expression to the interior commitment of faith. Paul presupposes that all believers have been baptized and have received instruction on its meaning. The disclaimer in 1 Corinthians 1:17 that Christ had not sent him to baptize but to proclaim the gospel does not downplay the sacrament. His commission from Christ is to elicit, through the power of the Spirit, a response in faith to the gospel. He appears to have left follow-up instruction and in due course baptism to other members of his team; the couple Prisca and Aquila come to mind in this regard (see Rom 16:3; 1 Cor 16:19; also Acts 18:26).

Actually, Paul's recounting of the slogans rife in the faction-ridden Corinthian community—"I belong to Paul," "I belong to Apollos,...Cephas,...Christ" (1 Cor 1:12)—sheds light on his understanding of baptism. The factions appear to have gathered around leaders from whom members received baptism. In the Greek form of the slogan, the first-person singular pronoun (*egō*) followed by the name of the leader in the genitive (e.g., *egō de Apollō*) indicates belonging. Paul's retort, "Has Christ been divided up?" (v. 13a), suggests that the only true slogan should be "I belong to Christ" (*egō de Christou*) because baptism initiates a belonging to or participation in the person of the risen Lord indicated elsewhere in Paul, for example, in the negative statement: "If a person lacks the Spirit of Christ, that person does not belong to him [*houtos ouk estin autou*]" (Rom 8:9cd).

The sense of belonging to Christ initiated through baptism appears in the phrase "baptized into," the directional sense indicated by the preposition *eis*, which retains its strong local thrust in Paul. Central to his theology is the understanding of the risen Lord as constituting a communal person "into" whom believers enter through faith and baptism, henceforth to live "in" him. This is clear toward the end of Galatians 3:

> 27 As many of you as were baptized into Christ have put on Christ [*hosoi gar eis Christon ebaptisthēte Christon enedysasthe*]. 28 There is no longer Jew or Greek,...slave or free,...male and female. For you are all one person [*heis*] in Christ Jesus.

Paul is arguing that believers are heirs of the promise made to Abraham (v. 29). That promise was focused simply and solely on one person: Christ (v. 16). Believers come under the scope of the promise by "entering into" Christ through baptism. In his person, they become part of the new creation (6:15; see 2 Cor 5:17), where the ethnic, social, and gender distinctions that mean so much in the present, passing age have fallen away.

In 1 Corinthians 12, defending the essential unity of the local community in which a variety of the gifts of the Spirit may flourish, Paul makes a similar appeal to the effect of baptism:

> [12] For just as the body is one and has many members, and all the members, though many, form one body, so it is the case with Christ. [13] For in the one Spirit we were all baptized into one body [*eis hen sōma ebaptisthēmen*]—Jews or Greeks, slaves or free—and we were all made to drink of the one Spirit.

Earlier in the letter, adducing the behavior and fate of the Exodus generation as a warning against presumption, he offers a curious parallel to this motif of a community being "baptized" into a corporate leader: "our ancestors were under the cloud, and all passed through the sea, and all were baptized into Moses [*eis ton Mōüsēn ebaptisthēsan*] in the cloud and in the sea" (10:1b–2). Although Paul does not, of course, speak of baptism in connection with Adam, passages such as Romans 5:12–21 and 1 Corinthians 15:22 show that he conceived of human existence, aside from the divine intervention in Christ, as existing "in Adam" in a similar corporate fashion, and caught up thereby in the legacy of sin and death stemming from the primal ancestor's sin. Baptism effects for believers a transfer from the death-dealing "body" of Adam "into" that of Christ.

Paul provides the deepest theological account of this transfer when countering any suggestion that his emphasis on the "overflow" of divine grace (Rom 5:15–21) could lead believers to continue in sin so as to give scope for even greater effusions of grace (6:1). Believers have "died" to sin, both to its guilt and to its control as an enslaving power (v. 2). To ground this sense of a "death" to sin Paul appeals to the baptism that all have undergone at the beginning of their existence in Christ (Rom 6:3–4):

> [3] Do you not know that all of us who have been baptized into Christ Jesus [*hosoi ebaptisthēmen eis Christon Iēsoun*] were baptized into his death [*eis ton thanaton autou ebaptisthēmen*]? [4] Therefore we have been buried with him by baptism into death [*synetaphēmen...autō dia tou baptismatos eis ton thanaton*], so that, just as Christ was raised from the dead by the glory of the Father, so we too might walk in newness of life.

This statement makes clear the dynamic nature of the union with Christ forged through baptism. It involves participation in his total "career": death, burial, and resurrection. Through baptism, believers have already shared in Christ's death (see 2 Cor 5:14). As participants in the legacy of sin stemming from Adam (literally, their "old man" [*ho palaios...anthrōpos*]) they have been "co-crucified with Christ" (*synestaurōthē*) to remove that sinful connection (literally, "the body of sin" [*to sōma tēs hamartias*]) (v. 6; see Gal 2:19c). Paul is careful to note (see the future tenses in Rom 6:5, 8) that bodily participation in Christ's resurrection remains outstanding. However, believers do participate in his risen life in the manner of life now incumbent on them: their "walk" in newness of life (vv. 4c, 11, 13; see also 1 Cor 6:11a): "You have been washed" [*apelousasthe*]—probably also a reference to baptism).

Baptism in the Later Pauline Letters

The allusion to baptism in Colossians 2:12 echoes the sense of dynamic involvement with the career of Christ set out in Romans 6:3–4. But now believers' involvement with the "burial" of Christ is followed by the assurance of having been "raised with him through faith in the power of God who raised him from the dead" (see also v. 13). The connection with Christ's risen life coheres with the more "realized" eschatology of Colossians, but, as in Romans 6, the main concern is to stress the total removal of believers from their former way of life. In the exhortation for unity in Ephesians 4:4–6, baptism appears as one of seven things qualified by "one" that serve to unite believers. Presumably, "one baptism" follows "one faith" (v. 5) in the sense that baptism gives social expression to the one faith (understood now in the sense of a body of truth) that all share. The reference to "the washing of rebirth" (*loutron palingenesias*) in the hymnic text in Titus 3:5 is generally taken to be a reference to baptism.

Baptism "for the Dead" (1 Cor 15:29)

An obscure reference to baptism occurs as a further brief argument for the resurrection of the dead in 1 Corinthians 15:29: "What do those who get themselves baptized for the dead think they are doing, if the dead are not raised? Why do they get themselves baptized on their behalf?" Multiple interpretations are on offer. The practice in view could reflect a belief that believers can vicariously effect the salvation of loved ones who have died without conversion by undergoing (a second!) baptism on their behalf. More congenial to Paul's overall theology would appear to be an interpretation that sees the desire to be reunited with loved believers who have died as a significant motive inducing some non-believers to request baptism.

ADAM; BODY OF CHRIST; DEATH; FAITH; "IN CHRIST"; MOSES; PROMISE; RESURRECTION

Reading

G. R. Beasley-Murray, *DPL*, 60–66; Byrne, *PES*, 140–43, 197–203; R. P. Carlson, "The Role of Baptism in Paul's Thought," *Int* 47 (1993): 255–66; Dunn, *Theology*, 442–49; Moo, *Romans*, 359–67; Schnelle, *Apostle Paul*, 300–301, 326–33; Thiselton, *1 Corinthians*, 669–73 (survey of interpretation), 1240–49 (on 1 Cor 15:29); A. J. M. Wedderburn, *Baptism and Resurrection: Studies in Pauline Theology against Its Greco-Roman Background* (Tübingen: Mohr Siebeck, 1987), 37–69, 368–71; Wolter, *Paul*, 125–46.

BLESSING, BLESS, BLESSED

Paul inherits the motif of blessing from his biblical patrimony where "to bless" (Heb *brk*; LXX Greek *[en]eulogeō*) is in first instance the prerogative of God, who communicates life, well-being, or success to human beings and other creatures (Gen 1:22, 28; 2:3; Deut 28:1–14). A "blessing" (*eulogia*) is a benefit acknowledged as received from God, a mark of divine favor and love (Gen 12:2–3). Human beings pronounce others as blessed on the basis of their having received such favors, or as having acted or being about to act in such a way as to place themselves in a position to receive them. When in prayers and other formulations human beings bless God they are not of course conferring a benefit on God but acknowledging and thanking God for benefits received. Expressions of blessing in Paul reflect this variety of usage.

Blessing God

First are simple blessings of God (expressed as "blessed be…" [*eulogētos*]), akin to the short doxologies prevalent in Judaism after mention of God or the holy name: Romans 1:25; 9:5; 2 Corinthians 11:31 (see also 1 Tim 1:11; 6:15). Discussing gifts inspired by the Spirit, specifically praying in tongues, Paul expresses a desire that the blessing of God so pronounced by an individual in the assembly will be intelligible so that an outsider can respond with "Amen" (1 Cor 14:16). In 2 Corinthians, the phrase "Blessed be God" introduces the thanksgiving element of the introduction (1:3–7), rendering it an extended expression of praise. This seems to serve as a model for a much longer eulogy or blessing in Ephesians 1:3–14, which reviews in sequence all the ways in which God, "the Father of our Lord Jesus Christ, has blessed us" (*ho eulogēsas hēmas*): from God's predetermined design, to the redemption in Christ's blood, to the full inheritance still to come.

Blessings from God: The Blessing Promised to Abraham

"Blessing" in the sense of a gift bestowed by God on human beings occurs in Paul chiefly in sequences in Romans and Galatians where Paul appeals to God's blessing of Abraham as a scriptural pointer to justification by faith. In Galatians 3:1–5, Paul reminds the community sharply that they received the gift of the Spirit simply on the basis of their response in faith to the gospel of the Crucified. He then points out (vv. 6–7) the parity between this and God's dealing with Abraham according to Genesis 15:6, where Abraham is pronounced righteous on the basis of having believed in God's promise that he would have a son and a vast progeny. It was in view of this that "Scripture preannounced to Abraham that in you (i.e., 'in your offspring') all the nations would be blessed [*eneulogēthēsontai en soi panta ta ethnē*]" (Gal 3:8). The "curse"—the very opposite of blessing—pronounced by the law over sinful human beings (Deut 27:26, cited v.

10) has been lifted by the redemptive act of Christ (v. 13) "in order that the Gentiles might receive the blessing (received by) Abraham, in order that we might receive the promised Spirit through faith" (v. 14). The "blessing," then, received by Gentile believers such as the Galatians (v. 9), would be the gift of the Spirit or, perhaps more accurately, the gift of justification attested by the Spirit.

In Romans 4:1–12, along with the witness to justification by faith provided by Genesis 15:6, a text from "the law" (the Pentateuch) (vv. 3–5), Paul adduces the further witness of a text from "the Prophets" (the Psalms), in the shape of LXX Ps 31:1–2 (see Rom 3:21b):

> [6] So too David pronounces a blessing [*makarismon*] on the person to whom God reckons righteousness apart from works. [7] "Blessed [*makarioi*] are those whose iniquities are forgiven, and whose sins are covered up. [8] Blessed [*Makarios*] is the person whose sin the Lord will not reckon."

The "blessing" (in this case indicated, in language taken from the psalm, by *makarismos/makarios*) consists in the gracious forgiveness of sin, corresponding here, as the parallel with verses 3–5 indicates, to justification. Paul concludes his case (vv. 9–12) by pointing out that Abraham received "this blessing" in a state of "uncircumcision" (*akrobystia*) and so could be "father" and paradigm of all who were to follow in his way of faith and so receive "the blessing"—the eschatological justification required for salvation at the judgment—along with him.

Human Beings Blessing Other Human Beings

Setting out his travel plans toward the end of his letter to Rome (15:14–33), Paul expresses confidence that his arrival will be accompanied by "the fullness of the blessing of Christ" (*en plērōmati eulogias Christou*) (v. 29); in view here may be the mutual encouragement mentioned in the introduction (1:12). On the other hand, when faced with hostility from outsiders, believers should have the freedom to respond to those who persecute them, not with a curse, but with a blessing (Rom 12:14), as is the practice of Paul and his suffering apostolic team (1 Cor 4:12b).

Speaking more in the mode of a beatitude, Paul declares "blessed" (*makarios*) the person who, concerning matters of food and drink, after correct discernment, acts with firm conviction flowing from faith (Rom 14:22b). While allowing a woman whose husband has died to remarry, in view of the shortness of the present time, he declares "more blessed" (*makariōtera*) the one who chooses to remain single (1 Cor 7:40; see v. 29b).

The brief allusion in 1 Corinthians 10:16 to the eucharistic cup as "the cup of blessing which we bless" (*to potērion tēs eulogias ho eulogoumen*) stands in parallel to the later recall of the supper tradition introduced with reference to the Lord's "giving thanks" (*eucharistēsas*) in 11:24. The eucharistic cup is a cup of blessing not just in view of the blessing pronounced over it but because it conveys the blessing of sharing in the benefits won by the blood of Christ (see EUCHARIST).

Urging the Corinthians to be generous in regard to contributing to the collection for the "saints" (Jerusalem church), Paul plays on the wider meaning of the word *eulogia* drawing in the sense of "generous, unforced gift" (2 Cor 9:5). He exploits an agricultural maxim to maintain that "the one who sows bountifully (*ep' eulogiais*), will also reap bountifully (*ep' eulogiais kai therisei*) (v. 6), that is, will receive a blessing in return. In Romans 16:18, *eulogia* has the entirely negative alternative sense of "flattery."

ABRAHAM; EUCHARIST; JUSTIFICATION; PRAYER; PROMISE; SPIRIT; THANKSGIVING

Reading

Byrne, *PES*, 191–96; D. D. Hopkins, *OEBT* 1:83–86; C.-C. Lee, *The Blessing of Abraham, the Spirit, and Justification in Galatians: Their Relationship and Significance for Understanding Paul's Theology* (Eugene, OR: Wipf & Stock, 2013), 34–60, 178–211; J. L. Martyn, *Galatians* (New Haven and London: Yale University Press, 1997), 294–328; P. T. O'Brien, *DPL*, 68–71; H. Patsch, *EDNT* 2:79–80; J. R. Wisdom, *Blessing for the Nations and the Curse of the Law: Paul's Citation of Genesis and Deuteronomy in Gal 3:8–10* (Tübingen: Mohr Siebeck, 2001), 139–200.

BOAST

"Boast," whether as a verb (*kauchaomai*) or a noun (*kauchēma, kauchēsis*), appears with remarkable frequency in Paul's letters. Whereas in secular Greek "boast" has the negative overtones of braggart self-praise that it has in English, Paul employs the word group not only in a pejorative but also in a positive sense, for which there is some precedent already in the Greek translation of the Old Testament (LXX Ps 31:11; see LXX Jer 9:22–23, part of which Paul loosely quotes in 1 Cor 1:31 and 2 Cor 10:17). For Paul the key thing is what you rest your boast on in order to bolster your sense of self-worth or gain approval, especially in the sight of God. The validity of the boast rests on the validity of the grounds on which it rests.

Negatively Rated Boasting

"Boasting" is an important theme in the first major section of Romans (1:16—4:25) where Paul is concerned to exclude any basis on which one might hope to find justification other than faith in God's action in Christ. Specifically excluded is boasting in the hope being found righteous on the basis of practice of the Jewish law (Rom 2:17, 23; see also Eph 2:9). Possession of the law is a flawed basis for boasting, not because a too zealous keeping of it leads to a self-regarding, legalistic mindset over against God (Bultmann, Käsemann), nor because it bolsters national pride over against the Gentile world (J.D.G. Dunn), but because it flies in the face of the divine verdict that *all* (Jews as well as Gentiles) have sinned (Rom 3:9, 23; 5:12). It is the universal prevalence of sin in a factual sense that undercuts boasting in the law. Even Abraham, because of his "ungodly" (Gentile) situation had no such grounds for boasting in God's sight (4:2). Likewise illegitimate would be "the boast in your flesh" on the part of the intruders in Galatia if they succeeded in their efforts to have the community adopt circumcision (Gal 6:13).

In the early part of 1 Corinthians, Paul criticizes the faction-ridden community for their tendency to "boast in human beings" (3:21; see 4:7), displayed in their preference for one teacher over another (1:12–13; 3:22). The lowly social status of the community (1:26–28) shows that God has chosen such a community in order that "no human being" (literally, "no flesh") should boast in the presence of God" (v. 29)—rather, "Let the one who boasts, boast in the Lord" (v. 31, citing LXX Jer 9:22–23). The Corinthians' tolerance of a community member living in a grossly immoral situation shows how little grounds they have for boasting (5:6).

Legitimate Boasting

Counter to the exclusion of boasting in Romans 1:18—4:25, Paul asserts that believers may boast in their suffering (5:3, 11) because associated with such suffering is the hope of glory (5:2; see 8:17). In a radical sense, Paul's only boast lies in the cross (Gal 6:14), in Christ Jesus (Phil 3:3; see also 1:26). Nevertheless, he has legitimate grounds for boasting in the wide-flung ministry of the gospel that Christ has worked in him (Rom 15:17–18; see 1 Cor 9:15, 16). He frequently mentions the communities he has formed as grounds for boasting on his part (1 Cor 15:31; 2 Cor 7:4, 14; 8:24; 9:2, 3), especially in the eschatological sense of what will stand him in good stead when called to account "on the day of the Lord" (2 Cor 1:14; Phil 2:16; 1 Thess 2:19).

"Boasting" becomes a sustained topic in the passionate defense of his apostleship and ministry that Paul mounts in 2 Corinthians 10–13. In the face of the criticisms launched against him, he feels compelled to boast of the authority that the Lord has given him for the building up of the community (10:8) and the labors he has undertaken in bringing the gospel to them. His boast, however, is within limits (v. 13) and does not rest on the work of others (v. 15). Although criticized as a weakness, his decision not to seek financial support is a "boast that will not be silenced" (11:10). In the face of the (false) boasts of the "pseudo–apostles," who wish to be considered his equals (11:12–13; see also 5:12), he feels compelled to embark on a series of boasts, even if in so doing he may appear a fool (11:16–18). He boasts of his Jewish credentials, which in every way match those of the adversaries (vv. 21b–22). He boasts in the labors and suffering he has endured that make him a better minister of Christ than they (vv. 23–29). He will even dare to boast in the visions and revelations of the Lord given him (12:1–7). He concludes by boasting even in his weaknesses, "for the power (of God) is made perfect in weakness" (v. 9b; see 11:30). Thus the "folly" of boasting in all these ways is tempered by the final boast in weakness because it shows that behind all the achievements mentioned is the power of Christ.

ABRAHAM; FAITH; JUSTIFICATION; LAW; SIN; SUFFERING; WEAKNESS

Reading

Bultmann, *Theology* 1:240–42, 262–67; Byrne, *Romans*, 97–99, 135–41; Dunn, *Romans 1–8*, 110–11, 217; *Theology*, 118–19, 362–64; C. Forbes, "Comparison, Self-Praise, and Irony: Paul's Boasting and the Conventions of Hellenistic Rhetoric," *NTS* 32 (1986): 1–30; S. J.

Gathercole, *Where Is Boasting? Early Jewish Soteriology and Paul's Response in Romans 1–5* (Grand Rapids, Cambridge: Eerdmans, 2002); E. Käsemann, *Commentary on Romans* (Grand Rapids: Eerdmans, 1980), 69–79, 102; D. F. Watson, "Paul and Boasting," in Sampley, *Paul*, 1:90–112; Wright, *PFG*, 847; J. Zmijewski, *EDNT* 2:276–79.

BODY

"Body" (*sōma*) is the most significant of all Paul's anthropological terms. The axes of virtually all his key concepts intersect at *sōma*. Since the middle of the last century there has been a strong tendency to emphasize that *sōma* in Paul, while certainly meaning the *physical body*, frequently goes beyond this to indicate the whole person under a particular aspect. What precisely this particular aspect consists in has itself long been a matter of discussion.

An existentialist approach (R. Bultmann), while not denying reference to the physical body, maintains that *sōma* in Paul represents the whole person from the perspective of being the object of one's own thought, attitude, and conduct. As *sōma*, one has the possibility of giving over oneself to an outside influence or power, whether to sin (personified by Paul), leading to final estrangement and death, or to the Spirit, leading to righteousness and (eternal) life.

Others (J. A. T. Robinson, W. D. Stacey), adopting a communal, social approach, see *sōma* indicating the human person as *bound in solidarity*—solidarity with the rest of creation and with other human beings, in particular. This solidarity can have either a negative or a positive direction, leading, respectively, either to sin and death, on the one hand, or to righteousness and life, on the other. In one variety of this approach (E. Käsemann), *sōma* denotes the human person as a non-isolable existence, that is, as in need of and capacity for communication—in brief, the human person "in touch" with others. Reacting to the tendency to see *sōma* as denoting the whole person, R. H. Gundry has argued that in Pauline usage the term denotes simply the *physical body* and hence is more or less synonymous with "flesh" (*sarx*) in the neutral sense.

Each of these approaches contributes something to the understanding of *sōma* in Paul. The key point of departure lies in perceiving its distinction from "flesh" (*sarx*). *Sōma* can accompany *sarx* across a broad range right down to the level of "flesh sold into slavery under sin" (Rom 7:14; see v. 5). But, in contrast to *sarx*, *sōma* can move in a positive direction where "flesh" does not go. The two concepts, although coextensive in a large range of meaning, are not identical. The following points may be made.

1. *Sōma* in Paul (and in the New Testament generally) is never used for "corpse" (dead body), as in secular Greek literature.
2. *Sōma*, like *sarx*, is used to denote the *physical body* in a neutral sense: Galatians 6:17 ("I carry the marks of Jesus branded on my body," NRSV); 1 Corinthians 9:27; 13:3; 1 Thessalonians 5:23; probably also 1 Corinthians 7:34; 2 Corinthians 4:10. For "body" in this sense with particular refer-

ence to its reproductive capacity, see Romans 4:19 (Abraham).

3. In close connection with the preceding usage, *sōma* can denote physical *presence*: 1 Corinthians 5:3; 2 Corinthians 10:10 ("His letters are weighty…, but his bodily presence [*hē parousia tou sōmatos*] is weak," NRSV). But even here the sense of the tangible, physical presence of the *whole person* may be operative. Similarly, in the expressions "in the body" and "out of the body" (2 Cor 5:6, 8, 10; 12:2–3), "body" seems to denote not just the physical component of a human being but the instrument whereby the whole person is joined to the present passing world.
4. In Romans 12:1, Paul exhorts his audience to "present your bodies as a living sacrifice, holy and acceptable, to God." While "your bodies" here is equivalent to "yourselves," the context contributes the overtone of yourselves as dealing with the surrounding world of persons and things, as also in 6:12–13; Philippians 1:20. Thus "body" can stand simply for "*self*" (as in English "somebody," "anybody") but often has the nuance of "self *in communication*," "self in touch."
5. Likewise, when Paul speaks of "body" in 1 Corinthians 7:4 and Romans 1:24 he may not mean simply the physical body with its sexual capacity but may have in mind the whole person with respect to that particular kind of communication that sexual union involves. Such a conception seems to underlie the instances of body that appear with unparalleled frequency in 1 Corinthians 6:12–20. Paul's initial argument (vv. 13–14) distinguishes "the body" from physical organs such as the stomach. Whereas the latter is destined for destruction, the "body" is "for the Lord" and destined for resurrection. In the remainder of the passage, "body" seems to stand for the physical (including the sexual) aspect of the whole person with a particular connotation of *union*. The personal union involved in relations with a harlot ("becoming one body with her" [v. 16]) is totally incompatible with the union believers have with Christ, wherein their bodies are his "members" (v. 15), that is, instruments of his tangible presence in the world. Fornication involves sinning "against one's own body" (v. 18) in that it directly abuses the faculty (the body) that is designed for personal union in the most intimate way (Byrne). The body is the "temple of the Holy Spirit within you" (v. 19a), the site of God's presence and power. Believers have been "bought for a price" (v. 20a), that is, redeemed from slavery to sin, at the cost of Christ's sacrifice on the cross. Their entire existence, including their bodily life, now belongs to him, as the bodies of slaves belong to their masters (see Rom 6:16–19). In this sense

the body is "for the Lord, and the Lord for the body" (1 Cor 6:13c). Hence, Paul's final injunction: "Glorify God in your body" (v. 20b; see Rom 12:1). "Body" emerges from this complex passage as the physical body but with a strong nuance of its being the instrument of personal union and communication.

6. The ***negative direction***: As an instrument of belonging to another party, "body" can be that whereby a person is given over to the old eon that lies under the domination of sin and death: "the body of sin" (Rom 6:6); "the mortal body" (6:12; see 8:10b, 11); the body whose "deeds" need to be "put to death" through the power of the Spirit (8:13); "the body of this death" (7:24b); the body that awaits "redemption" (8:23); "the body of our lowliness" that has to be "transformed" (Phil 3:21). Here "body" is coextensive with "flesh" in the full range of the negative meaning of *sarx*. It is to be noted, however, that no more than is the case with "flesh" can Paul's use of *sōma* in this negative sense be taken as indicating a negative evaluation on his part of the physical aspect of human existence (as in the unfortunate *JB* translation of Phil 3:21: "these wretched bodies of ours"). "Body" in this negative usage represents the person as bound up with the sinful, destructive existence of the present age, as part of the "body of Adam" ("the old man" [Rom 6:6]) destined for death.
7. The ***positive direction***: In contrast to "flesh," "body" in Paul can go in the opposite direction, namely, to be that whereby a person is associated with and at the service of the new epoch of grace and righteousness, destined for eternal life. In this sense "the body is for the Lord" (1 Cor 6:13c; see vv. 19–20). The same idea is implicit in Romans 6:13bc: "place yourselves at God's disposal [*parastēsate heautous tō theō*] …and your members [*melē*] to God as instruments of righteousness" ("bodies" and "members" stand in parallel across vv. 12–13; see also v. 19).

Ultimately, the bodies of believers are destined for resurrection, with the resurrection of Jesus as exemplar and guarantee. The parallel between the following statements is instructive: "the One who raised Christ from the dead will make alive also your mortal bodies [*ta thnēta sōmata hymōn*] through the Spirit dwelling in you" (Rom 8:11); "the One who raised the Lord Jesus will raise *us* also with Jesus" (2 Cor 4:14); see also Phil 3:21: "(the Lord Jesus Christ) who will change the body of our lowliness to be conformed [*symmorphon*] to his glorious body."

The "Resurrection" Body

A distinctive aspect of *sōma* in Paul emerges in 1 Corinthians 15:35–44 where Paul treats of the possibility and nature of life in the body postresurrection. The use of *sōma* in connection with the seed (vv. 37–38) and the heavenly bodies (v. 40) shows from the start that Paul is using the term in a frame of reference wider than that of "body" as applied to animate beings. He is arguing from the variety of ways in which things created by God can exist, appear, and present themselves. *Sōma* here seems to mean "way of existing and presenting oneself" (see the "glory" idea with reference to the heavenly bodies [v. 41]). With respect to the resurrection of human beings, Paul argues that, if there is a *sōma psychikon*, that is, a way of being human animated with natural life, as in present human existence, so we must grant that God, in the variety of possibility his power disposes, can create a *sōma pneumatikon*, that is, a way of being human animated with the Spirit of God (v. 44b), an existence totally transformed by and given over to the Spirit (not "spiritual body" in the sense of "immaterial body").

Paul's use of *sōma* here would seem to say very little about the nature of postresurrection existence. He avoids any crude "resuscitationist" view of resurrection and seems to envisage a "resurrection body" very different from present physical bodily existence. He does hold firmly, however, to the view that resurrection existence will be truly *human* existence, perhaps *the* truly human way of being (see the "Adam" Christology in vv. 45–49). As *sōma pneumatikon* such existence will involve communication with and through the Holy Spirit, an intimate sharing of the life of God.

Conclusion

Sōma in Paul can simply mean the "physical body." But beyond this it serves to indicate the *whole person*—sometimes simply as "self," but usually and perhaps always the whole person under the aspect of having the capacity to belong to, be in touch or communication with the world of persons, influences, events outside the self or inner core of the person. The link between the sense of *sōma* as simply the physical body and the more holistic sense of "person in communication" may lie in the fact that in the normal course of events it is the physical body that is the medium of daily communication. As "body," the human person can be joined to the old sinful, destructive association (Adam) leading to death, but in Christ the same person can "die" to this "body of sin" (Rom 6:6), this sinful, destructive solidarity, and acquire a new "body," an association with the "body of Christ," that will lead to (eternal) life.

Because of the "overlap" between the old age and the new in Paul's eschatology (see ESCHATOLOGY), believers have to live in a sense in two "bodies," in two spheres of association. While still physically "in" the (old) body, they have to be constantly "putting it to death" (Rom 8:13), so that the life of the new "body" (the "body of Christ") may dominate even the present earthly existence (Rom 6:12–13).

[For "body" in the deutero-Pauline letters see BODY OF CHRIST below.]

ADAM; BODY OF CHRIST; ETHICS; FLESH; "IN CHRIST"; RESURRECTION; SEXUALITY; SIN; SPIRIT

Reading

Barclay, *Gift*, 504–8; Bultmann, *Theology*, 1:192–203; B. Byrne, "Sinning against One's Own Body: Paul's Understanding of the Sexual Relationship in 1 Corinthians 6:18," *CBQ* 45 (1983): 608–16; Dunn, *Theology*, 54–61; R. H. Gundry, *Sōma in Biblical Theology* (Cambridge: Cambridge University Press, 1976), 51–80; Jewett, *Anthropological Terms*, 201–304, 456–58; E. Käsemann, "On Paul's Anthropology," in *Perspectives*, 1–31, here 17–23; L. J. Kreitzer, *DPL*, 71–76; J. A. T. Robinson, *The Body: A Study in Pauline Theology* (London: SCM, 1952), 17–26; Schnelle, *Apostle Paul*, 495–98; E. Schweizer, *TDNT* 7:1060–81; Stacey, *Pauline View of Man*, 154–80; Thiselton, *1 Corinthians*, 1276–81; N. T. Wright, *The Resurrection of the Son of God* (Minneapolis: Fortress, 2003), 340–56, 364–69.

BODY OF CHRIST

The use of "body" to designate the unity of a group or human society where individuals with diverse roles and gifts work toward a common purpose was well-known in the ancient world. Paul develops the image of community of believers as a "body" in this way in 1 Corinthians 12:12–30 and Romans 12:4–8. However, beneath and beyond the metaphor lies a distinctive, realistic conception indicating the union of Christians with and in the person of Christ. The "body of Christ" designates the risen Lord as constituting a personal, corporate sphere of salvation "into" whose person believers have "entered" through faith and baptism:

> [12] For just as the body is one and has many members, and all the members of the body, though many, are one body, so it is with the Christ. [13] For in the one Spirit we were all baptized into one body—Jews or Greeks, slaves or free—and we were all made to drink of one Spirit. (1 Cor 12:12–13 NRSV, with "the" added before "Christ" in v. 12)

> [27] As many of you as were baptized into Christ have clothed yourselves with Christ. [28] There is no longer Jew or Greek, there is no longer slave or free, there is no longer male and female; for all of you are one person in Christ Jesus. (Gal 3:27–28 NRSV, with "person" added after "one")

This entrance "into" Christ through faith and baptism is dynamic in the sense of an involvement in his entire "career": death, burial, and resurrection (Rom 6:3–11). It constitutes a corporate union with Christ that is totally incompatible with having relations with a prostitute (1 Cor 6:15–18), with participation in idolatrous feasts (1 Cor 10:16b–17), and with celebrating the Eucharist in such a way that fails to "discern" that when gathered for such a purpose the community constitutes, not just an assemblage of individuals, but in fact the "body" of Christ (1 Cor 11:29).

This sense of believers as constituting the body of Christ lies at the base of Paul's frequent designation of them as being "in Christ" (Rom 6:11; 8:1, 2; 12:5; 16:3; 1 Cor 1:2, 30; 15:18; 2 Cor 5:17; Gal 1:22; 2:4; 3:26; 5:6; Phil 2:1; 1 Thess 2:14), as being "of" him or belonging to him (Rom 8:9; Gal 3:29; 1 Cor 3:23).

Conversely, Christ is thereby "in" them (Gal 2:20; Rom 8:10); their bodies are the "limbs [*melē*] of Christ" (1 Cor 6:15; see also Rom 6:12–13).

The "Body of Christ" in the Deutero-Pauline Letters

The references to believers as constituting the "body of Christ" in the undisputed letters are normally considered to have the local communities rather than the worldwide collectivity of believers in view. In both Colossians and Ephesians, a distinctive shift in the latter direction has occurred. In Colossians, the worldwide church is now a "body" whose "head" is Christ (1:18). From him as head the whole body, nourished and held together by its ligaments and sinews, grows with a growth that is from God (2:19). The suffering that Paul endures are "completing" what is lacking in Christ's suffering for the sake of his body, which is the church (1:24; see 3:15).

This ecclesial imagery of Christ as "head" and the (worldwide) church as his "body" is greatly developed in Ephesians. The church is Christ's "body, the fullness of him who fills all in all" (1:23). Christ has reconciled Jews and Gentiles in one body to God through the cross (2:16; see also 3:6; 4:4). The various gifts that flourish in the church are all designed to "build up the body of Christ" into the perfect human being, to the "full measure" (*eis metron hēlikias*) in fact of Christ himself (4:12–13). The image plays out in an exhortatory sense when the image of Christ as "head" and the church as his "body" applies to the relationship that ought to prevail between husband and wife (5:21–33). In this connection, *sōma* can also refer to the individual human body (v. 28; see also Col 2:11, 23).

BAPTISM; BODY; "IN CHRIST"; CHURCH

Reading

Dunn, *Theology*, 548–60; R. Y. K. Fung, *DPL*, 76–82; E. Käsemann, "The Theological Problem Presented by the Motif of the Body of Christ," in *Perspectives*, 102–21; Y. S. Kim, *Christ's Body in Corinth: The Politics of a Metaphor* (Minneapolis: Fortress, 2008); Lincoln, *Ephesians*, 67–72; Matera, *GSG*, 134–42; C. F. D. Moule, *The Origin of Christology* (Cambridge: Cambridge University Press, 1977), 69–89.

BUILD, BUILDING (*see* Temple)

C

CALL, CALLING

"Call" (*kalō*) and "calling" (*klēsis*) in Paul has its origins in the biblical sense of Israel as a nation chosen out of all the nations on earth (Deut 7:6–8; 14:2; Pss 33:12; 105:43) and called to be God's own people (Deut 28:10; Hos 11:1, 2;

Isa 42:6; 43:1; 45:3; 48:1, 12; Jer 14:9; 2 Chron 7:14), who themselves call on the name of the Lord (Pss 79:6; 99:6; 105:1). "Call" follows closely on election in this sense.

Paul presents his own call to be an apostle in continuity with the calling of biblical prophets:

> But when God, who had set me apart before I was born and called me [*kai kalesas*] through his grace, was pleased to reveal his Son to me, so that I might proclaim him among the Gentiles.... (Gal 1:15–16a; see Isa 49:1; Jer 1:5)

Whereas those prophets addressed Israel, Paul sees himself as called to summon, through the gospel, those whom God was calling out of the nations of the world (Gentiles) to become, alongside Israel, God's eschatological people destined for salvation. Hence Paul will describe himself as "a called apostle" (*klētos apostolos* [Rom 1:1; 1 Cor 1:1]) and address those to whom he writes as "called saints" (*klētois hagiois* [Rom 1:6, 7; 1 Cor 1:2]) or simply as "saints" (2 Cor 1:1; Phil 1:1; see Eph 1:1; Col 1:2) since they have been incorporated through God's calling into the prerogative of Israel to be the holy people of God. Thus all believers, precisely as such, are "those called" (*klētoi* [1 Cor 1:24; see Rom 8:28]).

Although the gospel is preached by the apostle, the call itself comes from God (Gal 1:6; 5:8; see Rom 9:12; 1 Cor 7:15), whose call is an act of creation (1 Cor 1:26–28), rendering every believer "a new creation" (*kainē ktisis* [2 Cor 5:17; Gal 6:15]). The act of faith, on the model of that of Abraham, involves belief in God as One "who gives life to the dead and calls into being the things that do not exist" (*tou kalountos ta mē onta hōs onta* [Rom 4:17]). The "calling" enacted in the gospel is the first of a series of acts (calling, justification, glorification) whereby God's design (*prothesis*) for humanity, renewed after the image of the risen Lord, is being realized (Rom 8:28–30; 9:24–26). Paul assures the Corinthians that the God "through whom they have been called into fellowship [*di' hou eklēthēte eis koinōnian*] with (God's) own Son" is faithful and will see them through, blameless, to the "day of the Lord" (1 Cor 1:8–9; see 1 Thess 5:24).

The Moment of "Calling"

Although the believer remains a called person to the end, Paul assigns a particular significance to the moment when a person responds with faith to the gospel. At this moment the situation in which they are when the call comes to them becomes at that point their "calling" (*klēsis*). It is unrepeatable, unalterable (Gal 1:8–9), having brought about a radical transformation (justification) attested by the Spirit (Gal 3:1–9; see Rom 5:1). The call comes to people just as they are as a pure act of divine grace (Rom 9:12), without regard to preexisting worth or social status (see also 2 Tim 1:9). Paul reminds the Corinthians to "consider your own call [*blepete...tēn klēsin hymōn*], ...not many of you were wise, ...powerful, ... of noble birth" (1 Cor 1:26). God's choice and call landed on such people in order that no one should boast in the sight of God (vv. 27–29).

The same sense of "call" reappears later in 1 Corinthians in something of a digression (7:17–24) in Paul's overall instruction concerning marriage (7:1–40). Paul three times enunciates a general principle that each person "remain in the calling in which he or she was when called" (*en tē klēthē hē eklēthē*) (vv. 17a, 20, and 24). The principle is applied to two specific preexisting states: whether one was circumcised or not (vv. 18–19) and whether one was a slave or a free person (vv. 21–23). On one interpretation of a disputed phrase (*mallon chrēsai*) at the end of verse 21, Paul may allow those called as slaves to take advantage of an opportunity to gain their freedom (v. 21b) (see SLAVERY). However, the overall point is that the grace of God has grasped a person precisely in those circumstances (see v. 19b). A person who was a slave when called has become a freed person belonging to the Lord; a free person when called has become a slave of Christ (v. 22; see Rom 6:16–23). God's call has created a deeper sense of freedom and service that relativizes the existing ethnic and social distinctions even if for the time being they remain. They do remain, but the principle that Paul is affirming here must be understood in light of his view expressed again and again in the context that the present structure of the world is passing away (1 Cor 7:31b; see v. 29a). Aside from that conviction, the passage provides no basis for Christian passivity in the face of unjust social structures.

Personal Vocation

The distinctive Pauline sense of "calling" need not immediately be identified with the later Christian view that each and every believer has a personal "vocation" to discern and live out in the service of the Lord. Such a sense of vocation does, however, have a radical Pauline foundation in that each one belongs to a "called" community, in continuity with the calling of Israel. It also flows from the Pauline conviction that every believer has a distinctive gift (*charisma*) according to the gift (*charis*) given them for the building up of the body as a whole (Rom 12:6a; see 1 Cor 12:4–13).

Israel's Calling

The status of Israel as a called people has not lapsed because at the present time the majority of Israel has not responded positively to the gospel. In Romans 9—11, Paul undertakes a long exploration of Scripture to show that God's call does not rest on natural descent or personal merit but on the sovereign freedom of God. This freedom is displayed in the divine assurance to Abraham, "It is through Isaac that descendants will be called for you" (*en Isaak klēthēsetai soi sperma*; see Rom 9:7b, citing Gen 21:12 [LXX]), where "called" has the nuance of creation (see Rom 4:17b). Within that freedom God has borne for the time being with "vessels of wrath" (unbelieving Israel) and called into being "vessels of mercy" destined for glory, made up not only of Jews but also of Gentiles (Rom 9:22–24), thereby fulfilling the prophecy of Hosea:

> Those who were not my people,
> I will call "my people" [*kalesō... laon mou*] ....And in the very place

> where it was said to them, "You are not my people," they will be called "sons (and daughters) of the living God" [*klēthēsontai huioi theou zōntos*]. (Rom 9:25–26, loosely citing LXX Hos 2:25 and 2:1)

But Israel's "hardening" (*pōrōsis*) (11:25; see 11:7c) in unbelief is not irreversible. When the full number of the Gentiles has entered in, then "all Israel will be saved" (v. 26a), for "the gifts [*ta charismata*] and the calling [*hē klēsis*] of God are irrevocable [*ametamelēta*]" (v. 29). Thus, Paul rests the hope for the ultimate salvation of Israel, along with believers from the Gentile world, on the abiding validity of God's original call.

Consequences of Being a Called People

Once received, the privilege of being "called" has consequences. Paul makes clear in his earliest letter that believers must live (literally, "walk") in a way that is worthy of the God who has called them (1 Thess 2:12; see 4:7), a sense of the ethical consequences of vocation that is picked up in the later Pauline literature (Eph 4:1; Col 3:15; 2 Thess 1:11). Ephesians makes much also of the hope that attaches to calling (1:18; 4:4; see 2 Thess 2:14).

"Call" appears to have a strictly eschatological sense in Philippians 3:14 (see also 1 Tim 6:12), when Paul speaks of "pressing on to the prize of the upward call [*tēs anō klēseōs*] of God in Christ Jesus," although "call" here probably derives from the "race" image that is in play, with specific reference to the herald's summons of the winning athlete to the victory dais.

APOSTLE; ELECTION; ETHICS; FREEDOM; HOLY; ISRAEL; SLAVERY

Reading

B. R. Gaventa, "On the Calling-into-Being of Israel: Romans 9:6–29," in *Between Gospel and Election: Explorations in the Interpretation of Romans 9–11*, ed. R. Wilk and J. R. Wagner (Tübingen: Mohr Siebeck, 2010), 255–69; C. G. Kruse, *DPL*, 84–85; S. H. Polaski, *OEBT* 1:101–4; Schnelle, *Apostle Paul*, 214–17, 560–62; Thiselton, *1 Corinthians*, 544–65 (on 1 Cor 7:17–24); Wolter, *Paul*, 23–30 (on Paul's own call).

CHILDREN OF GOD (*see* Adoption)

CHRIST, MESSIAH

"Christ," *Christos* in Greek, means an anointed one, translating the Hebrew *meshiakh* "Messiah." The Israelite king is regularly referred to as "the Lord's anointed" in the Hebrew Bible. But the "messianic" usage of the phrase, as conventionally understood (to refer to a longed-for royal figure of Davidic lineage who will restore the fortunes of Israel), although attested in the late biblical and early Jewish period, is rare. In the gospels and for the most part in the Acts of the

Apostles, "Christ" does retain its messianic meaning ("the Messiah").

While the messianic meaning seems clear in some Pauline contexts (Rom 9:5; 15:8; 1 Cor 1:23; possibly also 12:12), "Christ" has become virtually a surname for Jesus, although Paul also uses it, along with "Jesus Christ," in a variety of combinations, including "Christ Jesus," "Lord Jesus Christ," "Christ Jesus, our Lord," and so on. Paul obviously believed that Jesus was the Davidic Messiah of Israel, as formulated in the creedal fragment he quotes in Romans 1:3–4. In 1 Corinthians 15:24–28, he depicts Christ's post-exaltation rule in the universe with the aid of quotations taken from Psalms 8 and 110 interpreted messianically. However, the revelation of the Crucified as the Son of God that he received on the Damascus road (Gal 1:16) has so transcended the bounds of conventional Jewish messianic expectation as to render the proclamation of Jesus as Israel's Messiah less meaningful than other categories, such as "Son of God" and "Lord," especially in the context of the Gentile mission.

Describing "Christ" as a quasi-surname does not really do justice to the intensely personal way in which it occurs in the context of Paul's relationship with the risen Lord. Where once he would have said, "For me to live is the torah," now he can simply say, "For me to live is Christ" (Phil 1:21). Paul thinks of himself as "crucified with Christ," so that, he himself no longer lives but Christ lives in him, and the life he lives in the flesh, he lives through faith in the Son of God, who loved him and delivered himself up for him (Gal 2:19–20; see also Rom 14:15; 1 Cor 8:11).

Whereas "Jesus" principally designates the Son of God in his earthly life and "Lord" (*kyrios*) his postresurrection status, "Christ" is a designation that ranges across all stages of his "career," so to speak: his preexistence with God (Phil 2:5–6; 2 Cor 8:9), his life as a human being up to his obedient death, his risen life and destiny to return as eschatological judge ("the day of Christ" [1 Cor 1:8; Phil 1:6, 10; 2:16]). That said, "Christ" appears particularly in connection with Jesus's death and resurrection, especially in the context of emphasizing the redemptive act of giving himself up in love for sinful humanity (Rom 5:6, 8; 14:15; 1 Cor 8:11; 15:3; see also Gal 2:19–20). Precisely as such Christ is the One God raised from the dead (Rom 6:4; 8:11; 1 Cor 15:3–4, 12–17, 20; 2 Cor 4:14), the "last Adam" in whom believers are destined to be "made alive" (15:22), sharing his image (1 Cor 15:45).

DEATH; LORD; RESURRECTION; SON OF GOD

Reading

A. Y. Collins and J. J. Collins, *King and Messiah as Son of God: Divine, Human, and Angelic Figures in Biblical and Related Literature* (Grand Rapids: Eerdmans, 2008), 101–22; N. A. Dahl, "The Messiahship of Jesus in Paul," in *Jesus the Christ: The Historical Origins of Christological Doctrine*, ed. D. H. Juel (Minneapolis: Fortress, 1991), 15–25; Dunn, *Theology*, 197–99; Matera, *GSG*, 56–60; F. J. Matera, *New Testament Christology* (Louisville: Westminster John Knox, 1999), 83–172; M. V. Novenson, *Christ among the Messiahs: Christ Language in Paul and Messiah Language in Ancient Judaism* (Oxford: Oxford University Press, 2012); Wright, *PFG*, 816–36; B. Witherington III, *DPL*, 95–100.

"IN CHRIST"

Paul expresses the solidarity of believers with Christ and one another in a variety of ways but especially through the frequently occurring phrase "in Christ," along with variants such as "in Christ Jesus," "in the Lord," or simply "in him." In some cases, the preposition appears to be simply instrumental, referring particularly to God's redemptive action through Christ (Rom 3:24; 8:2; 1 Cor 15:22; 2 Cor 3:14; 5:19; Gal 2:17; 3:14; 1 Thess 5:18). More distinctively, Paul uses the phrase in a locative sense to designate the environment or new sphere of salvation that believers inhabit following their coming to faith and reception of baptism. The solidarity thereby established stands over against the former solidarity of all human beings "in" Adam (Rom 5:12–21; 1 Cor 15:21–22, 49; see Col 3:9–11). The most explicit statement of the change appears in 2 Corinthians 5:17: "If anyone is in Christ, that person is a new creation" (see Gal 6:15). In this sense, to be "in Christ" is virtually a designation for being a "Christian," for example, in the greeting to Andronicus and Junia when Paul remarks that "they were in Christ before me" (Rom 16:7; see also 1 Cor 1:30; Gal 1:22; Phil l:1). Paul employs "in Christ" particularly in contexts where he is summoning his audience to allow their lives to be shaped by the values distinctive of their new existence (Rom 6:11; 1 Cor 4:17; 2 Cor 2:17; Gal 5:6; Phil 2:1, 5; 4:7; Phlm 20).

More than simply an environment, however, in situations where Paul is stressing the union of believers not only with Christ but also their union with one another through him, a more personal and indeed corporate sense of "Christ" emerges, possibly as a legacy from the messianic usage of the term (1 Cor 12):

> [12] For just as the body is one and has many members, and all the members of the body, though many, are one body, *so it is with (the) Christ.*
> [13] For in the one Spirit we were all baptized into one body—Jews or Greeks, slaves or free—and we were all made to drink of one Spirit. (NRSV; italics and "*(the)*" added; see also Rom 12:5; Gal 3:26–29)

These passages—along with 1 Corinthians 6:15–17—suggest that Paul thought of the risen Lord as a kind of communal person "into" whose person ("body) individual believers entered (note the directional sense of the preposition [*eis*]) through faith and baptism, henceforth to live one's life "in" him ("in Christ"). The union thereby forged is not simply static but involves an insertion into his total "career" (death, burial, resurrection [see especially Rom 6:3–5, 8]). Whether Paul thought of life "in" the person of Christ realistically and objectively or whether it is simply a metaphorical way of describing ongoing Christian existence has long been and continues to be a matter of dispute.

ADAM; BAPTISM; BODY; FAITH

Reading

C. R. Campbell, *Paul and Union with Christ: An Exegetical and Theological Study* (Grand Rapids: Zondervan Academic, 2012); C. R. Campbell et al., eds., *"In Christ" in Paul:*

Explorations in Paul's Theology of Union and Participation (Tübingen: Mohr Siebeck, 2014); Y. Chen, *The Ritual Dimension of Union with Christ in Paul's Thought* (Tübingen: Mohr Siebeck, 2022); Dunn, *Theology*, 396–401; R. N. Longenecker, *Paul: Apostle of Liberty*, 2nd ed. (Grand Rapids: Eerdmans, 2015), 146–55; Matera, *GSG*, 78–80; C. F. D. Moule, *The Origin of Christology* (Cambridge: Cambridge University Press, 1977), 47–89; B. Witherington III, *DPL*, 98–99; Wright, *PFG*, 832–35.

CHURCH

In secular Greek usage, the term *ekklēsia* refers to an assembly of people gathered for some purpose. It regularly designates an assembly of citizens called out from their homes by the civic herald for the purposes of hearing a solemn proclamation by the authorities or to decide on some matter of importance affecting the life of the community. The origins of the Christian usage of the term to describe local gatherings of believers, as so copiously illustrated in the letters of Paul, are obscure. Some (Dunn, Trebilco) have found a biblical background in the LXX's rendering of the Hebrew *qahal* by *ekklēsia* to designate the Exodus community of Israel as "the *ekklēsia* of the Lord" (Deut 23:2). But such usage is largely confined to references in historical books such as Chronicles and 1 Maccabees, whereas by far the most widespread LXX designation for gathered Israel is *synagōgē*, a term that early Christian believers appear to have avoided.

Paul uses *ekklēsia* with reference to the occasions when believers in a locality gather for worship and other communal activity (1 Cor 11:18; 14:19, 23, 28; see also 14:33–35). More frequently *ekklēsia* designates the community itself that exists beyond the actual occasions of gathering, sometimes with indication of the particular house or household in which the gathering is wont to meet (Rom 16:5, 23; 1 Cor 16:19; Phlm 2; see Col 4:15). Elsewhere, the community addressed is identified by the city or locality in which it exists: "the church at Cenchreae" (Rom 16:1); "the church of God in Corinth" (1 Cor 1:2; 2 Cor 1:1); "the church of the Thessalonians" (1 Thess 1:1; see 2 Thess 1:1). Romans is not addressed to a single church; however, the lengthy greetings that conclude the letter suggest that the believers in the imperial capital gathered in several house churches (Rom 16:5, 10, 11, 14, 15). Likewise, Galatians addresses "the churches of Galatia" (Gal 1:2; see 1 Cor 16:1), and there are similar regional references to churches in other letters: "the churches of Asia" (1 Cor 16:19); "the churches of Macedonia" (2 Cor 8:1); "the churches of Judea" (Gal 1:22; see 1 Thess 2:14). Elsewhere, Paul refers to the local communities of believers for which, as apostle to the Gentiles, he has particular responsibility simply as "all the churches" (Rom 16:4, 16; 1 Cor 7:17; 11:16; 2 Cor 8:18, 19, 23, 24; 11:28; 12:13; see 1 Cor 4:17; Phil 4:15; also 1 Cor 14:33; 2 Thess 1:4).

Along with these simple references there are places in the letters where a deeper theological sense attaching to *ekklēsia* emerges. The local communities constitute the "church of God" in a particular place. In Paul's eyes its members should have a distinctive sense of belonging to a community chosen, called, and sanctified by God through the Holy Spirit (1 Cor 1:2, 9; 6:4; 10:32; 11:22; 14:4; 2 Cor 1:1; 1 Thess 1:4; see Rom 8:29–30), on the way to salvation (1 Cor 15:2; 2 Cor 2:15; 3:18). With God as Father (Rom 8:15; Gal 4:6) and Christ as "firstborn brother" (Rom 8:29), the church is the family or household of God, in which all are brothers and sisters. Unlike the associations in the surrounding Greco-Roman society that gathered around the memory of a figure of the past or under the patronage of a particular god, the members of the *ekklēsia* gather to worship the one true God, in the living presence of the risen Lord, whom they collectively embody as "the body of Christ" (1 Cor 12:12–13) and whose values they are required to live out as they await his return (1 Cor 6:12–20; 11:17–34). In a series of rich images, the church in Corinth is a "field" that Paul has "planted" and Apollos has "watered," while its "growth" is entirely the work of God (1 Cor 3:6). Its members constitute a holy "building" (*oikodomē*), a "temple of God," indwelt by the Holy Spirit (3:16–17; 2 Cor 6:16b–18). The distinctive and diverse "gifts" (*charismata*) that the Spirit communicates to individuals in each community work together to "build up" (*oikodomein*) the church (1 Cor 14:4, 12; see 1 Cor 12–14 as a whole).

A Wider Sense of Church?

A key question in regard to "church" in Paul concerns whether his use of *ekklēsia* refers only to communities in a particular city or locality or whether there is some sense already in the undisputed letters (as is certainly the case in Colossians and Ephesians) that the term has a supra-local reference to the totality of the believing communities in a collective sense. There is perhaps a hint of this more universal reference when, recalling his past, Paul speaks of having persecuted "the church of God" (1 Cor 15:9; Phil 3:6; see Gal 1:13b), although if his brief career as a persecutor targeted only the primitive community in Jerusalem, the reference would still be strictly local. It could well be that it was in the mother church in Jerusalem that the disciples first began to describe themselves as "the assembly (*ekklēsia*) of God" and that this description, largely through the efforts of Paul, spread in due course to the communities established elsewhere. There could be a hint of a wider reference in his concluding admonition in 1 Corinthians 10:32, "Give no offense to Jews or Greeks or to the church of God," where "the church of God" appears as an entity set alongside the two ethnic groups that constitute humanity. In 1 Corinthians 12:28, Paul asserts that "God has appointed in the church first apostles, second prophets, third teachers." Whatever about prophets and teachers, it is unlikely that, as founder of the church in Corinth, Paul would accept the existence of any apostle there beside himself (see 1 Cor 3:6, 10; 4:15). Once again, a universal reference is more likely. Paul's hailing of particular communities as "the church of God" in a particular locality may indicate a sense that believers as a whole represent more than the sum total of all in the local communities; on the analogy perhaps of Israel's sense of "diaspora," they collectively constitute a unified "assembly of God," calling on the Lord's name in every place (Rom 10:12–13; 1 Cor 1:2).

"Church" in the Deutero-Pauline Letters

This "diaspora" understanding may have been the seed from which grew the use of *ekklēsia* in the more universal and indeed cosmic sense found in Colossians, notably in the hymnic text, Colossians 1:15–20, where the church is the "body" of which Christ is the "head" (v. 18; see also v. 24). Elsewhere in the letter, *ekklēsia* retains its reference to the local community (4:16), even to that gathering that meets in the house of an individual (Nympha [4:15]).

In the fully developed universal usage found in Ephesians, *ekklēsia* no longer refers to the local church. The distinction between Christ as head and the church as his body is pressed further: the church is the "fullness" (*plērōma*) or extension of Christ, the one who, as risen Lord, fills all things (1:22–23). The unity of Jews and Gentiles in the church following Christ's abolition of the age-old division and hostility through his work on the cross (2:11–22), has become a major theme, the fulfillment of a mystery, hidden from before the ages. The unified church makes known to the powers the manifold wisdom of God (3:9–10). The risen and exalted Lord has given gifts to each of the faithful in order to build up the body (the church) to the full measure of the "stature" of Christ (4:11–16). The Pauline author has adapted Paul's image of the church in Corinth as a pure virgin whom he had betrothed to Christ (2 Cor 11:2) into an explanation of the relationship between Christ and the universal church, and then made it a model for the relationship that should obtain between husbands and wives. As the church is subject to Christ its head, so wives should be subject to their husbands; as Christ loves and nourishes the church as his body, so husbands should love and nourish their wives (5:21–33). The joining together of man and woman in the sexual act in fulfillment of the design of the Creator according to Genesis 2:24, cited in v. 31, is a "great mystery" (v. 32a) in the sense that the Pauline author interprets it as foreshadowing the all-important unity between Christ and the church. The application of the ecclesiological image to the marital relationship has its challenges today but, in its own way, testifies to the high significance of ecclesiology in the letter as a whole.

According to the post-Pauline 1 Timothy, the well-governed household provides the model for how the church itself should be governed (3:5), it being the "household of God, the pillar and bulwark of the truth" (3:15).

ADOPTION; APOSTLE; BODY; BODY OF CHRIST; SPIRIT; TEMPLE; WOMAN

Reading

E. Adams, "The Shape of the Pauline Churches," (ch. 5) in *The Oxford Handbook of Ecclesiology*, ed. Paul Avis (Oxford: OUP, 2018), 119–46; E. Best, "Essay 1: The Church," in *Ephesians* (Edinburgh: T&T Clark, 1998), 622–41; Dunn, *Theology*, 537–52; Fitzmyer, *1 Corinthians*, 81–85; L. T. Johnson, *OEBT* 1:239–46; "Paul's Ecclesiology," in Dunn, *CCP*, 199–211; R. J. Korner, *The Origin and Meaning of* Ekklēsia *in the Early Jesus Movement* (Leiden: Brill, 2017), 150–264; R. Last, "*Ekklēsia* Outside the Septuagint and the *Demos*," *JBL* 137 (2018): 959–80; A. T. Lincoln, "Ephesians," in Dunn, *CCP*, 133–40; *Ephesians*, xciii–xcv, 161–63, 264–69, 387–90; Matera, *GSG*, 126–46; Y.-H. Park, *Paul's Ekklesia as a Civic Assembly* (Tübingen:

Mohr Siebeck, 2015); J. Roloff, *EDNT* 1:410–15; P. Trebilco, "Why Did the Early Christians Call Themselves *hē ekklēsia* [Greek]?" *NTS* 57 (2011): 440–60; G. H. van Kooten, "*Ekklēsia tou theou* [Greek]: The 'Church of God' and the Civic Assemblies (*ekklēsiai* [Greek] of the Greek Cities in the Roman Empire," *NTS* 58 (2012): 522–48; Wolter, *Paul*, 153–57.

CIRCUMCISION, CIRCUMCISE

Paul refers to circumcision (noun *peritomē*; verb *peritemnō*) in three ways: first, with respect to the practice itself; second, as a shorthand way ("the circumcision" [*hē peritomē*]) of referring to the people (Jews) who practice it, over against "the non-circumcision" (*akrobystia*), the Gentiles, who do not (Rom 3:30; 4:12; 15:8; Gal 2:7, 8, 9, 12; see also Col 3:11; 4:11; Titus 1:10); and third, in a figurative sense indicating a moral disposition ("circumcision of the heart" [Rom 2:29]).

As a Pharisaic Jew, Paul would have been totally committed to the necessity of circumcision as an essential mark of Jewish identity according to the unambiguous command imposed by God on Abraham (Gen 17:9–14). An intriguing remark of Paul, "If I am still preaching circumcision, why am I still being persecuted?" (Gal 5:11), suggests that at some stage, presumably before coming to faith in Christ, the zealous young Pharisee was insisting that all males who claimed or wanted to be part of God's holy people, specifically Gentile proselytes, must undergo circumcision, the sign and seal of the covenant regulated by the Mosaic law.

The encounter with the risen Lord and the concomitant grasp of the implications of Christ's death in regard to the universality of sin (Rom 3:23) shattered Paul's sense of a "holy nation" (Jews) set apart from "Gentile sinners" (Gal 2:15) and along with it the efficacy of covenant membership initiated by circumcision. His concern for the inclusion of Gentiles was confirmed but on a totally different basis: acceptance in faith of the gospel of the Crucified as the sole path to the righteousness required for salvation (Rom 1:16–17; Gal 2:16).

Circumcision in Galatians

Circumcision features prominently in Galatians because of the pressure being placed on the Gentile community by intrusive Christian Jewish teachers to take on circumcision and the full practice of the law. Paul's initial response (Gal 2:1–10) is to point out that the validity of his law-free gospel to the Gentiles ("the uncircumcision" [*akrobystia*]), alongside that of Peter ("Cephas") to the Jews ("the circumcision" [*peritomē*]), had been accepted by the leaders at a meeting in Jerusalem (Gal 2:6–9). Nor, at that meeting, had he yielded to pressure to have Titus circumcised, although he was known by all to be a "Greek" (Gentile) (vv. 3–5). Later (2:11–21), Paul recalls the response he gave publicly to Peter at Antioch when pressure from the James party had led him to abandon table fellowship with community members of Gentile origin, thereby in Paul's eyes re-erecting the Jew–Gentile barrier that God's act in Christ had thrown down (2:15, 18; see 3:28). Although circumcision as such was not an issue on this occasion, it was necessarily included in "the works of the law" that coming to faith in Christ excluded as a basis for justification (2:16). To continue to pursue justification by this route is to render the (supremely costly) death of Christ as of no purpose (*dōrean* [v. 21b])—in Paul's eyes, an utterly intolerable rejection of the grace of God (v. 21a).

In an extended sequence (Gal 3:1—4:7), Paul points to the gift of the Spirit as the key indication, preannounced in the Scriptures (3:6–9), that the Galatians have already been justified at the moment of coming to faith. To take on circumcision, along with the obligation to obey the law perfectly that it involves (5:3), means being "cut off from Christ" (v. 4); it means reverting to the slavery from which Christ has set them free (v. 1; see 4:1–3, 8–10). "In Christ Jesus neither circumcision [*peritomē*] nor the lack of it [*akrobystia*] mean anything but (only) faith finding expression through love" (5:6). Ultimately for Paul what is at stake, as earlier (2:20–21), is the efficacy of Christ's cross. Those who want to see the Galatians circumcised do so because they fear persecution (the kind Paul once inflicted) on account of Christ's cross (6:12). They want to "boast in your flesh" (i.e., the Galatians' circumcised state) (v. 13), whereas Paul's sole boast is in the cross (v. 14). For "neither circumcision [*peritomē*] nor the lack of it [*akrobystia*] is anything; rather, (there is) a new creation" (*kainē ktisis*) (v. 15). Circumcision belongs to the old age from which the Galatians have been set free. In the Spirit they live as members of the totally new order inaugurated by the death and raising of Christ.

Circumcision in Romans

Paul first mentions circumcision in the fictive dialogue with a Jewish teacher that excludes any route to justification other than by faith (Rom 1:18—3:20). Having relativized the value of the Mosaic law in this regard, on the grounds that performance rather than its possession was the key criterion (2:1–24), he turns more briefly to a similar argument in regard to circumcision (2:25–29). Transgression of the law renders circumcision "*un*circumcision" (*akrobystia*) (v. 25). By the same token, he asks, Will not the uncircumcision (*akrobystia*) of the Gentile who keeps the requirements of the law be reckoned as circumcision (*peritomē*) (v. 26)? With the last judgment in mind, Paul finally turns to the divine evaluation of who is "the real Jew" (v. 28). The real Jew in God's eyes will no longer be, as before, the external one marked by a circumcision made in the flesh but the one who is a "hidden Jew," whose circumcision is that "of the heart, wrought by the Spirit" (v. 29). Here we see the figurative usage of circumcision already found in the Old Testament (Deut 10:16; Jer 4:4; 9:25–26; Ezek 44:7), with echoes also of Jeremiah 31:31–34 (see Rom 7:6; 2 Cor 3:3).

In Romans 4, Paul faces the task of wresting the figure of Abraham away from the traditional view of him as a model of obedience to the depiction of him as a paradigm of one who found justification by faith, becoming in this respect the "father" of all subsequent believers. The all-important trump card in Paul's hand is Genesis 15:6, a text that, together with Psalm 31:1–2 (LXX), links being reckoned righteous by God simply and exclusively with Abraham's faith (Rom 4:3–8). Paul then (vv. 9–10) exploits the sequence in Genesis whereby the circumcision command to which the patriarch was obedient (Gen 17:9–14) appears only *later* in the story, making clear that his being declared righteous occurred when he was in a state of "un-circumcision" (*en akrobystia*). In that state he *subsequently* received circumcision as a "sign" (*sēmeion*) and "seal" (*sphragis*) of the righteousness he had already received through faith (v. 11a). This rendered him apt to be "the father," in first instance of all those (Gentiles) who in their lack of circumcision (*di' akrobystia*) would be reckoned righteous on the basis of faith (v. 11b), and "father of the circumcision" (Jews), who proceed not from circumcision only but who also follow the way of faith marked out by their father Abraham (v. 12). Thus, Paul has redefined Abraham's fatherhood—and with it the transmission of the promised inheritance in the messianic age (4:13)—away from circumcision and obedience to law, thereby allowing the inclusion of the Gentiles solely on the basis of faith.

Circumcision in Philippians

Writing from prison to the Philippians and facing the prospect of death, Paul feels the need to warn the community against an intrusion similar to that which had occurred in Galatia (3:2–4:1). "We are the (true) circumcision [*hēmeis... esmen hē peritomē*]," he insists (3:3), "serving God in the Spirit and boasting in Christ Jesus, with no confidence in the flesh" (i.e., in physical circumcision). He lists "circumcised on the eighth day" as the first of the impeccable Jewish credentials (v. 5) that he has come to regard as of no value in light of the supreme advantage of knowing Christ (vv. 7–8). Imitating his example, the community should hold firm to what has been attained (vv. 16–17), because "enemies of the cross of Christ" are abroad (v. 18), "whose belly is their god and whose glory lies in their shame" (v. 19ab). These "enemies" of the cross (see Gal 6:12–15) appear to be urging observance of Jewish food laws, on the one hand (see Gal 2:11–14), and circumcision, on the other (for "shame" [*aischynē*] as a reference to private parts see *ta aschēmona* in 1 Cor 12:23). The latter leads to an earthly belonging (v. 19c)—to Israel, presumably—whereas, as Paul continues, "our (true) citizenship" (*politeuma*) is a heavenly one (v. 20a) (see CITIZENSHIP).

Nonpolemical References to Circumcision

In contexts where observance of the Mosaic law is not an issue, Paul regards whether one is circumcised or not as a matter of no consequence. He invokes it as an illustration of the principle he advocates in the churches of remaining in the condition in which one is when called (1 Cor 7:17a; see vv. 20, 24): for "circumcision is nothing and the lack of it is nothing. (What matters) is keeping the commandments of God" (v. 19; see Gal 5:6).

Figurative Circumcision in Colossians

In Colossians 2:11, the readers are assured that in Christ they "have been circumcised with a circumcision not made with (human) hands [*en hō kai perietmēthēte peritomē acheiropoiētō*] but involving a stripping off of the fleshly body in the circumcision of Christ [*en tō peritomē tou Christou*]." The following verse (v. 12) suggests that believers' baptismal involvement in the (death), burial, and resurrection of Christ is a "circumcision" that has replaced their "uncircumcised state" (*akrobystia*) in the pre-conversion Gentile existence (v. 13). This figurative sense is taken up in Ephesians 2:11.

ABRAHAM; CROSS; GENTILES; JEW, JUDAISM; LAW; RIGHTEOUSNESS

Reading

J. M. G. Barclay, *Obeying the Truth*, 45–60; "Paul and Philo on Circumcision," in *Pauline Churches and Diaspora Jews* (Tübingen: Mohr Siebeck, 2011), 61–79; O. Betz, *EDNT* 3:79–80; T. L. Donaldson, *Paul and the Gentiles: Remapping the Apostle's Convictional World* (Minneapolis: Fortress, 1997), 275–92; Dunn, *Beginning*, 438–61; R. G. Hall, *ABD* 1:1025–31; T. W. Martin, "Paul and Circumcision," in Sampley, *Paul*, 1:113–42; N. J. McEleney, "Conversion, Circumcision and the Law," *NTS* 20 (1973–74): 319–41; T. R. Schreiner, *DPL*, 137–39; M. Thiessen, *Paul and the Gentile Problem* (New York: Oxford University Press, 2016).

CITIZENSHIP

Reference to citizenship in Paul occurs only in his letter to the Philippians (1:27 [the verb *politeuō*]; 3:20 [the noun *politeuma*]). Philippi was a Roman colony many of whose inhabitants would have enjoyed Roman citizenship. Allusions to this status would have resonated well with those who read or heard the letter. The noun *politeuma* can refer either to an organized state (commonwealth) to which citizens belong or to the "citizenship"—the privileges and rights—that such belonging confers. The verb, usually in the middle voice *politeuomai*, means to exercise the rights and privileges of living in such a commonwealth, often with the sense of doing so appropriately.

In Philippians 1:27, Paul moves from discussion of his own situation in prison to a more exhortatory passage, 1:27—2:18, encouraging the Philippians to stand firm in their commitment despite the hostility they incur. He urges them to "live worthily [*axiōs...politeuesthe*] of the gospel of Christ." Citizenship brings responsibilities and duties as well as rights. Paul's use here of the verb *politeuōmai* rather than the more usual *peripateō* (see Rom 6:4; 8:4; 13:13) communicates the sense that they should live as responsible citizens of a new commonwealth into which they have been incorporated through their adherence to the gospel.

The nature of this commonwealth becomes explicit toward the end of the sharp warning Paul gives in 3:2–4:1 against "evil doers, those who mutilate the flesh" (3:2). The warning seems directed against intrusive Christian Jewish teachers of a more conservative stamp who would seek to impose circumcision on the Philippians much as they or others of the same ilk had attempted in Galatia. Paul characterizes them as "enemies of Christ's cross" (v. 18), "whose God is the stomach and whose glory rests in their shame" (v. 19ab). If, as seems likely (see 3:2; Gal 6:12–15), the latter charge refers to circumcision, Paul would then have in mind the Jewish commonwealth, marked out as a people by the rite of circumcision. The adversaries he is warning against have "set their mind on earthly things" (v. 19c), in the sense that they have not responded to the announcement in the gospel of a divine intervention that is setting the present age and its institutions aside. Hence he continues with the contrasting claim, "Our citizenship belongs to the heavens [*hēmōn... politeuma en ouranois hyparchei*], from which we await a savior, the Lord Jesus Christ" (v. 20), "who will transform the body of our lowliness to make it conform to the body of his glory, according to the power that is his to subdue all things to himself" (v. 21). Believers have their names enrolled, as citizens, in a commonwealth that belongs to the realm of God. Although still living a bodily life determined by the mortality of the present age, they confidently await the arrival of a Savior from the heavenly realm. He will transform their present bodily incapacity to live there into the capacity to do so on the model of his own glorious risen existence (see 1 Cor 15:24–28, 35–55).

In expressing this hope, Paul is not necessarily setting the Christian sense of citizenship over against the Roman citizenship that the Philippians currently enjoy. Nor is he arguing from a totally otherworldly point of view. He is making the point that believers have a "dual citizenship" at the present time, one of which—the heavenly—determines how one lives here and now. The prospect of its full bodily realization (Phil 3:21) should ward off any invitation to "enroll" themselves through the bodily rite—circumcision—in the commonwealth (Israel) that belongs to a world already passing away.

Paul, a Roman Citizen?

Although Paul makes no mention of the subject in his letters, according to several references in the Acts of the Apostles, he did enjoy Roman citizenship (see Acts 16:37–38; 22:25; 23:27), as the Roman form of his name, "Paulus," along with the Jewish "Saul," suggests. Doubt has been cast on the historicity of this claim in Acts but the more recent tendency has been to accept it. Such citizenship could be inherited or acquired by other means such as purchase, by release from slavery, or military service. Most likely Paul inherited it because he belonged to a diaspora Jewish family taken into slavery decades before and subsequently freed.

BODY; CIRCUMCISION; ETHICS; ISRAEL; RESURRECTION

Reading

F. F. Bruce, *ABD* 1:1048–49; Holloway, *Philippians*, 104–6, 178–80; J. Murphy-O'Connor, *Paul: A Critical Life* (Oxford: Clarendon, 1996), 39–41; M. Reasoner, *DPL*, 140–42; Schnelle, *Apostle Paul*, 60–62; Wright, *PFG*, 1292–97.

COLLECTION (FOR THE SAINTS) (*see* Communion, Fellowship; Ministry; Riches, Poverty)

COMMUNION, FELLOWSHIP

"Communion" ("Fellowship") finds expression in Paul in various forms of the Greek word group, *koinōnos*, *koinōneō*, *koinōnia*, also the compounds *synkoinōnos*, *synkoinōneō*. The sense is that of participation or sharing, either in the passive sense of having a share in something or the active sense of sharing something with another person. The noun *koinōnia*, by far the most frequently occurring expression of the motif in Paul, has the basic sense of the union/fellowship/partnership created among individuals by their common participation in some experience or activity, for example, when people gather to celebrate the birthday of one of their number concretely enacted by sharing a cake. "Common participation in" would then be the most accurate translation of the Greek term *koinōnia*.

Paul uses *koinōnia* in a variety of contexts. Perhaps the most basic is the sense of Christian identity created by the common experience of the Spirit: *koinōnia tou pneumatos* (2 Cor 13:13; Phil 2:1; see also Eph 4:3–4) or by the sharing of the faith (Phlm 6). The *koinōnia* experienced by believers has both a "vertical" and a "horizontal" dimension, a duality perhaps best seen in Paul's brief reference to the Eucharist in 1 Corinthians 10:16–17 to exclude believers' participation in feasts tainted with idolatrous worship. The shared cup involves a "communion" (*koinōnia*) with the blood of Christ (v. 16a); the loaf that is broken and shared involves a "communion" (*koinōnia*) with his body (v. 16b). These more "vertical" aspects of union with Christ (see also 1 Cor 1:9) bring about the "horizontal" union among participants described in verse 17. Because there is one loaf, all are one because they share the one loaf. The *koinōnia* established in both respects is totally incompatible with anything smacking of union with the demons believed to be operative in pagan worship (vv. 20–22; see also 2 Cor 6:14; Eph 5:11; 1 Tim 5:22).

The basic *koinōnia* between believers finds expression in various ways. Paul acknowledges that the Philippians have been one with him in common service of the gospel (Phil 1:5, 7). The "right hand of *koinōnia*" given to Paul by the "pillar" apostles after the meeting in Jerusalem (Gal 2:9) represents an acknowledgment on their part that his distinctive mission to the Gentiles is a genuine sharing with them in the apostolic promulgation of the gospel. *Koinōnia* and cognates appear frequently in regard to the sharing of material resources between communities on the basis of their sharing in the spiritual benefits flowing from the gospel. This latter aspect is particularly prominent in respect to the obligation to support the mother community ("the saints," "the poor") in Jerusalem (Rom 15:26–27; 2 Cor 8:4; 9:13; Gal 2:9–10; see also Rom 12:13) or to the apostle himself (Phil 4:14–15) or another teacher (Gal 6:6). The collection for the saints is no mere gesture of economic relief but the most tangible expression of the *koinōnia* existing across all the churches, particularly, in Paul's eyes, that which existed or should exist between his Gentile communities and the mother church in Jerusalem. Hence his anxiety that his "ministry (the collection) in Jerusalem be acceptable to the saints" (Rom 15:31b).

The motif of *koinōnia* is so prominent in Philippians that it may reflect, as has been suggested, a formal partnership between the community and Paul (J. R. Sampley). It seems more likely, however, that it is simply the unique generosity of this church (4:14–20) that induces Paul to make much of the motif of "sharing" throughout the letter: the Philippians' "sharing" in the work of the gospel (1:5, 7), the shared experience of the Spirit (2:1), his own sharing in the sufferings of Christ (*koinōnian [tōn] pathēmatōn autou* [3:10]—afflictions that the Philippians have also shared when they supported him in his hardship (4:14).

All in all, the prominence of the concept of *koinōnia* in the Pauline literature as compared to the rest of the New Testament testifies to its significance for the apostle as an expression of the intimate bond between believers and Christ, and their union with each other, constantly attested by the experience of the Spirit, and given concrete expression in the generosity expected toward fellow believers particularly in need.

EUCHARIST; IDOLATRY; RICHES, POVERTY; SPIRIT

Reading

Dunn, *Theology*, 561–62; J. Hainz, *EDNT* 2:303–5; Holloway, *Philippians*, 74–75, 187–89; M. A. Jennings, *The Price of Partnership in the Letter of Paul to the Philippians: "Make My Joy Complete"* (London, New York: Bloomsbury, 2018); P. T. O'Brien, *DPL*, 293–95; J. M. Ogereau, *Paul's Koinonia with the Philippians: A Socio-Historical Investigation of a Pauline Partnership* (Tübingen: Mohr Siebeck, 2014); G. Panikulam, *Koinonia in the New Testament: A Dynamic Expression of Christian Life* (Rome: Biblical Institute Press, 1979), 8–108; J. R. Sampley, *Pauline Partnership in Christ: Christian Community and Commitment in Light of Roman Law* (Philadelphia: Fortress, 1980).

CONSCIENCE

"Conscience" (*syneidēsis*) came to Paul not from the biblical background but from popular Greek philosophy of the time. Originally meaning simply "consciousness," it came to have the sense of self-reflective awareness of what one has done or what one proposes to do, especially as regards whether such behavior is good or bad. It thus functions as an internal moral judge of what is right or wrong, both with respect to one's own behavior and also that of others. Paul's usage is indebted to that of Hellenistic Judaism (seen especially in Philo and the Wisdom of Solomon [LXX 17:10]), which had combined the popular usage in Greco-Roman culture with the strong Jewish sense of responsibility before God, especially as expressed in the Mosaic law. In this sense, conscience is that aspect of self-awareness that constantly evaluates one's behavior before that responsibility, for which one will be held accountable at the judgment.

The first occurrence of conscience in the Pauline corpus well illustrates this usage. In an attempt to relativize the value of possessing the Mosaic law (Rom 2:12–16), Paul points to the behavior of Gentiles. Although not possessing the law,

> 15 They show the work of the law written on their hearts, with their conscience providing confirmation [*symmartyrousēs autōn tēs syneidēseōs*] as their conflicting thoughts accuse or perhaps excuse them.

The fact that Gentiles can suffer pangs of conscience or, alternatively, feel good about what they have done, is testimony to the presence of a "law written on their hearts."

Elsewhere, Paul appeals to conscience in contexts where he is dealing with accusations or possible accusations against his own behavior. Introducing the sensitive issue of Israel's current rejection of the gospel (Rom 9–11), Paul adduces his conscience as a witness (*symmartyrousēs mou tēs syneidēseōs*) to the sincerity of his distress about the situation (9:1). He makes a similar affirmation via the verbal form in regarding the faithfulness of his apostolic ministry in Corinth. Although the final verdict rests with God, his conscience is clear (*ouden...emautō synoida*) (1 Cor 4:4; see also 2 Cor 1:12).

As well as appealing to the witness of his own conscience, Paul appeals to the consciences of those to whom he writes concerning his ministry. He ("we") does not employ shameful underhand measures that would distort the word of God but "by the open statement of the truth we commend ourselves to the conscience of everyone (*pros pasan syneidēsin*) in the sight of God" (2 Cor 4:2). The presupposition here is that every person has a capacity for moral judgment (conscience) and should respond positively to the open statement of the truth. The fact that so many do not do so is not the fault of the gospel or its proclaimers but, as the following sentences indicate, because "the god of this age" (Satan) has blinded their hearts" (v. 4). In this work of "persuasion," Paul claims to be entirely open to God and hopes that he is similarly open to the consciences of the Corinthians as well (5:11). The suggestion appears to be that, if they will set aside prejudice, the purity of his motives is something they will be obliged in conscience to accept. What emerges from these passages is Paul's respect for human freedom, along with the acknowledgment that conscience, functioning at its best, has the capacity to recognize and adhere to the truth.

In regard to the concrete issue of paying taxes and tariffs imposed by the civil authorities (Rom 13:1–7), Paul urges compliance with these requirements not simply out of fear of punishment but "for conscience' sake" (*dia tēn syneidēsin*) (v. 5). "Conscience" here reflects awareness that behind civic authority stands the rule of God (see vv. 1–4). Submission to such authority is part of the obedience that encompasses every aspect of a believer's life as a rational embodied being (12:1–2).

"Conscience" in the Matter of Eating Meat Sacrificed in Pagan Worship

"Conscience" appears in notable concentration in Paul's response to the Corinthians concerning the propriety of eating meat that has been used in pagan worship (1 Cor 8–10). In a first discussion of the matter (8:1–13), Paul concedes that, in light of belief in one God and one Lord (8:6), idols have no reality and that, other things being equal, this should allow for the freedom to consume such food without scruple. However, he points out that such robust knowledge stemming from faith is not universally shared. There are "weak" members who lack such knowledge (v. 7a). When they follow the example of those who eat with knowledge (v. 7b), they eat the food as genuinely sacrificed to idols and so are defiled in conscience (*hē syneidēsis autōn...molynetai*) (v. 7c; see v. 10), placing their salvation in jeopardy (v. 11). Hence, Paul insists, the freedom of those with knowledge to eat such meat should yield, in a deeper exercise of freedom, to refraining from eating in light of the paramount requirements of love and responsibility. By "sinning against the brothers (and sisters) in this way and wounding their weak conscience [*typtontes autōn tēn syneidēsin asthenousan*]" they would be "sinning against Christ" (v. 12). Here, as in Romans 2:15, conscience has its basic sense of the internal moral arbiter of what is right and wrong, especially in light of the accountability to God stemming from the key tenets of Christian faith.

After, by way of example, a "digression" concerning his own use of freedom (9:1–27) and a warning against having anything to do with idolatry (10:1–22), Paul returns directly to the issue as it arises in a slightly different circumstance (10:23–33). Believers may eat whatever is sold in the open marketplace without any scruple of conscience (*mēden anakrinountes dia tēn syneidēsin*) (v. 25). By the same token, when invited by an unbeliever to a social meal they may similarly eat without scruple what is placed before them (v. 27c). If, however, one of the company—obviously one with the weak conscience (see 8:7) is in view—says, "This has been sacrificed to idols," then one should not eat "on account of the one pointing this out and of conscience" (*di' ekeinon ton mēnysanta kai tēn syneidēsin*) (10:28). But Paul hastens to clarify: "I mean the other's conscience, not your own" (v. 29a) and adds "For why should my freedom be determined by the conscience of another?" (*hinati gar hē eleuthēria mou krinetai hypo allēs syneidēseōs*) (v. 29b). This last comment again shows Paul's respect for the moral autonomy of the individual. I do not curtail my freedom because I submit, contrary to the judgment of my conscience, to the faulty judgment of the weak conscience of the other person. I do so because, in this particular circumstance and without injury to my basic freedom to eat anything with thankfulness to God (v. 30), a deeper freedom flowing from responsibility and love calls me to refrain.

The Post-Pauline Letters

"Conscience," which does not appear in Ephesians, Colossians, or 2 Thessalonians, appears in the Pastoral Letters not so much in the sense of a moral arbiter but with its original sense of "consciousness," in this case consciousness of having behaved well, so that one has a "good" (1 Tim 1:5, 19a) or "clear" (1 Tim 3:9; 2 Tim 1:3) conscience. Contrary to this, the consciences of the false teachers condemned in the letters have been "seared with a hot iron" (1 Tim 4:2) or, along with the "mind," are "defiled" (Titus 1:15).

EUCHARIST; FREEDOM; IDOLATRY; LOVE

Reading

S. C. Barton, *ECB*, 1330–36 (on 1 Cor 8:1–13; 10:23–33); P. Bosman, *Conscience in Philo and Paul: A Conceptual History of the Synoida Word Group* (Tübingen: Mohr Siebeck, 2003),

191–275; Byrne, *Romans*, 93–94, 388–90; Dunn, *Romans 1–8*, 100–102, 105–6; Fitzmyer, *1 Corinthians*, 344–45; J. M. Gundry-Volf, *DPL*, 153–56; R. A. Horsley, "Consciousness and Freedom among the Corinthians: 1 Corinthians 8–10," *CBQ* 40 (1978): 574–89; Jewett, *Anthropological Terms*, 402–46, 458–60; C. A. Pierce, *Conscience in the New Testament* (London: SCM, 1955); Schnelle, *Apostle Paul*, 528–31; Thiselton, *1 Corinthians*, 640–44; M. E. Thrall, "The Pauline Use of SYNEIDĒSIS," *NTS* 14 (1967–68): 118–25.

COVENANT

"Covenant" (*diathēkē*) appears only nine times in Paul (including Eph 2:12) but is more significant in his theology than the paucity of reference might suggest. A reference to "the covenants" (*hai diathēkai*) appears among the six historical privileges of Israel Paul lists in Romans 9:4. The plural form could point to several covenants between God and Israel recorded in the Old Testament: with Abraham (Gen 15:18; renewed 17:2–14); the Mosaic covenant on Mount Sinai (Exod 19:1–8; 24:3–8; renewed 34:1–28; Deut 29–31; Jos 24:25); with David (2 Sam 23:5). It is likely, however, that the plural form, in a list that may well be a traditional formulation, simply indicates the abiding covenant relationship between God and Israel (from which the Gentiles have hitherto been "strangers" according to Eph 2:12). For Paul three moments of covenant making on God's part were crucial: the covenant God made with Abraham following his being found righteous through faith (Gen 15); the Sinai dispensation expressed in the obligations of the Mosaic law (Exod 24:3–8); the "new covenant" promised in Jeremiah 31:31–33.

"Covenant" in Galatians 3

The nub of Paul's argument in Galatians 3 against the Gentile Galatians taking on circumcision and the yoke of the Mosaic law lies in privileging the covenant with Abraham and the promise that accompanied it over the covenant dispensed to Moses on Mount Sinai. Paul sees the promise God made to Abraham as a divine will or testament (*diathēkē*) the clauses of which cannot be altered by a dispensation (Sinai) coming four hundred and thirty years later (Gal 3:15–17). The promise made to Abraham focused specifically on a singular "offspring" (*sperma*), namely, Christ (v. 16). Believers come under the scope of this promise simply and solely through their "entrance into" Christ by means of faith and baptism (3:27–29). Thus, Paul draws a straight line between Abraham and Christ, "leapfrogging" over the Sinai covenant and its imposition of the Mosaic law.

The Old Covenant and the New

Later in the letter (4:21–31), Paul constructs a second argument to the same effect drawing on the scriptural record concerning Abraham's two wives and the two sons to which they gave birth: one, Ishmael, from the slave girl Hagar (Gen 16:15); the other, Isaac, from the free woman Sarah (21:1–3). Through an ingenious wordplay (Gal

4:24–25) Paul finds here an allegory of "two covenants" (*dyo diathēkai*). The first, the covenant promulgated on Mount Sinai and currently promoted in "the present-day Jerusalem" (including by the Christian teachers disturbing the Galatians), he associates with Hagar and her slave status (v. 25). The second, he associates, not immediately with Sarah, as we might expect, but rather with the heavenly Jerusalem, who is free and is "our mother" (vv. 26, 31), giving rise to the covenant of freedom promoted by Paul (see JERUSALEM).

The same thought of two covenants runs through the extended midrash that Paul deploys in 2 Corinthians 3:1–18 in defense of the credibility and competence of his apostolic ministry. In the face of criticism in Corinth, he argues that "our" qualification (*hikanōtēs*) comes from God, "who has qualified us to be ministers of a new covenant [*diakonous kainēs diathēkēs*], not of letter, but of spirit [*ou grammatos alla pneumatos*]. For the letter kills but the Spirit gives life" (v. 6). Paul is here again setting up a contrast between the Sinai covenant (the one of "letter"; see v. 3) and the "new covenant" (foretold in Jer 31:31–33) promoted by the apostles. On an *a fortiori* logic that he often employs, he argues that, if, as told in Exodus 34:29, an accrediting glory attended Moses's administration of the former covenant, which was one of condemnation, how much greater must be the accrediting glory attending the administration of righteousness (2 Cor 3:7–11). Paul makes play (3:12–16) with the detail in Exodus 34:33–35 recording that Moses, when he had finished promulgating the law, placed a veil over his face to shield the Israelites from the divine glory reflected on it (2 Cor 3:13). The veil, Paul argues, continues to lie over the hearts of Israelites "to this very day" when the old covenant (*palaia diathēkē*) is read out to them, preventing them from seeing that in Christ it is being removed (v. 14). It is not clear whether what is being removed ("it") is the veil over the hearts or the covenant itself. Both readings are possible but the overall thrust of the argument points to the temporary and provisional nature of the old covenant, which human sin has rendered a dispensation of condemnation (v. 9a). Christ's saving work on the cross has lifted that condemnation for those who "turn to the Lord" through faith. In the power of the Spirit they enter the "new covenant" of freedom foretold by Jeremiah (v. 17).

Finally, the "new covenant" features in Paul's recalling of the eucharistic tradition in 1 Corinthians 11:23–26, specifically Jesus's words over the cup: "This cup is the new covenant in my blood" (*hē kainē diathēkē estin en emō haimati*) (v. 25b). By partaking of the cup believers participate in the saving benefits won by the shedding of Christ's blood on the cross. The repeated eucharistic rite enacts their entrance into and continuing existence within the new covenant.

Covenant features in Paul's vision of the final inclusion of Israel within the community of salvation (Rom 11:25–32). He cites, with considerable modifications and omissions, a composite text made up from Isaiah 59:20–21 and 27:9 (Rom 11:26–27):

> [26] …The deliverer will come from Zion; he will banish ungodliness from Jacob. [27] And this will be my covenant with them [*kai hautē autois hē par' emou diathēkē*] when I take away their sins.

Paul sees the prophet foreseeing a time when God's abiding covenant fidelity will at last be realized (note the force of "this") when, as in the case of believers presently, Israel will enter fully into and benefit from into the saving work of Christ ("the deliverer from Zion"). In this sense, the covenant relationship between God and Israel endures.

ABRAHAM; EUCHARIST; ISRAEL; JERUSALEM; LAW; MINISTRY; MOSES; SPIRIT

Reading

F. Avemarie, "The Notion of a 'New Covenant' in 2 Corinthians 3: Its Function in Paul's Argument and Its Jewish Background," in *Second Corinthians in the Perspective of Late Second Temple Judaism*, ed. R. Bieringer et al. (Leiden: Brill, 2014), 59–78; Byrne, "Glory," 13–30; "Jerusalems," 215–31; W. S. Campbell, *DPL*, 179–83; "Paul's Covenantal Theology and Participation in Christ: Pauline Perspectives on Transformation," in *Paul and Judaism: Crosscurrents in Pauline Exegesis and the Study of Jewish–Christian Relations*, ed. R. Bieringer and D. Pollefeyt (London: T&T Clark, 2012), 41–60; Dunn, *Theology*, 146–50; Gorman, *Apostle*, 166, 172–73, 354–57; S. Grindheim, "The Law Kills but the Gospel Gives Life: The Letter-Spirit Dualism in 2 Corinthians 3.5–18," *JSNT* 84 (2001): 97–115; S. J. Hafemann, *Paul, Servant of the New Covenant: Pauline Polarities in Eschatological Perspective* (Tübingen: Mohr Siebeck, 2019); Wolter, *Paul*, 406–13; N. T. Wright, *The Climax of the Covenant: Christ and the Law in Pauline Theology* (Edinburgh: T&T Clark, 1991), 137–56; *PFG*, 781–92, 795–815, 846–51, 860–79.

CREATION, NEW CREATION

Apart from the reference to the act of creation—"from the creation of the world" (*apo ktiseōs kosmou*)—in Romans 1:20, "creation" (*ktisis*) in Paul refers to that which God has created. (For God as Creator see GOD.) In Romans 1:19–25, Paul portrays the human lapse into idolatry as an inexcusable failure to recognize the revelation of the divine power and deity manifest in the created world. Instead of responding by glorifying and thanking God (v. 21), human beings worshipped and served the creature (*tē ktisei*) rather than the Creator (*ton ktisanta*) (v. 25).

In Romans 8:18–22, Paul personifies creation (*ktisis*) and appeals to its "groaning" for liberation as one of the grounds for hope amid the suffering of the present time. But what is meant here by "creation"? Multiple suggestions are on offer: the entire creation, human beings included; the created world apart from human beings; the entire creation, believers alone excepted; the human world as a whole. Reference to the entire creation is excluded because in verse 23 Paul mentions a new subject "we," clearly distinct from creation, which also rules out reference to the human world as a whole. The inclusion of any human beings would seem to be excluded by the antithesis between creation and fallen humanity described in verses 20–21. It is thus widely agreed that by creation here Paul means the nonhuman created world. Drawing on a biblical tradition that sees the fate of creation in this sense intimately bound up with that of human beings (Gen 1:26–28; Ps 8:5–8), he interprets the cursing of the earth following Adam's sin (Gen 3:17–19) as the unwilling involvement of creation in the consequences of human sin. Subdued against its will in this way, creation, on the same principle of being bound up in a common fate with humankind, cherishes a hope that, if and when human beings as "sons (and daughters) of God" are set free from slavery to decay (mortality), it too would share this glorious liberation (vv. 20–21). Hence creation, thus personified, groans in one great act of giving birth to this longed-for new world (v. 22; see v. 19). What precisely Paul understands by the groaning of creation in this sense and how it functions as an index of hope is far from clear. Within an apocalyptic frame of reference, the passage is an appeal to imagination rather than theological reasoning. Needless to say, the passage features prominently in contemporary theological discussion of the environmental crisis.

The New Creation

Paul shared the Jewish apocalyptic expectation based on passages such as Isaiah 43:18–19 and 65:17–19 that the present creation, irrevocably soiled by human sin, would come to an end and God would usher in a new creation. Paul differed from conventional Jewish expectation in holding that the new creation had already dawned in the resurrection of Christ. In their existence "in Christ" through faith and baptism, believers are already experiencing the Spirit as the power of the new creation while still anchored bodily in the old. Stressing the radical break from the past and the new ways of thinking and evaluating required, Paul maintains, "So if anyone is in Christ, there is a new creation (*kainē ktisis*): everything old has passed away; see, everything has become new!" (2 Cor 5:17 NRSV). In similar vein at the end of Galatians he insists: "Neither circumcision [*peritomē*] nor the lack of it [*akrobystia*] is anything; rather, there is a new creation [*kainē ktisis*]" (6:15; see also Gal 3:28, where the copula "and" between the third pair of opposites that have ceased to have relevance in Christ—"male and female"—in contrast to "or" between the first two, indicates allusion to the creation story [Gen 1:27c]).

Creation in the Deutero-Pauline Letters

The "creation" theme emerges strongly in the later Pauline literature. The christological hymn early in Colossians (1:15–20) begins by describing Christ as "the firstborn of all creation" (*prōtotokos pasēs ktiseōs*) (v. 15b) and as instrumental in the creation of all else (v. 16; see 1 Cor 8:6). In what would appear to be an Adamic reference, the audience are reminded that they have "put off the old man" (*ton palaion anthrōpon* [Adam]; see Rom 6:6) and have "put on the new (*ton neon* [Christ]), the one being renewed in knowledge according to the image of the one who created it" (Col 3:9–10; see Gen 1:26–27).

Ephesians takes the motif of humanity created anew in Christ even further. Reviewing the whole scope and totally gratuitous nature of God's redemptive work in our regard (2:1–10), the Pauline author describes believers as "(God's) work of art [*poiēma*], created [*ktisthentes*] in Christ Jesus for good works" (v. 10). God has abolished the divisive "law of commands and ordinances" that he might create in himself "one new man" (*hina tous duo ktisē en autō eis hena kainon anthrōpon*) in place of the two (Jews and Gentiles), "thus making peace" (v. 15). Following the lead of Colossians 3:9–10 (see above), the author urges the audience to "put aside the old man [*ton palaion anthrōpon*]" (4:22) and "to put on the new man, the one created according to (the likeness of) God [*ton kata theon ktisthenta*] in true righteousness and holiness" (v. 24). Here, the author is drawing out the ethical implications of Paul's concept of every believer as a "new creation," being transformed through the Spirit into the image of God that Christ, as risen Lord, is (Rom 8:29; 2 Cor 3:18; 4:4).

ADAM; GOD; IDOLATRY; IMAGE; NEW; SPIRIT

Reading

B. Byrne, "A Pauline Complement to *Laudato Si'*," *TS* 77 (2016): 308–27; *PES*, 203–4, 213–15, 244–45; *Romans*, 66–69, 254–62; N. Elliott, "Creation, Cosmos, and Conflict in Romans 8–9, in Gaventa, *Apocalyptic Paul*, 131–56; M. V. Hubbard, *New Creation in Paul's Letters and Thought* (Cambridge: Cambridge University Press, 2002); T. R. Jackson, *New Creation in Paul's Letters* (Tübingen: Mohr Siebeck, 2010), 83–185; G. W. H. Lampe, "The New Testament Doctrine of *Ktisis*," *SJT* 17 (1964): 449–62, esp. 455–62; J. J. J. Leese, *Christ, Creation and the Cosmic Goal of Redemption: A Study of Pauline Creation Theology as Read by Irenaeus and Applied to Ecotheology* (London, New York: T&T Clark, 2018), 23–88; J. R. Levison, *DPL*, 189–90; P. S. Minear, *Christians and the New Creation: Genesis Motifs in the New Testament* (Louisville: Westminster John Knox, 1994), 62–81; G. Petzke, *EDNT* 2:325–27.

CROSS, CRUCIFY

The cross stands at the absolute center of Paul's theology and the gospel he preached. His references to the cross concern not so much the implement of execution itself as what the shameful crucifixion of Jesus Christ represented: the saving outreach of God in the person of the Son for the reconciliation and salvation of the world (Rom 3:21–26; 4:25; 5:6–10; 8:3–4; 1 Cor 15:3–5; 2 Cor 5:18–21; Gal 3:13; 4:4–5).

Paul's preoccupation with the cross, presumably stemmed from his pre-conversion view that the proclamation of the Crucified Nazarene as Messiah represented a blasphemous outrage to the faith of Israel, particularly in light of the application to this mode of execution of the curse rained down, according to Deuteronomy 21:22–23 (see Gal 3:13). His persecution of those engaged in such proclamation came to a halt when the Crucified One was revealed to him as God's Son (Gal 1:16), shining the light of divine glory on the face of (the Crucified) Christ (2 Cor 4:6; see also v. 4: "the illumination of the gospel of the glory of Christ, who is the image of God").

Henceforth, Paul felt himself called to proclaim what hitherto he had so vigorously persecuted: the Crucified Messiah (*Christon estaurōmenon*) (1 Cor 1:23). In the account of the divine project of salvation contained in the hymn quoted in Philippians 2:6–11, Christ's embrace not only of the slave-like human condition, but even an obedience unto the death—crucifixion—reserved for slaves (*hypēkoos mechri thanatou, thanatou de staurou*) (vv. 7–8), represents the polar opposite not only of his (preexistent) being "in the form of God" (v. 6) but also of the "lordship" of the universe to which God subsequently exalted him in view of that obedience (vv. 9–11).

Paul's Preaching of the Cross in Corinth

On his first coming to the Corinthians, Paul proclaimed "nothing other than Jesus Christ (i.e., Jesus as Messiah) and him crucified" (2:2). The Crucified Messiah, a stumbling block to Jews and foolishness to Gentiles (1:23), represents for those who are called the power and the wisdom of God (v. 24). Had "the rulers of this age"—that is, the demonic powers hostile to God and the worldly rulers (such as Pilate and Herod), whose tools they were—not been ignorant of this true wisdom, they would not have crucified "the Lord of glory" (i.e., Christ), since it was precisely through his cross that, in the wisdom of God, their efforts were thwarted (2:8) (see WISDOM).

The Cross in Galatia

In the Galatian churches, the problem threatening the efficacy of Christ's work on the cross, was not, as in Corinth, a false wisdom of the world, but an attempt by intrusive Christian missionaries to supplement the faith of Paul's Gentile converts by inducing them, as a condition for acquiring the righteousness (justification) necessary for salvation, to take on circumcision and the practice of the Jewish law ("works of the law"). For Paul this represented a going back on the justification they had already received when, as attested by the Spirit, they responded in faith to his preaching of the Crucified (3:1–9). If justification were to come through practice of the law, it would render in vain Christ's (costly) death on the cross (Gal 2:21).

Speaking personally ("I"), although representatively as of all believers, Paul describes himself as "co-crucified with Christ" (*Christō synestaurōmai* [Gal 2:19c). Those who have been baptized "into Christ" have been "baptized into his death" (Rom 6:3). Their old (Adamic) self has been "co-crucified with" Christ (*synestaurōthē*) in order to destroy the body of sin (v. 6). In similar ethical vein, Paul will insist to the Galatians that "those who belong to Christ Jesus have crucified the flesh [*tēn sarka estaurōsan*] with its passions and desires" (5:24).

Toward the end of the letter, Paul returns to insist on his costly proclamation of the Crucified Messiah. He asks why he is still being persecuted if he were still preaching circumcision, since that would remove the "scandal of the cross" (5:11). Those who are urging circumcision are trying to avoid being persecuted for the cross of Christ (6:12), persecuted, that is, by Jews as zealous he once was. In a warning staving off a similar threat to the Philippians from the circumcision party Paul describes them as "enemies of the cross of Christ" (Phil 3:18).

The personal cry on which letter to the Galatians ends shows how the cross has entered not only into Paul's preaching but into the deepest level of his personal spirituality: "May I never boast of anything except the cross of our Lord Jesus Christ, by which the world has been crucified to me, and I to the world" (6:14 NRSV). It seems that God's "illumination" of the glory of God on the face of the Crucified (2 Cor 4:4) on the Damascus road never ceased to work in him a profound and unparalleled mysticism of the cross.

The Cross in the Deutero-Pauline Letters

In the Pauline tradition, the apostle's association of Christ's death with the divine act of reconciliation (Rom 5:10; 2 Cor 5:18–21) is broadened at the close of the christological hymn in Colossians 1:15–20 to embrace the reconciliation of the entire universe: "making peace by the blood of his cross" (v. 20b), a motif echoed in Ephesians 2:14–16 with respect to the coming together of Jews and Gentiles in the "one body" (the church). Colossians 2:14 offers the striking image whereby the readers are assured that indictment against their former sinful way of life has been "nailed to the cross" of Christ, signifying its being rendered null and void through his expiatory death.

BAPTISM; DEATH; FAITH; GOSPEL; POWER; SIN; WISDOM

Reading

Beker, *Paul the Apostle*, 182–211; C. B. Cousar, *A Theology of the Cross: The Death of Jesus in the Pauline Letters* (Minneapolis: Fortress, 1990); Dunn, *Theology*, 208–12; Gorman, *Apostle*, 144–48, 287–93; J. B. Green, *DPL*, 197–99; M. Hengel, *Crucifixion in the Ancient World and the Folly of the Message of the Cross* (London: SCM, 1977); H.-W. Kuhn, *EDNT* 3:270–71, 313; A. E. McGrath, *DPL*, 192–97; L. Morris, *The Cross in the New Testament* (London: Paternoster, 1967), 180–269; G. O'Collins, *ABD* 1:1207–10; G. Samuelsson, *Crucifixion in Antiquity*, 2nd ed. (Tübingen: Mohr Siebeck, 2013); Schnelle, *Apostle Paul*, 100–102, 199–203, 255–58, 429–34; Wolter, *Paul*, 113–24.

D

DEATH

"Death" (*thanatos*; "die" [*apothnēskein*]) is a prominent topic in Paul and one that he understands in a variety of ways: (1) death in the physical sense, the term of human life on earth; (2) death in the more radical sense of final extinction and separation from God; (3) death personified as a "power" looming over human beings; (4) the saving death of Christ; (5) death in the sacramental sense of dying with Christ in baptism; (6) death in the ethical sense of being "dead to" malevolent powers and influences from which one has been set free. (7) The prospect of death in Paul's personal spirituality.

1. For Paul, as for the writer of the Book of Wisdom, physical mortality was not the original intention of the Creator for human beings. Both read an account of death's origins out of Genesis 2—3. For Wisdom it came through the "envy" of the devil (2:23–24), for Paul it is legacy of the sin of Adam (Rom 5:12a–c, 15b; 1 Cor 15:21–22),

that all his descendants in his train have ratified (Rom 5:12d; 6:23a). For Paul, then, death in the sense of physical mortality is a penalty incurred by sin (Rom 8:10b; see Rom 1:32; 2:5, 8–9).

2. Although all human beings die as a legacy from Adam that they have ratified in their personal sinning, God has intervened in Christ (the "last Adam" [1 Cor 15:45]) to create the possibility of a life beyond physical death ("eternal life"). Those who in faith accept the free gift of righteousness made available through faith in Christ and live out that righteousness through the power of the Spirit (Rom 5:17b; 8:4, 5–13) will pass through death to eternal life and, ultimately to the resurrection of their bodies, modeled on thc risen life of Christ. For those, however, who do not avail themselves of this divine offer, physical death will become death in the complete sense of final separation from life and from God.
3. Although the distinction between "death" in these two senses seems necessary, it is also important to note that it is a distinction that for the most part lies in the background. Especially in the central chapters of Romans (5—8) Paul personifies death as an alien power that, in the train of sin (equally personified), looms over human beings and, in fact, "reigns" (Rom 5:14, 17a, 21a; see 8:38; 1 Cor 3:22).

Against this potent nexus between sin and death, the law is impotent (Rom 3:20; 8:3). In fact, its arrival on the scene, whether in the shape of the "commandment" given to Adam or the Sinai dispensation, served not to provide the righteousness required to escape death but, in fact, exacerbated sin and hence the destiny to suffer it (Rom 4:15; 5:20a; 7:5; 7:7–13, 14–25); the law's promulgation was, in fact, an administration of death (2 Cor 3:7). The divine intervention in the person of the Son rescued the situation in that his "obedience unto death" (Phil 2:8; see Rom 3:21–26; 5:19), vindicated in resurrection, sufficed to deal with human sin (Rom 8:3). As such it opened up the way for believers to have the righteousness that will ensure that their "mortal bodies" will be raised to share his resurrection (Rom 4:25; 8:4, 9–11; 1 Cor 15:3–5, 12–22, 49; see also Rom 14:7–9; 2 Tim 1:10). This will represent the final victory over death, the last of the powers hostile to God that Christ will overcome (1 Cor 15:26). Hence, the believer can cry, "Where death is your victory? Where death is your sting?" (15:55). It is sin that gives death its fatal "sting." For believers, death retains its "bite" in the sense of physical mortality (Rom 8:10b), but it has lost the sting that renders it fatal in an eternal sense.

4. Paul's references to the death of Christ have in mind not so much the simple objective fact of his death but the obedience (Rom 5:19; Phil 2:8), love, and self-

sacrifice that it displayed (Rom 5:6–8; 14:15b; 15:3; 1 Cor 8:11b; 2 Cor 5:14–15; 8:8–9; Gal 2:20; Phil 2:5–8). Paul reminds the Corinthians that when they celebrate the Lord's supper they are "remembering" his death in this sense (1 Cor 11:26), hence the total lack of congruence between the self-sacrifice involved in that death and their unsocial behavior at the meal (vv. 20–22, 33–34). The self-gift of Christ in death stems, in total continuity, from the love and action of the Father, who "sent" him (Rom 8:3; Gal 4:4; see also Rom 5:6–9, 15), who "gave him up" for us all (Rom 4:25; 8:32), in a divine act of expiation (Rom 3:24–26; 8:3–4) and reconciliation (Rom 5:10; 2 Cor 5:18–21; see Col 1:20, 22; Eph 1:7; 2:13–16). Thus Paul's multiple references to Christ's death invariably have its soteriological effects in mind, sometimes—in line with more primitive Christian tradition—appealing to imagery taken from the sacrificial cult of Israel (*hilastērion* [Rom 3:25]; *kai peri hamartias* ("sin-offering") [8:3]; see also 1 Cor 5:7).

5. Paul presents baptism as an entrance "into (Greek *eis*) Christ," conceived of as a corporate personal sphere of salvation, involving a participation not simply in his person in a static sense (1 Cor 12:12–13; Gal 3:27) but into the dynamic of his total "career": his death, burial, and (in due course) his resurrection (Rom 6:3–8; see also 2 Cor 5:14).
6. An ethical sense of "death" flows from this baptismal "death" with Christ (Rom 6:2). Believers should consider themselves "dead to sin and living for God in Christ Jesus" (Rom 6:11); they have been "put to death to the law through the body of Christ" (Rom 7:4, 6), as Paul has "died to the law...being crucified with Christ" (Gal 2:19). Those who belong to Christ "have crucified the flesh with its passions and desires" (Gal 5:24; see Rom 8:13).
7. Death, Paul's constant "companion" and likely fate, enters deeply into his own personal spirituality. The apostles think of themselves as "exhibited...as last of all (in the triumphant procession), as though sentenced to death [*epithanatious*]" (1 Cor 4:9), as "always carrying in the body the death [*nekrōsin*] of Jesus...always being given up to death for Jesus' sake...so that death is at work in us, but life in you" (2 Cor 4:10–12). Confidence in the divine pledge of resurrection (4:13–18) leads Paul to wonder whether it would, in fact, be better to leave the body for the dwelling not made by hands prepared for him in the heavens (5:1–10). Philippians contains extended reflections in a similar vein as Paul, in prison, confronts the prospect of execution (1:12–26). For him, while living means Christ, to die would be "gain" (v. 21), although to "remain" is more "necessary" for the sake of his ministry (v. 24). His deepest aspiration is to be fully

conformed to Christ in suffering and death so as to gain a share in his resurrection (3:10–11).

ADAM; BODY; LAW; LIFE; LOVE; PRINCIPALITIES AND POWERS; RESURRECTION; SIN

Reading

Becker, *Paul*, 399–411; Beker, *Paul the Apostle*, 221–34; C. B. Cousar, *A Theology of the Cross: The Death of Jesus in the Pauline Letters* (Minneapolis: Fortress, 1990); M. de Boer, *The Defeat of Death: Apocalyptic Eschatology in 1 Corinthians 15 and Romans 5* (Sheffield: JSOT Press, 1988), 93–188; "Paul's Mythologizing Program in Romans 5–8," in *Apocalyptic Paul*, 1–20; Dunn, *Theology*, 124–27; J. B. Green, *DPL*, 201–9; Harris, *2 Corinthians*, 175–82; J. L. Sumney, *Steward of God's Mysteries: Paul and Early Church Tradition* (Grand Rapids: Eerdmans, 2017), 20–40, 70–95; Wolter, *Paul*, 95–124.

DEATH OF CHRIST (*see* Death)

DESIRE

In itself "desire," as expressed in Greek by the noun *epithymia* and the verb *epithymein*, does not have a negative connotation but simply expresses powerful longing. However, Paul's usage aligns with that of Hellenistic Judaism, where, under Stoic influence, the connotation of "covetousness," "lust," or "inordinate passion" was predominant, so that "desire" almost always has a negative tone in his letters.

Positive Desire

The two exceptions where "desire" has a positive connotation in Paul both appear as expressions of strong feeling in a situation of absence from the communities he founded. In Philippians 1:23, awaiting the outcome of his imprisonment, Paul speaks of the dilemma he faces because of the desire he has (*echōn epithymian*) to depart and be with Christ, on the one hand, and the consideration that to remain alive ("in the flesh") would be more apostolically fruitful ("more necessary for you" [v. 24]). In 1 Thessalonians 2:17, recalling his forced departure and continued separation from the community, he speaks of how eager he was, "with great desire" (*en pollē epithymia*) to see them face-to-face.

Negative Desire

More typically, Paul speaks of "desire" in connection with covetousness or the longing for forbidden things that arises out of fallen human nature ("flesh") and leads to sin. In Romans 1:19–23, he describes how, in response to human lapse into idolatry, God "gave them up in the lusts of their hearts [*en tais epithymiais tōn kardiōn*] to impurity and the degrading of their bodies among themselves" (v. 24). Here the overweening desire itself becomes a captivity into which God has delivered human beings (see v. 27c). In a similar vein, he warns in Romans 6:12 against allowing "sin" (personified as an enslaving force) to set up its "rule in your mortal body" to make you obey its desires (*tais epithymiais autou*). The bodily life of believers, though already belonging to Christ and destined for resurrection (1 Cor 6:13–14), is still affected by the weakness and temptation of the present age. Hence the continuing necessity to check its "desires" lest sin set up its "reign" in this sphere (see Rom 6:13). Here "body" as the seat of ill lustful desires comes very close to what Paul otherwise describes as "flesh," as in the warning in Romans 13:14: "and do not carry out the intent of the flesh to gratify its desires" (*tēs sarkos pronoian mē poieisthe eis epithymias*). The same sense of evil desires proceeding from the flesh finds expression again and again in the extended contrast between living according to the flesh and living according to the Spirit that Paul sets up in Galatians 5:16–26. Flesh and spirit are utterly opposed to each other in what they "desire" (vv. 16–17). Those who belong to Christ have "crucified the flesh with its passions and desires" (*syn tois pathēmasin kai tais epithymiais* [v. 24]).

It is important to note that what is meant by "desire" in such contexts is not restricted to sexual lust but, as shown by the list of the "works of the flesh" in Galatians 5:19–21a, ranges well beyond to include all kinds of self-centered and evil behavior, some instances of which (e.g., idolatry) have no immediate connection with the sexual area. In fact, Paul inherited a tradition where the prohibition against "coveting" in the final commandments of the Decalogue, expressed in LXX Greek by the verb *epithymein* (*ouk epithymēseis* [Exod 20:17; Deut 5:21]) was understood more generally as the prohibition of all sin, of which "covetousness" or "desire"—both expressed by *epithymia* in Greek—was seen as the root cause. Paul evokes the "fall" narrative (Gen 3) as a first-person account in Romans 7:7–13 to illustrate how the law ("the commandment"), instead of suppressing sin, actually provokes it. The "I" claims, "I would not have known desire (*epithymian*), if the law had not said, 'You shall not covet'" (*ouk epithymēseis* [v. 7d]). Sin "sprang to life" when the imposition of the commandment (in Adam's case the prohibition against eating from a particular tree [Gen 2:17; 3:3, 11]; in Israel's case the Mosaic law) provoked "all manner of desire" (*pasan epithymian* [v. 8]), the instinct to rebel against creaturely limit seen as the root of all evil. In Romans 13:9, Paul cites the prohibition against coveting (*ouk epithymēseis*) alongside those forbidding adultery, murder, and stealing. Although the object of the coveting is not specified, the parallel with the other behaviors prohibited suggests that the more specific sense is in view. In 1 Corinthians 10:1–11, Paul recalls the rebellion of Israel in the golden calf episode (Exod 32:1–6) as a typological warning: "so that we might not become desirous of evil things [*epithymētas kakōn*] such as they desired [*kathōs k'akeinoi epethymēsan*]" (v. 6). As the following verses (vv. 7–8) suggest, the "evil things" desired went beyond idolatry to the orgiastic behavior associated with pagan worship.

Desire in the Later Pauline Literature

Aside from the commended desire to obtain the office of bishop (1 Tim 3:1), "desire" in the later Pauline literature retains the negative tone characteristic of Paul (Eph 2:3; 4:22). The qualifications attached in some cases—"bad" (Col 3:5); "senseless and harmful" (1 Tim 6:9); "youthful" (2 Tim 2:22)—suggest that "desire" in itself could be neutral. However, the overwhelming tone is negative (see also 2 Tim 3:6; 4:3; Titus 3:3).

BODY; FLESH; IDOLATRY; LAW; SIN; SPIRIT

Reading

Byrne, *Romans*, 216–22; Dunn, *Theology*, 91–92, 98–100, 119–20; H. Hübner, *EDNT* 2:27–28; H. Räisänen, "The Use of *epithymia* and *epithymein* in Paul," in *Jesus, Paul and Torah: Collected Essays* (Sheffield: JSOT Press, 1992), 95–111; Schnelle, *Apostle Paul*, 334–36; S. Stowers, "Paul and Self-Mastery," in Sampley, *Paul*, 2:270–300, esp. 280–300; Thiselton, *1 Corinthians*, 731–35; J. A. Ziesler, "The Role of the Tenth Commandment in Romans 7," *JSNT* 33 (1988): 41–56.

DEVIL (*SEE* SATAN)

DISCERN, TEST

In Paul, discernment finds expression through two Greek verbs: *diakrinō* and *dokimazō*, which overlap to some extent in meaning, while in other respects go their own way.

Diakrinō

The verb *diakrinō* has the basic sense of sifting through two or more possibilities, making a distinction between, and then of arriving at a judgment or simply judging (as in 1 Cor 6:5). Berating the Corinthians for the divisions that exist in the community, Paul asks (1 Cor 4:7), "Who makes you different one from another?" (*tis se diakrinei*). Later in the letter, calling their celebration of the Lord's supper to account (11:17–34), he warns that anyone eating (the bread) or drinking (the cup) without discerning the body (*mē diakrinōn to sōma*) eats and drinks judgment to himself or herself (v. 29). The failure in question could be that of not distinguishing between the ordinary bread that the blessed loaf once was and the presence of Christ that it now is. Alternatively, the failure could lie in not recognizing that the gathered assembly is not just a collection of individuals but the corporate body of Christ (see 12:12–13). Paul cautions each one to examine (*dokimazetō*) himself or herself (11:28). If they judge themselves (*diakrinoumen*), they will not incur judgment (*ouk an ekrinometha*) (v. 31).

While Paul recognizes that the gift of tongues, so highly prized in Corinth, is a genuine gift of the Spirit, he lists before it both prophecy and "the discernment of spirits" (*diakriseis pneumatōn*) (1 Cor 12:10). Just as tongues should be accompanied by interpretation (14:26–28), so the utterances of prophets themselves must be "discerned" (*diekrinetōsan*) by other prophets (14:29). In all cases, the aim should be the building up of the community.

In quite a different and less favorable direction, *diakrinō* has the sense of "wavering" between commitment and noncommitment (denied in regard to Abraham's faith in God's promise [Rom 4:20]) and of "hesitation" (about whether to eat meat or not [Rom 14:23]).

Dokimazō

The verb *dokimazō* also has the sense of coming to a judgment but doing so on the basis of testing. In Paul, it can mean simply "test" (1 Cor 3:13 [tested by fire]) and, especially in the case of persons, to prove their worth on the basis of test (1 Cor 16:3; 2 Cor 8:8, 22; see also 1 Tim 3:10) or simply to approve (Rom 14:22; 1 Cor 16:3; 1 Thess 2:4). Paul calls for self-examination in such terms (1 Cor 11:28; 2 Cor 13:5; Gal 6:4).

In a singular usage Paul employs *dokimazō* in the final, summarizing statement about the lapse of the world into idolatry in Romans 1:28–31: "Since they did not accept knowledge of God as proved [*kathōs ouk edokimasan ton theon echein en epignōsei*], God gave them up…" (v. 28). The sense is not that human beings did not recognize God but that, having awareness of God (vv. 19–20), they refused to hold on to such knowledge as something proven and to be taken into account in how life should be lived.

The verb *dokimazō* comes closest to *diakrinō* in passages where the discernment of God's will is at stake. In Romans 2:18, Paul mocks the boast of the Jewish teacher that, instructed by the law, he can discern what is right and what is wrong (*dokimazeis ta diapheronta*). The positive counterpart to this appears at the beginning of the letter's paraenesis where Paul appeals to the readers to be "transformed by the renewing of your minds, so that you may discern what is the will of God [*eis to dokimazein hymas to thelēma tou theou*]—what is good and acceptable and perfect" (12:2d). Whereas the Jewish teacher looked to the law for an indication of God's will, in the situation where the law no longer applies (10:4), believers have to use the capacity of their "renewed mind" (12:2c) to make this discernment of God's will. The use of *dokimazō* conveys the sense of test, suggesting that a process, even a measure of trial and error, may be required to determine what is best (see ETHICS). See also in this vein the use of *dokimazō* in Philippians 1:10 and 1 Thessalonians 5:21.

EUCHARIST; ETHICS; GIFT(S) OF THE SPIRIT; JUDGE, LAST JUDGMENT; MIND; PROPHECY

Reading

Byrne, *Romans*, 362–64; G. Dautzenberg, *EDNT* 1:305–7 (*diakrinō*); Dunn, *Romans 1–8*, 66, 111; *Romans 9–16*, 714–15; A. Munzinger, *Discerning the Spirits: Theological and Ethical Hermeneutics in Paul* (Cambridge: Cambridge University Press, 2007); G. Schunack, *EDNT* 1:341–43 (*dokimazō*); Thiselton, *1 Corinthians*, 891–94, 965–70.

E

ELECTION, PREDESTINATION

The Pauline base on which the closely related and historically controversial doctrines of election and predestination rest is largely confined to a few short passages in Romans 8 and 9, and the opening eulogy of salvation in Ephesians 1 (vv. 3–14). Election is expressed in the cognate word group consisting of the verbal form *eklegomai*, the noun *eklogē*, and the adjective *eklektos*; the verb *proginōskō* (literally, "foreknow"), following a biblical idiom (see below), also appears to have this meaning. Predestination is expressed by the verb, otherwise rare in Greek, *proorizō*.

Election

The biblical concept of election stems from the tradition of Israel as the chosen people of God (Deut 7:6–8; 14:2; 28:10; Pss 33:12; 105:43). Coming to faith in Christ led Paul to understand that God's choice in this respect was, as foreshadowed in the promise to Abraham, to be extended beyond Israel to the nations of the world (see PROMISE). His own role (Gal 1:15–16) was to proclaim the gospel as widely as possible so that all those God had chosen would have the opportunity to respond and become part of the inclusive end-time people of God (Rom 15:15–21).

Paul believed that a positive response to the gospel of the Crucified, so paradoxical in human terms (1 Cor 1:21–24), could only come about through the power of God as displayed in the Spirit. He interpreted the assent of faith to the gospel as indicating God's choice. In line with biblical thought generally, he saw no conflict between the aspect of divine choice and power on the one hand and human freedom on the other. Hence his grateful recall to the Thessalonians: "We are aware, brothers (and sisters), beloved of God, of your choice [*tēn eklogēn hymōn*], because our gospel did not come to you in word only but with power and in the Holy Spirit and with full conviction" (1 Thess 1:4–5a; see 2 Thess 2:13). Far more sharply he reminds the Galatians of their similar experience of the Spirit when responding in faith to the Crucified (Gal 3:1–2; see v. 5).

Paul enlarges on this theme when defending his presentation of the gospel in Corinth (1 Cor 1:17—4:13). The Crucified Messiah may be "a stumbling block to Jews and sheer folly to Gentiles," but "to those who have been called [*klētois*], Jews and Greeks alike, (it is) Christ the power of God and the wisdom of God" (1:23–24). God's choice of the Corinthians was not because they were wise or strong or wellborn. On the contrary, God chose (*exelexato* [stated three times]) what is foolish, weak, and lowly in the world to shame the wise, strong, and significant, "so that no one might boast in the presence of God" (1:26–29). Accordingly, Paul's preaching in Corinth was not by way of persuasive words of wisdom but through demonstration of the Spirit and of power (2:4–5).

Paul can describe an individual believer (Rufus) as "chosen in the Lord" (Rom

16:13), but this description applies to all. To believers who may think that the sufferings of the present time (Rom 8:18, 35–36) could indicate that they are liable to be accused at the judgment, Paul defiantly asks, "Who will bring accusation against the chosen of God [*kata eklektōn theou*]? (granted that) God is acquitting (us)!" (8:33). For "the elect" as a general designation of believers see also Col 3:12 ("As God's chosen ones [*hōs eklektoi tou theou*], holy and beloved"; 2 Tim 2:10; Titus 1:1).

In Romans 9—11, Paul wrestles with the issue of Israel's continuing resistance to the gospel. If so few have responded positively, where does this leave God's original choice in their regard? In a long rereading of Scripture (9:6–18), he points out passages that indicate the freedom with which God's elective plan (*hē kat'eklogēn prothesis* [v. 11b]) has operated, quite independently of human merit. This pattern is presently operative in the existence of "a remnant (of Israel) chosen by grace" (*leimma kat'eklogēn charitos* [11:5; see vv. 6, 7]), that is, the minority of believers of Jewish origin, of which he himself is a notable example (see 11:1). Insisting (v. 2) that "God has not rejected those whom he foreknew" (*proegnō*—used in the sense of "choose"), he foresees the salvation of "all Israel" (11:26) on the basis that, while currently "enemies" for the sake of the proclamation of the gospel to the Gentiles (v. 28a; see vv. 11–12, 15), "as regards election they are beloved because of the fathers" (*kata...tēn eklogēn agapētoi dia tous pateras* [v. 28b]). And Paul adds in explanation, "For the gifts and the calling [*hē klēsis*] of God are irrevocable [*ametamelēta*]" (v. 29). Thus, despite the prevalence of Israel's current resistance to the gospel, Paul cannot countenance the thought that the divine election of Israel has fallen away (see 9:6a).

Predestination

Predestination flows from election—or perhaps actually precedes it—in the sense that God has a plan in mind for those who have been chosen. In more strictly theological terms, predestination refers to an eternal and effective determination of God by which the salvation of those to be saved will be accomplished. But theological speculation in this area has gone well beyond what Paul appears to have had in mind in the few passages where his use of the verb *proorizō* appears. Most notable in this regard is the sequence in Romans 8:28–30 where Paul, to give hope to the faithful in view of the sufferings of the present time, sets out the sequence of divine saving acts that are—inexorably—unfolding for the benefit of "those called according to (God's) plan [*tois kata prothesin klētois ousin*]" (v. 28c):

> 29 Because those whom he chose beforehand [*proegnō*], he also predestined [*proōrisen*] that they should become shares in the image of his Son, so that he might become the firstborn among many brothers (and sisters). 30 And those whom he predestined, these he also called [*ekalesen*], and those whom he called, these he also justified [*edikaiōsen*], and those whom he justified, these he has also glorified [*edoxasen*].

The first verb *proegnō*—literally, "foreknew"—according to a biblical idiom (see Gen 18:19; Exod 33:12; Hos 13:5; Amos 3:2; Jer 1:5; Gal 1:15), indicates choice. Only in regard to the second verb *proōrisen* does Paul break into the set steplike pattern to indicate the content of God's predestination of the elect: it is that they, presently caught up in the sufferings of the present age (v. 18), should share the risen existence of the divine Son. The process is already well under way—with "calling" (through the gospel) and "justification" already achieved; even "glorification" is expressed in the past tense in view of the certainty of the final outcome. The perspective is entirely positive and inclusive. There is no sense of a divine fixation of individual human lives in a set direction toward salvation on the one hand or damnation on the other. Paul is asserting the ultimate grounds for hope in the midst of suffering on the basis that what God has already brought about for believers at great cost (see 5:6–10; 8:32) guarantees their ultimate arrival at the goal predetermined for them (8:29b; see 1 Cor 2:7: "that which God decreed before the ages for our glory [*hēn proōrisen ho theos pro tōn aiōnōn eis doxan hēmōn*]"; see also Eph 1:5, 11). But the sure hope of salvation that Paul draws here from consideration of the inexorable working out of the pretemporal divine decree has to be set alongside the strong warning against loss of salvation in Romans 8:13—and, in fact, alongside the entire sequence 6:1—8:13, where Paul insists on the necessity of living righteously if salvation is to be gained. His theology holds together both the hope emanating from the divine decree *and* the necessity of human cooperation if salvation is to be achieved. Any theology of predestination derived from his work must take into account the wider context of the text (Rom 8:28–30) from which it has been principally drawn.

Another passage in Romans (9:22–23) has featured in the same connection. Wrestling with the current paradoxical situation where Israel is largely unbelieving in regard to the gospel while many Gentiles have accepted it, Paul begins a long question formulated as a conditional sentence of which the main statement (apodosis) is wanting and has to be supplied:

> [22] What if God, desiring to show his wrath and to make known his power, endured with much patience vessels of wrath ripe for destruction [*skeuē orgēs katērtismena eis apōleian*] [23] and in order to make known the riches of his glory for the vessels of mercy [*skeuē eleous*], which he had prepared beforehand for glory [*ha proētoimasen eis doxan*]...?

The "vessels of wrath" refer to currently unbelieving Israel. They are "ripe" for destruction but not as yet inescapably consigned to it; the final part of this section of the letter, 11:11–36, will refute such a conclusion. What is then said of the "vessels of mercy" (the Gentiles)—that they have been prepared beforehand for glory—simply repeats the divine intention as expressed in Romans 8:29–30 but in a phrase more closely aligned with 1 Corinthians 2:7. Particularly in regard to the "vessels of wrath" it must be kept in mind that Paul is reviewing the current situation not the final outcome. Moreover, he is likely thinking of collectivities—Israel and the Gentiles—not individuals. The text hardly affords grounds for theological conclusions in a predestinarian sense concerning the ultimate fate of individuals in the divine scheme of salvation.

CALL; FREEDOM; GENTILES; GOD; GOSPEL; HOPE; ISRAEL; SALVATION

Reading

Byrne, *Romans*, 266–74, 289–307, 329–36, 348–57; Dunn, *Theology*, 500–501, 512–13; J. Eckert, *EDNT* 1:416–19; W. A. Elwell, *DPL*, 225–29; Moo, *Romans*, 531–37, 585–88, 596–609; Schnelle, *Apostle Paul*, 342–46, 400–403, 588–92; Wright, *PFG*, 774–1042.

ENCOURAGE, EXHORT, CONSOLE

The frequent appearance in Paul's letters of the word group *parakaleō/ paraklēsis* suggests a conviction on his part that encouragement was what communities of believers needed to receive above all else. The word group itself has a wide range of meaning in Greek, all centered around the basic idea of bringing an effect on another in a way that has a positive impact: whether that be to console, encourage, exhort, dispose them to grant a favor, or catch their attention. The much rarer word group *paramytheomai/ paramythion–ia* also has the sense of "console"/"encourage" and always appears in Paul in close connection with *parakaleō/ paraklēsis* (1 Cor 14:3; Phil 2:1; 1 Thess 2:12; 5:14).

Encouragement and Consolation

While "consolation" may be a valid translation of *paraklēsis*, the more subjective overtones of the word in English in the direction of sympathy and compassion are less applicable in Paul's usage than "comfort" in the strict sense, that is (as in the Latin *confortare* ["strengthen"]), to give strength to someone in adversity. In the midst of the suffering and persecution that was so often the lot of the early communities, Paul speaks of consolation as a gift from "the God of steadfastness and encouragement" (*paraklēseōs*) (Rom 15:5; see also 2 Thess 2:16, 17). It is possible that the opening words of (deutero-) Isaiah 40: "Comfort [LXX *parakaleite*], O comfort, my people, says your God" (v. 1), lie behind his frequent assurances to this effect, since "whatever was written in former days was written for our instruction, so that by steadfastness and the encouragement of the scriptures [*tēs paraklēseōs tōn graphōn*], we might have hope" (Rom 15:4).

Paul expands on this theme at remarkable length in the introductory blessing of 2 Corinthians (1:3–7):

> [3] Blessed be the God and Father of our Lord Jesus Christ, the Father of mercies and the God of all consolation [*theos pasēs paraklēseōs*], [4] who consoles us [*ho parakalōn hēmas*] in all our affliction, so that we may be able to console [*parakalein*] those who are in any affliction with the consolation [*dia tēs paraklēseōs*] with which we ourselves are consoled [*parakaloumetha*] by God. [5] For just as the sufferings of Christ are abundant for us, so also our consolation [*hē paraklēsis hēmōn*] is

> abundant through Christ. [6] If we are being afflicted, it is for your consolation [*hyper tēs hymōn paraklēseōs*] and salvation; if we are being consoled [*parakaloumetha*], it is for your consolation [*hyper tēs hymōn paraklēseōs*], which you experience when you patiently endure the same sufferings that we are also suffering. [7] Our hope for you is unshaken; for we know that as you share in our sufferings, so also you share in our consolation [*tēs paraklēseōs*]. (NRSV)

Later in the same letter (7:6–7, 13), Paul recounts how, in the midst of the affliction he endured in Macedonia, the arrival of Titus was for him a gift of consolation from God:

> [6] But God, who consoles [*ho parakalōn*] the downcast, consoled [*parekalesen*] us by the arrival of Titus, [7] and not only by his coming, but also by the consolation with which he was consoled [*tē paraklēsei hē pareklēthē*] about you,… [13] In this we find comfort [*parakeklēmetha*]. In addition to our own consolation [*tē paraklēsei hēmōn*], we rejoiced still more at the joy of Titus. (NRSV)

Earlier, Paul had sent Timothy to Thessalonica in the hope that his visit would have a similar effect (1 Thess 3:2; see also Eph 6:22; Col 4:8 [the mission of Tychicus in both cases]). Paul himself has been encouraged (*pareklēthēmen*) by the faith of the Thessalonians (1 Thess 3:7; see also Phlm 7).

Comfort is not only something passively received. It is incumbent on believers to comfort and encourage one another. Paul has longed to visit Rome in the hope that his presence will lead to a mutual encouragement (Rom 1:12 [expressed through the compound *symparaklēthēnai*]). Those in Thessalonica grieving for the dead should encourage one another through the hope of resurrection (1 Thess 4:18; 5:11). Encouragement (*paraklēsis*) and the consolation (proceeding) from love (*paramythion agapēs*) should be a feature of existence in Christ (Phil 2:1). It should be given to an errant brother lest his punishment overwhelm him (2 Cor 2:7). It is a role for which some have a special gift (Rom 12:8; see also 1 Tim 4:13). Paul prefers prophecy to speaking in tongues since those who prophesy speak to others for their building up and encouragement (*paraklēsin*) and consolation (*paramythian*) (1 Cor 14:3; see v. 31).

Exhortation

Beyond the more passive sense of consolation, Paul employs *parakaleō* where the adoption of a fresh attitude or a spur to action is required. The exhortation rests on acceptance of the gospel, which requires a life lived in a way that is worthy of it (see Eph 4:1). Paul sees himself and his apostolic team as "ambassadors for Christ, through whom God is making appeal" (*presbeuomen hōs tou theou parakalountos di' hēmōn*) (2 Cor 5:20). Hence he can exhort (*parakaloumen*) the Corinthians "not to accept the grace of God in vain (6:1; see 1 Thess 2:3, 12). Having expounded the gospel at length in Romans (1:16—11:36), he now exhorts them (*parakalō hymas*) "through the mercy of God," to present their life in the body as a sacrifice, holy and acceptable to God (12:1; see 1 Thess 4:1, 10).

The exhortation becomes more urgent when addressed to specific situations of concern: as in the call for unity in the community in Corinth (1 Cor 1:10; 4:16; 16:15) or for displaying love toward an errant brother (2 Cor 2:8; see 1 Thess 5:14) or urging individuals to a particular course of action (1 Cor 16:12 [Apollos]; 2 Cor 8:6; 12:18 [Titus in both cases]; see also 9:5; Phil 4:2; Rom 16:17). Such injunctions expressed with *parakaleō* become still more pressing and authoritative in the post-Pauline letters (2 Thess 3:12; 1 Tim 1:3; 2:1; 6:2; 2 Tim 4:2; Titus 1:9; 2:6, 15).

Elsewhere, *parakaleō* has the sense of a personal appeal, almost with the meaning "beg" (2 Cor 8:4; 10:1; Phlm 9, 10). Three times Paul "begged the Lord" (*tris ton kyrion parekalesa*) for the removal of the "thorn" in his flesh (2 Cor 12:8). In view of the likely hostility awaiting him in Jerusalem, Paul appeals (*parakalō*) to the community in Rome to join him in earnest prayer that he be rescued from the unbelievers in Judea and that his ministry in Jerusalem may be acceptable to the saints (15:30–31).

Along with this already broad range of meaning, *parakaleō* has the quite distant sense of "respond graciously" (to slanderers) in 1 Corinthians 4:13 and this may also be the meaning in 1 Timothy 5:1. Ultimately, Paul's wide-ranging use of the word group *parakaleō/paraklēsis* would seem to reflect his sense that "in Christ" all human interaction should be lived within the warm and gracious "atmosphere" established by the supremely gracious act of God (see Phil 2:1–5).

ENDURANCE; GIFT(S) OF THE SPIRIT; GOD; PRAYER; SUFFERING

Reading

Byrne, *Romans*, 361–67; V. P. Furnish, *II Corinthians* (New York: Doubleday, 1984), 108–25; K. Grayston, "A Problem of Translation: the Meaning of *Parakaleo*, *Paraklesis* in the New Testament," *ScrB* 11 (Winter 1980): 27–31; B. Kaplan, "Comfort, O Comfort, Corinth: Grief and Comfort in 2 Cor 7:5–13a," *HTR* 104 (2011): 433–45; J. Lambrecht, "Paul's Appeal and the Obedience to Christ: The Line of Thought in 2 Corinthians 10,1–6," *Bib* 77 (1996): 398–416; G. Smiga, "Romans 12: 1–2 and 15:30–32 and the Occasion of the Letter to the Romans," *CBQ* 53 (1991): 257–73; J. Thomas, *EDNT* 3:23–27.

ENDURANCE, PATIENCE, PERSEVERANCE, STEADFASTNESS

These four English words all translate the Greek word *hypomonē* and its cognate verb *hypomoneō*, which has the basic sense of remaining or standing fast in a difficult situation. The relatively frequent appearance of the words in Paul's letters undoubtedly reflects the situation of the communities addressed, which, perhaps with the exception of those at Corinth, faced persecution and misunderstanding from many sides.

Endurance in General

The word group can appear with reference to perseverance in the face of difficulty or challenge in a more general sense: so with respect to perseverance in good works (*kath' hypomonēn ergou agathou* [Rom 2:7]), as a characteristic of love (*panta hypomenei* [1 Cor 13:7]), as a quality of hope (1 Thess 1:3; see also Col 1:11). In a little excursus on hope in Romans 8:24–25, Paul writes that we do not hope for that which is already in view; on the contrary, we hope for what we do not yet see (v. 24bc). In such a situation what is required is a perseverance in hope: "we await (what is hoped for) with endurance [*di' hypomonēs apekdechometha*]" (v. 25).

In Romans 15:1–5, Paul concludes his plea for tolerance on the part of "the Strong" of the scruples of "the Weak" in the matter of Jewish dietary law with an appeal to the example of Christ, who "did not please himself" (Rom 15:3a), illustrating this with a quotation from LXX Psalm 68:10, christologically interpreted. He then makes the point that such texts, indeed all Scripture, "was written for our instruction so that by steadfastness [*dia tēs hypomonēs*] and by the encouragement [*dia tēs paraklēseōs*] of the Scriptures we might have hope" (v. 4). The reasoning here is cryptic. Paul seems to be suggesting that, when we learn from Scripture that God fulfills promises, we find the strength and encouragement to endure the sacrifices presently asked of us. The hope is that God will be faithful to us as God was indeed faithful to Christ, raising him from the dead after he had borne, innocent though he was, the insults that (rightly) fell on us. God is "the God of steadfastness and encouragement" (*theos tēs hypomonēs kai tēs paraklēseōs*) in the sense of communicating these qualities to believers through the Scriptures (v. 5).

Endurance in the Face of Suffering

The connection between "endurance"/"steadfastness" and "hope" (see Rom 8:25; 15:4; 1 Thess 1:2–3) emerges in striking fashion in the "chainlike" sequence that Paul deploys in Romans 5:3–4:

> 3 ...we also boast in our sufferings [*en tais thlipsesin*], knowing that suffering produces endurance [*hē thlipsis hypomonēn katergazetai*] 4 and endurance produces character [*hē hypomonē dokimēn*], and character produces hope [*hē de dokimē elpida*]. (NRSV)

It is not immediately obvious how suffering could produce hope and do so via endurance and character. Stoics would probably agree that endurance can form character, but Paul goes beyond the Stoic view to the specifically Christian virtue of hope. What he is beginning to formulate here is a case for hope in the face of the sufferings of the present time that he will pursue right up to the rhetorical climax of 8:31–39. Suffering is not to be interpreted as a sign of divine disfavor. On the contrary, it is a sign that the messianic transformation is already under way (8:18–22). Believers suffer in union with Christ and for his cause (8:36); sharing his suffering is a guarantee that they will share his glory (8:17, 37–39), hence its capacity to increase both the longing for and the assurance of gaining what God has in store (see 1 Cor 2:9). "Enduring in (the midst of) affliction" (*tē thlipsei hypomenontes*) also appears alongside "rejoicing in hope" in the long list of commended Christian attitudes and dispositions in Romans 12:12 (see also 2 Thess 1:4; 1

Tim 6:11; 2 Tim 2:12; Titus 2:2). The "steadfastness of Christ" (*tēn hypomonēn tou Christou*) mentioned in a final blessing in 2 Thessalonians 3:5 refers either to Christ's own exemplary steadfastness in his passion or, more likely, to the steadfastness that he presently communicates to believers in their trials.

Apostolic Endurance

The apostolic life calls for endurance in multiple situations of suffering and peril. This is a constant theme in 2 Corinthians. Paul begins the letter recalling the near-fatal afflictions he had suffered in Asia (1:3–11). He assures the Corinthians that in sharing his afflictions with patience (*en hypomonē tōn autōn pathēmatōn*) they also share his God-given consolation (v. 6). He and his fellow workers, as servants of God, strive to present no obstacle to their ministry (6:3) but "with great patience" (*en hypomonē pollē*) adopt the attitudes and responses listed at length in verses 4–10 (see also 4:7–12; 11:23–33). It is in the endurance of such trials (*en pasē hypomonē*) that Paul displays the "signs of an apostle" (12:12; see also 2 Tim 2:10; 3:10–11).

APOSTLE; HOPE; SCRIPTURE; STRONG, WEAK; SUFFERING

Reading

Byrne, *Romans*, 166–67, 170, 423–27; D. R. Denton, "Hope and Perseverance," *SJT* 34 (1981): 313–20; Dunn, *Romans 1–8*, 251–52; A. Gieniusz, *Romans 8:18–30: "Suffering Does Not Thwart the Future Glory"* (Atlanta: Scholars Press, 1999); F. J. Matera, *Romans* (Grand Rapids: Baker Academic, 2010), 132–33, 320–22; W. Radl, *EDNT* 3:404–6; Wolter, *Paul*, 177–201.

ESCHATOLOGY (*see* READ ME FIRST)

ETHICS

Paul brings to his ethical thinking the Jewish tradition that saw relationship with God underpinning all reality. For Jews, the relationship took the form of a covenant that God had made with them, the obligations of which found expression in the Mosaic law. To live according to the requirements of the law was to live "righteously." The law was thus both a way of life and a path to life according to an axiom pervasive in the biblical tradition that righteousness leads to life (Deut 30:19; Ezek 33:10–16; Wis 1:15).

For Paul, the believer in Christ the law of Moses had ceased to have this role with regard to righteousness and the attaining of life. Faith in the Crucified Messiah (Gal 1:15–16) involved recognizing the pervasiveness of sin in the entire world, Israel included (Rom 3:9, 23; 5:12; Gal 3:22). The law had not succeeded in preserving Israel from sin because it proved impotent to deal with the human instinct to rebel against God, which Paul dubs "flesh" (*sarx*) (Rom 7:7–25; 8:3a, 5–8). In the face of this universal human alienation, however, God had graciously intervened, sending the Son to deal with "sin in the flesh" (v. 3bc), thereby creating a new possibility for living righteously through the power of the Spirit (vv. 4–11).

Paul's ethical thought, then, is, on the one hand, profoundly pessimistic concerning human capacity to live righteously, and, on the other hand, deeply hopeful about the capacity to do so through the power of divine grace, made effective through the Spirit. A continuing quest to find righteousness and life through practice of the law flies in the face of this truth about fallen human nature. Above all, it nullifies the gracious gift of God enacted in the costly death of Christ on the cross (Rom 10:1–4; Gal 2:15–21).

That being said, the fundamental ethical values and precepts expressed in the law, especially the Ten Commandments, remain in place for Paul (see Rom 1:24–31; 7:7–13, 16, 22; 1 Cor 5:1; 6:9–11, 12–20; 7:1–2, 9; Gal 5:19–21; 1 Thess 4:1–8; see also Eph 4:17—5:20; Col 3:5–11; 2 Tim 3:1–5). He did not, it seems, think it wrong for believers of Jewish origin to continue living according to the law on a practical level (Rom 14:1–12, 17–19; 1 Cor 9:20). What he strongly opposed was the imposition on his converts from the Gentile world of the ritual precepts of the law—circumcision, food laws, observance of the Sabbath, and so on. To adopt such measures would mean that Gentile believers were taking on Jewish identity as a means to righteousness and life, the very aspiration that had been overthrown by the costly death of Christ. It would mean rebuffing the grace of God (Gal 2:21a).

The chief challenge Paul had to confront in the ethical area was to find a rationale for continued obedience on the part of believers within his emphasis on the overwhelming grace of God (see Rom 5:15, 17, 20b, 21). He faced criticism that refusal to impose observance of the law on his Gentile converts along with his great stress on grace would lead to a moral free-for-all (Rom 3:8; 6:1). His efforts to ground a life of continuing righteous living go in several directions.

Pauline Passages of Ethical Significance

Apart from the exhortatory (paraenesis) sections of the letters (see Rom 12:1—15:13; Gal 5:13–6:10; Phil 2:1–18; 4:1–9; 1 Thess 4:1–5:11; see also Eph 4:1–6:20; Col 3:1–4:6), Paul's ethical theory chiefly emerges in the context of asserting the superseding of attempts to find righteousness through practice of the law ("works of the law") by the "righteousness of God" available to all believers (Rom 1:17; 3:21–26; 10:3–4; Gal 2:15–5:26; Phil 3:2–11).

1. *Romans 6:1–14:* Sin is now the "impossible possibility" for believers. Through their existence "in Christ" constituted through faith and baptism (vv. 3–5) they have radically "died" to the claims of "sin" (*hamartia*, imaged as slave master) (vv. 6–7). They now "live to God," as Christ "lives to God" (vv. 10–11). Hence Paul's ethical thought has a totally christological base: "in Christ" believers allow the "obedience" of the risen Lord to well up within them, molding their lives according to the pattern manifested by him (Phil 2:5–11). They should place their entire bodily existence at the dis-

posal of the gift of "righteousness" they have received.

2. *Romans 6:15–23:* This second argument for living righteously rests on the image of a slave's transfer from one master to another. In both situations—under both the former master and the new—an "obedience" is required; there is no "obedience-free" form of existence (v. 16). But the obedience is totally different in the two situations. In their former slavery to sin, those who have now become believers were compelled to obey its dictates whether they wanted to or not (see 7:14–25), with the outcome, first, of "uncleanness" (*akatharsia*) and ultimately (eternal) death (6:19–21). In the new situation a willing obedience ("from the heart" [v. 17]) to righteousness brings forth "sanctification" (*hagiasmos*), and ultimately eternal life (vv. 22–23).
3. *Romans 7:4–6:* Paul applies a marital image that he has formulated (7:1–3). Having "died" to the claims of the law through Christ's death (v. 4a), believers are now "joined" to him as risen Lord in a union the "fruit" of which, as "offspring," are the good works of believers (v. 4b). In this new situation believers render "service" (*douleuein*) in "newness of Spirit," as contrasted with the "oldness of letter" (v. 6).
4. *Romans 7:7—8:13:* In this key sequence, Paul describes the ethical "impossibility" of life under the law as a negative background ("foil") against which to highlight all the more tellingly the freedom (from sin) and the ethical "possibility" created by God's gift of the Spirit (8:1–4). Being merely external, the law is incapable of combating the tyranny of sin in human life (7:7–25; 8:3a). When sin as indwelling power (7:17, 20b, 23) is replaced by the Spirit as indwelling power (8:2, 4, 9, 11), a moral capacity (righteousness) is created that holds out the genuine possibility of gaining (eternal) life: "the Spirit means life because of righteousness" (8:10c).

   Where the law ineffectively laid down commands and prohibitions from "outside," actually making matters worse (7:7–13), the Son's costly entrance into the heart of the human situation ("the flesh" [8:3c]) dealt with sin at its noxious core, providing the capacity for fulfillment through the Spirit (v. 4). Indications elsewhere in the letters suggest that Paul saw the superseding of the law by the Spirit as the eschatological fulfillment of the promises made by God as recorded in Jeremiah 31:31–33 (see 2 Cor 3:6; 1 Cor 11:25) and Ezekiel 36:26–27 (see Rom 2:29; 7:6; 2 Cor 3:3). There is no need for a new external moral code: the Spirit (the impact of the risen Christ [see 1 Cor 15:45; 2 Cor 3:17–18]) is now the supreme norm for ethical decision.
5. *Romans 13:8–10; Galatians 5:14: Love:* In the place of a new external moral code, Paul speaks of "love" (*agapē*) as the "fulfillment of the law" (*plērōma...nomou*

agapē) (Rom 13:10b; see Gal 5:14); all the commandments of the law dealing with one's fellow human beings are "summed up" (*anakephalaioutai*) in the statement, "You shall love your neighbor as yourself" (Rom 13:9; see Lev 19:18; Matt 22:39; Mark 12:31; Luke 10:27). Believers' love is the extension in their lives of the love of Christ who, "at the right time," gave his life "for the ungodly," as an outreach of God's love for sinful human beings (Rom 5:6–10). The totally unpayable "debt" of love that believers have thereby incurred (13:8) they discharge in their love for others (1 Thess 4:9–12), even at the price of their own freedom in certain areas (Rom 14:1—15:12; 1 Cor 8:1–13; 10:23–24, 28–29; Phil 2:1–5; see also Eph 5:1–2; Col 3:14).

6. *Romans 12:1–2: Discerning God's Will:* A short passage introducing the paraenesis of Romans indicates how believers ought to confront the ethical dilemmas of living as the community of the new creation:

> 1 I appeal to you therefore, brothers [and sisters], by the mercies of God, to present your bodies as a living sacrifice, holy and acceptable to God, the worship you owe as rational beings. 2 Do not be conformed to this world but be transformed by the renewal of your mind, that you may discern [*dokimazein*] what is the will of God: what is good and acceptable and perfect.

This appeal had a brief foreshadowing in 6:12–14 where Paul urged the community to "offer… (their) members [*melē*] as instruments of righteousness to God" (v. 13). Now, once again, he makes his ethical appeal in terms of life in the body, which embraces the entire existence of believers, with particular emphasis on relations within the community and interaction with the surrounding external world. Believers are to offer their bodies (*parastēsai ta sōmata hymōn*) as "a living sacrifice pleasing to God" (*thysian zōsan euareston tō theō*) (12:1b). Initiating his prophetic accusation (Rom 1:18—3:20), Paul had depicted the fallen existence of the Gentile world as something stemming from a "suppression of the truth about God" (v. 18). Instead of employing their minds to pass from perception of the created world to the giving of glory and thanks to the Creator, human beings "became futile in their thinking and their senseless hearts were darkened" (1:21). Their idolatrous worship and service of the creature rather than the Creator" (vv. 23, 25, 28) had ruinous effects on their bodily life (vv. 24b, 26b–27), along with a "worthless mind" (*adokimon noun*) (v. 28). The present appeal (12:1–2), with its stress on "bodily worship" and "renewal of mind," makes a positive response to that earlier picture. Faith, which for Paul is always faith in God as Creator (see 4:17b), finds expres-

> sion in a bodily obedience that is the "rational worship" owed by human beings to God. The "worship" is "rational" (*logikēn*), not in the sense of "spiritual" (immaterial) as opposed to the physical, but in the sense, familiar from Hellenistic-Stoic usage, of proceeding from that which is distinctive of human beings as rational, reflective creatures whose highest powers (reason, will) are or ought be engaged in the homage they bring to the Creator (1:21–23).

Paul completes this description of Christian life as rational worship by indicating how believers are to know what it requires in practice (v. 2). Negatively (v. 2a), it means not being conformed to the pattern of this world. Presupposed here is Paul's eschatological sense of living in the "overlap of the ages." While the new age inaugurated by the resurrection of Christ has become palpable in the experience of the Spirit, attesting a new relationship with God (Rom 5:1–5; 8:15–16, 23; Gal 3:2–5; 4:6–7), the conditions of the sin-laden old era endure for the time being and will continue to do so till Christ's victory is complete (1 Cor 15:24–28). Believers have to live out the values of the new era in the conditions of the old. To do so, they must allow their "minds" to undergo the "renewal" (*anakainōsis*) required by life in the new era. Far from simple conformity to a blueprint provided by external law or sanction, the new moral life proceeds from the inner core of the person (see Rom 6:17: "from the heart"), now capable of discerning (*dokimazein*) the "will of God." (The casting of the appeal in the second person plural suggests that Paul has communal rather than individual discernment principally in view.)

Significantly, then, Paul's fundamental principle of moral discernment, laid down here prior to any concrete norms or maxims, is that Christian obedience involves a constant quest for God's will in the confusing and difficult circumstances of the present, "overlap" time. He displays a remarkable confidence in the capacity of the "renewed mind" to determine God's will and so arrive at behavior that, echoing popular Greco-Roman ethical discourse, is "good, pleasing (to God) and perfect" (12:2c). The principle set out here stands in sharp contrast—in all likelihood intentional—to what he had written earlier when lampooning the claim of the Jewish teacher to "know the will (of God) and discern (*dokimazein*) what is essential, instructed by the law" (2:18). Believers have no need to be instructed by such a law, just as they have no need to go to a temple to offer sacrifice to God. The bodily obedience flowing from discernment makes their lives a continual "sacrifice" pleasing to God.

These two sentences contain a theory of ethical discernment that is suggestive and open-ended. Granted the vast cultural gap between the biblical world and the present, Scripture provides contemporary believers with little concrete guidance for the ethical dilemmas of modern life. The abiding values of the gospel have to be discerned and lived out in totally different circumstances, with science and technology in particular throwing up ethical challenges unimaginable in Paul's day. Under these circumstances, his stress on the capacity of the "renewed mind" to discern; his sense of the need to test (*dokimazein*), allowing for some measure of trial and error; his use of the language of the surrounding secular world ("good and acceptable and perfect") offer an important charter for contemporary ethical thought.

BODY; ESCHATOLOGY; DISCERN, TEST; FLESH; HEART; LAW; LOVE; MIND; OBEDIENCE; RIGHTEOUSNESS; SIN; SPIRIT; WORLD

Reading

Barclay, *Gift*, 493–519; *Obeying the Truth*, 220–35; Barrett, *Freedom*, 53–70; Beker, *Paul the Apostle*, 272–94; Byrne, "Living Out," 567–81; Dunn, *Theology*, 625–712; V. P. Furnish, *Theology and Ethics in Paul* (With a New Introduction by R. B. Hays; Louisville, KY: Westminster/John Knox, 2009); Gorman, *Apostle*, 140–62; Horrell, *Introduction*, 110–15; Matera, *GSG*, 156–85; S. C. Mott, *DPL*, 269–75; S. E. Porter, "Paul, Virtues, Vices, and Household Codes," in Sampley, *Paul*, 2:368–90; B. S. Rosner, ed., *Understanding Paul's Ethics: Twentieth-Century Approaches* (Grand Rapids: Eerdmans, 1995); J. P. Sampley, *Walking in Love: Moral Progress and Spiritual Growth with the Apostle Paul* (Minneapolis: Fortress, 2016); Schnelle, *Apostle Paul*, 546–58.

EUCHARIST, LORD'S SUPPER

Paul does not explicitly discuss the Eucharist ("the Lord's Supper" [*kyriakon deipnon*]). He alludes to the eucharistic practice that he has passed on to communities (see 1 Cor 11:23) in the context of correcting behavior he finds questionable. Three passages, all in 1 Corinthians, are relevant.

1. In 1 Corinthians 10:1–13, Paul warns the Corinthians against the danger of falling into idolatry when they participate in social meals in the precincts of pagan temples. His warning takes the form of evoking the experience of the Israelites ("our fathers") in the wilderness, drawing a parity between what they experienced and the sacramental practice—baptism and Eucharist—of the church. The Israelites were "baptized into Moses" when they passed under the cloud and through the sea (vv. 1b–2). In the gift of manna (Exod 16:4, 35; Deut 8:3) and water from the rock (Exod 17:6; Num 20:7–11), they ate the same "spiritual food" and drank the same "spiritual drink" (1 Cor 10:3–4). Yet this quasi-sacramental participation in food and drink divinely provided did not preserve them from falling into the idolatry and immoral behavior that led 23,000 of them to die in a single day (vv. 7–8). Paul points to this biblical episode—the Golden Calf episode (Exod 32:1–6)—as offering a typological warning (1 Cor 10:6) against over-confidence that sacramental participation will preserve the Corinthians from a similar fate. While couched as a negative warning, the typological comparison with the experience of the Israelites does communicate a sense of the Eucharist as "bread for the journey" akin to what emerges from the "Bread of Life" sequence in John 6.
2. Within the same warning about idolatry ("Flee idolatry!" [v. 14]), Paul evokes the Christian

Eucharist more explicitly in 1 Corinthians 10:16–17:

> [16] The cup of blessing which we bless, is it not a communion with the blood of Christ? The bread that we break, is it not a communion with the body of Christ? [17] Because there is one bread we, though many, are one body, for we all share in the one bread.

Presumed here is the belief that communal meals shared in a sacral context promote union (*koinōnia*) between the participants and the deity in question. The union created thus goes in two directions: "horizontal" between the participants and "vertical" between them and the deity. Participation in the blessed cup means "communion with the blood of Christ" (*koinōnia…tou haimatos tou Christou*) in the sense of sharing in the saving benefits won by his death. Participation in the broken bread means "communion with the body of Christ" (*koinōnia tou sōmatos Christou*) (v. 16b). The added explanatory comment, "Because there is one bread we, though many, are one body, for we all share in the one bread" (v. 17), suggests that "body of Christ" here does not refer simply to the physical body of Christ given up at the time of his death but to the risen Lord as constituting a communal person "in" whom believers collectively exist ("in Christ"). Thus participation in the Eucharist involves for believers the deepest union between themselves and Christ, and with one another "in" him. Despite the emphasis on union in a "horizontal" sense in the added comment (v. 17), the following examples of the union created in sacral meals—with the altar of sacrifice in the Jerusalem temple (v. 18) and with demons in a pagan setting (vv. 19–20a)—suggest that the "vertical" sense of union with Christ is paramount here. The danger inherent in taking part in meals in temples stems from the utter incompatibility between the union with demons thereby created and the union with the risen Lord stemming from the eucharistic participation. (vv. 20b–22).

3. In the more extended reference to the Eucharist in 1 Corinthians 11:17–34, Paul's chief concern is not the with the eucharistic rite as such but with the way in which the Corinthians were conducting the shared meal (later known as the Agape), which was its wider context. Their behavior was creating social divisions completely at odds in his view with the meaning Christ had imprinted on the rite at its institution. What they are coming together to eat is not "the Lord's supper" (*kyriakon deipnon*) (v. 20). Whether the problem is that the food is not being shared—in the sense that each one goes ahead with his or her own supply of food, leaving hungry those who have nothing or little (see v. 21)—or whether it is more a matter of not waiting for everyone to arrive (see

v. 33) is not entirely clear. In either case the poorer members would be deprived since they would either have little to bring or else, as servants or slaves, not being masters of their time, they would not arrive until the celebration was well under way and the food largely consumed. What Paul finds particularly reprehensible is not just that the poor are deprived of food but that they are "shamed" (v. 22c).

To show the utter incompatibility between this state of affairs and the meaning Christ imprinted on the eucharistic rite, Paul recalls the institution narratives (1 Cor 11:23–26; see Matt 26:26–29; Mark 14:22–25; Luke 22:15–20):

> [23] For I received from the Lord what I also handed on to you, that the Lord Jesus on the night when he was given up took a loaf of bread, [24] and when he had given thanks, he broke it and said, "This is my body that is for you. Do this in remembrance of me." [25] In the same way he took the cup also, after supper, saying, "This cup is the new covenant in my blood. Do this, as often as you drink it, in remembrance of me." [26] For as often as you eat this bread and drink the cup, you proclaim the Lord's death until he comes. (NRSV, with "betrayed" replaced by "given up")

The broken loaf of bread over which thanks is given is "my body that is for you" (*to sōma to hyper hymōn*): that is, it is the body of Jesus given up for the salvation of the world on the cross. The cup is "the new covenant in my blood" (*hē kainē diathēkē en tō emō haimati*). In the shedding of his blood on the cross Jesus inaugurated the new covenant—announced in Jeremiah 31:31—as Moses had inaugurated the old by sprinkling the blood of sacrificed oxen on the Israelites (Exod 24:8). By sharing in the cup believers seal or reaffirm their inclusion in the new covenant and its saving benefits won by the shedding of Christ's blood.

After both pronouncements—over the bread and over the cup—the Lord issues the remembrance command: "Do this in remembrance of me" (*eis tēn emēn anamnēsin* [see also Luke 22:19c]). The Passover ritual, which Jesus has here transformed, celebrated the Israelites' deliverance from Egyptian slavery. In the rich biblical sense of a "memorial" (Hebrew *zikkaron*), it allowed Israelites of later generations to participate in the liberation their ancestors had experienced. Likewise, the "remembrance" effected in the Eucharist enables believers of subsequent generations to participate in the experience of those who were with Jesus at the Supper and in the liberation (from sin, from death) achieved by his death the following day. It reenacts those saving effects for the benefit of all who participate in the meal.

Hence, Paul's concluding comment, "As often as you eat this bread and drink this cup you proclaim the death of the Lord until he comes" (v. 26), is not referring to his death as a simple fact. It is a proclamation of his death as an offering of self-sacrificial love for the world (see 2 Cor 5:14). This means that when believers share in the Eucharist, the union with the Lord thereby created is not static but dynamic. In the space of time until his return (see 1 Cor 16:22c: "Our Lord, come!" [*marana tha*]), they are being caught up in and celebrating the ongoing resonance of his love—something utterly at odds with their unsocial behavior in the communal meal. To eat the bread and drink the cup "unworthily" (*anaxiōs*) in this sense is to become guilty of the body and blood of the Lord (v. 27). They should "examine" (*dokimazein*) themselves, therefore, and only then proceed to eat and drink" (v. 28). For if they do so, "not discerning the body" (*mē diakrinōn to sōma*), they will eat and drink judgment (*krima*) to themselves (v. 29).

The meaning of "not discerning the body" has been much discussed. "Body" here has been taken, especially in the Catholic tradition, as a reference to the real presence of Christ in the Eucharist. In favor of this would be the sense of *sōma* as "personal presence" in texts such as 1 Corinthians 5:3; 2 Corinthians 10:10 (see also Col 2:9, 17). Alternatively, in view of the context, where divisions in the community gathering are being exposed, *sōma* can also be interpreted in a "social" sense, that is, as referring to the community as the "body of Christ." It may be possible to hold both interpretations together in the sense that in the Eucharist Christ is present as the One who gave himself in death for others and who, as "body," draws believers into dynamic association with this self-giving pattern of his entire life (Rom 15:3; Gal 2:20; Phil 2:6–8). To celebrate the Eucharist in a context of selfishness and social shaming as the Corinthians are doing (1 Cor 11:17–22, 33–34) is to distort the whole nature and purpose of Christ's presence in the eucharistic gathering.

BODY; COMMUNION; DEATH; IDOLATRY; "IN CHRIST"; LOVE; MOSES

Reading

P. F. Bradshaw, *Eucharistic Origins* (Oxford and New York: Oxford University Press, 2004), 1–15; P. Duff, "Alone Together: Celebrating the Lord's Supper in Corinth (1 Cor 11:17–34)," in *The Eucharist: Its Origins and Contexts. Vol. 1: Old Testament, Early Judaism, New Testament*, ed. D. Hellholm and D. Sänger (Tübingen: Mohr Siebeck, 2017), 555–75; Dunn, *Theology*, 599–623; E. Käsemann, "The Pauline Doctrine of the Last Supper," in *Essays*, 108–35; E. LaVerdière, *The Eucharist in the New Testament and in the Early Church* (Collegeville, MN: Liturgical Press, 1996), 21–45; I. H. Marshall, *DPL*, 569–75; F. J. Moloney, *A Body Broken for a Broken People: Divorce, Remarriage and the Eucharist*, 3rd ed. (London: Darton, Longman and Todd, 2015), 41–69; Wolter, *Paul*, 264–80.

EXALTATION (OF CHRIST) (*see* Lord)

EXPIATION (*see* Propitiation)

F

FAITH, BELIEVE, BELIEF

The Greek word *pistis* serves to express both the subjective disposition expressed by "faith" and also the virtue or quality of "faithfulness." In Paul's usage the former sense, along with the cognate verb *pisteuein*, prevails. Faith has great moment in his theology because of its link with justification, the issue being whether justification is gained by performance of the "works of the (Mosaic) law" or whether, as Paul insists in light of the gospel, through believing in the saving effects of God's intervention in Christ.

As a zealous Pharisee before his encounter with Christ, Paul doubtless shared the conventional Jewish belief in God as Creator and in Israel's special position as the chosen people of God. He likely also, in a more apocalyptic vein, shared the belief that God would soon intervene to rescue Israel's current distress and bring in the promised blessings of the messianic age, at least for those faithful (righteous) in the practice of the law. He vigorously persecuted a small movement within Judaism whose members were making blasphemous messianic claims concerning a Jew crucified by the Romans, Jesus of Nazareth.

For Paul, the vision of "the glory of God on the face of (the crucified) Christ" (2 Cor 4:6) meant a total revaluation of his personal standing before God and of the law's capacity to bring about the required eschatological righteousness. If the messianic intervention of God came in the form of a crucified person revealed as God's Son (Gal 1:16), what was the state of Israel and of himself as a devout Israelite that warranted such a form of redemption? It could only be a state of sinfulness in so profound a degree as to erode the distinction between Israel as a holy nation and the sinful remainder of humankind (Gal 2:15–17; see Rom 2:1–24; 3:9, 23). The God who reached out to him at this moment was a God acting out of pure grace, without regard to merit of any kind—a God who asked simply a trusting belief that he, Paul, was accepted simply as he was in virtue of the reconciliation effected in the death and resurrection of Christ, "who was given up for our trespasses and raised for our justification" (Rom 4:25).

This experience was undoubtedly the origin of Paul's conviction that the God of Israel, in fidelity as Creator to all humankind, was reaching out to the nations of the world who lacked the law just as graciously as the same God was reaching out to Jews such as Paul himself (Rom 3:29–30). More particularly, Paul was being called and sent, as apostle, to summon the nations to respond in faith to this good news (gospel) of God's grace. Hence Paul begins his exposition of the gospel in Romans with the thematic statement (Rom 1:16–17):

> [16] I am not ashamed of the gospel. It is the power of God leading to salvation for all who come to faith, the Jew first, but also the Greek (Gentile). [17] For in it a righteousness of God is being revealed, from faith to faith, as it is written, "*The person righteous by faith will live*" [Hab 2:4].

In the following section (Rom 1:18—3:20), Paul sweeps aside any other grounds on which human beings can claim to be righteous before God; all, Jew and Gentile alike, are under the power of sin (3:9). He then restates in Romans 3:21–26 the basic content of the gospel in terms more explicitly focused on the saving death of Christ. In the Christ event, acting as a sacrifice for sin, God has graciously made available to believers a righteousness that will avail for salvation, in a way that at once deals effectively with sin and demonstrates God's faithfulness both to Israel and, as Creator, to the rest of the world (3:29–30).

Hence not only the prominence of faith in Paul but also its single-minded focus on God's action in the death and resurrection of Jesus. Faith is not a meritorious work. It is a divinely facilitated acceptance of one's sinfulness, revealed in the cross of Christ, and at the same time a conviction that God is reaching out to me precisely as a sinner and graciously drawing me into a new relationship (righteousness), which, granted perseverance, will lead to salvation (Rom 10:9–13; Gal 2:16; see also Eph 2:8).

Paul's single-minded insistence on faith as the gateway to membership of the community destined for salvation, including Gentiles, inevitably led to clashes, not only with Jews not won to faith in Christ but also with fellow believers who maintained that observance of the law ("works of the law"), including circumcision for male Gentile converts, remained necessary for salvation. Hence the prominence of faith as a topic in those letters, Galatians and Romans, where he particularly addresses this issue, along with the prominence of Abraham as the biblical figure to whom, in his argument, he makes particular appeal (Rom 4:1–25; Gal 3:1–29; 4:21–31).

Abraham as a Paradigm of Faith

Because Abraham was regarded in the Jewish tradition, not only as the "father" of all destined to be saved, but also the one whose behavior and interaction with God was paradigmatic for the messianic age, to establish his case Paul had to claim the patriarch as primarily a person of faith rather than obedience and merit. He extradites Abraham from his own time and claims him entirely for the gospel. Crucial here was the text of Genesis 15:6, which states, according to the Septuagint, that, following a divine assurance that he would have a son and a progeny as numerous as the stars of heaven, Abraham believed God and this was "reckoned to him as righteousness," forging, in Paul's view a direct link between faith and righteous standing before God, prior to any mention of circumcision or other legal requirement. It was as an "ungodly" Gentile that Abraham received this assurance, paving the way for him to model divine acceptance of Gentiles simply on the basis of faith (see ABRAHAM; PROMISE).

To drive home the parity between the faith of Abraham and that of his believing "progeny" Paul, in Romans 4:17b–22, explores the nature of Abraham's faith in responding to the promise, that he would have a son and heir. Because of the "deadness" of his aged reproductive capacity and that of the womb of his wife Sarah (v. 19), to believe that God would fulfill this promise meant believing in a God who, as Creator, has the capacity to raise the dead (v. 17b). The parity with the faith of present believers consists in the fact that the focus of their faith lies on God's raising of Christ from the dead. Hence righteousness is "reckoned" to them on the same basis as it was reckoned to Abraham, their "father in faith" (vv. 23–24; see vv. 11b–12).

In Galatians 3, Paul points to the community's experience of the Spirit as a sure sign that, again, like their "father" Abraham, they have received the blessing of justification simply on the basis of their faith in the Crucified (vv. 1–9; see also Eph 1:13). The law was simply a temporary provision to deal with transgressions (Gal 3:19–24). It could not disturb the divine promise to Abraham that the Gentiles would be justified through faith and entry, through baptism, into the singular "offspring" (Christ) on whom the promise was uniquely and directly focused (vv. 15–18, 25–29).

Faith Finding Expression in Love

While faith for Paul marks the beginning of life "in Christ," of belonging to the messianic community destined to "inherit" the full promise of salvation, he also speaks of it as an ongoing disposition. Earlier in Galatians, his rejoinder to Peter and those in Antioch who had reverted to the separation between Jew and Gentile set up by adhering to the prescriptions of the law in regard to food concludes on the stirring note: "it is no longer I who live, but it is Christ who lives in me. And the life I now live in the flesh I live by faith in the Son of God, who loved me and gave himself for me" (2:20; see also Rom 15:13). Later he will write, "For in Christ Jesus neither circumcision nor lack of it counts for anything; the only thing that counts is faith finding expression through love" (Gal 5:6). The replacement of the law by faith in no way leads to an ethical vacuum. Through the power of the Spirit, the values enshrined in the law are "fulfilled" as faith is lived out in love (see Gal 5:14; Rom 8:4; 13:8–10; see also Eph 1:15; Col 1:4).

Granted the significance of faith (externally enacted in baptism) as the disposition initiating membership of the community destined for salvation (Rom 13:11), it is not surprising that the members can simply be designated "believers" (*hoi pisteuontes* [1 Cor 14:22; 1 Thess 1:7; 2:10, 13]). In due course, *pistis* also came to be used not only in respect to the subjective disposition but also as a summary of the *content*, the body of teaching, that is believed: "the faith." Beginning already in Paul (Gal 1:23; Phil 1:27; 1 Cor 16:13), this usage becomes regular in the later Pauline literature (Eph 4:5, 13; Col 1:23; 2:7; 1 Tim 3:9; 4:1).

While "faith" is the predominant meaning of *pistis* in Paul, the sense "faithfulness" is not entirely lacking. This is certainly the case in Romans 3:3 where *pistis* is used, in parallel with "truth" (v. 4) and "righteousness" (v. 5) to indicate the faithfulness of God, as also with reference to the human virtue of faithfulness in Galatians 5:22.

ABRAHAM; BAPTISM; BLESSING; FAITH IN/OF CHRIST; GENTILES; JUSTIFICATION; LOVE; PROMISE; RIGHTEOUSNESS; SIN

Reading

Bultmann, *Theology*, 1:314–30; Byrne, *Romans*, 141–62; D. A. Campbell, *OEBT* 1:327–36; Dunn, *Theology*, 371–79; Käsemann, "The Faith of Abraham in Romans 4," in *Perspectives*, 78–101; L. Morris, *DPL*, 285–91; Schnelle, *Apostle Paul*, 521–27; Westerholm, *Perspectives*, 352–407; Wolter, *Paul*, 71–99.

FAITH IN/OF CHRIST

The openness of the word *pistis* to the alternative meaning of "faithfulness" has led to a view, now widely held especially in North America, that the Greek genitive phrase *pistis Christou* in Paul (Rom 3:22 [see also 3:26: *ek pisteōs Iēsou*]; Gal 2:16 [*dia pisteōs Iēsou Christou*; see also 2:20: *en pistei…tē tou huiou theou*]; 3:22 [*ek pisteōs Iēsou Christou*]; Phil 3:9 [*dia pisteōs Christou*]) should be understood in a subjective sense, that is, as referring to the faith or faithfulness of Christ, rather than as "faith in Christ," just as in Romans 4:16 the phrase *ek pisteōs Abraam* must refer to Abraham's faith, not faith "in" him. While, viewed aside from the context, the subjective sense seems more natural, grammatically the genitive construction is open to the more traditional objective understanding, which is unambiguously expressed in phrases where a preposition expresses the object of faith (Rom 3:25; see also Col 1:4; 2:5; Phlm 5; Eph 1:15) or phrases with the verb *pisteuein* (see Rom 4:24; 10:10; Gal 2:16). Because grammatical considerations are not decisive, the meaning in each case must rest on the context and a sense of Paul's overall theology. The parallel constituted by the phrase *ek pisteōs Abraam* is of little help to the objective understanding since Abraham appears in Paul as a model of faith rather than faithfulness. The two occurrences of the phrase in Galatians 2:16 favor the objective understanding since between them stands the verbal phrase: "we too have put our faith in Christ," with its undeniably verbal sense. In Romans 3:21–26 and 3:27–31, just as in Galatians, the issue turns on the appropriate *human* response (faith as opposed to works of the law) to God's action in Christ, rather than on Christ's personal faith or faithfulness, even if his obedience is presupposed, and this antithesis to going the way of the law supports taking the remaining instances of the phrase (Gal 3:22; Phil 3:9) in an objective sense. The matter is likely to remain controversial in Pauline studies for some time. In fact, however, understood objectively, the phrase more precisely expresses faith in *God's action* in Christ rather than simply faith in Christ personally (see Rom 4:24).

Reading

Barclay, *Gift*, 378–82, 476–77; M. F. Bird and P. M. Sprinkle, eds., *The Faith of Jesus Christ: Exegetical, Biblical and Theological Studies* (Milton Keynes: Paternoster, 2010); Byrne, *PES*, 93, n.5; Dunn, *Theology*, 379–85; B. C. Dunson, "Faith in Romans: The Salvation of the Individual or Life in Community?" *JSNT* 34 (2011): 19–46; R. B. Hays, *The Faith of Jesus Christ* (Chico, CA: Scholars, 1983), 157–76; Holloway, *Philippians*, 165–68; Horrell, *Introduction*, 107–110;

C. Kugler, "*PISTIS CHRISTOU*: The Current State of Play and the Key Arguments," *CurBR* 14 (2016): 244–55; Moo, *Romans*, 224–25; J. H. Pifer, *Faith as Participation: An Exegetical Study of Some Key Pauline Texts* (Tübingen: Mohr Siebeck, 2019); Westerholm, *Perspectives*, 305–6, n.18; Wright, *PFG*, 836–51.

FELLOWSHIP (*see* Communion)

FLESH

Of all the terms most commonly used by Paul, the Greek word *sarx* is perhaps the most difficult to translate. The common rendering "flesh" makes sense only within already established Christian discourse and, outside that context, is quite misleading. The most common misunderstanding is to regard *sarx* as equivalent to "body" in the sense of the material aspect of the human person as opposed to the immaterial ("soul") or spirit. *Sarx* can have that meaning in Paul but it is only one meaning within a wide range and is not at all the most common in his writing or theology.

"Flesh" as Neutral

Sarx appears in Paul in a neutral sense simply to indicate the *human* aspect or origin, for example, in Romans 9:5, "the Messiah according to the flesh," locating the Jewish origins of the Messiah among the key privileges of Israel (see also Rom 1:3). Speaking as a Jew, Paul can introduce Abraham as our "forefather" according to the flesh (Rom 4:1; see also 9:8; 1 Cor 10:18) and he can indicate his own Jewish origins in similar terms (Rom 9:3; 11:14). Likewise, in a neutral sense and coming close to "body" (*sōma*), *sarx* serves to indicate the physical makeup of animals and human beings (1 Cor 15:38–39; 2 Cor 7:5; 12:7 ["thorn in the flesh"—with reference presumably to some physical ailment]; Gal 4:13–14). *Sarx* can also simply indicate present human life in the body, seemingly without negative connotation (1 Cor 7:28; Gal 2:20; Phil 1:22, 24; see Col 2:1, 5).

"Flesh" as Pejorative

Behind Paul's most characteristic usage of *sarx* and to a large degree determining his usage is the biblical (Old Testament) usage of *basar* in Hebrew to indicate, not a part of the person, but the whole person, a human being, or humanity as such ("flesh and blood" [see 1 Cor 15:50; Gal 1:16]; "all flesh" [see Rom 3:20; Gal 2:16, both citing Ps 142 (LXX 143):2]). Prominent in this biblical usage are the aspects of frailty, mortality, vulnerability to sin that characterize mere human existence over against God, and to some extent in opposition to God. Paul takes up this biblical language to indicate the human person from the aspect of *external*, *visible*, *physical* existence, as opposed to what is internal, spiritual (Rom 2:28; 1 Cor 7:28; 2 Cor 4:16). Here the sense is not really neutral: a note of weakness, frailty, distance from God hovers round *sarx*. Where Paul will speak of the resurrection of the "body" (*sōma*), there is never any suggestion of a "resurrection of the flesh." "Flesh and blood cannot inherit the kingdom of God" (1 Cor 15:50).

Exacerbating this negative tone is the apocalyptic cast of Paul's theology, in which there is a sharp distinction between the present, evil age and the age that is to come, following a redemptive intervention of God. For Paul as a believer that decisive intervention has already occurred in the sending of the Son and the release of the Spirit for those who through faith and baptism have come to live "in Christ." Although "right with God" (Rom 5:1) and destined to share Christ's risen life, believers are still bodily anchored in the old age, waiting in hope for the "redemption" of their bodies (Rom 8:23). In this sense, they live in an "overlap of the ages" situation, still feeling the pull of the old age in the shape of suffering, temptation, and physical death. The term *sarx* comes to denote everything that characterizes life in the present, evil age: its conditions, its attitudes (see 2 Cor 5:16), its values—above all, its hostility to God (Rom 8:7). The challenge for believers is that they have to live in the physical conditions of the present age—"in" the flesh in this sense—while striving *not* to live "in the flesh" in the sense of living according to its attitudes and values, which have been outdated by the Christ event. Hence the frequency in Paul of the dichotomy "according to the flesh" (*kata sarka*)/"according to the Spirit" (*kata pneuma*) in passages such as Romans 7:1—8:13 and Galatians 5:16–26 (where Paul contrasts the "works of the flesh" with the "fruit of the Spirit"; see also 3:3; 4:29; 6:8). Paul uses the adjective "fleshly" (*sarkikos* or *sarkinos*)—better translated "worldly"—in the same negative way (Rom 7:14; 1 Cor 3:1, 3; 2 Cor 1:12), although the less pejorative sense of "merely human" (2 Cor 10:4) or "material" (Rom 15:27; 1 Cor 9:11) also appears.

"Flesh" and "Sin"

One can gain the impression that Paul virtually identifies "flesh" and "sin." Certainly, he thinks of the flesh as prone to sin, especially and paradoxically in the presence of the law/"the commandment," which, contrary to its basic intention, serves to provoke rather than inhibit sin (Rom 7:7–13; see also 5:20a; 8:3a). But he presupposes a key distinction across Romans 7—8: "flesh sold (into slavery) under sin" (Rom 7:14) and "flesh" where sin has been "condemned," following the entrance of the Son "in the likeness of the flesh of sin" (*en homoiōmati sarkos hamartias*) (Rom 8:3–4). In the former existence (Rom 7), the person "in" the flesh *had* to live "according to the flesh" because of the enslavement to sin that had a firm and crushing foothold in the flesh. But those "in Christ" (Rom 8:1–2), although still bodily living "in" the flesh, do not *have* to live "*according* to the flesh." The grip of sin has been broken (Rom 8:3), introducing the possibility as well as the necessity to live "according to the Spirit" (vv. 4–11). "Flesh" for Paul is the remnant of the passing, evil age as it impinges on the present life of the believer. Its essence is the *tendency to oppose God* (v. 8).

From the above it should be clear that the "works of the flesh" for Paul are by no means confined to what have been traditionally dubbed "sins of the flesh": sexual vice, gluttony, drunkenness, and so on. Along with these, Paul ranges as "works of the flesh," vices and tendencies that have their seat in human imagination and will: idolatry, sorcery, jealousy, selfishness, party spirit, and so on (see Gal 5:16–21).

ABRAHAM; BODY; ESCHATOLOGY; ISRAEL; LAW; RESURRECTION; SIN; SPIRIT

Reading

Barrett, *Freedom*, 71–90; D. Boyarin, *A Radical Jew: Paul and the Politics of Identity* (Berkeley: University of California Press, 1994), 57–85; Byrne, *PES*, 52–53, 151–60, 219–22; Dunn, *Theology*, 62–73; Jewett, *Anthropological Terms*, 49–166, 453–56; Schnelle, *Apostle Paul*, 498–99; E. Schweizer, *TDNT* 7:125–35; Stacey, *Pauline View of Man*, 154–86; Wells, *Grace and Agency*, 224–53; J. Ziesler, *Pauline Christianity*, rev. ed. (Oxford: Oxford University Press, 1990), 77–83.

FORGIVE, FORGIVENESS

References to "forgiveness" as such are very rare in Paul. The normal word for "forgive" in the New Testament, *aphiēmi*, appears only once in Paul with this meaning and then in a quotation from Scripture: LXX Ps 31:1, cited in Romans 4:7, while the cognate noun *aphesis* ("forgiveness") appears only in the deutero-Pauline letters of Colossians (1:14) and Ephesians (1:7).

There is no doubt that Paul understood God's action in Christ as centrally concerned with the barrier to salvation created by human sin and therefore as effecting the removal of that barrier through forgiveness. This is abundantly clear when the essential message of the gospel is described as "reconciliation": "God was in Christ reconciling the world to himself, not counting (*mē logizomenos*) their sins against them" (2 Cor 5:19; see v. 21; Rom 4:25; 5:6–10; 1 Cor 15:3b). It seems, however, that the apocalyptic cast of his thought and, in particular, the thought of the last judgment as the looming horizon against which he proclaimed the gospel, led Paul to speak of God's action regarding human sin in the more forensic language of justification and "not reckoning," as in 2 Corinthians 5:19, cited above, and Romans 4:3–8. The union of believers with the obedience of Christ forged through faith and baptism has brought about the expiation of their sins in the present time, as also the sins formerly committed but passed over in the time of God's "patience" (Rom 3:25–26).

Human Forgiveness

The forgiveness received from God is something that, as expressed so memorably in the parable of the Unmerciful Servant (Matt 18:23–35), believers must pass on to one another. In this connection Paul employs the verb *charizomai* in the sense of "be gracious to" and hence "forgive." He urges the Corinthians that they should forgive (*charisasthai*) and console the brother who has offended and been punished lest he be overwhelmed by sorrow (2 Cor 2:7). He continues, "Anyone whom you forgive [*charizesthe*], I also forgive [*k'agō*]. What I have forgiven [*ho kecharismai*], if I have forgiven anything [*ei ti kecharismai*], has been for your sake in the presence of Christ" (v. 10 NRSV). The risen Lord himself, whose gracious act (Rom 5:15) won forgiveness for all, presides over the mutual exchange of forgiveness in the community. In 2 Corinthians 12:13, Paul's "Forgive me" (*charisasthe moi*) is actually a defensive response to criticism, not without a touch of sarcasm.

Forgiveness in the Deutero-Pauline Letters

In the deutero-Pauline letters the word *aphesis* appears in hymnic material with its usual New Testament meaning. In Colossians, the "redemption" (*apolytrōsis*) wrought by God's act in the beloved Son is described as "the forgiveness of sins" (*tēn aphesin tōn hamartiōn*) (1:14). This is expanded in Ephesians: "in whom (the Beloved [Christ]) we have redemption through his blood, the forgiveness of our trespasses [*tēn aphesin tōn paraptōmatōn*] according to the riches of his grace" (1:7). In Colossians 3:13, and almost identically in Ephesians 4:32, the audience is enjoined to pass on to each other the forgiveness they have received from God in Christ, the verb *charizomai* appearing in each case, as also in Colossians 2:13 (*charisamenos hēmin panta ta paraptōmata*). The Pauline authors, following Paul himself, exploit the sense of "gracious gift" (*charis*) inherent in the verb to draw believers in their dealings with one another into the atmosphere of the supremely generous gift of Christ (see 2 Cor 8:9).

GRACE; JUSTIFICATION; RECONCILIATION; SIN

Reading

Byrne, *PES*, 92–102, 177–78, 231–33; R. P. Martin, "Reconciliation and Forgiveness in Colossians," in *Reconciliation and Hope*, ed. R. Banks (Exeter: Paternoster, 1974), 104–24; L. Morris, *DPL*, 311–13; J. B. Prothro, *Both Judge and Justifier: Biblical Legal Language and the Act of Justifying in Paul* (Tübingen: Mohr Siebeck, 2018), 79–81, 172–81; S. Westerholm, *NIDB* 2:484–85.

FREEDOM, SET FREE

Freedom describes the situation of not being constrained or held captive by any force. In the social setup of Paul's day, freedom stood over against the situation of slavery that was the lot of so large a proportion of the population in the Greco-Roman world. A more interior sense of freedom—freedom from passions and fears—was promoted by popular Stoic philosophy. Although freedom as such is not a topic in the Old Testament, the sense of God as the liberator of Israel from Egyptian slavery was central to the national identity (Exod 12:13, 25–27; 13:3–10; Deut 6:20–24; Pss 78:11–12; 105:36–39; 135:8–9; 136:10–15; Jer 2:6; Hos 11:1) and was reprised by prophets such as Jeremiah (16:14–15 and 23:7–8) and (deutero-) Isaiah, who pointed to a "new exodus" from captivity and exile in Babylon (41:17–20; 43:16–21; 51:10–11). The contribution of passages in (deutero-) Isaiah to the Christian concept of "gospel" (see GOSPEL) ensured that the essential message of the Christian gospel would be one of freedom.

For Paul, the gospel message of freedom addresses a universally prevalent human situation of slavery. The slavery in question, very much part of the apocalyptic cast of Paul's thought, is fundamentally a slavery to sin and resultant alienation from God. When Christ "emptied himself" of a divine way of being (*en morphē theou*) to enter the human realm, he took on the way of being of a slave (*morphēn doulou*) (Phil 2:6–7; see Rom 8:3).

The freedom that believers gain as a result of Christ's redemptive act has several facets in Paul, reflecting the various contexts and needs he addresses in the letters.

Freedom from Sin

In Romans 1:18—3:20, as a background to the hope contained in the gospel (1:16–17), Paul charges that all humankind, Jews as well as Gentiles, are "under sin" (*hyph' hamartian* [3:9]; see 3:23; 5:12d). The preposition *under* suggests that sin is a slavery from which all need to be set free. The following passage, Romans 3:21–26, describes how, in the face of this situation, God has wrought a "redemption" through the death of Christ (v. 24). The word translated "redemption"—*apolytrōsis*—is chiefly used to express the liberation of those who have been enslaved after being taken captive in war. In an extended sequence across Romans 5:12—8:13, Paul more explicitly personifies sin as an enslaving power from which human beings need to be set free (7:14). In the union with Christ's death established by faith and baptism believers have been radically freed from the power of sin (6:1–14). Set free (*eleutherōntes*) from this slavery (vv. 18, 22) they are now free for a service (literally, "slavery" [*douleia*]) of righteousness, which leads to sanctification and, ultimately, to eternal life (vv. 22–23). Paul seems to apologize or at least reach for an excuse for applying the image of slavery to the present as well as the past situation of believers (v. 19a). However, he points out that freedom does not mean license (6:1–2, 13): an obedience to righteousness has replaced an obedience to sin. The crucial difference, however, is that a former imposed obedience to sin has given way to an obedience "from the heart" (*hypēkousate...ek kardias* [v. 17c]), that is, a willing obedience proceeding from liberty and love.

Freedom from the Law

The freedom won by the redemptive act of Christ means that believers have been set free from the Mosaic law (Rom 7:1–4). The law, especially in the shape of the Ten Commandments, enshrines the key values by which human beings should live. These values remain valid and obligatory but only in the sense that they are all "summed up" by love (see Rom 13:8–10; Gal 5:14). The Mosaic law, with its myriad specific requirements, had become a law of "letter" (*gramma* [Rom 7:6c; 2 Cor 3:6]). When addressed to unredeemed human beings, still in the grip of "the flesh" (*sarx*), the law actually elicited transgression (Rom 5:20a; 7:5, 7–11), and hence, while "holy and righteous and good" in itself (7:12), had become an unwilling accomplice of sin.

Paul depicts the enslaving encounter with the law to this effect at length in Romans 7:7–25 (see LAW). Over against this negative background he goes on to describe the breakthrough into freedom in Romans 8:1–4, tracing it back to the divine act of sending the Son: "There is now no condemnation for those in Christ Jesus (v. 1), for the law (in the shape) of the Spirit of life has set you free [*ēleutherōsen se*] from the law of sin and death" (v. 2). The Son's full entrance into the realm of the flesh (human alienation from God), broke the grip of sin and released the Spirit, so that those "in Christ" can live (literally, "walk") now, "not according to the flesh but according to the Spirit" (vv. 3–4). The Spirit has created the freedom to live righteously (see 6:13, 18, 19, 22) and so be set in line to share the bodily risen life of Christ (8:10–11).

The association of freedom with the Spirit also emerges from the extended midrash on the account of Moses's promulgation of the law that Paul deploys in defense of his apostolic ministry in 2 Corinthians 3:4–18. He and his coworkers are ministers of a "new covenant," which is not one of "letter" but of the Spirit (v. 6). When one "turns to the Lord" (v. 16), that is, responds in faith to the ministry of the new covenant, one encounters the Lord as Spirit and there finds freedom—from sin, from the law—because "where the Spirit of the Lord is, there is freedom" (*hou...to pneuma kyriou eleutheria*) (vv. 17–18).

Freedom from the law is the principal theme in Galatians. Paul is combatting an attempt on the part of intrusive Christian teachers to pressure his Gentile converts to take on the "works of the law," specifically in this case, circumcision. For Paul, to follow this path is to render otiose the supremely costly work of Christ on the cross (2:19–21). For Jews, it would mean reverting to a situation of slavery under the law from which Christ has set them free (4:1–3); for Gentiles, it would mean reverting to the parallel situation of slavery of their former worship of "things that by nature are not gods" (4:8). In a complex scriptural allegory working from Abraham's two sons—Ishmael, born of the slave girl Hagar (Gen 16:1–15), and Isaac, born of the free woman, Sarah (Gen 21:1–13)—Paul argues (4:21–31) that, believers, in the line of Isaac, are children of the free woman. Their present "mother" is the heavenly Jerusalem, whereas those who are disturbing them remain in the enslaved line of Hagar (see JERUSALEM). Hence Paul's strong conclusion: "For freedom Christ has set us free [*tē eleutheria hēmas Christos ēleutherōsen*]. Stand firm, then, and do not submit again to the yoke of slavery" (5:1; see Gal 2:4).

Freedom from Death and Decay

Both in Romans and Galatians freedom is closely associated with the filial status that believers now enjoy, as attested by the Spirit (Rom 8:14–16; Gal 3:26; 4:5–7). The entire creation "groans" in expectation that, in the reversal of the subjection to futility it suffered at the fall, it too will be "set free from its bondage to decay to enjoy the freedom associated with the glory of the children of God" (Rom 8:21). Believers are already "children of God," but in a hidden way; bodily they are still tied to the physical mortality that is the legacy of sin (Rom 8:10b). The "redemption" (*apolytrōsis*) of their bodies that they hope to receive when they share Christ's risen life (v. 23; see v. 11) will mean their sharing in his freedom from death and corruption (see 1 Cor 15:53–54).

Freedom in Christian Life

While insisting that believers have been set free from the law in Christ, Paul is equally concerned that this freedom is to be preserved and lived out. Hence he continues to the Galatians (5:13):

> …you were called to freedom [*ep' eleutheria eklēthēte*] brothers and sisters; only do not use your freedom to give opportunity to the flesh but through love become slaves to one another [*dia agapēs douleuete allēlois*]. (NRSV, slightly altered)

Paradoxically, the freedom from slavery to sin and to the law means a further "slavery" (*douleuete*) but this time one proceeding entirely from love. "For," he continues, "the entire law is fulfilled [*peplērōtai*] in the (commandment), 'You shall love your neighbor as yourself'" (v.14). The provocative nature of describing this fulfillment in terms of "slavery" (see above on Rom 6:16–23) is alleviated when one understands it in light of Christ, who, in a free act of self-emptying love, embraced the "slave" existence of humankind in order to win it freedom (Phil 2:6–8; see Gal 4:4–5). The loving "service" (*douleia*) that believers should exercise toward one another is nothing other than an extension in their lives of this redemptive love of Christ, a freedom "in him" that wells up within them through the Spirit (see 2 Cor 3:17).

For the subtle exercise of freedom that Paul calls for in his lengthy treatment of the issue concerning eating food sacrificed to idols and attending social meals in pagan temples (1 Cor 8:1—11:1), see CONSCIENCE.

Social Freedom

Although Paul writes that (in Christ) "there is neither slave nor free [*ouk eni doulos oude eleutheros*]" (1 Cor 12:13; Gal 3:28), he has long been criticized for not following through with this principle in regard to freedom for those in his own churches who were slaves. His advice in 1 Corinthians 7:21–22, although not entirely clear, seems to suggest that those who are slaves should remain content with their condition and not seek freedom. Existence "in Christ" has completely relativized this key social disadvantage since the Christian slave is "a free person of the Lord" (*apeleutheros kyriou* [v. 22]) (on this passage, see SLAVERY). Likewise unclear is whether his appeal to Philemon on behalf of the slave Onesimus (Phlm 8–21) implied the latter's release from slavery. In the deutero–Pauline letters, the instructions concerning slaves in the household codes (Col 3:22—4:1; Eph 6:5–9) contain not a hint that such a condition is one from which a believer might aspire to be set free. The sense that the structure of the present world was fast passing away (1 Cor 7:31b) seems to have prevented Paul and his followers from grasping the social consequences of the freedom—from sin, from law, from the demands of the flesh—that he otherwise so strongly endorsed.

ADOPTION; CONSCIENCE; DEATH; GOSPEL; LAW; LOVE; RESURRECTION; SIN; SLAVERY; SPIRIT

Reading

Barrett, *Freedom*, 1–52; M. A. Beavis, *OEBT* 1:377–84; Byrne, "Glory," 16–26; *PES*, 143–65, 173–78; *Romans*, 216–47; J. K. Chamblin, *DPL*, 313–16; W. Coppins *The Interpretation of Freedom in the Letters of Paul: With Special Reference to the "German" Tradition* (Tübingen: Mohr Siebeck, 2009); G. W. Dawes, "'But If You Can Gain Your Freedom' (1 Cor 7:17–24)," *CBQ* 52 (1990): 681–97; Dunn, *Theology*, 396–401; R. N. Longenecker, *Paul: Apostle of Liberty*, 2nd ed. (Grand Rapids: Eerdmans, 2015), 142–90; K. Niederwimmer, *EDNT* 1:431–34; Schnelle, *Apostle Paul*, 211–17, 538–45; Thiselton, *1 Corinthians*, 669–73, 779–87; Wolter, *Paul*, 362–66.

G

GENTILES

"Gentiles" (*ethnē*) is the Jewish way of referring to all the non-Jewish people and nations of the world. For stylistic reasons Paul occasionally uses "Greek(s)" as a substitute for "Gentile(s)" (Rom 1:16; 2:9–10; 10:12; Gal 3:28; see also Col 3:11). The prominence of this term in his writing is, of course, due to his sense of being called by God to the unique role of apostle to the Gentiles (Rom 1:5, 13; 11:13; 15:15–21; Gal 1:16; 2:2, 7–9; see also Eph 3:1, 8; 1 Tim 2:7; 2 Tim 4:17).

Whether this particular aspect of his calling was made known to Paul at the moment of his encounter with the risen Lord or emerged more gradually as he along with Barnabas became involved in the missionary outreach of the Antioch church (see Gal 2:11–15; Acts 13:1–3) is disputed. However, the linkage is certainly there in his own mind in the allusion to his call in Galatians 1:16 ("But when God… was pleased to reveal his Son to me, so that I might proclaim him among the Gentiles…" [NRSV]). Moreover, it is hard to account for the radicality of Paul's view of the terms on which the Gentiles are to be accepted into the end-time people of God—that is, simply as Gentiles, without any taking on any of the ritual prescriptions of the Mosaic law—if this conviction does not stem from his conversion vision of the Crucified Messiah, an experience that he describes in 2 Corinthians 4:6 as akin to the act of creation itself.

In Romans 3:29–30, Paul rounds off his case that the eschatological justification is by way of faith rather than pursuit of the works of the law (3:21–28) with a similar appeal to God as sole Creator, echoing the Shema text (Deut 6:4). If God is one, God cannot have "two faces," as it were, to the world, granting to one group (Israel) a salvation denied to the rest. God's covenant faithfulness to Israel must be matched by a similar faithfulness as Creator toward the rest of humankind. So it is out of the heart of Israel's faith in the one God that Paul rests the validity of his mission to the nations, a validity acknowledged by the leading figures ("pillars") among the community in Jerusalem (Gal 2:7–9).

The revelation of the Crucified as Israel's Messiah and Son of God led Paul to question the distinction between a holy nation (Israel) and the unholy rest (Gentiles) (see Gal 2:15; see also Eph 2:14–22). All alike were "under sin" (Rom 3:9; see also 3:23; 5:12) and, at the same time, God was in Christ reaching out graciously, offering justification and the hope of salvation to all, simply on the basis of faith (Rom 3:21–26). To compel Gentiles to, in effect, become Jews by taking on circumcision and other ritual practice of the law—as was the case in Galatia—was to render Christ's costly death in vain (Gal 2: 21), something unthinkable for Paul.

Abraham as "Father" of Gentiles

To place this inclusive view of salvation on a scriptural foundation, Paul turned to the figure of Abraham, introduced from his very appearance in the Bible as the one "in whom all the families of the earth will be blessed" (Gen 12:3). The Jewish tradition, by and large, saw in Abraham a model of obedience, especially in regard to implementation of the circumcision command and the sacrifice of Isaac. Paul, however, in extended sequences in Romans 4 and Galatians 3—4, through a skillful exegesis of Genesis 15, especially verse 6 (Rom 4:3; Gal 3:6), presents the patriarch as a paradigm of one who found justification simply on the basis of faith. Abraham believed in God's assurance that he would have a son and an heir (Gen 15:4–5) *before* there was question of circumcision, that is, while he was still in effect a Gentile. Moreover, it was in this state of righteousness before God that he received the further promise (the "land" promise [vv. 18–19]; see PROMISE), on which, in the developed Jewish tradition, all the blessings of salvation were seen to be contained (Rom 4:13). Paul can then present Abraham's "fatherhood" as based primarily on his faith (v. 16; see Gen 17:5). His numberless "progeny" (see Gen 12:2; 13:16; 15:5) destined to "inherit" the promise he received (Gal 3:29; 4:7) consists of those, Jews *and* Gentiles, who follow him in his faith (Rom 4:11–12, 16–25; Gal 3:6–9). In this way, Paul made the "Gentile" mode of response to the gospel, simply in terms of faith, paradigmatic for all who would be members of the eschatological people of God, those of Jewish background included.

Israel and the Gentile Mission

This inclusive vision of the gospel, set out thematically in Romans 1:16–17, while privileging Gentile believers, leaves in jeopardy the status of Israel as covenant people of God and, in particular, raises the question of God's faithfulness to that bulk of Israel that has not responded positively to the gospel. Paul addresses this issue at length in Romans 9—11. The wide-ranging discussion, based largely on the sovereign freedom of God to operate completely independently of human response or merit, concludes (11:11–32) with a vision of the ultimate salvation of "all Israel" according to an eschatological program hitherto totally unforeseen: not, before the salvation of the Gentiles, but only *after* the "full number" of the latter destined for salvation has entered in (v. 25), and on the same basis of faith in the saving death of Christ (vv. 26–27). In fact, Paul cautions Gentile believers in Rome against writing off the salvation of as yet unbelieving Israel (vv. 17–24). God has brought about a temporary "hardening" of Israel in order to reach out to the Gentiles (vv. 7–16). But the "mercy" they have received as once "disobedient" Gentiles will operate with equal effect toward Israel's current disobedience to the gospel in order that God may be merciful to all (11:28–32).

In this way, Paul's tireless mission to the Gentiles (see especially the attractive summary in Romans 15:15–21) is not at the expense of or contrary to mission to the Jews but serves an inclusive vision of God's plan as Creator directed to the salvation of all. It is ultimately founded on the "service" of Christ, who "became a servant of the circumcised on behalf of the truth of God in order to confirm the promises given to the patriarchs, and in order that the Gentiles might glorify God for his mercy" (15:8–9). Paul's rounds off (vv. 10–12) this inclusive vision with a string of biblical quotations (Ps 18:49; Deut 32:43; Ps 117:1; Isa 11:10), all of which point to the inclusion of Gentiles alongside Israel among those who praise God.

In Ephesians, a letter written in Paul's name to Gentile believers (1:13–14; 2:11–13; 3:1), the union of Jews and Gentiles within the church is the primary manifestation of the divine design to draw all things into unity through Christ (1:10; 2:14–16; 3:1–14).

ABRAHAM; APOSTLE; BLESSING; FAITH; GOD; GOSPEL; ISRAEL; MERCY; PROMISE

Reading

Byrne, *Romans*, 144–62, 348–57, 428–33; T. L. Donaldson, *Paul and the Gentiles: Remapping the Apostle's Convictional World* (Minneapolis: Fortress, 1997); Dunn, *Theology*, 177–79; P. Fredricksen, *Paul: The Pagans' Apostle* (New Haven and London: Yale University Press, 2017); M. Thiessen, *Paul and the Gentile Problem* (New York: Oxford University Press, 2016); S. Winter, "Paul's Attitude to the Gentiles," in *Attitudes to Gentiles in Ancient Judaism and Early Christianity*, ed. D. C. Sim and J. S. McLaren (London: Bloomsbury, 2013), 138–53.

GIFT (*see* Grace)

GIFT(S) OF THE SPIRIT

Gifts of the Spirit are designated in Paul by the word, rare outside his usage, *charisma*. The *-ma* ending adds the sense of impact or effect. Thus, where *charis* basically means "favor" or "gift" bestowed as an expression of favor, *charisma* has the sense of the way in which the favor or gift is embodied or impacts on others. This is very attractively illustrated by a couple of sentences from Paul's comparison/contrast between the effects on humanity of Adam and Christ respectively in Romans 5:15–16:

> [15] But it is not a case of, "As (was) the trespass, so (is) the gracious gift [*charisma*]." For if through one man's trespass, many died, much more have the grace of God [*hē charis tou theou*] and the gift in grace [*hē dōrea en chariti*] of the one man, Jesus Christ abounded for many.... [16] ....the gracious gift [*charisma*], following many trespasses, brings justification.

Paul here stresses the absolute continuity between the grace of God and the self-sacrificial death of the incarnate Christ as the embodiment or fine point of impact of divine grace.

In Romans 6:19–23, Paul offers a similar negative/positive contrast in terms of a "service" of sin and of righteousness respectively. He concludes: "For the wages of sin is death but the gracious gift [*charisma*] of God is eternal life in Christ Jesus our Lord" (v. 23).

Eternal life is the *charisma* of God in the sense that the grace of God has created in believers the righteousness that leads to this positive outcome. In Romans 11:29, the *charismata* (plural) are the inalienable privileges God has graciously bestowed on Israel, a guarantee of her final salvation (see v. 26).

Gifts of the Spirit in the Community

Predominantly, however, *charisma* appears in the sequences where Paul addresses the gifts that should flourish in the believing community to build up its growth and strength (Rom 12:3–8; 1 Cor 12:1—14:40). It is customary to refer to these as "gifts of the Spirit," although it is not certain that the term *charisma* connotes *in itself* the sense of the gift given by the Spirit. Hence the apparent necessity for Paul to add the qualification *pneumatikon* to *charisma* when speaking of the particular spiritual gift he wants to share with the community in Rome (Rom 1:11). The explanation that heads the list in Romans 12:6–8, "Having gifts [*charismata*] that differ according to the grace [*charin*] given us" (v. 6a), shows, again, the relationship between *charis* and *charismata*. The gifts are the particular instances of grace that God has bestowed on individuals in the community for the building up of all.

In both sequences devoted to the gifts of the Spirit, although far more extensively in 1 Corinthians 12:12–27, Paul draws on the image of the community as a "body" (*sōma*), specifically "the body of Christ" (vv. 12, 27; Rom 12:4–5). In 1 Corinthians 12, he attributes the gifts to the working of the Spirit, heading his response as "concerning gifts of the Spirit" (*peri...tōn pneumatikōn* [v. 1]), presumably because of the predilection of the community for that divine agency. It is unlikely that permanent offices are in view—more likely, gifts that are evident in various individuals to a significant degree. It is noteworthy that preeminence in what would nowadays be regarded as gifts for administration—"assistance" (*antilēpseis*); "leadership" (*kybernēseis*) (1 Cor 12:28)—are regarded as gifts of divine grace (*charismata*).

Putting the Gift of Tongues in Its Place

Whereas the Corinthians appear to have prized the gift of tongues above all, Paul insists that just as the human body, though one, has many limbs and organs working to a common purpose, so the community, as the body of Christ, is endowed with many kinds of gifts through which the one Spirit works toward a common goal. It is not clear that he is actually ranking the eight gifts listed in 1 Corinthians 12:8–10 (utterances of wisdom, utterances of knowledge, faith, gifts of healing, working of miracles, prophecy, discernment of spirits, various kinds of tongues) but, in the context, it is significant that the gift of tongues appears last. This position still obtains in a later list that does begin with explicit ranking: "God has appointed in the church": "first apostles, second prophets, third teachers, then gifts of healing, forms of assistance, forms of leadership, various kinds of tongues" (v. 28).

The further development in 1 Corinthians 14 makes clear, however, that Paul's main concern is to deal with the issue of tongues—that is, utterance, unintelligible to hearers, arising from below the level of consciousness. The intervening sequence on the preeminence of love in chapter 13 prepares the way for dealing with this issue (see 13:1–2, 8). Paul esteems the gift of tongues, which he himself shares (14:18–19, although he may be speaking ironically), but expresses a clear preference for prophecy (14:1, 5). Prophecy communicates a Spirit-inspired message of God to the community for guidance, edification, encouragement, or consolation. Where persons who speak in tongues "build up" themselves as individuals, the prophetic gift "builds up the church"; tongues can do that only if followed by interpretation (v. 5). When assessing the relative value of gifts in the community the key considerations are discernment (v. 29; see "discernment of spirits" [12:10]) and right order in the assembly (14:23–33, 40).

The echo of this extended treatment of gifts appearing early in the paraenesis of Romans 12:3–8, again images the community as "one body in Christ" (v. 5) but makes no mention of the Spirit. After each reference to a gift (prophecy, service [*diakonia*], teaching, exhortation, almsgiving, leadership, mercy), Paul lists the quality with which it should be exercised so that, as the *–ma* ending suggests, it really becomes for the recipient an expression and experience of God's grace.

BODY; CHURCH; GRACE; LOVE; PROPHECY; SIGNS AND WONDERS; SPIRIT

Reading

D. E. Aune, *Prophecy in Early Christianity and the Ancient Mediterranean World* (Grand Rapids: Eerdmans, 1983, repr. 1991), 203–5, 219–22; Byrne, *Romans*, 368–74; Dunn, *Theology*, 552–61; G. D. Fee, *DPL*, 339–47; *God's Empowering Presence*, 32–35, 886–89; E. Käsemann, "Ministry and Community in the New Testament," in *Essays*, 63–94; Matera, *GSG*, 142–44; C. M. Robeck Jr., *DPL*, 755–62 (Prophecy), 939–43 (Tongues); Thiselton, *1 Corinthians*, 956–65 (Prophecy), 970–88 (Tongues), 1087–94 (Prophecy).

GLORY, GLORIFY

The Greek word for "glory" (*doxa*) as used in biblical Greek (the Septuagint and the New Testament) diverges notably from its usage elsewhere in Greek literature. In secular usage *doxa* has the basic sense of what appears or seems to be the case, and hence "what one expects" or "reckons" to be the case on that basis. So *doxa* means "expectation," "opinion," or "judgment"; then, on the basis of the opinion others have of a person, it acquires the objective sense of "reputation" or "honor" or even "glory." The most frequent meaning of *doxa* in secular literature, namely, "notion" or "opinion," is entirely lacking in biblical Greek whereas the LXX's regular employment of *doxa* to translate the Hebrew *kabōd* has led to it carrying much of the meaning of that Hebrew term, in particular "glory." As such, it can refer to the "weight" of esteem or honor in which a person is held, especially a ruler and notably the supreme ruler, God. In this connection glory attends the heavenly realm as the abode of God and manifests closeness or belonging to that realm.

Giving Glory to God

When apparent on earth, glory denotes the outward splendor of divine power seen in the works of creation and historical acts of salvation. In this sense, particularly in regard to the manifestation of the divine, *doxa* recaptures its most basic meaning of "what appears." The cognate verb *doxazein* ("glorify") then means acknowledging the manifestation of the divine, evoking admiration and praise.

In Romans 1:21–23, Paul depicts the human lapse into idolatry as a failure to "glorify" the Creator in this sense. Abraham, on the contrary, in his faith in the creative power of God, "gave glory" (*doxa*) to God (Rom 4:20c). The work of salvation will consist in a display of divine glory (Rom 9:23; see 3:7), with Jews and Gentiles glorifying God together (15:6, 7, 9). The lordship of Christ (see 1 Cor 12:3b) will culminate in the subjection of the universe to the glory of God the Father (Phil 2:11; see 1:11), and of course such acknowledgment of God's power and wisdom features above all in doxologies (Rom 11:36; 16:27; Gal 1:5; Phil 4:19–20; see also 2 Cor 1:20; Eph 3:21 [see also 1:6, 12, 14]; 1 Tim 1:17). The daily life of believers should be directed entirely to the glory of God (1 Cor 10:31), as is their obedience to the gospel and their generosity in supporting the relief of the saints (2 Cor 9:13; see also 8:19).

Glory as Apostolic Accreditation: 2 Corinthians 3:1—4:18

The motif of "glory" appears in unparalleled concentration in 2 Corinthians 3:1—4:18 within the wider context of Paul's "apology" for his apostolic ministry in 2 Corinthians 2:14—7:4. Here, "glory" has the basic sense of the manifestation of the divine and the heavenly that lends authority and credibility to human ministry on behalf of God. In a running midrash on Exodus 34:29–35,

Paul contrasts Moses's ministry of the old covenant (one of condemnation and death) unfavorably with his own apostolic ministry of a new covenant of righteousness and life (2 Cor 3:6). If the glory on the face of Moses in his ministry of death was nonetheless so splendid that he had to utilize a veil to shield the Israelites from its harmful effects, how much more glory must attend the ministry of the new life-giving covenant carried on by Paul (vv. 7–11). Believers who see, as in a mirror, the glory of God on the face of the risen Lord are being transformed, through the Spirit, into the image of God that he is, "from one degree of glory to another" (3:18; see 4:6; Rom 8:29–30).

Glory as Human Transformation

It is at this point that the anthropological sense of "glory" comes to the fore. According to Genesis 1:26–28, as the culmination of God's creation, human beings bear the divine image (LXX *eikōn*) and likeness (LXX *homoiōsis*), and in this respect, function as God's "viceroys," exercising authority over the remainder of creation. There is a poetic reflection of this in Psalm 8:5–8, where the same "governance" role is expressed in terms of being "crowned with glory" (*doxa* [LXX v. 6]; see also Wis 9:2; 1 Cor 11:7). Glory is one of the privileges of Israel (Rom 9:4). For Paul all human beings have forfeited this "glory" through sin (Rom 3:23). A central aspect of the saving work of Christ will be the eschatological restoration of this "glory" in the new creation. For believers this process is already under way in a hidden sense as a consequence of justification (Rom 8:30; 2 Cor 3:18). Its full, visible manifestation awaits the resurrection of the body, in line with the already visible glory of the risen Christ (Rom 8:17, 18–23; 29–30; Phil 3:21).

Thus, "glory" acquires the eschatological sense of the heavenly destiny of the faithful (Rom 2:7, 10; 5:2; 2 Cor 4:17; 1 Thess 2:12; see also Eph 1:18; Col 1:27; 3:4; 2 Thess 2:14). This destiny is not necessarily to be understood as totally "otherworldly," since what Paul appears to foresee is not so much the replacement of the present creation but its transformation into the original design of the Creator as set out in the creation accounts of Genesis 1—2 and Psalm 8 (see Rom 8:18–22; 1 Cor 15:22–28). However, the sense of glory as the manifestation of the heavenly never entirely slips away, as is clear from Paul's attempt to describe the risen bodily existence of believers in 1 Corinthians 15:35–49. Here he speaks of the heavenly bodies (sun, moon, and stars) as differing from one another in "glory" in the sense of their visible manifestation (vv. 40–41).

Glory as Repute

Paul can speak of "glory" in the more secular sense of honor or repute (1 Cor 12:26; 2 Cor 6:8; 1 Thess 2:6) and also, more positively, of that in which one may rightly—or wrongly (see Phil 3:19)—rejoice or boast (2 Cor 8:23; 1 Thess 2:20; see also Eph 3:13). Glory is, therefore, a motif in Paul that goes in many directions. Predominantly, however, he retains the biblical sense of glory at that which pertains to and manifests God and as the heavenly existence that God wishes to share with human beings.

ABRAHAM; BODY; CREATION; GOD; HOPE; IMAGE; MINISTRY; MOSES; RESURRECTION

Reading

L. L. Belleville, *Reflections of Glory: Paul's Polemical Use of the Moses-Doxa Tradition in 2 Corinthians 3,1–18* (Sheffield: JSOT Press, 1991); Byrne, "Glory," 13–30; *PES*, 60–65; *Romans*, 257–58, 268–70; R. B. Gaffin Jr., *DPL*, 348–50; Harris, *2 Corinthians*, 275–92, 314–19; H. Hegermann, *EDNT* 1:344–48; G. Kittel and G. von Rad, *TDNT* 2:232–55; C. C. Newman, *Paul's Glory Christology: Tradition and Rhetoric* (Leiden; New York: Brill, 1992; repr. Waco, TX: Baylor University Press, 2017); "Paul on Christ and Glory," *PRSt*, 47 (2020): 399–413; Wolter, *Paul*, 186–89, 388–92.

GOD

Paul brought to his faith in Christ his Jewish belief in the one God as Creator of the universe and, in particular, as the God who had rescued a people from slavery and forged with them a covenant as a people set apart. By the same token, Paul was heir to the apocalyptic expectation characteristic of the Judaism of his time. This worldview foresaw an imminent intervention and reckoning on the part of the Creator to deal with the evil of the present age and bring the righteous into possession of a renewed creation. Within that apocalyptic perspective, the revelation on the Damascus road of the crucified Jesus of Nazareth as Messiah and Son of God (Gal 1:16; see also 2 Cor 4:4, 6) drastically reshaped Paul's image of God and the special position of Israel within that image. God for Paul was no longer just the God who had brought Israel out of Egypt but, more immediately, the God who had raised Jesus from the dead, designating him Messiah and divine Son (Rom 1:3–4; 4:24; 8:11; 1 Cor 6:14; Gal 1:1), and as such, eschatological judge (Rom 2:16; 2 Cor 5:10). God was now the "Father of our Lord Jesus Christ" (Rom 15:6; 2 Cor 1:3; 11:31; see Col 1:3), who is "the image of God" (2 Cor 4:4c; see 3:18; Col 1:15).

Paul ranges the risen Lord alongside God in greetings, blessings, prayer wishes, thanksgivings, and final salutations (Rom 1:7; 1 Cor 1:3; 2 Cor 1:2; 13:13; Gal 1:3; Phil 1:2; 1 Thess 1:1; 3:11; Phlm 3; see also Eph 1:2, 17; 6:23; 2 Thess 1:1, 2; 2:16; 1 Tim 1:2; 2 Tim 1:2; Titus 1:4). In 1 Corinthians 8:6, Paul recites what appears to be an early Christian creed, acknowledging "the one God and Father, from whom are all things and for whom we exist" and then adds "and one Lord Jesus Christ, through whom are all things and through whom we exist" (NRSV), associating Christ with the work of creation. The final stanza of the Philippians hymn (2:9–11) describes the universal acknowledgment of Christ's lordship as directed "to the glory of God the Father" (v. 11), while Paul in 1 Corinthians 15:22–28 outlines the same subject as a work in progress until "the Son himself will also be subjected to the one who put all things in subjection under him, so that God may be all in all" (v. 28). These texts display an unhesitating capacity on Paul's part to attribute exalted and indeed divine status to Christ (see Phil 2:6) without injury to Judaism's basic monotheism.

As "called apostle to the Gentiles" (Rom 1:1, 5), Paul stressed that God was not only the God and covenant partner of Israel but the God of all nations as well. God's faithfulness to Israel was matched by a similar fidelity, as Creator, to the whole world. To this end, Paul privileges the prior covenant and promise that God made to Abraham, with its inclusive pledge that "all the nations would be blessed in his offspring," over the more exclusive Sinai covenant made with Israel through Moses (Rom 4:1–25; Gal 3:1–4:7, 21–31). In a telling theological move, Paul appeals to the very text most expressive of Israel's monotheism, the Shema (Deut 6:4), to claim that the one God cannot have "two faces" to the world in regard to justification—one based on performance of the law and the other on faith. The "blessing" promised to Abraham was the blessing of justification, to be made available equally and necessarily to Jews and Gentiles alike, on the sole basis of faith (Rom 3:29–30).

In order to exclude any basis for justification other than faith, Paul presents God in more traditional terms as eschatological judge, whose wrath is already revealed not only against Gentile idolatry but also Jewish wrongdoing (Rom 1:18–3:20). But the same God has intervened in Christ to mount an "eleventh hour" rescue of humanity in a way that both deals with the evil of human sin (Rom 3:21–26) and at the same time creates the possibility, through faith and baptism, for human beings to enter "into" Christ (6:3; 1 Cor 12:13; Gal 3:26–28), and so find justification and ultimately salvation in him. In so doing God has displayed "righteousness" ("righteousness of God") in both a juridic and salvific sense (Rom 3:21–26; see 1:16–17). Paul stresses both the divine initiative and also the absolute continuity between Father and Son in the work of redemption and reconciliation (Rom 5:8–10; 8:3–4; Gal 4:4–5; 2 Cor 5:18–21).

Paul sees the divine decision to justify human beings simply on the basis of grace and faith, without regard to human merit or desert, as a sovereign exercise of the freedom that belongs to God as Creator (Rom 9:6–29; 11:5–6), on the pattern of God's dealing with Abraham (Rom 4:16). Granted the "deadness" of his own reproductive organs and that of his wife Sarah's womb (v. 19), Abraham's faith in the divine promise that he would have a son and heir meant believing in a God who "raises the dead and calls into being things that do not exist" (v. 17b). As such, Abraham "models" the faith of believers who, similarly, believe in a God who raised the Christ from the dead (v. 24), and who will raise their own mortal bodies through the power of the Spirit dwelling within them (8:9–11) (see FAITH).

God's action in Christ represents the unfolding of a predetermined plan focused entirely on Christ, whose risen glory believers are destined to share as God's sons (and daughters) and "co-heirs" (Rom 8:14–17, 29–30). Although that destiny remains for the present outstanding, the experience of the Spirit, in which like Christ in his earthly life (Mark 14:36) they address God as "*Abba*, Father" (Rom 8:15; Gal 4:6), confirms their righteous status, their experience of divine love (Rom 5:5, 6–10; see Gal 4:9); it is also the pledge that all is unfolding for their good (8:23, 28–30). Romans 8 culminates with a vision of the final judgment (vv. 31–39) headed by the presupposition, "If God is for us" (*ei ho theos hyper hēmōn* [v. 31]). "God is for us" well sums up Paul's sense of God as revealed in Jesus Christ. What God did not in the end require of Abraham (see Gen 22:16), God did require of Godself, the "not-sparing," the "giving up of the beloved Son" (Rom 8:32; see 4:25a) in order to give us the fullness of salvation. Nothing that hostile powers can throw against the elect, including the sufferings of the present time, will ever be able to separate them from the love of God that comes to us in Christ Jesus, our Lord" (v. 39).

The fact that believers are enveloped within this unfolding divine plan stemming from God's grace and love does not mean that they no longer remain accountable at a final judgment. All will have to stand before the judgment seat of God (Rom 14:10b–12) and receive the recompense for their conduct in their present life in the body (2 Cor 5:10; see also Rom 2:6–11, 16; 3:6). Paul's theology can hold human accountability within an overall sense of the victorious grace and sovereign freedom of God. In his vision of the inclusion of as yet unbelieving Israel in the community destined to be saved (Rom 11:11–32), it is mercy that emerges as the most prominent attribute of God:

> 30 Just as you (Gentiles) were once disobedient to God but have now received mercy because of their disobedience, 31 so they (Israelites) have now been disobedient in order that, by the mercy shown to you, they too may now receive mercy. 32 For God has imprisoned all in disobedience so that he may be merciful to all. (NRSV)

Paul can then bring his exposition of the inclusive gospel of divine faithfulness to a festive end with a doxology acclaiming the depth of the richness and wisdom of God (Rom 11:33–36).

ABRAHAM; CREATION; FAITH; IMAGE; JUDGE, LAST JUDGMENT; LORD; MERCY; RESURRECTION; RIGHTEOUSNESS; SON OF GOD

Reading

Becker, *Paul*, 379–86; Byrne, *PES*, 225–45; N. A. Dahl, "The One God of Jews and Gentiles (Romans 3.29–30)," in *Studies in Paul* (Minneapolis: Augsburg, 1977), 178–91; Dunn, *Theology*, 27–50; D. Guthrie and R. P. Martin, *DPL*, 354–69; Matera, *GSG*, 215–49; T. Milinovich et al., *God in Paul's Letters* (Washington, DC: Catholic Biblical Association of America, forthcoming); N. Richardson, *Paul's Language about God* (Sheffield: Sheffield Academic, 1994); Schnelle, *Apostle Paul*, 392–402, 407–9; J. L. White, *The Apostle of God: Paul and the Promise of Abraham* (Peabody, MA: Hendrickson, 1999), xx–xxv, 1–18, 139–72; Wright, *PFG*, 619–773.

GOSPEL

Christian usage of the word group "gospel"/"evangelize" (*euangelion/euangelizomai*) to announce the saving benefits of God's intervention in Jesus Christ likely predated the conversion of Paul. However, it was in his writings that the motif "gospel" (understood as a message as distinct from the later literary genre: "a gospel") assumed a prominence out of all proportion to its appearance elsewhere in the New Testament. It is true that Luke employs the verb slightly more often than Paul (twenty-five times, compared to twenty-one). However, of the seventy-six appearances of the noun *euangelion* in the New Testament, eight are in the gospel of Mark, while the Pauline literature accounts for no less than sixty. The "gospel" had become absolutely central to his self-understanding and mission.

The Origins of the "Gospel"

In tracing the origins of the "gospel" motif, we have to reckon with two sources: one biblical and one stemming from the Greco-Roman milieu. In the biblical background, a participial form *mebasser* appears in the sense of "one who brings good news" (1 Sam 31:9; 1 Kgs 1:42; Jer 20:15). Particularly noteworthy is a cluster of texts from Second (and Third) Isaiah (40:9; 52:7; 61:1–2; see also Ps 96:2; Nah 1:15), all of which (with the LXX employing *euangelizomai*) announce a coming liberation associated with a saving intervention (rule) of God. Evidence from Qumran (11Q13; 4Q521) and elsewhere (Pss Sol 11:1) suggests that "tell good news" later became a quasi-technical usage for announcing the onset of the messianic age. It was natural, then, for the early Christian community, in continuity presumably with the practice of Jesus himself (see Mark 1:14–15 and parallels; Matt 11:4–5//Luke 7:22), to reach for this terminology in regard to the saving intervention of God in Christ. Their post-resurrection faith led them to draw the person and fate of Christ into the center of the proclamation, so that "the gospel of God" (Mark 1:14; see also Rom 1:1; 15:16; 1 Thess 2:8, 9) became more specifically the good news about Jesus, whom God had installed as Messiah by raising him from the dead (see Rom 1:3–4).

The Greek-speaking milieu into which the early messianic community spread then provided the noun *euangelion* as an apt designation for the content of the proclamation. This word (normally in the plural form *euangelia*) featured in the announcement of significant imperial events, such as the birth of an heir, the beginning of a reign, or a notable victory in war. Alongside and to some extent over against the rule of the emperor, commitment to the gospel meant acknowledging the "lordship" (*kyrios*) of the crucified and risen Jesus (Rom 10:9; 1 Cor 12:3; 2 Cor 4:5; Phil 2:11).

Paul, Minister of the Gospel

Paul's brief allusion to his encounter with the risen Lord on the Damascus road goes immediately to the heart of his distinctive relationship to the gospel: "When God...was pleased to reveal his Son to me that I might 'gospel' [*euangelizōmai*] him among the Gentiles" (Gal 1:15–16). The text reveals Paul's conviction that the revelation to him of the risen Lord was by the same token a call to become an apostle, a minister of the gospel (1 Cor 9:1; 15:8–11), with a ministry directed specifically to Gentiles (Rom 1:1–5; 15:15–21; see also Eph 3:8). His credentials in all these respects were recognized by the "pillar" apostles in Jerusalem (Gal 2:2, 6–9).

The Judgment as Context of the Gospel

Within the apocalyptic cast of Paul's theology, the context for the proclamation of the gospel is the divine wrath looming over sinful humankind. This is made clear not only in his recall of his initial proclamation in 1 Thessalonians 1:10 (see also Gal 1:4) but also in the fact that the thematic announcement of the gospel in Romans (1:16–17) is followed immediately by a parallel announcement of the revelation of God's wrath (1:18). The gospel is the power of God leading to salvation for all who respond to it in faith because it reveals and communicates the divine righteousness that alone can ensure salvation from the wrath at the judgment. As proclaimed in the summary of the gospel cited in 1 Corinthians 15:3–5, Christ died "for our sins" (v. 3c) in the sense that his death represented a divine atonement for human sin on a universal scale (Rom 3:23–26), opening up the way for all to receive, through faith, the eschatological justification required for salvation: Christ "was given up" (by God) "for our transgressions" and "raised for our justification" (Rom 4:25; see 5:6–10).

Faith: The Only Valid Response to the Gospel

Implying, as it does, universal human sinfulness (Rom 3:9, 23; 5:12; 11:32; Gal 3:22), the gospel of the Crucified Messiah excludes the possibility of salvation on any basis other than faith—in particular, any hope for justification stemming from performance of the requirements of the Jewish law (Rom 3:19–20, 27–30). Scolding the Galatians for yielding to the suggestion that justification required taking on the works of the law, Paul recalls his proclamation to them of the Crucified Messiah (Gal 3:1; see also 1 Cor 1:22–24). The experience of the Spirit that attended their response in faith was the guarantee of justification *already* received (Gal 3:2–9).

An Inclusive Gospel

In regard to salvation, the gospel overthrows the former distinctions between Jew and Gentile, slave and free, male and female (Gal 3:28; see also 1 Cor 12:13; Eph 2:11–18; Col 3:11). Hence Paul can accuse Peter ("Cephas") of "not walking a straight line in regard to the truth of the gospel" when, under pressure from the faction associated with James, he effectively re-erected the barrier between ("holy") Jews and "Gentile sinners" by going along with separate tables at the community gathering at Antioch (Gal 2:11–15; see vv. 16–18). The gospel, not the law, has become the supreme criterion for how believers are to live on their way to salvation (1 Cor 15:1–2; Phil 1:27).

The Gospel as Proclaimed by Paul

The gospel as proclaimed by Paul, its validity attested by "signs and wonders" and the power of the Spirit (Rom 15:19; 1 Cor 2:4–5; Gal 3:3–5; 1 Thess 1:5), is unalterable. Paul castigates the Galatians for turning aside to "another gospel," contrary to the one he had proclaimed among them (Gal 1:6–9; see also 2 Cor 11:4). In a totally different direction, he rejoices that the Philippians have themselves become sharers in the grace given to him to proclaim the gospel (Phil 1:5–7; see 4:15).

Paul's intense personal identification with the gospel emerges from texts such as 1 Corinthians 9:16d: "Woe to me if I do not proclaim the gospel" (see Rom 1:14–15). He foregoes his right as an apostle to receive support from the churches in order to place no hindrance to the gospel (1 Cor 9:3–18; see 2 Cor 11:7; 1 Thess 2:9). Passionate commitment lies behind the vast scope of his ambit to complete the proclamation as far as Spain to the west (Rom 15:18–24), so that the full number of the Gentiles may be garnered for the harvest. His hope is that at that point the current "hostility" of Israel to the gospel (Rom 11:28) will cease, so that "all Israel" will be saved (v. 26), bringing about a united glorification of God for the mercy shown to all (15:8–12).

"Gospel" in Later Pauline Literature

In the later Pauline literature (Col 1:5, 23; Eph 1:13; 3:6–8), as elsewhere in the New Testament (Heb 4:2, 6; 1 Pet 1:12, 25), the "gospel" motif has receded from central focus to become, in rather stereotyped fashion, Christian "in-language" for the original preaching. An explicit retrieval of the Isaianic tradition does, however, appear in Ephesians 2:14–17, where Christ is described as having come proclaiming a "gospel of peace" to those near and those far off (see Isa 52:7; 57:19).

APOCALYPTIC; APOSTLE; CHRIST; FAITH; FREEDOM; GENTILES; JUDGE, LAST JUDGMENT; RESURRECTION; SALVATION; SON OF GOD; WRATH

Reading

Byrne, *OEBT*, 432–37; *PES*, 71–76; *Romans*, 42–43; J. D. G. Dunn, "The Gospel According to St. Paul," in Westerholm, *Paul*, 139–53; *Theology*, 164–69; A. B. Luter Jr., *DPL*, 369–72; Schnelle, *Apostle Paul*, 403–9; J. H. Schütz, *Paul and the Anatomy of Apostolic Authority* (Cambridge: Cambridge University Press, 1975; repr. Louisville: Westminster John Knox, 2007), 35–78; G. N. Stanton, *Jesus and Gospel* (Cambridge: Cambridge University Press, 2004); "Paul's Gospel," in Dunn, *Companion*, 173–84; G. Strecker, *EDNT* 2:69–74; P. Stuhlmacher, "The Pauline Gospel," in *The Gospel and the Gospels*, ed. P. Stuhlmacher (Grand Rapids: Eerdmans, 1991), 149–72; Wolter, *Paul*, 51–69.

GRACE

The Greek word *charis* most basically has the sense of the grace and beauty of a person that renders them attractive, eliciting favor and goodwill. (It corresponds to and regularly appears in the LXX as the translation of the Hebrew *hēn* in this sense, as in the expression "to find favor in the eyes of….") Reciprocally then *charis* can indicate the *favor* and goodwill thereby elicited in others by a person's charm and attractiveness. More concretely, *charis* can denote a *gift* given as an expression of favor in this second sense. Finally, *charis* can denote the *gratitude* created in the recipient of the favor or gift.

Paul's use of *charis* does not include the first sense (see, however, Col 4:6; see also Eph 4:29) but ranges widely across the remaining senses outlined above. While his usage, reflecting his sense of the sheer gratuity of God's intervention in Christ, has bequeathed to the Christian theological tradition a sense of the absolutely unmerited quality of divine grace, it is important to be aware that this note stems from his theological understanding and is not necessarily inherent in *charis* as more widely understood at the time. Benefactors and others in the ancient world could bestow gifts as a sign of favor but this did not mean that the recipients were undeserving nor that it was without expectation of some service in return.

The "Overflow" of God's Grace into the World

Paul sees the divine intervention in Christ as the expression of an immense wave of God's *charis*, in the second sense above, flowing over an undeserving world. Over against the sin of Adam and its consequences "much more surely have the grace of God [*hē charis tou theou*] and the free gift in the grace [*hē dōrea en chariti*] of the one man, Jesus Christ, abounded for the many" (Rom 5:15; see also 5:17; Col 1:6; Eph 1:6, 7; 2:7; 2 Thess 2:16; 1 Tim 1:14). The redemption and justification that flows from Christ's self-gift is an expression of divine grace in this totally unmerited sense (Rom 3:24; Gal 1:6; see also Eph 2:5, 8; 2 Tim 1:9; Titus 3:7), foreshadowed for believers in God's dealing with Abraham (Rom 4:4, 16; see also 11:5–6). Henceforth therefore believers live in an "atmosphere" of divine grace (Rom 5:2), which has replaced the death-dealing existence under the law (Rom 6:14; Gal 2:21; 5:4).

Grace as Empowering Force

Paul depicts God's *charis* in this sense as a triumphant force, over against the force, equally personified, of sin (Rom 5:20, 21; see Titus 2:11). It empowers him personally (2 Cor 12:9), lies behind his apostolic achievements (1 Cor 15:10), and is communicated through them (2 Cor 1:12; 4:15; 6:1; 8:1). Paul's replacement of the standard Hellenistic greeting *chairein* with "grace" (*charis*) both in the greetings (Rom 1:7; 1 Cor 1:3; 2 Cor 1:2; Gal 1:3; Phil 1:2; 1 Thess 1:1; Phlm 3; see Col 1:2; Eph 1:2) and conclusions (Rom 16:20; 1 Cor 16:23; 2 Cor 13:13; Gal 6:18; Phil 4:23; 1 Thess 5:28; Phlm 25; see Col 4:18; Eph 6:24) of his letters reflects the sense that the communities of believers live within and are themselves expressions of the grace of God that has come to them in Christ Jesus (1 Cor 1:4; 2 Cor 8:1; 9:14; Gal 1:6; Phil 1:7).

Grace as Personal Gift

Paul sees his apostolic calling as a very distinctive instantiation of God's grace (Gal 1:15; see Rom 1:5; 12:3, 15:15; 1 Cor 3:10; Gal 2:9; see also Eph 3:2, 7, 8; 1 Tim 1:12, 14). But other believers also receive their own gift of grace (Rom 12:6; see Eph 4:7). Still within the sense of *charis* as gift, Paul, especially in connection with the collection for the saints (2 Cor 8—9), uses the term in the sense of "a generous gift," whether on the part of God (2 Cor 8:1), of Christ (8:9), or of others inspired by the generosity of God (8:4, 6, 19; 9:8, 14).

Grace as Gratitude

Finally, in the third sense outlined above, *charis* features in expressions of gratitude to God, whether in regard to God's own action (Rom 6:17; 7:25; 1 Cor 10:30; 15:57; 2 Cor 2:14; 9:15; see also Col 3:16) or in regard to the generosity divinely inspired in fellow believers (2 Cor 8:16). Paul describes the fundamental human lapse into idolatry in terms of a failure to "honor God or give thanks to him" (Rom 1:21). He formulates a most attractive expression of the reversal of this when indicating the goal or consequence of his apostolic ministry as "so that grace [*charis*], as it extends to more and more people, may increase thanksgiving [*eucharistian*] to the glory of God" (2 Cor 4:15). Giving thanks, then, is the truly appropriate human response to the redemptive outpouring of God's *charis* that has come to the world in the person of the Son.

Grace in the Later Pauline Letters

The immeasurable riches of God's grace features strongly in the hymnic sections of the Ephesians (1:6–7; 2:7; see Col 1:6; also 2 Thess 1:12; 2:16; Titus 2:11), along with a repeated insistence on the Pauline doctrine that salvation is by grace and not by human achievement (Eph 2:5, 8; see 2 Tim 1:9; Titus 3:7). Likewise, "Paul" makes repeated mention of the distinctive grace that was given him as the apostle to the Gentiles (Eph 3:2, 7–8; see 1 Tim 1:12, 14), while acknowledging that each believer has been given grace according to the measure of Christ's gift (Eph 4:7; see Rom 12:3). Every word that comes from the mouth should communicate a sense of God's grace to those who hear (Eph 4:29; see Col 4:6).

ABRAHAM; ADAM; FAITH; GOD; GENTILES; LAW; RIGHTEOUSNESS; SIN; THANKSGIVING

Reading

Barclay, *Gift*, 11–78, 562–65, 575–79; *Paul and the Power of Grace* (Grand Rapids: Eerdmans, 2020); Dunn, *Theology*, 319–23; B. Eastman, *The Significance of Grace in the Letters of Paul* (New York: Peter Lang, 1999); J. R. Harrison, *Paul's Language of Grace in Its Graeco-Roman Context* (Tübingen: Mohr Siebeck, 2003); J. A. Linebaugh, *God, Grace, and Righteousness in Wisdom of Solomon and Paul's Letter to the Romans: Texts in Conversation* (Leiden; Boston: Brill, 2013); A. B. Luter Jr., *DPL*, 372–74; O. McFarland, *God and Grace in Philo and Paul* (Leiden; Boston: Brill, 2016), 1–24, 103–232; Rainbow, *Way of Salvation*, 132–40; Schnelle, *Apostle Paul*, 482–84; Wells, *Grace and Agency*, 20–21, 295–311.

H

HAND OVER

Paul uses the Greek verb *paradidōmi* in a considerable variety of contexts, all of which are worthy of note. The verb has the basic sense of handing over something precious or significant to another party or force, or simply surrendering it altogether.

Divine Giving Up

The most significant usages of *paradidōmi* in Paul have God or Christ as subject. In a formal pattern in Romans 1:18–32 the "revelation of God's wrath" (v. 18) is depicted as the consequences of God's "handing over" (*paredōken*, stated three times: vv. 24a, 26a, 28b) of the idolatrous world (vv. 19–23, 25, 28a) to a variety of passions described in ever-increasing length and intensity (vv. 24b, 26b–27, 28b–31). In an extremity of love and grace, to remedy the human situation thus enslaved, God "did not spare his only Son but gave him up [*paredōken auton*] for us all" (Rom 8:32). The passive expression of Christ's being "given up [*paredothē*] for our trespasses" in Romans 4:25a likewise indicates the action of God in the saving death of Christ, as does also the location of the eucharistic institution as occurring "on the night on which he was given up" (*hē paredideto*) (1 Cor 11:23). In this latter case the passive verb is regularly translated "betrayed" (e.g., the NRSV), which is certainly defensible in light of the use of the verb with reference to the action of Judas in the passion narratives of the gospels. However, Paul makes no explicit mention of Judas, and it is equally likely and perhaps more probable that he has a divine passive in mind: Christ given up in a soteriological sense by God (besides Rom 4:25 and 8:32, see also 3:25; 5:8, 10).

Christ himself is the subject of the loving self-gift in Galatians 2:20, where Paul passionately insists that he "lives now through faith in the Son of God, who loved me and delivered himself up for me" (*paredontos auton hyper emou*; see also Rom 5:6; 15:3; Gal 1:4). There are echoes of this allusion to Christ's loving self-gift in Ephesians 5:2, 25. Finally, the thought of being "given up" by God—to suffering and possibly to death—in union with Christ seems to be operative in Paul's portrayal of the perilous nature of the apostolic ministry in 2 Corinthians 4:11 (*eis thanaton paradidōmetha*; see Rom 8:36; see also Phil 3:10–11).

Without reference to imminent death, Paul gives thanks to God in Romans 6:17 that those to whom he is writing, who once were slaves of sin, "now have given obedience from the heart to the pattern of teaching [*eis typon didachēs*] to which you were handed over [*eis hon paredōthēte*]." The allusion is obscure, but the passive construction may, again, indicate the action of God. Coming to faith and being baptized meant for believers being consigned totally to Christ: his death and resurrection (6:3–4), and, consequently, his self-giving pattern of life (see Phil 2:5).

In Paul's description of the events of "the End" (1 Cor 15:24–28), after Christ has subjected all things, including death, "the last enemy" (v. 26), to himself, he will "hand over" (*paradidō*) the kingdom to the God and Father" (v. 24), having completed his redemptive task of reclaiming the universe for the rule of God (v. 28; see Phil 2:10–11; Isa 45:23).

Human Handing Over

Dismayed that the Corinthians are tolerating the continued existence in the community of a man living in an overtly immoral situation (1 Cor 5:1), Paul instructs them to "hand this man over to Satan for the destruction of his flesh, so that his spirit may be saved on the day of the Lord" (v. 5; see 1 Tim 1:20). To emphasize the centrality of love, Paul posits that one might hand over (*paradidō*) one's body to be burned (there is textual uncertainty about the allusion), but, unless accompanied by love, even so extreme an act would amount to nothing (1 Cor 13:3). One may also, in a negative direction, surrender oneself to licentiousness (*paredōkan tē aselgeia*) (Eph 4:19).

The Tradition

A distinctive usage of "handing over" occurs in contexts where Paul speaks of handing over to the community traditions that he himself had received. He introduces an instruction about women's attire when praying in the assembly (1 Cor 11:2–16; see WOMAN) with a more general commendation to the effect that the community hold fast to the traditions (*paradoseis*) that he had handed over (*paredōka*) to them (v. 2). Recalling the eucharistic tradition to correct the community's celebration of the Lord's Supper, he speaks of what "I received from Lord [*egō...parelabon apo tou kyriou*], I passed on to you [*ho kai paredōka hymin*]" (v. 23). "From the Lord" does not necessarily mean that Paul received the tradition directly from the Lord himself but that the tradition passed on in the community goes back ultimately to the Lord himself. Likewise, though himself a recipient of an appearance of the risen Lord, albeit the last (15:8), he reminds the Corinthians of how he passed on to them the tradition that he had himself received (*paredōka...hymin... ho kai parelabon*), the tradition that traced the witness to the resurrection right back to Cephas (vv. 3–5).

DEATH; EUCHARIST; LOVE; SATAN; SON OF GOD; WRATH

Reading

O. Büchsel, *TDNT* 2:169–71; Byrne, *Romans*, 63–79, 202, 275–81; Dunn, *Theology*, 174–77; Hurtado, *Lord Jesus Christ*, 126–33; N. Perrin, "The Use of *(para)didonai* in Connection with the Passion of Jesus in the New Testament," in *Der Ruf Jesu und die Antwort der Gemeinde*, ed. E. Lohse et al. (Göttingen: Vandenhoeck & Ruprecht, 1970), 204–12; W. Popkes, *EDNT* 3:18–21; Thiselton, *1 Corinthians*, 866–71, 1186–87; Wells, *Grace and Agency*, 227–29.

HEART

Paul inherits and brings to his writing the rich biblical concept of the "heart" (Hebrew *lēb*; Greek *kardia*), which has a broader reference than in English. As well as indicating the physical organ and, in a figurative sense, that organ as a source of feeling, the heart was also considered the seat of thinking, willing, and decision-making. It appears in the Bible in places where English would speak of "mind" or "will."

This wide range of meanings accounts for a certain overlap in Pauline usage between "heart" and "mind" (*nous*), a term that he owed to the Hellenistic rather than the biblical background. Where the element of knowing is strongly present in *nous*, the volitional is more to the fore in *kardia*. "Heart" in Paul's usage designates the inmost center of a person, the dynamic source of all thinking, willing, and feeling, the site of decision-making and commitment, whether in a positive or negative sense.

Loosely citing phrases from (LXX) Isaiah 64:3 and 65:16, Paul avers that what God has in store for those who love him has not entered "into the human heart" (*epi kardian anthrōpou*) (1 Cor 2:9). With reference to the idolatry of the Gentile world, he writes (Rom 1:21) that though knowing God, they did not respond with glorification or thanks, but "their thoughts were rendered futile and their senseless hearts were darkened" (*eskotisthē hē asynetos autōn kardia*); here a failure in knowledge is solidified in the heart. In a positive sense, with respect to righteousness by faith, in Romans 10:6 Paul uses a phrase from Deuteronomy 9:4 ("Do not say in your heart [*mē eipēs en tē kardia sou*]") to introduce Deut 30:12, "Who will ascend into heaven…?" What is "in" the heart is the "word of faith" (v. 8). The fundamental commitment of faith that is made in the heart finds outward expression on the lips (vv. 9–10). But as well as being open to the light of the gospel that God has shone in the hearts of believers (2 Cor 4:6; see also Eph 1:18), the human heart can be hardened against it (Rom 2:5; 2 Cor 3:15; see also Eph 4:18).

The sense of the heart as the hidden source of human commitment in distinction to mere external appearance is widespread in Paul. "Real circumcision is a matter of the heart in the Spirit [*peritomē kardias en pneumati*], rather than in the letter" (Rom 2:29). Paul wants the Corinthians to be able to counter those "who boast in outward appearance [*en prosōpō*] and not in the heart [*mē en kardia*]" (2 Cor 5:12). In response to a demand for letters accrediting his apostolic ministry, Paul tells the community in Corinth that they themselves are "a letter of Christ, written by the Spirit of the living God not on tablets of stone but on tablets of human hearts [*en plaxin kardiais sarkinais*]" (2 Cor 3:2–3). God searches (Rom 8:27), tests (1 Thess 2:4), and will reveal the secrets of the human heart (1 Cor 4:5); prophecy causes the "the secrets of the heart" (*ta krypta tēs kardias*) to be disclosed (1 Cor 14:25). The Spirit has been "poured out in the hearts [*en tais kardiais*]" of believers, communicating to them a sense of God's love (Rom 5:5; see 2 Cor 1:22; Gal 4:6; see also Eph 3:17).

The heart is also the source of human will and desire (Rom 1:24; 10:1; 1 Cor 7:37). The renewed person obeys "from the heart" (*ek kardias*) in this sense (Rom 6:17; see also 2 Cor 9:7; see also Col 3:22; Eph 6:5). Paul prays that God may "strengthen the hearts" (*stērixai…tas kardias*) of the Thessalonians in holiness (1 Thess 3:13; see also 2 Thess 2:17; 3:5). He assures the Philippians that "the peace of God,…will guard their hearts [*phrourēsei tas kardias*] and minds in Christ

Jesus" (4:7). He thanks God for having put in the heart of Titus (*en kardia Titou*) the same eagerness that he himself has for the Corinthians (2 Cor 8:16; see also Eph 6:22; Col 2:2; 4:8).

As in English, the heart is the source both of strong feeling and of affection. Paul has "unceasing anguish in his heart" (*adialeiptos odynē tē kardia*) for Israel (Rom 9:2); it was with "anguish of heart" (*synoxēs kardias*) that he wrote severely to the Corinthians (2 Cor 2:4). His heart is "wide open" (*hē kardia hēmōn peplatyntai*) to them (6:11b); they are "in his heart" (7:3; see Phil 1:7). He has been separated from the Thessalonians "in person but not in heart [*prosōpō ou kardia*]" (1 Thess 2:17).

> When Paul uses the word *kardia*, he designates the deepest inner core of the person, the seat of the understanding, feelings and will, the place where the ultimate decisions of life are made and where God's act through the Spirit begins. (Schnelle)

DESIRE; FLESH; MIND; IDOLATRY; SPIRIT

Reading

Bultmann, *Theology*, 1:220–27; J. K. Chamblin, *DPL*, 765–75; Dunn, *Theology*, 73–75; Jewett, *Anthropological Terms*, 305–33, 447–48; A. Sand, *EDNT* 2:249–51; Schnelle, *Apostle Paul*, 533–34; Stacey, *Pauline View of Man*, 194–97; Wells, *Grace and Agency*, 231–33, 255–60, 269–75.

HOLINESS, SANCTIFICATION

The concept of "the holy" (Greek *hagios*) stems from the cult, designating that which pertains to the gods or the sphere of the sacred. In secular usage outside the Bible the primary sense is not ethical goodness but closeness to the deity, consecration, and separation from the worldly and the profane.

As chosen, freed, and set apart by God, Israel is a holy nation in this sense (Exod 19:6; Wis 17:2). Paul's frequent address to local communities of believers as "saints" reflects Christian inheritance of the "holiness" privilege of Israel. Gentile believers, sanctified by the Spirit (Rom 15:16), have been grafted onto the "holy root" (presumably the patriarchs) of Israel (11:16–17) and hence, like Israel, are "called to be saints" (Rom 1:7; 8:27; 12:13; 16:2, 15; 1 Cor 1:2, 6:1–2; 14:33; 2 Cor 1:1; 13:12; Phil 1:1; 4:21–22; 1 Thess 3:13; Phlm 5, 7), although "the saints" seems to have been a particular designation of the mother community in Jerusalem (Rom 15:25, 31; 1 Cor 16:1, 15; 2 Cor 8:4; 9:1, 12).

Holiness (Sanctification) as Ethical Transformation

While the relational aspect of closeness to God remains primary regarding "holiness" in the biblical tradition, an ethical note inevitably enters in. Israel must preserve and live out her status as the holy people of God: "You shall be holy, for I the Lord your God am holy" (Lev 19:2; see 11:44; 20:7–8). In line with this, Paul appeals to holiness in contexts where he wishes to stress the radical difference between the way of life now required of believers and that of their past (Rom 6:19, 22; 1 Cor 1:30; 6:11; 2 Cor 7:1). Thus "sanctification" in the sense of holiness lived out features as a major theme in the paraenesis of 1 Thessalonians, where Paul sets the summons to live a life of holiness over against the sexual immorality of the surrounding world (4:3–8). He reminds the Corinthian community that "God's temple is holy, and you are that temple" (1 Cor 3:17; see 6:19; 2 Cor 6:16).

Justification and Sanctification

The relationship between sanctification and justification has been a major topic of discussion between Catholic and Protestant interpreters of Paul since the Reformation. Whereas Catholics, following Augustine, have held that justification in itself involves moral transformation, the Protestant tradition has viewed justification as restricted to a legal or forensic declaration, with sanctification indicating the subsequent process of ethical transformation worked by the Spirit (Rom 8:4–11; 15:16; see Gal 5:13–26). Passages such as Romans 6:20–23, where Paul sets up a "progression" from righteousness to holiness with the outcome of "eternal life" over against a negative progression in the former existence from sin to "uncleanness" to eternal death, suggest that the Protestant understanding is more accurate to Paul, at least in the sense that sanctification represents a stage of Christian existence subsequent to the initial divine act of justification. That said, on the one hand, believers are already "saints"; from the moment of their baptism, they belong to a people "sanctified in Christ Jesus, called to be saints" (1 Cor 1:2; see 6:11). On the other hand, their sanctification is an ongoing process being worked by the Spirit. It seems that Paul mainly reserves the Greek word *hagiōsynē* for holiness in the first sense (2 Cor 7:1; 1 Thess 3:13), while *hagiasmos*, as the ending (*-m*) suggests, refers more to the process of sanctification, the end result of which will the sanctified state required for gaining eternal life at the eschaton (Rom 6:19, 22; 1 Thess 4:3, 7–8; see also 5:23). "The believer *both* lives in holiness *and* grows into holiness" (S. E. Porter, italics original).

Holiness in the Later Pauline Letters

The sense of believers constituting a holy community continues in the later letters (Eph 1:1, 15; 3:8, 18; 4:12; 5:3; 6:18; Col 1:2, 4; 2 Thess 1:10; 1 Tim 5:10), with a particular ecclesiological note in Ephesians (5:25–27). When in this literature believers are said to be destined to "inherit the lot of the saints" (Col 1:12; see Eph 1:18; 2:19), the reference is likely to be to sharing the life of angels, the citizens of God's heavenly realm.

ETHICS; ISRAEL; GENTILES; JUSTIFY, JUSTIFICATION; LIFE; RIGHTEOUSNESS; SEXUALITY; SPIRIT; TEMPLE

Reading

J. A. Adewuya, *Holiness and Community in 2 Cor. 6:14–7:1: Paul's View of Communal Holiness in the Corinthian Correspondence* (New York: Peter Lang, 2001); H. Balz, *EDNT*

1:16–20; K. B. Brower and A. Johnson, eds., *Holiness and Ecclesiology in the New Testament* (Grand Rapids: Eerdmans, 2007), 148–292; V. P. Furnish, *Theology and Ethics in Paul*, with new introduction by R. B. Hays (Louisville: Westminster John Knox, 2009), 153–57; Matera, *GSG*, 118–20; S. E. Porter, *DPL*, 397–402; Rainbow, *Way of Salvation*, 141–54.

HOMOSEXUALITY (*see* Sexuality)

HOPE

The significance of hope (noun *elpis*; verb: *elpizō*) in Paul stems from the apocalyptic cast of his theology in which the present situation is a stage in a process moving rapidly toward an end. In the death and resurrection of Christ, God has dealt the decisive blow to the forces ranged against the realization of the divine plan for humankind, but the final consummation—"salvation"—is still outstanding. It awaits the return of Christ ("the day of the Lord") to complete his messianic work (Rom 2:16; 1 Cor 1:8; 3:13; 5:5; 2 Cor 1:14; Phil 1:6, 10; 2:16; 1 Thess 5:2; see also 2:19). Believers at the present time, thus find themselves in what has been aptly dubbed an "overlap" situation where the final age (the "new creation") has dawned, but where the old or present age is still around, with believers in their bodily life feeling its effects in the shape of weakness, suffering, and physical death. Thus believers "are saved but only in hope" (Rom 8:23).

In 1 Thessalonians 1:3, Paul ranges hope alongside faith and love in a triad of "virtues" distinctive of Christian life, a triad that reappears in the more familiar order—faith, hope, and love—at the close of the encomium to love in 1 Corinthians 13:13 (see also Col 1:4–5). Whereas one thinks of Abraham as a model of faith in Paul (Rom 4:1–13; Gal 3:6–9), it is significant that the analysis of the patriarch's faith in Romans 4:17–22 presents him equally as a paradigm of hope. This was because his faith involved believing in God's *promise* that, despite, the "deadness" of his own reproductive capacities and those of his wife Sarah, he would have a son and heir, and a vast progeny: "Hoping against hope, he believed that he would become 'the father of many nations,' according to what was said, 'So numerous shall your descendants be'" (v. 18 NRSV; see Gen 15:5). As Abraham believed in a God who could raise life from death in order to fulfill the promise that he would have a son, so believers put their faith in God who raised Jesus from the dead in the hope that God will also raise their own mortal bodies through the power of the Spirit (8:11).

Hope as the Theme of Romans 5—8

The presentation of Abraham's faith blending into hope because focused on a promise prepares the way at the end of Romans 4 for what is in effect the overall theme of Romans 5—8: the hope of salvation for those justified by faith: "Justified therefore by faith...we boast in our hope of sharing the glory of God,... and hope does not disappoint us, because God's love has been poured out into our hearts through the Holy Spirit that has been given us" (5:1–5).

Two things in particular emerge from these sentences. First, the object of hope is "sharing the glory of God," that is, attaining the heavenly existence intended by God for human beings from the start but lost by sin (Rom 3:23; see also 1:22–23); second, the guarantee of the hope to come is the experience of the Spirit, because God's gift of the Spirit is the indicator of the righteous status (righteousness) that believers presently enjoy in Christ (see also 8:23; 2 Cor 1:22; Eph 1:13–14). The attainment of the hope ("eternal life") rests on righteousness once received and preserved through the power of the Spirit up to the judgment: "the Spirit (means) life because of righteousness" (Rom 8:10c; see also Gal 5:5).

Toward the end of Romans 8, there is a little "excursus" on hope, addressing the difficulty that what believers hope for is neither seen nor imagined: "We are saved but only in hope. Now hope that is seen is not hope. For who hopes for what is seen? But if we hope for what we do not see, we wait for it with patience" (vv. 24–25; see also 1 Cor 2:9–10). Ultimately, behind the hope cherished by believers is the pretemporal design of God, already set in motion and inexorably unfolding, that they should share the "image" way of being already seen in the risen Christ (Rom 8:29–30; 1 Cor 15:49; 2 Cor 3:18). If the hope of believers concerned this world only, they would be "of all people most to be pitied" (1 Cor 15:19); they should not grieve over their dead "as others do who have no hope" (1 Thess 4:13).

Hope for Human and Cosmic Transformation

How the hoped-for risen existence is to be thought of in bodily terms is the subject of extensive discussion in 1 Corinthians 15:35–57 (see RESURRECTION). That this hope is not imagined in entirely otherworldly terms emerges from the celebrated apocalyptic passage in Romans 8:19–22. Paul presents "the whole of creation" (the created world aside from human beings) as cherishing a hope that it would one day be set free from its bondage to decay and share the freedom of the glory of the children of God (vv. 20–21); to that end it is groaning in the act of giving birth (v. 22). What appears to be envisaged is the eschatological transformation of the entire cosmos, human beings included (v. 23), into the original design of the Creator (see Gen 1:26–28; 1 Cor 15:22–28; Phil 3:21). The whole thematic assertion of hope in Romans 5—8 comes to a triumphant conclusion in 8:31–39, where Paul evokes the last judgment to conclude that, if God is "for us" (v. 31), nothing can ultimately separate believers from the love of God made visible in Christ Jesus (v. 39).

Hope in the Later Pauline Letters

In the later Pauline letters, hope is not so much a subjective Christian attitude but, more objectively, the content of the salvation that is its object (see 2 Cor 3:12; Gal 5:5). The fact that it is already "laid up in heaven" (Col 1:5, 23) underscores the sense of it as an assured reality in the present, just waiting to be revealed, to which believers are already "called" (Eph 1:18; 4:4). The presence of Christ as living Lord is the "hope of the glory" to come (Col 1:27; see 1 Tim 1:1), while the future manifestation of his glory is the object of present hope (Titus 2:13).

ABRAHAM; APOCALYPTIC; ESCHATOLOGY; FAITH; GLORY; LOVE; RIGHTEOUSNESS; RESURRECTION; SALVATION

Reading

Becker, *Paul*, 440–49; Byrne, *PES*, 130–40, 161–68, 211–24; D. R. Denton, "Hope and Perseverance," *SJT* 34 (1981): 313–20; Dunn, *Theology*, 461–72; J. M. Everts, *DPL*, 415–17; A. T. Lincoln with A. J. M. Wedderburn, *The Theology of the Later Pauline Letters* (Cambridge: Cambridge University Press, 1993), 114–19; Matera, *GSG*, 186–214; B. Mayer, *EDNT* 1:437–41, esp. 438–440; Schnelle, *Apostle Paul*, 577–97; Wolter, *Paul*, 177–220; Wright, *PFG*, 1061–95.

I

IDOLATRY

Paul brought to his faith in Christ the traditional Jewish abhorrence of the worship of idols pervasive in the Greco-Roman world. In Romans 1:18–32, he depicts the alienation of the Gentile world from God as a refusal to acknowledge the revelation of the unseen Creator's power and glory in the created world, and a turning to the manufacture and worship of idols. In a formal threefold pattern the lapse into idolatry is followed in each case by God's "giving up" human beings to all manner of vicious behavior, which has become the evidence for the revelation of God's wrath against the world (1:18) (see HAND OVER). The depiction of human lapse into idolatry here bears striking resemblance to tracts against idolatry to be found in contemporary Jewish literature, notably the Wisdom of Solomon (see chapters 13—14). Paul shares with the Jewish authors of such tracts a firm belief in a causal connection between the idolatry and the sexual depravity of the Gentile world, which they found equally abhorrent. It is interesting, however, to note that the language in which the lapse into idolatry is first described (v. 23) echoes the allusions to Israel's lapse into the worship of the Golden Calf (Exod 32:1–10) in Psalm 106:20 (LXX 105:20). This subtle allusion to lapse into idolatry on Israel's part may be intended to prepare the way for Paul's subsequent accusation in diatribe mode that Jews, as well as Gentiles, are not immune from the threat of the eschatological wrath (Rom 2:3–11).

Paul would have had to confront Gentile idolatry in every city where he proclaimed the gospel. The depiction of his evangelization of Athens in Acts 17 is probably accurate in this regard (see v. 17). Early in his first letter to the Thessalonians, Paul recalls how they "turned to God from idols to serve a living and true God" (1:9). In a far less favorable frame of mind, he points out to the Galatians that their submission to the practice of the Jewish law is tantamount to returning to the enslaving "service [*edouleusate*] to beings that by nature are not gods [*tois physei mē ousin theois*]" (Gal 4:8; see 1 Cor 12:2).

Eating Food that Has Been Sacrificed to Idols

Paul includes worshippers of idols (*eidōlolatrai*) in a long list of those who will not inherit the kingdom of God in 1 Corinthians 6:9–10 (see Gal 5:19–21). Before their conversion the Corinthians lived in a world where such practice and the sexual immorality that went with it prevailed (see 1 Cor 5:10–11). They still live in that world and have to have dealings with it, but they have been claimed for a totally new allegiance and way of life (6:12).

How to navigate through this situation of conflicting claims is the problem Paul deals with at length (1 Cor 8:1—11:1) in response to the specific issue of eating meat sold in the marketplace after having been used in pagan sacrifices. Whether such meat may be eaten or not threatens the unity of the community. Some, "strong" in their knowledge that idols have no reality (8:4–6), feel completely free to eat such food. Paul agrees in principle but points out that not all have such "knowledge" in sufficient degree (v. 7a). Some, accustomed to thinking of such food as really offered to idols, would eat with bad conscience, placing their salvation in jeopardy. Hence, a deeper exercise of freedom, proceeding from love, would require refraining from such food (8:7–13).

After exemplifying the freedom he is talking about through reference to his own apostolic practice (1 Cor 9:1–27), Paul returns to the issue at hand (10:1—11:1), prefacing it with a stern warning about idolatry (vv. 1–13). He appeals to the scriptural example of Israel in the wilderness as a typological illustration of what can happen through presumption. The Israelites had quasi-sacraments of baptism ("in the cloud and in the sea") and Eucharist ("spiritual food") (vv. 2–4), yet they fell into idolatry (the golden calf) and immorality (Exod 32:1–10), incurring the wrath of God and their own destruction (1 Cor 10:5). After indicating further lapses on the part of the Israelites with similar consequences (vv. 8–13), Paul issues a preliminary emphatic conclusion: "Flee from idolatry" (v. 14). With the typological warning from the story of Israel still in view, he then points to the total incompatibility between participation in the Christian Eucharist and having anything to do with idolatry. Participation in eucharistic worship involves "communion" (*koinōnia*) with Christ and with one's fellow worshippers (vv. 16–17). Idolatrous worship may not involve worship of a real deity (v. 19; see 8:4), but it does involve communion with demons (v. 20), who manipulate it for their own evil purpose. It is totally inappropriate, then, to share the cup of the Lord and the cup of demons, the table of the Lord and the table of demons (v. 21; see 2 Cor 6:16).

Thus Paul excludes any Christian participation in table fellowship in pagan temples where the worship of idols takes place. It is a different matter, however, when eating as a guest in private homes where meat that has been bought in the marketplace and may have been used in pagan worship is served. In such cases, Paul reverts to much the same advice as he gave earlier (8:1–13). Such food may be eaten provided that the conscience of a fellow guest is not injured thereby (10:25—11:1).

"Idolatry" features among the vices that the recipients of the letter to the Colossians should "put to death," but now it is no longer pagan worship that is in view but "the greed [*pleonexia*] that is idolatry" (3:5). The same metaphorical usage is repeated in Ephesians 5:5.

COMMUNION; CONSCIENCE; GENTILES; GOD; SLAVERY; WRATH

Reading

S. C. Barton, *ECB*, 1330–31, 1334–36 (on 1 Cor 8, 10); P. Borgen, "'Yes,' 'No,' 'How far?': The Participation of Jews and Christians in Pagan Cults," in *Paul in His Hellenistic Context*, ed. T. Engberg-Pedersen (Minneapolis: Fortress, 1995), 30–59; Byrne, *Romans*, 63–79 (on Rom 1:18–32); P. W. Comfort, *DPL*, 424–26; G. Fee, "*Eidolothyta* Once Again: An Interpretation of 1 Corinthians 8–10," *Bib* 61 (1980): 172–97; H. Hübner, *EDNT* 1:386–88; R. L.-S. Phua, *Idolatry and Authority: A Study of 1 Corinthians 8.1–11.1 in the Light of the Jewish Diaspora* (London: T&T Clark, 2005); Thiselton, *1 Corinthians*, 719–49; Wolter, *Paul*, 135–36, 266–70, 324–25.

IMAGE

The Greek term *eikōn* ("image") expresses likeness in various shades of meaning. It can mean a manufactured likeness as in a statue or the imprint of a ruler on a coin (see Mark 12:16; Matt 22:20; Luke 20:24); in this sense it appears predominantly in the LXX to designate an idol (also ten times in Revelations). It can simply designate the likeness of one thing to another or, more particularly, that which outwardly manifests the being or inner quality of something in a representational way.

Human Creation in the Image of God

Paul uses *eikōn* with respect to human lapse into idolatry in Romans 1:23 when, echoing the language of (LXX) Psalm 105:20, he writes "… and they exchanged the glory [*doxa*] of the immortal God for the likeness of an image [*en homoiōmati eikonos*] of a mortal human being" or various kinds of animals. Although *eikōn* is used here with reference to idolatry, the sense of "exchange" and the negative parallel with "glory" make possible, if not necessarily probable, a reference to the loss, on the part of idolatrous human beings, of the likeness to God in which they were created according to Genesis 1:26 (*kat' eikona hēmeteran kai kath' homoiōsin*) and 1:27 (*kat' eikona theou*), a human prerogative that receives more poetic expression in (LXX) Psalm 8:6 in terms of "glory [*doxa*] and honor [*timē*]."

Paul does explicitly appeal to the motif of man (literally) created as the image of God in his (rather desperate) attempt to require women to appear as women (see WOMAN) when praying and prophesying (1 Cor 11:2–16). Whereas a man ought not to have his head covered, "being the image [*eikōn*] and glory [*doxa*] of God," a woman ought not be uncovered since "she is the glory of the man" (v. 7). Behind the distinction between the sexes lies the temporal sequence of Genesis 2, where the creation of the woman is subsequent to and derivative from that of the man. The same appeal to the creation story finds an exhortatory echo in Colossians 3:9–10, where the Colossians are urged to put off the old "self" (literally, "man" [*anthrōpon*]) with its practices and to "put on the new self, which is being renewed in knowledge according to the image of its creator" (*kat' eikona tou ktisantos auton*).

Human Transformation into Christ, the Image of God

It is likely, however, that the Genesis 1:26–28 motif of human beings created in the image of God played a more significant role in Paul's Christology than the paucity of explicit allusions suggests. We have already noted the parallel between "image" and "glory" in Romans 1:23 (also 1 Cor 11:7). The loss of the "glory of God" mentioned in Romans 3:23 as a consequence of sin could suggest the loss or tarnishing of the divine image, which the gift of righteousness in Christ is set to restore. This would appear to be the case in the transformation being described in 2 Corinthians 3:18:

> And we all, with unveiled faces, seeing as in a mirror the glory of the Lord, are being transformed into the same image [*tēn autēn eikona*], from one degree of glory to another, as from (the action) of the Spirit.

Here Paul is describing the ongoing effect on believers of their "turning to the Lord" (see v. 16) in response to the promulgation of the new covenant. The "mirror" in which they contemplate the glory of the Lord is the glory of the risen Christ, himself described as "the image of God" (*eikōn tou theou*) a few lines further on (4:4; see also Col 1:15). Through the action of the Spirit believers are being transformed into "the same image." Although not all interpreters agree, this last phrase ("the same image") and the subsequent designation of Christ as image of God suggest that, beyond mere likeness to Christ, believers are being transformed into the image (of God) that Christ actually *is*. What is being restored in them, "from one degree of glory to another," in the new creation is the Adamic imaging of God and its attendant glory (Gen 1:26–28; Ps 8:6) that had been lost through sin (Rom 3:23). The same eschatological outcome for human beings according to the eternal design of the Creator finds expression in Romans 8:29:

> For those whom he foreknew he also predestined to be conformed to the image of his Son [*symmorphous tou eikonos tou huiou autou*], in order that he might be the firstborn within a large family.

Beyond likeness in a general kind of way, the qualifier *symmorphous* expresses participation in the same way of being; the addition of *eikōn* would be redundant if mere likeness was in view. As is the case in 2 Corinthians 3:18, what Paul has in mind here is eschatological participation in the image of God that Christ is, and hence the regaining in the lineage of the new Adam of the likeness to God lost through the old.

In 1 Corinthians 15:35–49, Paul discusses the future bodily existence of believers when they fully share the resurrection of Christ. With explicit allusion to the creation of Adam (Gen 2:7), Paul maintains that "as we have borne the image of the man of dust [*tēn eikona tou choïkou*], so we shall bear the image of the man of heaven [*tēn eikona tou epouraniou*]" (v. 49). Here, it is a matter of bearing the image of Christ rather than the image of God. Since, however, Christ is himself the image of God (2 Cor 4:4), the overt Adamic allusion suggests an implication at least of human beings bearing the image of God.

Bearing the image of God has to do with the exercise of authority. Images of rulers were set up at the gates of cities to make clear to all who entered whose writ ran therein. In Genesis 1:26–28, human beings are created in God's image to "have dominion" over all other living creatures on the face of the earth. In 1 Corinthians 15:24–28, Paul applies the expression of this in Psalm 8:5–8 to Christ's subjection of all things, death included, to the rule of God (vv. 25, 27–28). Although Christ is not described in this sequence as the image of God, it is likely that his authority to subdue all things (see Phil 3:21) represents a messianic extension of the motif of human beings created in the image of God. According to the hymn in Colossians 1:15–20, Christ, as image of God (v. 15), has authority to reconcile all things to himself (v. 20), including the spiritual powers whose influence the Colossians are far too prone to recognize (see 2:8–23).

AUTHORITY; BODY; CHRIST; GLORY; IDOLATRY; SIN; SPIRIT

Reading

Byrne, *PES*, 62–63; 216, 221–22; D. J. A. Clines, *DPL*, 426–28; Dunn, *Romans 1–8*, 483–84; J. J. J. Leese, *Christ, Creation and the Cosmic Goal of Redemption: A Study of Pauline Creation Theology as Read by Irenaeus and Applied to Ecotheology* (London, New York: T&T Clark, 2018), 89–130; Lincoln, "Colossians," 597–98; Matera, *GSG*, 120–23; S. V. McCasland, "The 'Image of God' according to Paul," *JBL* 69 (1950): 85–100; T. R. Middleton, *OEBT* 1:516–21; G. H. van Kooten, *Paul's Anthropology in Context: The Image of God, Assimilation to God, and Tripartite Man in Ancient Judaism, Ancient Philosophy and Early Christianity* (Tübingen: Mohr Siebeck, 2008); Wright, *PFG*, 438–41.

ISRAEL, ISRAELITES

Paul's references to "Israel," with just a few exceptions, are confined to Romans 9—11, where he deals with the issue of the tension between God's fidelity to the chosen people and the failure of the majority of that people to accept the gospel. For the most part, Paul seems to refer to the Jewish people as "Israel" and its members as "Israelites" when writing from a theological rather than a social or national point of view. The sense of Israel as the chosen, privileged people of God is never entirely absent.

The sense of privilege is clear in contexts where Paul points out his belonging to and continuing concern for his own people, "his brothers according to the flesh" (Rom 9:3). They are "Israelites," to whom belong the six privileges listed in verse 4, also the "fathers" (patriarchs), and the Messiah (Christ) according to his human origin (v. 5). Paul defends his peerless Jewish credentials as an "Israelite" (2 Cor 11:22), from the "race of Israel" (*ek genous Israēl*) (Phil 3:5).

Present-Day Israel

In biblical parlance, Paul refers to the Sinai generation as "the sons of Israel" (2 Cor 3:7, 13). However, the dominant reference of "Israel" in his writing is to the people of his own time. Paul begins the discussion in Romans 9—11 with a startling distinction: "Not all who are from Israel [*ex Israēl*] are 'Israel'" (9:6b). Paul justifies the distinction by appealing to the narrative of Genesis, where the line of descent through Isaac, whose birth was the result of a promise, is privileged over that of the elder son, Ishmael (vv. 7–9), and where, in the following generation, Jacob is preferred over Esau (vv. 10–13). That this preference proceeds without regard for any human merit provides scriptural warrant for the divine prerogative to act with sovereign freedom in bringing about an end-time Israel on the basis of promise and grace.

Thus Paul can cite Scripture with reference to the present situation of Israel where the greater part is subject to a "hardening" (*pōrōsis* [11:25; see v. 7]), while a considerable number of non-Israelites have responded positively to the gospel. The whittling down of the numbers of Israel to a faithful remnant was foretold by Isaiah (9:27–29, citing Isa 10:22–23; 28:22). The rejection of the gospel on the part of the majority Paul attributes to their "stumble" on the rock of the Crucified Messiah (Rom 9:32–33, citing Isa 28:16; see 1 Cor 1:23). Clinging to a pursuit of righteousness based on practice of the law, they ignored and failed to submit to the righteousness of God (Rom 9:30—10:3–4). This failure cannot be attributed to the gospel, which has gone out to all the world (10:14–18); rather, it is a failure on the part of Israel to understand rightly (see "know" [10:19]).

Israel's Ultimate Salvation

Eventually (11:1), Paul raises and instantly dismisses the suggestion that God has rejected Israel ("his people"). The first evidence to the contrary, again indicated in Scripture (Elijah's entreaty to God against Israel; see 1 Kgs 19:10, 14; cited Rom 11:3–4), is the present existence of a "remnant chosen by grace" (vv. 5–6) made up of believers of Jewish origin such as Paul himself, even though the rest (of Israel) may be hardened (vv. 7–10). Finally (v. 11), the discussion turns in a positive direction as Paul begins to deploy a soteriological explanation for the current hardened situation of Israel: it is to provide a space for the inclusion of Gentiles, an inclusion that will provoke Israel to "jealousy" (vv. 13–14) and so lead to her final reconciliation and salvation (vv. 25–27). The ultimate basis for this hope is that, despite her current unbelief, Israel remains "chosen" and "beloved because of the fathers" (v. 28; see v. 16), "for the gifts and calling of God are irrevocable" (*ametamelēta*) (v. 29). The reason for this totally unexpected reversal of the priority of Israel in the program of salvation is that God may act toward all, both Israel and the Gentile world, on the basis of mercy (vv. 30–32) (see MERCY).

Within this broad outline of Paul's comprehensive vision of salvation in

11:11–32, the reference of the phrase "all Israel" in verse 26 ("And so all Israel will be saved [*kai houtōs pas Israēl sōthēsetai*]") has been controversial. The longstanding view that the phrase encompassed all believers, Jewish and Gentile collectively, has now largely been abandoned. It flies in the face of the unambiguous reference to ethnic Israel in the immediately preceding sentence (v. 25) and the nine mentions of Israel with that meaning in the sequence in Romans 9—11 up to that point. Paul clearly has in view here salvation of ethnic Israel as such, though this need not mean the salvation of all Jews on an individual basis.

What emerges from this survey of "Israel" in Romans 9—11 is the fluidity with which Paul can use the term. Without cutting its essential tie to ethnic Israel—described in 1 Corinthians 10:18 as "Israel according to the flesh"—he has to project a vision of an eschatological Israel that will come into being as a result of the sovereign freedom and covenant fidelity of God, constituting along with believers from the nations a composite people that, together, will "glorify God for the sake of mercy" (Rom 15:7–12). This is not a "replacement" of ethnic Israel but an eschatological incorporation of Israel in a joint human acknowledgment and praise of God. It is possible that a similarly inclusive view lies behind the prayer wish Paul expresses in the, otherwise highly polemical, letter to the Galatians: "Peace on them (i.e., those who have taken to heart his instructions) and on the Israel of God (*ton Israēl tou theou* [6:16]), that is, on the Israel that God is bringing into being as a "new creation" (v. 15) through the proclamation and power of the gospel.

In the deutero-Pauline letters, "Israel" occurs only in Ephesians, in reference to the erstwhile condition of Gentile believers as "aliens from the commonwealth of Israel" and "strangers to the covenants of promise" (2:12). However, the overcoming of the division between Jews and Gentiles through the saving work of Christ and their union in the one body, the church, is a major theme of the letter (see especially Eph 2—3). Paul's ultimately positive hope for as yet unbelieving Israel has dropped from view.

ABRAHAM; CALL, CALLING; CHRIST; GRACE; JEW; MERCY; PROMISE; RIGHTEOUSNESS

Reading

Barclay, *Gift*, 520–61; "Paul, Israel, and the Jewish People," in Westerholm, *Paul*, 188–201; Beker, *Paul the Apostle*, 328–47; R. Bieringer and D. Pollefeyt, eds., *Paul and Judaism: Crosscurrents in Pauline Exegesis and the Study of Jewish-Christian Relations* (Edinburgh: T&T Clark, 2012); Byrne, *Romans*, 109–21; 328–47; W. S. Campbell, *DPL*, 441–46; Dunn, *Theology*, 499–532; S. Eastman, "Israel and Divine Mercy in Galatians and Romans," in *Between Gospel and Election: Explorations in the Interpretation of Romans 9–11*, ed. R. Wilk and J. R. Wagner (Tübingen: Mohr Siebeck, 2010), 147–70; Matera, *GSG*, 147–53; J. M. Scott, *DPL*, 796–805 ("Restoration of Israel"); J. Sievers, "God's Gifts and Call Are Irrevocable," in *Reading Israel in Romans*, ed. C. Grenholm and D. Patte (Harrisburg, PA: Trinity Press International, 2000), 127–73.

J

JEALOUSY (*see* Zeal)

JERUSALEM

This topic does not consider the city of Jerusalem from a historical point of view. Rather, it discusses how Jerusalem and, in particular, the community of believers there featured in Paul's apostolic consciousness and theology.

Paul himself was a product of Diaspora—and hence, Greek-speaking—Judaism, as his proficiency in Greek readily attests. Yet his claim to be a Pharisee, and indeed one of the strictest kind (Phil 3:5; see Gal 1:14), suggests a significant period of formation in Jerusalem, since Pharisaic education was unlikely to have been available outside Palestine. Presumably at some stage in his late teens or early adult years he moved to Jerusalem, from which it is also likely that his brief persecuting career had its base, even if—as suggested by Acts 9:1–2—it involved excursions to other places.

Paul's Independence from Leaders in Jerusalem

In the early chapters of Galatians (1—2), Paul recounts the history of his relationship with Jerusalem in order to convince his Galatian converts of his full and independent status as an apostle, called and appointed directly by the risen Lord (Gal 1:15–16). At no stage did he receive a commission from the leading apostles in Jerusalem during the period of fourteen (or possibly seventeen) years between his call and his going up to Jerusalem, with Barnabas and the Gentile convert Titus, for the meeting with the apostles recorded in 2:1–10 (see 1:17, 18, 19, 21–23).

The Apostolic Meeting in Jerusalem

Paul's account of this meeting (see also Acts 15:1–29) suggests that its chief agenda was to resolve a dispute about the legitimacy of the law-free Gentile mission as conducted by himself and Barnabas (Gal 2:2). What Paul received at Jerusalem was not approval or delegation from the Jerusalem church but recognition.

Paul's part of the agreement, which he says he readily accepted, was "to remember the poor" (v. 10). This "remembrance" is generally understood to refer to the collection from the Gentile churches for the relief of the mother church in Jerusalem (Rom 15:25–28; 1 Cor 16:1–4; 2 Cor 8–9). Beyond economic relief, the collection had high symbolic significance for the unity of the community of believers as a whole. Through it, the Gentile churches acknowledged their debt to the mother church in Jerusalem (Rom 15:27), while gracious acceptance of it on the part of that church would signal recognition of the Pauline communities as full members of the renewed people of God.

Subsequent Relations with the Community in Jerusalem

Whether the collection was graciously received in Jerusalem when Paul eventually delivered it there we do not know. His request for prayers to this effect in Romans 15:31b suggests apprehension on his part in this regard. Moreover, the Jerusalem church—or at least certain parties within it—continued to dog his path for the remainder of his apostolic career. Not long after the meeting in Jerusalem, emissaries from James, presumably therefore from Jerusalem, caused the issue of table fellowship between Jewish and Gentile believers to blow up at Antioch, forcing Paul to issue a severe public rebuke to Peter (Cephas) in order to preserve the truth of the gospel (Gal 2:11–14). The incident in all likelihood led to the severing of his ties with the Antioch church, which up till then had been his base. The intrusive teachers denigrating his apostolic authority and pressurizing his Galatian converts to take on circumcision, also, it would seem, stemmed from Jerusalem and, although the evidence is less clear, this may also have been the case in regard to those responsible for the disaffection from him in Corinth that occasioned his responses in 2 Corinthians 1—7 and 10—13. Writing from prison, possibly at the end of his life, to his beloved community at Philippi, he suddenly turns aside to issue a sharp warning against the possible intrusion of teachers of a similar stamp to those in Galatia, also likely emanating from Jerusalem (Phil 3:2—4:1).

Hence Jerusalem likely had an ambiguous status in Paul's eyes. Doubtless he acknowledged it as the location of the saving events described in the gospel and seat of the primary community of faith. However, this community was also the source from which sprang questioning of the gospel he preached to the Gentiles and at times downright opposition to his apostolic mission.

The Earthly and Heavenly Jerusalem

The ambiguity of Paul's attitude to Jerusalem from a theological point of view is patent in the allegory he deploys in Galatians 4:21–31 to reinforce his plea that the Galatians stand firm in the freedom Christ had won for them (see 5:1). Paul draws on the scriptural record concerning Abraham's two wives and the two sons to which they gave birth: one, Ishmael, from the slave girl Hagar (Gen 16:15); the other Isaac, from the free woman Sarah (21:1–3). Through an ingenious wordplay (Gal 4:24–25), Paul finds here an allegory of "two covenants" (*duo diathēkai*). The first, the covenant promulgated on Sinai and currently promoted in "the present-day Jerusalem" (*tē nyn Ierousalēm*), he associates with Hagar and her slave status (v. 25); it is from this Jerusalem that the law with its, in his eyes, enslaving effects (4:1–3, 9) is promulgated. The second covenant, he associates, not immediately with Sarah as we might expect, but with "the above Jerusalem" (*hē...anō Ierousalēm*), who is free and is "our mother" (vv. 26, 31). The epithet "above" points to the heavenly, transcendent origin of the community to which this "mother" gives birth: the community of the new creation that is now coming to be through the mission of the Son and the summons of the gospel. The words of Isaiah 54:1 (cited in verse 27) summon this heavenly "mother," to rejoice because, previously barren, she is now giving birth to a multitude of children. In Paul's theological vision "Jerusalem" no longer applies to the earthly Jerusalem from which emanated most of the opposition to his apostolic work but to a heavenly Jerusalem giving birth to a host of free citizens drawn from the nations of the world (see Phil 3:20).

ABRAHAM; APOSTLE; FREEDOM; GENTILES; LAW; SLAVERY

Reading

Byrne, "Jerusalems," 215–31; R. B. Hays, "The Letter to the Galatians," *NIB* 11:131–348, here 302–7; Schnelle, *Apostle Paul*, 121–37; P. W. L. Walker, *Jesus and the Holy City: New Testament Perspectives on Jerusalem* (Grand Rapids: Eerdmans, 1996), 113–60; Wright, *PFG*, 1136–39.

JESUS (*see* Christ)

JEW, JUDAISM

The term *Jew* (Greek *Ioudaios*) goes back to the Hebrew *yehudi* to indicate a member of the tribe of Judah and then an inhabitant of Judea, where that Israelite tribe was historically located. In the postexilic period, the Aramaic form came to designate more generally those who lived in the land of the Southern Kingdom of Israel and lived by the Mosaic law. Greek-speakers employed the term *Ioudaioi* for this purpose. As such, *Ioudaios* was for some centuries a designation used by non-Jews, rather than Jews themselves, who preferred to speak of themselves as "Israelites" or "Hebrews." In due course, however, beginning in the Maccabean period, *Ioudaioi* became an accepted way for Jews to refer to themselves in distinction from members of other nations. By Paul's day, "Jew" had lost its sense of an "outsider" designation and had become a way in which people would identify themselves proudly as members of the chosen people of God. Paul's riposte to Peter at Antioch, "We are Jews by birth and not Gentile sinners" (Gal 2:15) suggests the pride that attached to the designation, which of course, as he immediately goes on to make clear (v. 16), was thoroughly relativized on coming to faith in Christ.

"Jew/Jews" as Used by Paul

Paul uses the term "Jew/Jews" principally to designate members of the people to whom he belonged over against the rest of humanity, that is, the Gentiles (*ethnē*), although he will often use the term "Greek" (*hellēnos*) as a synonym for "Gentile," to balance the ethnic designation "Jew" (the singular *ethnos* refers to a nation as a whole, not to individuals). The pairing "Jew–Greek" in this sense is frequent in the letters (Rom 1:16; 2:9, 10; 3:9; 10:12; 1 Cor 1:22, 24; 10:32; 12:13; Gal 3:28; see Col 3:11).

To the end of his life—post-faith in

Christ as well as before—Paul would have described himself as a "Jew." Significantly, however, "Jew" does not occur among the extended list of his impeccable Jewish credentials in Philippians 3:5–6 ("Hebrew from Hebrews" is preferred), nor in that of 2 Corinthians 11:22 ("Hebrews," "Israelites"). In defense of his apostolic freedom he claims, "I have become as a Jew to Jews in order to win Jews; to those under the law as under the law, though not myself under the law, in order to win those under the law" (1 Cor 9:20). The note of "becoming" here suggests the later adoption, for apostolic purposes, of a way of life (observing Jewish customs), from which radically he had been set free; it does not signal any return to the practice of the law as a way of salvation.

The ethnic dichotomy "Jew–Greek ("Gentile") features in both Galatians 3:28 and 1 Corinthians 12:13 as the first of the socio-ethnic divisions that no longer apply "in Christ" (see also Col 3:11), that is, in the existence in the new creation that believers have entered through faith and baptism. Of course, Paul does not mean believers in either case cease to be of Jewish or Gentile origin—any more than they cease to be male or female and, it would seem, slave or free. The point is that these categories that once were so significant have essentially been swallowed up in the unity that now exists in the communal body of Christ: "There is (now) no distinction between Jew and Greek; the same Lord is Lord of all" (Rom 10:12).

The "Real" Jew

In one sequence Paul does address the designation "Jew" as an honorific title—or self-designation—and, as part of his prophetic "accusation" of the entire world (Rom 1:18—3:20), appears to undermine it as a claim to privileged status before God. Addressing the fictive Jewish teacher with whom he is in "dialogue" in this section of Romans, he begins, "If you call yourself a Jew [*ei de sy Ioudaios eponomazē*]" (2:17), and then lists multiple claims and purported roles that go along with this self-designation: "guide to the blind, light in darkness, instructor of the foolish, teacher of little ones, having the embodiment of knowledge and truth in the law" (vv. 18–20). All these claims, however, are undercut by failure to keep the law oneself (vv. 21–23). The value of circumcision, likewise, is similarly rendered null by such failure (vv. 25–27). The "real" Jew, Paul concludes, is not the one who is so outwardly, marked by an outward (visible) circumcision in the flesh (v. 28). No, the real Jew is one who is one inwardly (*ho en kryptō Ioudiaos* [literally, "the one in secret"]), whose circumcision is one "of the heart [*peritomē ek kardias*], wrought by the Spirit, not the letter, and whose commendation is not from human beings but from God" (v. 29). Here, the reference to the Spirit—in contrast to "the letter" (see also 7:6; 2 Cor 3:6)—has taken the honorific title "Jew" and redefined it in light of prophetic pronouncements of what God would do in the eschatological age (Jer 31:33; Ezek 36:27). The "true" Jew, in effect, is the believer, in whom the Spirit brings about a fulfillment of the righteous requirement of the law (Rom 8:4).

Although Paul may appear to have annihilated Jewish identity here, this is of course, only an early stage in the long presentation of the gospel in Romans. He, in fact, immediately goes on to ask, "What then is the advantage of being a Jew?" (3:1), and replies, "Much and in every way…" (v. 2). However, he doesn't really resolve this issue until he returns to it, at great length, in Romans 9—11. There, however, especially in the positive hope for Jewish salvation that he eventually arrives at (11:11–32), his preferred designation is "Israel" rather than "the Jews" (see vv. 25–26).

"Judaism"

Around the time of the Maccabees (second century BCE), the Greek term *Ioudaismos* had come into being to refer to the Jewish way of life, specifically the keeping of the practices prescribed by the Jewish law (see 2 Macc 2:21; 8:1; 14:38); the adverb *ioudaïkōs* (see Gal 2:14d) describes living in this way. In his autobiographical references early in Galatians, Paul employs *Ioudaismos* to refer to his full embrace and practice of his ancestral religion (Gal 1:13, 14). It is anachronistic, however, to regard this term as corresponding to "Judaism" in the sense that later evolved and remains today as referring to a distinct religio-ethnic identity parallel to "Christianity."

CIRCUMCISION, CIRCUMCISE; GENTILES; ISRAEL; LAW; SPIRIT

Reading

Dunn, *Beginning*, 524–28; *Romans 1–8*, 109–10; *Theology*, 346–50, 504–9; Fitzmyer, *Romans*, 129–31; W. Gutbrod, *TDNT* 3:380–91; H. Kuhli, *EDNT* 2:193–97; Wells, *Grace and Agency*, 209–223 (on Rom 2:17–29).

JOY, REJOICE

Considering the extent to which suffering was Paul's lot, the frequency with which "joy" finds mention in the letters—in the form of both the Greek noun *chara* and the verb *chairō*—is remarkable. Most remarkable of all is the fact that no letter contains more references to joy than Philippians, written by Paul from captivity in the face of likely condemnation and death.

Paul tells of the joy occasioned by things turning out well (Phil 1:18), the welcome arrival of persons (1 Cor 16:17; Phil 2:28–29), the receiving of a gratifying report (Phil 4:10), the knowledge of the love a fellow believer (Philemon) has for him (Phlm 7). He hopes that, his ministry to the saints in Jerusalem successfully accomplished, he will arrive in Rome with joy (Rom 15:32). What gives him joy above all is the progress of the communities he has nurtured (2 Cor 2:3; 7:4; Phil 2:2; 1 Thess 3:9; see also Col 2:5) and their personal attachment to him, especially after a period of disaffection (2 Cor 7:7, 9, 16). He prays for the Philippians with joy (1:4); they are his "joy [*chara*] and his crown" (4:1). The Thessalonians will be his "hope or joy or crown of boasting before our Lord Jesus Christ at his coming" (1 Thess 2:19–20).

Joy should be a hallmark of Christian life (see 1 Cor 13:6; 2 Cor 1:24). Paul's command to the Philippians is, "Rejoice in the Lord always; again I say, 'Rejoice'" (4:4; see 1:25; 3:1; 1 Thess 5:16; see

Rom 12:15). It is the fruit of the Spirit (Gal 5:22; 1 Thess 1:6), an anticipation of the kingdom of God (Rom 14:17). Joy and hope go together because "the Lord is near" (Phil 4:5b; contrast 1 Cor 7:30b, although the joy in question is more natural happiness than true Christian joy). Paul's prayer for the Roman community is that "the God of hope" will fill them "with all joy and peace in believing," so that they "may abound in hope by the power of the Holy Spirit" (Rom 15:13).

Most remarkable is the close association of joy with suffering. Paul acknowledges that, despite persecution, the Thessalonians received the word with joy inspired by the Spirit (1 Thess 1:6, as also noted in 2 Cor 8:2). The sorrows attending the apostolic life do not prevent him and his coworkers from "always rejoicing" (*aei...chairontes*) (2 Cor 6:10). He rejoices in weakness because it is through his weakness (see 12:9–10) that the Corinthians are made strong through the power of Christ (13:9; see Phil 2:17, 18).

There is a striking reflection of this in Colossians when the author, in Paul's name, speaks of "rejoicing in my sufferings for your sake [*chairō en tois pathēmasin hyper hymōn*], completing in my flesh what is lacking in Christ's afflictions for the sake of the body, that is, the church" (1:24). This seems to draw out Paul's conviction that suffering can be cause for rejoicing in that, for believers, it is always suffering in union with Christ (see Rom 8:17, 35–37; 2 Cor 4:8–12; Phil 1:12–14; 3:10–11), whose suffering brought such benefit to the world.

The verb *chairō* in the imperative can also mean "Farewell," and, although not likely, this could be the meaning in Philippians 3:1; 4:4.

COMMUNION; HOPE; PRAYER; SPIRIT; SUFFERING

Reading

K. Berger, *EDNT* 3:451–52, 454–55; H. Conzelmann, *TDNT* 9:369–70; L. R. Hogan, *I Live, No Longer I: Paul's Spirituality of Suffering, Transformation, and Joy* (Eugene, OR: Wipf & Stock, 2017); Holloway, *Philippians*, 1–10; F. J. Matera, "Philippians," *PBC*, 1419–28; W. G. Morrice, *DPL*, 511–12.

JUDGE, LAST JUDGMENT

The motif of the last judgment plays a more substantial role in Paul's theology than the comparatively few explicit appeals to it in the letters might suggest. Along with most New Testament authors, Paul writes within the overarching framework of the Jewish apocalyptic theology prevalent at the time, a key feature of which was the expectation of a more or less imminent final reckoning (see APOCALYPTIC). God would intervene to wind up the present age, instituting a great judgment in which all would be judged according to their works. The righteous would be vindicated and brought into a transformed new world, while the unrighteous, especially those persecuting the faithful and practicing idolatry, would experience the divine wrath and be condemned. A summons to repentance in view of this looming judgment is the essential burden of Paul's sermon before the Areopagus according to Acts 17:22–31 (see vv. 30–31).

The Last Judgment as Backdrop to the Gospel

It is likely that this sermon in Athens placed on Paul's lips by a later writer is not all that far removed from the kind of appeal that Paul would have made to a Gentile audience in his apostolic ministry of the gospel. Early in 1 Thessalonians, he reminds the community how they "had turned to God from idols, to serve a living and true God, and to wait for his Son from heaven, whom he raised from the dead—Jesus, who rescues us from the wrath that is coming" (1:9b–10 NRSV). That the prospect of the last judgment is the essential backdrop to the proclamation of the gospel in Romans is clear from the fact that a statement concerning the revelation of God's wrath (1:18) follows immediately on the thematic announcement of the revelation of God's righteousness (1:17).

Where Paul and the early believers differed from other apocalyptic movements in Judaism lay in the belief that God's action in the death and resurrection of Jesus represented both a judgment on the sinfulness of the entire world, Israel included, *and* at the same time a gift of divine righteousness that would ensure rescue from condemnation at the judgment and entrance into the promised blessings of salvation (Rom 3:21–26; 8:1–4; 2 Cor 5:21). In this way the gospel of the Crucified Messiah confronted its hearers not only with the prospect of judgment but also with the means of finding justification, that is, acquittal, at the judgment. Hence believers find themselves in a more complex eschatological situation than was otherwise envisaged in apocalyptic Judaism. In virtue of the righteousness ("righteousness of God") already graciously gifted to them through faith, they are already justified (Rom 5:1; 8:30), as attested by the Spirit (5:5; Gal 3:1–9). In this sense they have passed through the judgment. Now through the power of the Spirit (Rom 8:4, 9–11), they must "live out" the righteous status they have received so as to experience "salvation from the wrath" (Rom 5:9) at the final judgment.

Hence the frequent expressions in Paul's letters of his hopes that the believing community will be found "blameless on the day of our Lord Jesus Christ" (1 Cor 1:8; see 2 Cor 1:14; Phil 1:10; 2:16; 1 Thess 5:2, 4). Justification already received does not eliminate all sense of an accountability to come. Reference to the future judgment in this sense finds explicit reference in 2 Corinthians 5:10:

> For all of us must appear before the judgment seat of Christ [*tou bēmatos tou Christou*], so that each may receive recompense for what they have done in the body, whether good or evil.

A similar accountability—this time to God rather than to Christ—appears in the exhortation to tolerance in the matter of dietary practice in Romans 14:10c–12:

> 10 …For we will all stand before the judgment seat of God. 11 For it is written, "*As I live, says the Lord, every knee shall bend before me, and every tongue shall confess to God*" (Isa 45:23). 12 So then, each one shall give an account of themselves to God.

Likewise, individual ministers will be accountable for the quality of the "work" they have performed in building up the community, for the day of the

Lord will disclose it (1 Cor 3:10–15). Paul knows of nothing "against" himself but is not thereby "acquitted," as it is the Lord who judges him and who will bring to light the things now hidden in darkness. On that day, "each one will receive commendation [*epainos*] from the Lord" (4:4–5).

The Judgment in Romans 2

Paul's most explicit evocation of the last judgment appears in Romans 2, as the backdrop to the proclamation of the gospel (1:16–17). To exclude the possibility of attaining the righteousness that will be required at the judgment on any basis other than faith in God's gracious action in Christ, Paul launches, in diatribe mode, a prophetic accusation against a fictive Jewish teacher who hopes to be justified on the basis of successful practice of the law (Rom 2):

> [5] In your hardness and impenitence of heart you are storing up wrath for yourself against the day of wrath, when God's righteous judgment will be revealed, [6] who (God) *will repay according to each one's deeds* [LXX Ps 61:13; see Prov 24:12]: [7] to those who through perseverance in good work seek glory and honor and immortality (there will be) eternal life; [8] To those who through ambitious self-seeking disavow the truth and follow wickedness, there will be wrath and fury....
>
> [12] All who have sinned apart from the law will also perish apart from the law, and all who have sinned under the law will be judged by the law. [13] For it is not the hearers of the law who are righteous in God's sight, but the doers of the law who will be justified.... [16] on the day when, according to my gospel, God, through Jesus Christ, will judge the secret thoughts of all.

This extended passage unambiguously asserts that the last judgment will be strictly according to one's works. The formulation is not hypothetical. Aside from faith and the God-given righteousness to which faith gives access, the judgment will proceed on the basis of works. There is no tension between justification according to works and justification by grace and faith in Paul (see JUSTIFICATION). The former is the presupposition of the latter, which is why the revelation of God's wrath (1:18) and the looming judgment is a key element of the gospel (2:16). However, for those "in Christ Jesus" through faith and baptism, provided that through the power of the Spirit they live out and preserve the righteousness gifted to them (Rom 8:4–11), there is (will be) "no condemnation" (Rom 8:1). Although not all interpreters would agree, it is possible to read Romans 8:31–39, especially verses 31–34, as an evocation of the last judgment, presenting it as nothing other than the final victory of God's love against accusation that could be brought against God's elect (v. 33).

APOCALYPTIC; ESCHATOLOGY; GOSPEL; JUSTIFICATION; LAW; RIGHTEOUSNESS; SALVATION; SPIRIT; WRATH

Reading

J. Barclay, "Believers and the 'Last Judgment' in Paul: Rethinking Grace and Recompense," in H.-J. Eckstein et al., *Eschatologie–Eschatology* (Tübingen: Mohr Siebeck, 2011), 195–208; Byrne, *PES*, 43–70, 78–82, 126–27, 237–42; K. P. Donfried, "Justification and Last Judgment in Paul," *ZNW* 67 (1976): 90–110; reprinted in *Paul, Thessalonica, and Early Christianity* (London: Clark, 2002), 253–78, with a further reflection, "Justification and Last Judgment in Paul—Twenty-Five Years Later," 279–92; Dunn, *Theology*, 41–43, 490–93; K. R. Snodgrass, "Justification by Grace—To the Doers: An Analysis of the Place of Romans 2 in the Theology of Paul," *NTS* 32 (1986): 72–93; C. VanLandingham, *Judgment and Justification in Early Judaism and the Apostle Paul* (Peabody, MA: Hendrickson, 2006); Westerholm, *Justification*, 4–17; Wolter, *Paul*, 210–17; Wright, *PFG*, 1078–90; K. L. Yinger, *Paul, Judaism, and Judgment according to Deeds* (Cambridge: Cambridge University Press, 1999).

JUSTIFY, JUSTIFICATION

An account of justification in Paul has first to confront the fact that English employs two quite distinct word stems—"righteous"/"righteousness" and "justify"/"justification"—to express concepts that are derivatives of the one verbal stem *dikai-* in Greek. One has then to keep in mind that "righteous"/"righteousness" and "justify"/"justification" are more closely connected in Greek than reference in English to "pronouncing" or "making righteous" might suggest. This means that consideration of justification in Paul has to take into account the essentially related concept of "righteousness," which is in many respects primary (see RIGHTEOUSNESS).

In secular (as distinct from biblical) Greek usage, the verb *dikaioō* almost invariably has the meaning of "render justice" in the negative sense of punishing someone convicted of a crime. This meaning is totally absent from the Greek Bible. The usage of *dikaioō* in the Septuagint appears to have been influenced by the Hebrew verbal stem *sdq*, which it regularly translates in the more positive senses of acknowledging or declaring that someone is "in the right" ("righteous"). In the legal/forensic contexts in which it frequently occurs it has the sense of "acquit" or "find innocent." Just as a negative verdict does not "make" persons guilty but declares them to be such on the basis of conduct found wanting, so a verdict of justification does not "make" a person righteous in an ethical sense but declares her or him to be so on the basis of their conduct, in this case good. Presupposed in either case is a principle, norm, or law—often not made explicit—in view of which the conduct is assessed as either righteous or unrighteous. Thus, justification requires three things: a principle against which conduct is assessed; a person who has behaved in a certain way; another party who assesses this conduct in light of the principle and declares it to be positive.

Justification and the Judgment

The prominence of "justification" language in Paul stems from the apocalyptic cast of his theology, in which the prospect of the last judgment bulked large. In the view of Jewish apocalypticism of the time, the present evil age would soon be brought to an end by a divine intervention in which God (or God's agent) would institute a great judgment to deal with evil, condemn the oppressors (inflicting on them "the wrath"), and vindicate the righteous, who would then enter the "age to come," in which the original design of the Creator for human beings and the world would at last be realized. "Justification" has an essential reference to this process of being found "righteous" or "acquitted" at the last judgment, leading to the gaining of "(eternal) life." It is thus intrinsically "forensic" in nature and, in a Jewish context, the Mosaic law provided the key norm or standard against which righteousness would be assessed.

Justification in Christ

For Paul, as a convert to faith in Christ and apostle to the nations, the key difference from the wider Jewish expectation of judgment was the conviction that, in the Crucified Messiah, God had already rendered a negative verdict on all human conduct, that of Israel included (Rom 3:9, 23; 5:12d; 11:32; Gal 3:22), while at the same time offering, totally gratuitously, a gift of righteousness ("righteousness of God") accessed simply by faith, which would ensure a favorable verdict at the judgment. This was the essential message of the gospel preached by Paul (Rom 1:16–17; 2:16; 3:21–30).

The reason that justification looms so large in Galatians and Romans and scarcely at all elsewhere (see 1 Cor 4:4; 6:11) is that in the former Paul is countering a threat to impose on his Gentile converts observance of the Jewish law as a basis for justification, while in Romans he is attempting to provide an accurate account of his law-free gospel to a community that has not heard it from his own lips and that he aims to visit with any misunderstanding cleared up. Where law observance on the part of Gentiles is not an issue, as would seem to have been the case in Corinth and Thessalonica, justification is not a topic. Hence, the now centuries-old debate as to how central the matter is to Paul's theology as a whole.

The Time Reference of Justification in Paul

While justification does have an essential reference to the last judgment, the fact that in the Christian view the judgment has been brought forward for believers creates a complex situation in regard to its time reference in Paul. When Paul is writing within the frame of reference of a Jew who has not yet come to faith, as in the fictive dialogue with a Jewish teacher in Romans 2:1–29, justification appears as a *future* process and one based on works:

> [12] All who have sinned apart from the law will also perish apart from the law, and all who have sinned under the law will be judged by the law. [13] For it is not the hearers of the law who are righteous in God's sight, but the doers of the law who will be justified [*dikaiōthēsontai*].

The same future reference appears in the exclusion of the factual possibility of justification by works in 3:20 and in other contexts where justification is considered aside from the divine intervention in Christ, or, as in Galatians, where the implications of that intervention are in Paul's view insufficiently taken into account by fellow believers (Gal 2:16a; 3:11; 5:4). As something that believers have already experienced justification appears in the *past* tense in Romans 5:1 (*dikaiōthentes*…); 5:9; 8:30; 1 Corinthians 6:11 (see Rom 6:7). It is something *presently* going on or being made available through the gospel in Romans 3:24 (*dikaioumenoi*…), 26c, 28; 4:5; 9:30; Galatians 2:16b. Paul can, however, also refer justification to the future in regard to believers, as in 5:19b (*dikaioi katastathēsontai*) and, albeit in the present tense, in 8:33b (*theos ho dikaiōn*).

These references to a justification yet to come even for believers, together with references to an accountability to be rendered, presumably at the last judgment (Rom 14:10–12; 2 Cor 5:10; see also 1 Cor 3:12–15; 4:4–5), have led to the question as to whether we should think of two justifications in Paul: one at the moment of coming to faith and one at the last judgment. Then there is the further question of the tension that arises if the latter is seen to be on the basis of works in view of the former being indisputably on the basis of grace and faith. Has justification by works reentered through the back door?

Justification by Faith and Justification by Works

First, it must be said that justification on the basis of one's works remains an abiding principle for all outside the response required by the gospel. As Romans 2:12–13 makes clear, it is the essential presupposition for the divine intervention to rescue sinful humanity through the mission and saving death of the Son. In grace and mercy, through the sending of the Son and the expiatory function of his death (Rom 3:24–26; 4:25; 8:1–4; Gal 3:13; 2 Cor 5:18–21), God has found a way to justify sinful humanity without compromising that principle or the divine righteousness in judgment. To justify the guilty or to convict the innocent is a heinous crime denounced in the biblical tradition (Exod 23:7; Prov 17:15; 24:24; Isa 5:23; Sir 42:2; see also CD I, 19). God's justification of the "ungodly" Abraham (Rom 4:5) does not transgress this principle. It occurs entirely in light of the Christ event and of faith in that event, for which Abraham has been "co-opted" as paradigm believer (see Gal 3:8, where Paul states that Abraham had the gospel "pre-preached" to him).

Thus there is no essential tension between justification by works and justification through grace and faith in Paul. Christ, for Paul, is the only individual truly justified on the basis of his works—more correctly, his obedience (Rom 5:19; Phil 2:8)—a justification displayed in his resurrection/exaltation (see Phil 2:9). Through faith and baptism, believers "enter into" his person (Rom 6:3; 1 Cor 12:13; Gal 3:27) and into his obedience, finding justification, graciously, in and through him, "who was given up for our transgressions and raised for our justification" (Rom 4:25).

Although an accountability remains for believers, it is unlikely that Paul thought of two "moments" of justification, one at initial coming to faith, one at the last judgment. The task for believers is to live out and so preserve the justification already graciously received. Although not itself identical with transformation of life, justification requires such transformation, which is wrought in believers through the power of the Spirit and manifests itself in particular through love (Rom 8:4–11; 13:8–10; Gal 5:5–6, 13–14). Where justification refers primarily to the initial moment of coming to faith, Paul appears to reserve the term *sanctification* for the ethical transformation through the Spirit that should follow in order that justification be preserved and lived out up to the judgment (Rom 6:19b–23).

The post-Pauline tradition has echoes of the principle of justification/salvation by grace and faith (Eph 2:8–9; 2 Tim 1:9; see also Acts 15:11), but the emphasis lies more on the living out of the faith righteously than on the initial act.

ABRAHAM; FAITH; CHRIST; ESCHATOLOGY; GRACE; HOLINESS; JUDGE, LAST JUDGMENT; LAW; RIGHTEOUSNESS; SIN

Reading

Byrne, *PES*, 35–41, 233–45; Dunn, *Theology*, 334–89; C. L. Irons, *The Righteousness of God: A Lexical Examination of the Covenant-Faithfulness Interpretation* (Tübingen: Mohr Siebeck, 2015); Matera, *GSG*, 103–17; A. E. McGrath, Iustitia Dei*: A History of the Christian Doctrine of Justification*, 3rd ed. (Cambridge: Cambridge University Press, 2005), 18–31; *DPL*, 517–23; J. B. Prothro, *Both Judge and Justifier: Biblical Legal Language and the Act of Justifying in Paul* (Tübingen: Mohr Siebeck, 2018); Rainbow, *Way of Salvation*, 97–115, 155–212; M. A. Seifrid, *Christ, Our Righteousness: Paul's Theology of Justification* (Downers Grove, IL: Intervarsity, 2000); *Justification by Faith: The Origin and Development of a Central Pauline Theme* (Leiden; New York: Brill, 1992); C. VanLandingham, *Judgment & Justification in Early Judaism and the Apostle Paul* (Peabody, MA: Hendrickson, 2006); Westerholm, *Justification*, 4–17; Wolter, *Paul*, 210–17; Wright, *PFG*, 1078–90; K. L. Yinger, *Paul, Judaism, and Judgment according to Deeds* (Cambridge: Cambridge University Press, 1999).

K

KINGDOM OF GOD/CHRIST

References to "the kingdom of God" (*hē basileia tou theou*), so central to the message of Jesus in the Synoptic gospels (Matt 4:17; Mark 1:14–15; Luke 4:43), are rare in the letters of Paul. As also in the Synoptic tradition, the kingdom has both present and future aspects, with the latter more dominant in Paul.

Whereas "kingdom" in English suggests a political institution of some stability and spatial extent, "rule" or "regime" might be a more accurate rendering of *basileia*. That said, "the kingdom of God" can refer in a more spatial sense to the heavenly realm: the "place" where God rules. Such is the reference when Paul speaks of "inheriting"—usually *not* inheriting—the kingdom of God (1 Cor 6:9, 10; Gal 5:21; see also Eph 5:5). With reference to risen bodily existence, Paul maintains that "flesh and blood," that is, human bodily life in the present, is unable, without substantial change, to inherit the kingdom of God in the sense of sharing the heavenly life of the risen Lord (1 Cor 15:50). Here "kingdom of

God" has an entirely future reference and denotes the eschatological goal of human existence otherwise dubbed "eternal life" (Rom 2:7; 5:21; 6:22, 23; Gal 6:8). This future destiny may also be in view when Paul reminds the Thessalonians of his having encouraged them to "lead a life worthy of the God, who calls you into his own kingdom and glory" (1 Thess 2:12).

Full attainment of the kingdom may for the present remain a hope, but the call into it requires, as in the Synoptic tradition, transformation of life here and now. Addressing differing attitudes as to what is legitimate in the matter of diet, Paul writes that "the kingdom of God is not food and drink but righteousness and peace and joy in the Holy Spirit" (Rom 14:17). Here, there is the sense of the rule of God as a present reality in the community—its presence palpable not in specific actions of eating and drinking, but in the "atmosphere" of the righteousness, peace, and joy that is the fruit of the Holy Spirit (see Gal 5:22; also 1 Cor 4:20).

The Messianic Reign of Christ

A unique reference to divine rule appears in the eschatological scenario described in 1 Corinthians 15:24–28. The description proceeds in neither logical nor temporal order but the basic program is clear enough: Christ must "reign" (*basileuein*) until he has put under his feet all "enemies," the last of which is death (vv. 25–26); the subjection of this final enemy will herald the general resurrection. Then, his messianic task accomplished, Christ will "hand over the kingdom [*paradidō tēn basileian*] to the God and Father" (v. 24b), so that "God may be all in all" (v. 28c). As risen and exalted Lord, Christ is presently exercising his messianic reign until he has reclaimed the universe entirely for the rule of God (see Isa 45:23; Phil 2:9–11). (This interpretation does not, with appeal to Revelation 20:5–6, find in verse 25 an allusion to an interim ["1000 year"] reign of Christ, between his *parousia* and the handing over of the kingdom to the Father.)

The Kingdom of God in the Later Pauline Letters

The christological hymn in Colossians 1:15–20 is introduced by a thanksgiving to God who "has rescued us from the power of darkness and transferred us to the kingdom of his beloved Son [*eis tēn basileian tou huiou tēs agapēs autou*]" (1:13). Here, in the more realized eschatology of Colossians, the rule of the Son is already accomplished (contrast 1 Cor 15:25–26) and so, in the sphere where he "reigns" ("the kingdom"), believers have been rescued from the alien powers and should have nothing to fear from them (see Col 1:20; 2:6–15). Later, however, the greetings mention "co-workers for the kingdom of God [*synergoi eis tēn basileian tou theou*]" (4:11), suggesting that the extension of God's realm in the universe remains an ongoing cause. Elsewhere in these letters the "kingdom of God" basically has the future reference of the eschatological destiny awaiting the faithful provided they live lives worthy of the calling they have received (Eph 5:5; 2 Thess 1:5; 2 Tim 4:1, 18). They will, in fact, share Christ's reign (*symbasileusomen*) (2 Tim 2:12; see Rom 5:17; 1 Cor 4:8).

BODY; CHRIST; ESCHATOLOGY; GLORY; LIFE

Reading

Byrne, *PES*, 217–19; Dunn, *Theology*, 190–92; G. Johnson, "'Kingdom of God' Sayings in Paul's Epistles," in *From Jesus to Paul: Studies in Honour of Francis Wright Beare*, ed. P. Richardson and J. C. Hurd (Ontario: Wilfred Laurier University, 1984), 143–56; L. J. Kreitzer, *DPL*, 524–26; M. J. Vlach, "The Kingdom of God in Paul's Epistles," *MSJ* 26 (2015): 59–74 (millenarian); Wolter, *Paul*, 217–20.

KNOW, KNOWLEDGE

The word group "know ([*epi-*]*ginōskō*)/"knowledge" ([*epi-*]*gnōsis*) has in Greek, as in English, a wide range of reference. It is not necessary to review all its occurrences in Paul but simply to indicate areas where his usage is particularly distinctive.

Knowing and Being Known by God

Beyond simple awareness of a fact or state of affairs, knowledge in Paul reflects the biblical sense of "know" that connotes experience and deep personal relationship. This is particularly the case in relation to God. In Romans 1:18–32, Paul describes the radical human failure to know God. Although human beings could conclude to the existence of God through observation of the created world (vv. 19–20), they failed to respond with glorification and thanks (Rom 1:21a), lapsing instead into all manner of idolatry (vv. 23, 25). In this sense, they did not "know" God (1 Cor 1:21; see Rom 1:28). On the contrary, those who have responded to the gospel have turned away from worship of idols (1 Thess 1:9) and come to "know God" or, rather, to be known *by* God (Gal 4:9; see 1 Cor 8:3; 13:12). The reciprocity in knowledge expressed here goes to the heart of the experience of God proclaimed in the gospel. The initiative lies with God, whose knowing involves in a biblical sense foreknowledge and election (Isa 49:1; Jer 1:5; Gal 1:15). Those who truly come to know God have been drawn into an experiential reciprocity of love and knowledge made palpable through the experience of the Spirit (Rom 5:5; 8:15–16; Gal 4:6).

Knowing Christ

Besides knowledge of God, coming to faith brings knowledge of Christ. Alluding it seems to the moment of his own coming to faith (see Gal 1:15–16), Paul writes, "The God who said, 'Out of darkness let light shine,' has shone in our hearts to light up knowledge of the glory of God [*pros phōtismon tēs gnōseōs tēs doxēs tou theou*] on the face of Jesus Christ" (2 Cor 4:6). Only through the Spirit can one truly know the revelation of God on the face of the Crucified (1 Cor 2:8–11; see vv. 14–15). Had those who encompassed his death known the wisdom of God, "they would not have crucified the Lord of glory" (2:8). If once Paul knew Christ according to the flesh (which was not in fact the case), that is no longer how he knows him now (2 Cor 5:16b). The Jewish credentials that previously meant so much to him (Phil 3:4b–6) he regards as loss and rubbish compared to "the surpassing value of knowing Christ Jesus [*dia to hyperechon tēs gnōseōs Christou Iēsou*], my Lord" (vv. 7–8). His desire is "to know him [*tou gnōnai auton*] and the power of his resurrection and the sharing of his sufferings, becoming conformed to his death in the hope of attaining resurrection from the dead" (vv. 10–11). Knowing Christ is more than a one-off discovery. It involves ongoing experience of ever-deeper union and companionship with the one "who loved me and gave himself up for me" (Gal 2:20). The apostolic ministry serves to make known in every place "the fragrance that comes from knowing (Christ)" (*tēn osmēn tēs gnōseōs autou*) (2 Cor 2:14).

Knowledge as a Feature of Christian Life

Paul also speaks about "knowledge" in the more absolute sense of an understanding of God and God's action in Christ that he himself and believers as such possess. He is confident that the recipients of his letter to Rome are "filled with all knowledge" and so are capable of admonishing each other (15:14; see 2 Cor 6:6; 8:7; 10:5; 11:6; Phil 1:9; also Col 1:6). Noteworthy in the deutero-Pauline letters are prayers and expressions of hope that this knowledge will develop and grow as life in Christ proceeds (Eph 1:17; 3:19; 4:13; Col 1:9–10; 2:2; 3:10).

The Gift of Knowledge at Corinth

Although the view that Paul had to counter incipient Gnosticism at Corinth is no longer current, the language of "knowledge" (*gnōsis*) clearly struck a chord in the community. Early in 1 Corinthians, Paul gives thanks that the community has been "enriched in speech and knowledge of every kind" (*en panti logō kai pasē gnōsei*) (1:5). This is something of a *captatio benevolentiae*, however, as later he will point out that claims made in the name of having knowledge need to be carefully assessed. In the matter of eating meat that has been used in the worship of idols (1 Cor 8:1–13), some claim that their knowledge that there is only one God and that idols have no reality (vv. 4–6) gives them the freedom to eat such meat without further concern. Paul points out, however, that not all possess knowledge to such a liberating degree (v. 7). Lest the example of those who eat cause a brother or sister to eat against their conscience and so jeopardize their salvation (vv. 9–12), a higher degree of freedom, inspired by love, should lead those claiming knowledge to refrain (v. 13). Whereas knowledge "puffs up" (*gnōsis physioi*), love "builds up" (v. 1b) (see FREEDOM; IDOLATRY).

A similar relativization of knowledge appears later where Paul is attempting to lead the community to a more balanced appreciation of the gifts of the Spirit (1 Cor 12–14). He includes "a word of knowledge" as one gift among many that, according to the same Spirit, a person may contribute for the common good (12:8). But the encomium to love that intervenes (13:1–13) before the presenting issue (tongues) returns in 14:1–40 asserts the superiority of love above all other gifts and qualities: "I may understand all mysteries and all knowledge," but without love, "I am nothing" (13:2). Whereas knowledge, along with prophecies and tongues, will have an end, love never ends (v. 8). Present knowledge now is partial (*ek merous*) (v. 9), dim as in a mirror (v. 12a), and destined to come to an end (v. 10). Whereas "I know now only in part; then I shall know as I am known" (v. 12cd). Thus for Paul, knowledge is a gift to be prized (see 14:6) but in the present time what it conveys about God is limited. Only love transcends the barrier between the present and what is yet to come (13:8, 13).

Inadequate Knowledge

Over against the knowledge of God communicated in the gospel, Paul sets the claims of the fictive Jewish teacher portrayed in Romans 2:17–24 to know the will of God (v. 18) and to have "the embodiment of knowledge and truth in the law" (*tēn morphōsin tēs gnōseōs kai alētheias en tō nomō*) (v. 20). He concedes that Israel has "a zeal for God," but it is "not according to knowledge" (*ou kat' epignōsin*) (10:2). It is "not according to knowledge" because, involving a quest to establish righteousness by purely human effort (*tēn idian dikaiosynēn*), it has failed to recognize—literally, "not knowing" (*agnoountes*)—the righteousness of God revealed in the Christ event (v. 3; see 9:30–33). For Paul, true knowledge stems from and retains its focus on the cross (1 Cor 2:2).

Knowledge of Sin

Paul speaks of knowledge in the experiential sense in regard to sin. No one finds justification through practice of the law ("works of the law") because "through the law (comes) knowledge of sin" (*epignōsis hamartias*) (Rom 3:20). "I would not have known sin [*tēn hamartian ouk egnōn*] except through the law" (7:7). By qualifying wrongdoing as transgression of the explicit will of God, the law communicates the sense of what it is, in essence, to sin.

Knowledge of the Truth

In the Pastoral Letters a set phrase "knowledge of the truth" (*epignōsis alētheias*) (1 Tim 2:4; 4:3; 2 Tim 2:25; 3:7; Titus 1:1) has become a stock way of referring to the body of truths that, according to the concern of these letters, must be preserved and defended as the basis for salvation and right living.

CROSS; GIFT(S) OF THE SPIRIT; GLORY; GOD; IDOLATRY; LAW; LOVE; SIN; SPIRIT; WISDOM

Reading

C. K. Barrett, "Christianity at Corinth," *BJRL* 46 (1964): 269–97, reprinted in *Essays on Paul* (London: SPCK, 1982), 1–27; Fee, *1 Corinthians*, 37–38, 401–15, 714–19; Fitzmyer, *1 Corinthians*, 339–40, 466, 493; R. A. Horsley, "Gnosis in Corinth: 1 Corinthians 8.1–6," *NTS*

27 (1980): 32–51; C. M. Robeck Jr., *DPL*, 526–28; W. Schmithals, *EDNT* 1:248–51; Thiselton, *1 Corinthians*, 92–93, 620–27, 1267–71.

L

LAST JUDGMENT (*see* Judge, Last Judgment)

LAW

In Paul, "law" (*nomos*) almost always refers to the law of Moses, given on Mount Sinai to Israel as the covenant people of God (Exod 20:1–21; 24:1–8; 34:10–35). Through obedience to the commandments of the torah, Israel is preserved within the covenant and finds life (Lev 18:5; Deut 30:15–20). Prior to his encounter with the risen Christ (Gal 1:16), Paul the Pharisee, by his own description, was "blameless" in regard to righteousness in keeping the law (Phil 3:6; see also Gal 1:14). As such he would doubtless have said, "For me to live is the torah"; after coming to faith in Christ, he can say, "For me to live is Christ" (Phil 1:21; see Gal 2:20).

Faith in the Crucified Messiah shattered Paul's view of the law. If such was the Messiah God sent to Israel, the alienation from the Creator created by sin was universal, Israel included (Rom 1:18–3:20; 3:23; 5:12; Gal 3:22). The righteousness required for salvation could not be gained through practice of the law (see Gal 2:15–16); the law had proved impotent against the proneness to sin of unredeemed human nature ("the flesh" [Rom 8:3]). But, in the face of this universal lack of righteousness, God had graciously intervened in the person of the Son to create a new possibility of righteousness ("righteousness of God"), on an equally universal scale, a righteousness accessed solely through faith in the divine action itself (Rom 1:16–17; 3:21–30; Gal 2:16, 19–21; see Phil 3:8–9). In the marital analogy Paul deploys in Romans 7:1-3, every believer has "died" to the law in order to be "betrothed" to the risen Lord in a union that will be "fruitful (in righteousness) for God" (v. 4; see 10:4).

For Paul, the law in itself is "holy, and the commandment is holy, just, and good" (Rom 7:12). Obedience to the law is the criterion of judgment, but, as Paul notes, "it is not the hearers of the law who are righteous in God's sight, but the doers of the law who will be justified" (Rom 2:13). The problem is, however, that there is no one who practices what the law requires, whether by possession of the law (Jews [2:12b, 17–24]) or following the requirement of the law written on the heart (Gentiles [2:14–15]). Hence, the inevitable conclusion that through practice of the works of the law, no one will be justified (3:20a); rather, "through the law comes "knowledge of sin" (3:20b).

This last phrase ("knowledge of sin") reveals Paul's distinctive view of the law. At one level the law's role is to specify various kinds of wrongdoing as infringement of the explicit will of God, thereby rendering the wrongdoing "transgression" (*parabasis* or *paraptōma*). But beyond simply indicating what is sin in this sense, the law rains down on sin its curse (Gal 3:10), and "works wrath" (Rom 4:15), that is, the prospect of condemnation at the judgment. Likewise, although the word *nomos* does not occur in 2 Corinthians, the characterization of the Sinai covenant as "a ministration of death" (3:7) and "of condemnation" (3:9), implies this same negative function of the law. In a striking image, Paul speaks of the law in Galatians 3:24 as "our *paidagōgos* to Christ," not in the sense of a "teacher" as the word might suggest to present-day ears but as a harsh guardian, making clear that there is no hope of avoiding condemnation other than through faith in Christ.

The Law and the Spirit in Romans 7:1—8:13

Romans 7:7–25 is often described as an *apologia* for the law and at one point (v. 12) this is true. But Paul is really here drawing out the most provocative aspect of his view of the law. Far from restraining or preventing sin, it actually provokes and increases it (Rom 5:20a; 7:5; see also 6:15; Gal 3:19). Paul brings this out in Romans 7:7–13 by presenting Israel's confrontation with the law promulgated on Mount Sinai in the guise of Adam's confrontation with "the commandment" according to Genesis 3. The parity between the two situations consists in the fact that both involved/involve the possibility of sinning against an explicit ruling of God (see also Rom 5:14). The law is not identical with sin (7:7a) but it provides the opportunity for sin, latent in the flesh, to gain mastery and so lead, not to life, but to death (7:7b–11). In an extended rhetorical sequence in the present tense (7:14–25), Paul describes how sin's mastery leading to death arises through the law. The law itself may be "spiritual" (*pneumatikos*) but "I" (the person confronted by the law/commandment) am "fleshly (*sarkikos*), sold into slavery under sin (*pepramenos hypo hamartian*)" (v. 14). "I" may acknowledge the goodness of the law (see v. 12) and want to fulfill it but the regime of sin in my flesh constantly frustrates that will. The reiterated description of the tension thereby created builds up to the anguished cry, "Who will deliver me from this body of death?" (v. 24a), preparing the way (especially if v. 25a is regarded as an anticipatory gloss) for the positive response to be given in 8:1–11.

For Paul, then, the law has become the unwilling accomplice of sin, leading to (eternal) death rather than life. As such, however, it is not totally disconnected from the divine purpose. The complex statement in Romans 7:13 places the operation of thc law within the wider overall design of God: "But sin, in order that it may appear as sin, was working death for me through this good thing, in order that sin might become sinful beyond measure through the commandment" (v. 13b). Thus Paul sees the law as having the role of unmasking sin—bringing it to the surface, so to speak—in order that it may be dealt with once and for all through the divine redemptive act in Christ.

The depiction in Romans 7:7–25 of the ethical "impossibility" under the law functions as a rhetorical foil preparing the way for Paul's triumphant announcement (8:1–2) of the possibility for righteous living created by the redemptive mission of the Son. There is now "no condemnation" hanging over those in Christ (v. 1) because the "law" (*nomos*) consisting of the Spirit leading to life has replaced "the law of sin and death" (v. 2). By describing the replaced factor on the negative side as "the law of sin and death," Paul is not necessarily categorizing the Mosaic law in such terms. He occasionally uses *nomos* in a more general sense to indicate whatever is a controlling factor in a situation (see especially 7:23; see also 3:27). Hence, while *nomos* usually designates the Mosaic law, it can also refer, as here, both to the regime of sin and death, on the one hand, and the impact of the Spirit, on the other. By speaking of the controlling power in both cases as "law" Paul preserves a certain continuity in regard to the law. In so doing he likely has in mind the fulfillment of the divine promise contained in Jeremiah 31:33 and Ezekiel 36:26–27 to place "the law" (the Spirit) within the people, granting the capacity to live righteously (see also Rom 2:29; 7:6; 2 Cor 3:6).

This capacity is wholly traceable to God's sending of the Son "in the likeness of sinful flesh" and the "condemnation" of sin in the flesh" (8:3). The Spirit brings about within believers a fulfillment (*plērōthē*) of the righteousness that the law required of human beings (*to dikaiōma tou nomou*) but could not deliver (v. 4). The law is thus not summarily dismissed. There is even a hint in verse 7b of its abiding validity as an indication of God's will. However, as passages such as Romans 13:8–10 and Galatians 5:14 suggest, its fulfillment now is totally encompassed in the single commandment of love.

The Law in Galatians 3:1—4:7

Paul's comments about the law are more polemical in Galatians than in Romans because he sees the imposition of its requirements ("the works of the law") on his Gentile converts as discounting the supremely costly death of Christ (2:20–21). His riposte to Cephas at the Antioch incident (2:11–14) implies that, even for believers of Jewish background such as Cephas and himself, coming to faith in Christ required recognition that the eschatological righteousness was to be gained solely by faith and not by doing "the works of the law" (2:16). To impose the works of the law, specifically circumcision and food laws, on Gentiles is to re-erect the division between "holy nation" (Israel) and "Gentile sinners" that the cross of Christ had overthrown (2:18). In an extended sequence (3:1–29), Paul privileges the covenant God made directly with Abraham on the basis of his faith, with its promise of bestowing the Spirit on Gentile believers as guarantee of their justification, over the later Sinai covenant, where the law was ministered not directly by God but by angels and through a mediator (Moses) (v. 19d). This subsequent dispensation could not write new conditions into the original covenant, focused directly and solely on Christ (v. 16), and on those "in" him through faith and baptism, and hence heirs of the promise Abraham received (vv. 26–29). Christ has done away with the law's curse on sin (3:13; see v. 10), bringing to all believers the freedom from the law indicated by the Spirit (5:1–6; see Rom 8:1–4).

The "Law" as Scripture

Adding to the complexity of Paul's statements about the law is the fact that he also uses *nomos* to refer not to the legal code but to "the law" as Scripture. The ambiguity is patent in Romans 3:19–20, where *nomos* appears with reference both to the preceding chain of scriptural quotations (vv. 10–18) and to the legal requirements ("works of the law"). Immediately following (v. 21), Paul affirms that a righteousness of God has been revealed "aside from" (*chōris*) the law (as code), but "with the law (presumably the Pentateuch) and the prophets bearing witness." In verse 31, he claims to be "upholding" rather than doing away with the law through faith, and then goes on (4:1–12) to deploy an extensive scriptural witness to justification by faith centered on the figure of Abraham, citing "the law" (Gen 15:6) and "the prophets" (LXX Ps 31:1–2). Paul seems to exploit this ambiguity also in Galatians 4:21–22 (see JERUSALEM). In the less polemical context of 1 Corinthians 14:21, "law" (*nomos*) introduces a quotation from a prophetic book (Isa 28:11–12).

The Law in Paul Aside from Romans and Galatians

Aside from Romans and Galatians, references to the law in the remaining letters are few and uncontroversial. In 1 Corinthians 9:8–9, Paul cites the law about not muzzling the ox (Deut 25:4) in order to justify the right of missionaries to receive support from the churches—a right he himself forgoes. In an exercise of apostolic adaptability (9:20–21), although personally not "under the law" (*hyper nomon*), he is prepared to live "as one under the law" (i.e., as a Jew) in order to win for Christ "those under the law" (i.e., Jews). Only in 1 Corinthians 15:56 do we hear something of an (arbitrary) passing shot at the law's complicity in the onset of sin and death, and as previously noted, Philippians 3:6–9 records his abandonment of seeking righteousness through the law consequent on being "captured" by Christ (v. 12).

"Works of the Law"

The phrase "works of (the) law" (always in the form *ex* [or *chōris*] *ergōn nomou*) appears to be a technical phrase operative in the controversy concerning the terms on which Gentiles may be admitted into the community destined for salvation. As such it appears frequently in Galatians (2:16 [three times]; 3:2, 5, 10) and Romans (3:20, 28; in shortened form [*ex ergōn*]: 4:2; 9:12, 32; 11:6; see also 4:6 [*chōris ergōn*]; 2:15 [*to ergon tou nomou*]). Interpretation of the phrase has become controversial in recent decades in that representatives of the New Perspective on Paul have tended to confine its reference primarily to ritual prescriptions of the torah that functioned as "boundary-marking" statements of Jewish identity (circumcision, Sabbath observance, food laws). Such a reference is particularly congenial to the context addressed in Galatians where observance of the food laws (Gal 2:11–14) and the requirement of circumcision (5:2–12; 6:12–16) are the presenting issues. In both letters, however, the basic question concerns how one obtains and preserves the righteousness required for salvation and this for Paul involves the status of the law *as such*, rather than particular prescriptions. Hence the more traditional interpretation of the phrase as referring simply to deeds prescribed by the law and hence as indicative of a quest to find justification through practice of the law remains cogent.

The Law in the Pauline Tradition

Although not explicitly mentioned, the law seems to be in view in the reference to God's nailing "the record that stood against us with its legal demands" to the cross in Colossians 2:13–14. According to Ephesians 2:15–16, God has created "peace" between Jews and Gentiles by abolishing in Christ the law with its commandments and ordinances that formed a barrier between them. For the Pauline author of 1 Timothy the law appears to remain in force as a moral guide, although it must be understood as laid down, not for the innocent, but for the godless and sinful (1:8–10).

DEATH; FAITH; FREEDOM; GRACE; JUDGE, LAST JUDGMENT; JUSTIFICATION; LOVE; RIGHTEOUSNESS; SIN; SPIRIT

Reading

Beker, *Paul the Apostle*, 235–54; Byrne, *PES*, 145–59; "The Problem of *Nomos* and the Relationship with Judaism in Romans," *CBQ* 62 (2000): 294–309; J. D. G. Dunn, *Paul and the Mosaic Law* (Grand Rapids: Eerdmans, 2001); *Theology*, 128–61; J. D. G. Dunn, ed., "Paul and the Torah," in *The New Perspective on Paul*, rev. ed. (Grand Rapids: Eerdmans, 2008), 448–67; Horrell, *Introduction*, 126–36; A. J. Hultgren, "Paul and the Law," in Westerholm, *Paul*, 202–15; Moo, *Romans*, 207–17; E. P. Sanders, *Paul, the Law, and the Jewish People* (Philadelphia: Fortress, 1983); F. Thielman, "Law," *DPL*, 529–42; M. J. Thomas, *Paul's "Works of the Law" in the Perspective of Second Century Reception* (Tübingen: Mohr Siebeck, 2018), 23–60, 219–30; Westerholm, *Perspectives*, 297–340; Wolter, *Paul*, 342–73.

LIFE, LIVE

As in English, the Greek terms for "life" (*zōē*) and "live" (*zaō*) have a broad range of reference in Paul. Most basic is the reference simply to present or past earthly existence (Rom 7:1–3, 9; 1 Cor 7:39; 9:14; 15:19; see Col 2:20; 3:7; 2 Tim 4:1), although sometimes with a particular nuance of life over against death (Rom 8:38; 1 Cor 3:22; 2 Cor 1:8; 2:16; 4:11–12; 5:4; 6:9; Phil 1:20, 22; 1 Thess 4:15, 17).

However, Paul inherited the Old Testament idea of life as the gift of God, who brought the first human being to life by breathing into him the breath of life (1 Cor 15:45, citing Gen 2:7). Behind Paul also stood the scriptural tradition that fullness of life flowed from righteous living (Pss 34:15–22; 37:28–29; Ezek 3:20–21; 18:5–9, 19–20) and, in particular, observance of the covenantal obligations set out in the Mosaic law (Lev 18:5 [cited by Paul in Rom 10:5; Gal 3:12]; Deut 30:6, 15–20; Ps 119:33–40, 93). In the mainstream biblical tradition, the life in view lay totally within the bounds of an enhanced earthly life. However, in the Wisdom of Solomon the fruit of righteousness is immortality: "For righteousness is immortal" (1:15; see also 5:15; 15:3), and this sense of righteousness leading to a life beyond death became pervasive in works of the Jewish apocalyptic tradition that formed the matrix of Paul's theology.

The axiom that life in this sense flows from righteousness is, however, rendered more complex in Paul because of the unprecedented eschatological situation in which believers in Christ find themselves. Christ's resurrection has inaugurated the age to come. Participation through faith and baptism in his ongoing life as risen Lord (Rom 5:10; 6:10–11; 14:9; 2 Cor 4:10–12; 13:4) means that believers, while still bodily anchored in the present passing age and in this sense awaiting resurrection (Rom 8:23), are already sharing in his risen life as far as relations with God are concerned. "Righteous through faith" (Rom 5:1), they are already "walking in newness of life" (Rom 6:4) or ought to be so living (6:2; 8:12; Gal 5:25). "Dead to sin and alive to God" as Christ himself is "alive to God" (Rom 6:10–11, 13), they are living not for themselves but for the one who died and rose for them (2 Cor 5:15; see Rom 14:7–9).

Life Both Present and to Come

Thus Paul can refer "life" in this eschatological sense to the present life of believers (Rom 6:2, 4, 11, 13; 8:6; 14:7; Gal 2:19–20; 5:25; Phil 1:21; 1 Thess 3:8; see Titus 2:12), and at the same time refer to it in the future tense as something yet to come following the general resurrection (Rom 11:15; see 1 Cor 15:20–28): "those who receive the abundance of grace and the free gift of righteousness will reign in life [*en zōē basileusousin*] through the one man Jesus Christ" (Rom 5:17); "one man's righteous act (has brought about) a justification leading to life [*eis dikaiōsin zōēs*] for all" (v. 18; see also 2:7; 8:13; 2 Cor 13:4; Phil 4:3; 1 Thess 5:10). This eschatological sense of "life"/"live" seems to be the way in which Paul understood the phrase "will live" (*zēsetai*) in the quotation from Habakkuk 2:4 that provided for him an all-important link between faith and the righteousness that leads to life: "The person righteous by faith will live" (Rom 1:17; Gal 3:11). (The issue across Romans 1:16—4:25 is not how the righteous person now lives [i.e., by faith], but with what kind of righteousness a person should be clad in order to gain eschatological life—Paul's response being: a righteousness based on faith.) At times Paul will make clear the future reference of the life that flows from righteousness by qualifying the "life" in question as "eternal": *zōē aionios* (Rom 2:7; 5:21; 6:22, 23; Gal 6:8; see also 1 Tim 1:16; 6:12; Titus 1:2; 3:7).

The Spirit as Agent of Life

As in the original creation God "breathed" life into the first human being (Gen 2:7), so in the already inaugurated new creation (2 Cor 5:17; Gal 6:15), the Spirit is the agent of eschatological life for those in Christ ("the Spirit of life" [Rom 8:2; see v. 7]). Although the body is mortal as a legacy of sin, "the Spirit means life because of righteousness" (*to...pneuma zōē dia dikaiosynēn* [v. 10c]) because it brings about in believers the capacity to live the righteous life that will lead God who raised Jesus from the dead to raise their mortal bodies through the Spirit dwelling within them (v. 11). In this passage (8:9–11), Paul speaks interchangeably between the impact of the risen Lord and the Spirit as the indwelling power creating the righteousness that leads to life. This coheres with the description (1 Cor 15:45) of "the last Adam" (Christ) as "life-giving Spirit" (*pneuma zōopoioun*).

Ultimately, the gift of life in the fullest sense derives from worship of a "living God" (Rom 9:26 [citing Hos 2:1]; 14:11 [citing Isa 49:18b]; 2 Cor 3:3; 6:16), whom believers from the Gentile world, having turned from demons, now serve (1 Thess 1:9; see Gal 4:8; see also Eph 4:18; 1 Tim 3:15; 4:10). Following their "father" Abraham, they put their faith in a God "who makes the dead alive [*tou zōopoiountos tous nekrous*] and calls into being things that do not exist" (Rom 4:17; see also 8:11; 1 Tim 4:10).

"Life" in the Later Pauline Letters

In Colossians, the continuity between the present and future life is strongly pressed. Believers are already raised with Christ (2:12–13; 3:1), their "life" is hidden with Christ in God and awaits simply to be revealed (3:3), although this does not necessarily exclude eventual bodily conformity to Christ, the "*first*born [*prōtotokos*] from the dead" (1:18). In the post-Pauline letters, the distinction between the present life and the life to come remains (1 Tim 1:16; 6:19; Titus 1:2; 3:7), with strong emphasis on the need to live a godly life and endure the trials of the present in order to gain the (eternal) life to come (1 Tim 4:8; 6:12, 19; 2 Tim 3:12; Titus 2:12).

ADAM; BODY; DEATH; GOD; LAW; RESURRECTION; RIGHTEOUSNESS; SPIRIT

Reading

Barclay, *Gift*, 500–503; Bultmann, *Theology* 1:345–52; Byrne, *PES*, 32, 132–33, 143–45, 159–67, 237–39; Schnelle, *Apostle Paul*, 577–88; L. Schottroff, *EDNT* 2:105–9; J. J. Scott Jr., *DPL*, 553–55; Wolter, *Paul*, 159–64.

LORD

Paul refers to God as "Lord" (*kyrios*) only in biblical quotations. Elsewhere, he reserves the title for Christ, usually in the wider formula "our Lord Jesus Christ." Whereas "Son of God" applies to Christ primarily regarding his relationship with God, "Lord" has to do with his relationship with believers and the universe as a whole.

"Lord" in Early Christian Usage

Paul's letters offer the earliest evidence for Christian use of "Lord" in relation to Christ. However, the very frequency of the title, its appearance in the opening grace and concluding formulas (Rom 1:7; 1 Cor 1:3; 2 Cor 1:2; 13:13; Gal 1:3; Phil 1:2; 1 Thess 1:1; Phlm 3; see also Eph 1:2; 6:23; 2 Thess 1:1; 1 Tim 1:2), and the fact that it never requires explanation suggest that it was something Paul inherited rather than coined himself. A significant clue to the origin of the address to Jesus as "Lord" is provided by the invocation *Maran–atha* in the closing greeting of 1 Corinthians

(16:22c). *Maran–atha* is a transliteration in Greek of an Aramaic phrase meaning "Our Lord, come!" suggesting that the invocation to Jesus in these terms goes back to the early Aramaic speaking community. No scriptural quotation occurs more frequently in the New Testament than the opening of Psalm 110: "The Lord said to my lord, 'Sit on my right hand'" (v. 1a). Interpreted in a messianic sense with reference to the postresurrection exaltation of Jesus, the text played a key role in the community's understanding of the resurrection as indicating or confirming his messianic status (see Rom 1:3–4). If this conviction was abroad already in the Aramaic-speaking community, the acknowledgment of Jesus as *mareh* and in due course in Greek as *kyrios* is likely to have had his status as Messiah particularly in view.

Christ as Lord in Relation to God

Beyond the messianic usage, however, the fact that the Aramaic *mareh* and its Greek equivalent *kyrios* were being used respectively by Semitic-speaking and Greek-speaking Jews as reverential substitutes for the sacred name for God (the tetragrammaton YHWH) points to the already high status accorded to the risen Jesus from the earliest moments of the Easter faith. *Kyrios* occurs 188 times in the undisputed Pauline letters (204 times if Colossians in included). In the clear majority of cases the reference is to Christ. In the minority of cases where the reference is to God, this, as noted above, always occurs in quotation from the Old Testament (Rom 4:8; 9:28–29; 11:34; 15:11; 1 Cor 3:20; 2 Cor 6:17–18); there are also cases where Paul supplies *kyrios* as a title for God where the equivalent is lacking in the original (Rom 11:3; 12:19; 1 Cor 14:21). Of high christological significance, however, is the fact that Paul applies to Christ as *kyrios* Old Testament texts where the original reference was to God (Rom 10:13; 1 Cor 1:31; 10:26; 2 Cor 10:17; possibly also Rom 14:11; 1 Cor 2:16). In 2 Corinthians 3:16–18, Paul applies Moses's "turning to the Lord" (Exod 34:34) as a paradigm of believers "turning to the Lord" in the sense of conversion to the risen Lord as Spirit. This interchangeability of reference to both God and Christ as "Lord" indicates that Christ enjoys a status closely and uniquely related to God.

Other Pauline texts confirm this. In 1 Corinthians 8:6, without further explanation, Paul cites an early Christian reformulation of the Shema confession from Deuteronomy 6:4. In the surrounding pagan milieu worship may paid to "so-called gods and lords" (v. 5), but

> 6 …for us there is one God, the Father, from whom are all things and for whom we exist, and one Lord [*heis kyrios*], Jesus Christ, through whom are all things and through whom we exist. (NRSV)

If God, as Creator, is source and goal for whom all exist, Christ as Lord is both mediator of creation and also the divine agent whereby that goal is attained (see Col 1:16; John 1:1–2). The supreme statement of Israel's monotheism has been adjusted to include Christ as Lord within the divine realm and operation.

Still more striking in connection with associating Christ as Lord with God is the concluding stanza of the hymnic passage in Philippians 2:6–11, which is generally considered to predate the composition of

Philippians and perhaps itself to be a rendering of an Aramaic original. The third stanza, verses 9–11, describes the divine response to the obedience of Christ (v. 8):

> 9 Wherefore God has highly exalted him
> and given him the name that is above every name,
> 10 so that at the name of Jesus every knee should bend,
> in heaven and on earth and under the earth,
> 11 and every tongue confess that
> Jesus Christ is Lord [*hoti kyrios Iēsous Christos*],
> to the glory of God the Father.

The "name that is above every name" is the divine title of "Lord" bestowed on the obedient Christ, risen and installed at God's right hand. The title is not simply honorific, it designates an active role in the universe. The phrases in verses 10a and 11a are taken from Isaiah 45:23 in a context where Israel's God as sole Creator invites all peoples to turn and be saved, acknowledging the divine dominion over all. What is now described is a universal acknowledgment of the lordship of Christ in virtue of his bearing the divine name. But Christ is not requiring the universal acclaim for himself. As the final statement makes clear, it is all "for the glory of God the Father" (v. 11b), the One who has exalted and bestowed the name upon him. As in 1 Corinthians 8:6, there is complete unity between what is said of God and the status and function of Christ as Lord. What is set out in 1 Corinthians 15:23–28 as a process yet to be completed—Christ's "subjection" of all powers to the rule of God, to whom he will himself become "subject" (vv. 27c–28)—is stated here in the timeless perspective of a liturgical hymn.

Implications of Commitment to Christ as Lord

It is to this lordship of Christ that believers commit themselves in their fundamental act of faith: "If you confess with your lips that Jesus is Lord and believe in your heart that God raised him from the dead, you will be saved" (Rom 10:9; see also 1 Cor 12:3b: "No one can say 'Jesus is Lord' except by the Holy Spirit"). Moreover, the lordship of Jesus implies that those for whom he is Lord "belong" to him as slaves belong to their master; they have been "bought at a price" (1 Cor 6:20; see 7:23a)—the price of his costly death. They have exchanged a slavery to "weak and beggarly elements" (Gal 4:9) to become slaves of Christ, but in reality freed persons who belong to the Lord (1 Cor 7:22; see also Rom 6:16–23; 12:11; 14:8, 18; 16:18; see Col 3:24), to whom alone each one will have to give an account concerning their service (2 Cor 5:10; see Rom 14:12).

Contexts Where "Lord" Is Prominent

While "Lord" appears widely across the letters of Paul, it is prominent in three contexts in particular. It occurs with some frequency, first, in passages of ethical exhortation. Belonging to the Lord makes demands on how one lives and relates to others. Hence the multiple references to Christ as Lord in passages such as the plea for tolerance in the matter of dietary observance previously noted, Romans 14:1–23, and the series of instructions concerning sexual behavior in 1 Corinthians 5:1–8; 6:12–20; 7:1–40.

Second, "Lord" is prominent in passages of an eschatological nature. Significant in this connection are the frequent references to "the day of the Lord," an Old Testament phrase originally applying to God but now used with reference to the end-time return of Christ (1 Cor 1:8; 5:5; 2 Cor 1:14; 1 Thess 5:2; see also 2 Thess 1:9–10; 2:2). In 1 Thessalonians 4:13–18, Paul comforts those who mourn the loss of loved ones who have died with a description of the eschatological scenario at the coming of the Lord.

Finally, "Lord" appears in contexts discussing situations of worship, the most notable example being Paul's castigation of the Corinthians for the totally inappropriate way in which they are celebrating the Lord's Supper (1 Cor 11:17–34). Paul recalls the tradition he had received "from the Lord" (v. 23a) in order to remind the community of the meaning that "the Lord Jesus," on the night of his betrayal, had imprinted on it (vv. 23c–25). Hence, whenever they eat the bread or drink the cup they "proclaim the death of the Lord until he comes" (v. 26).

The triple occurrences of "Lord" in the eucharistic passage illustrate the wide range of time reference in which the title appears. The eschatological reference, which is perhaps primary, can be retrojected back to the sense of the Lord's presence in the community, whereby believers' current existence "in Christ" can equally be represented as "in the Lord" (Rom 16:2, 8, 11, 22; 1 Cor 4:17; 7:22; 9:1, 2; 11:11; 15:58; 2 Cor 2:12; Gal 5:10; Phil 2:29; 4:1, 4, 10; 1 Thess 5:12; Phlm 16). By the same token, Paul can refer to sayings, rulings, and instructions given by Jesus in his pre-passion ministry as derived from "the Lord" (1 Cor 7:10 [regarding divorce]; 9:14 [regarding support for preachers of the gospel]; 11:23–25 [eucharistic institution at the Last Supper]).

Hence "Lord" encompasses a wide range of contexts and situations in which believers in the Pauline churches referred to, called on, and worshipped Jesus, not precisely as equal to God but as participating in the transcendence of God in a unique degree, and worthy, on that account, of sharing the title (Lord) otherwise reserved to God alone. At the same time, more than any other title, *kyrios* expresses the depth of belonging and closeness to Jesus that characterizes the existence of believers and sets them on the path to salvation (Rom 10:9–13). The extent to which, if at all, the confession of Jesus as "Lord" in the Pauline churches represented a conscious challenge to the supreme earthly lordship vested in the Roman emperor (Horsley, Wright) remains a matter of controversy in Pauline scholarship at the present time.

"Lord" in the Deutero-Pauline Letters

The usage of "Lord" in Colossians and Ephesians does not notably differ from that in the earlier letters, save that the cosmic dimension of Christ's lordship, already seen in passages such as 1 Corinthians 8:6 and Philippians 2:9–11, is notably developed, as in the hymnic passages Colossians 1:15–20 and in the sevenfold "one" statement in Ephesians 4:4–6 summarizing the foundation on which the unity of the worldwide church rests: "One Lord, one faith, one baptism; one God and Father of all" (vv. 5–6a).

CHRIST; FAITH; GOD; PRINCIPALITIES AND POWERS; RESURRECTION; SON OF GOD

Reading

J. M. G. Barclay, "Why the Roman Empire Was Insignificant to Paul, " in *Pauline Churches and Diaspora Jews* (Tübingen: Mohr Siebeck, 2011), 363–87; Dunn, *Theology*, 244–52, Fee, *Pauline Christology*, 41–55, 120–41; 254–69, 393–401, 558–88; J. A. Fitzmyer, *EDNT* 2:328–31; "The Semitic Background of the New Testament *Kyrios*-Title," in *A Wandering Aramean: Collected Aramaic Essays* (Missoula, MT: Scholars Press, 1979), 115–42 (highly technical but classic study that remains indispensable); R. A. Horsley, ed., *Paul and Empire* (Harrisburg, PA: Trinity Press International, 1997); *Paul and the Roman Imperial Order* (Harrisburg, PA: Trinity Press International, 2004); L. W. Hurtado, *DPL*, 560–69; *Lord Jesus Christ*, 108–18; C. F. D. Moule, *The Origin of Christology* (Cambridge: Cambridge University Press, 1977), 35–46; J. L. Sumney, *Steward of God's Mysteries: Paul and Early Church Tradition* (Grand Rapids: Eerdmans, 2017), 41–69; Wright, *PFG*, 661–70, 680–90, 701–6, 1271–1319.

LORD'S SUPPER (*see* Eucharist)

LOVE

"Love" in Paul is expressed by the Greek noun *agapē* and various forms of the cognate verb *agapaō*. The topic features in all the letters and, as is well known, receives a sustained description as the "greatest" of the Spirit's gifts in 1 Corinthians 13. Paul thinks of a cascade of divine love descending from God the Father, supremely displayed in the sending and self-gift of the Son, and palpable in the experience of the Spirit. The experience of divine love calls forth a return of love on the part of human beings—to God, to fellow believers, and even to the wider society as well.

God's Love

God's love is basic to the argument for hope in the face of the sufferings of the present time that Paul offers in Romans 5—8, a section of the letter that in fact begins and ends with love (5:1–11; 8:31–39). Those justified through faith (5:1) have hope because God's love (not human love for God) has been "poured out into our hearts through the Holy Spirit that has been given us" (5:5). To bolster this sense of divine love communicated through the experience of the Spirit, Paul recalls the Christ event in two "waves" of argument resting on an *a priori* logic (vv. 6–9 and 10):

1. What supremely shows God's love for us is that it was while we were *sinners* that Christ died for us (vv. 6, 8). How much more, then, now that we have been jus-

tified through the shedding of his blood, can we be certain that "we shall be saved from the wrath," that is, final condemnation at the judgment (v. 9)?

2. If when we were at *enmity* with God, we have been reconciled to God through the death of God's Son, how much more, now that we are reconciled (is it certain that), "we shall be saved by his life" (v.10), that is, his resurrection.

Noteworthy here is the total continuity between the love of God the Father and the self-sacrificial act of Christ (see also Eph 1:6).

The same continuity of divine love returns in the concluding passage (Rom 8:31–39), which begins with the defiant challenge, "If God is for us, who can be against us?" (v. 31) and continues in a way that recalls the argument of 5:6–10: "(God) who did not spare his own Son but gave him up for us all, how could it be that he would not with him give us all things?" (v. 32), that is, the fullness of salvation. The phrase "did not spare his own Son" alludes to Abraham's near sacrifice of his son Isaac (Gen 22:16). What God did not in the end require of the patriarch, God, in an extremity of love for sinful humanity, required of Godself. What, Paul asks, could separate us from the love of Christ (v. 35a)? He lists (v. 35b) trials that might be thought to do so, but then, with the aid of Scripture (LXX Ps 43:23, cited in v. 36), claims that "in all these things we are more than conquerors through the one who has loved us" (*dia tou agapēsantos hēmas*, v. 37), presumably alluding once again to the divine love displayed in the Christ event (see v. 32; see 1 Thess 1:4; Col 3:12). The sequence concludes asserting that nothing—certainly none of the spiritual powers listed at length (vv. 38–39a)—will separate us from the love of God that has come to us in Christ Jesus (v. 39b), that is, in the costly love displayed in his death.

Paul draws 2 Corinthians to a conclusion with the hope that if the community live in peace with one another, "the God of love and peace" will be with them (13:11a). The celebrated "trinitarian" grace formula at the end places "the love of God" between "the grace of our Lord Jesus Christ" and "the communion of the Holy Spirit" (v. 13).

Christ's Love

While the love of Christ is ultimately inseparable from that of God the Father, there are places where Paul singles out Christ's own love. The most personal expression comes in Galatians 2:19–20: with his old self "co-crucified" with Christ (v. 19), he now lives "by faith in the Son of God, who loved me and gave himself up for me" (v. 20). Paul again recalls the love of Christ when defending his apostolic behavior in the face of criticism from members of the community in Corinth (2 Cor 5):

> [14] For the love of Christ [*hē agapē tou Christou*] urges us on, because we are convinced that one has died for all; therefore all have died. [15] And he died for all, so that those who live might live no longer for themselves, but for him who died and was raised for them.

The love that Christ displayed in dying "for all" is not just a memory of a generous act in the past. It continues to be the driving and motivating force of how Paul lives and how all believers should live: not for themselves, but for him who died and was raised for them (see Rom 15:3: "Christ did not please himself").

Human Love

Paul obviously understands that the love believers have received from God in Christ will be reciprocated by their loving God in return (1 Cor 8:3). However, this God-directed love finds expression mainly in rather stock phrases from the Jewish tradition such as "those who love God" (Rom 8:28; 1 Cor 2:9), where it refers simply to the elect community.

Paul presumably is aware of Jesus's bringing together the twin commandment of love of God and neighbor (Matt 22:37–39; Mark 12:29–31; Luke 10:27; see Deut 6:4–5; Lev 19:18). His reference in Romans 13:8 to love fulfilling "the other law" (*ton heteron nomon*)—that is, the commandments concerning the neighbor—implies the existence of a primary law requiring loving God. However, the vast majority of references to love in Paul have to do with the love that believers should have for one another in response to the grace and love they have received from God. The extended sequence in Romans 13:8–10, where he speaks of the whole law as being summed up (*anakephalaioutai*) by the commandment, "You shall love your neighbor as yourself" (v. 9) and of love as the "fulfillment [*plērōma*] of the law" (v. 10), is skillfully introduced by a play on the word *debt* introduced from the preceding instruction (13:1–7). The only "debt" believers should have is the totally unpayable debt stemming from the immensity of the love they have received from God. They discharge this debt owed to God by love of the neighbor. The same sense of the entire law being fulfilled in the single command to love one's neighbor as oneself appears more briefly in Galatians 5:14 and is perhaps also implied in the fulfillment through the Spirit of the "righteous requirement of the law" (*to dikaiōma tou nomou*) in Romans 8:4 (see also Gal 5:22, where "love" appears first in the list of the "fruit" of the Spirit). Distinctions promoted by the law (such as circumcision or the lack of it) do not count for anything; the only thing that matters is "faith finding expression in love" (*pistis di' agapēs energoumenē*) (5:6).

The paraenetic portions of Paul's letters are replete with injunctions to love (Rom 12:9; 14:15; 1 Cor 8:1; 14:1; 16:14; 2 Cor 2:8; 6:6; 8:7–8, 24; Gal 5:13; Phil 1:9; 2:1–2; 1 Thess 1:3; 3:6; 3:12; 4:9; 5:8, 13; Phlm 5, 7; see Col 1:4, 8; 2:2; 3:14, 19). In several places, Paul also protests his love for the community (1 Cor 4:21; 16:24; 2 Cor 2:4; 11:11; 12:15; 1 Thess 3:12; Phlm 9).

All comes to a head, however, in 1 Corinthians 13, where Paul mentions love (*agapē*) nine times in a rhetorical "praise" (encomium) of love in order to place the Corinthians' estimation of the gifts of the Spirit in a perspective where, as is right, love is supreme. Paul first (vv. 1–3) goes one by one through gifts and virtues highly esteemed by the Corinthians (tongues, prophecies, knowledge of mysteries, faith sufficient to move mountains, and even extremities of virtue and self-sacrifice) and in each case, reduces them to nothing if they are not accompanied by love. There follows (vv. 4–7) a description of love in action—what it does and what it refrains from doing. Fundamental is the principle expressed earlier in the letter: "Love builds up" (1 Cor 8:1c). Love does not look to its own advantage but always serves to build up the other person. The final section, 13:8–13, is a sustained comparison between love and other gifts such as tongues, prophecies, and knowledge. The virtues listed in the famous triad "faith, hope, and love" (see Gal 5:5–6; 1 Thess 1:3; 5:8; see also Col 1:4–5) all, for the present, "remain" (v. 13a), but love is "greater" than the other two (v. 13b), presumably because it will never fall away (v. 8a): it alone already partakes of the eternity of God. Hence the conclusion (14:1): "*Pursue* [*diōkete*] love"—not, as the verb might at first suggest, as a virtue to be acquired by human effort, but rather in the sense of valuing and seeking love as the highest of all divine gifts.

Love in the Later Pauline Letters

Colossians locates the origin of the love that should flourish in the believing community in the love of the Father, "who has rescued us from the power of darkness and transferred us into the kingdom of the Son of his love ("his beloved Son") (1:13), so that believers should think of themselves as "God's chosen ones, holy and beloved" (*ēgapēmenoi*) (3:12; see 2 Thess 2:13, 16; 1 Tim 1:14; 2 Tim 1:13), responding in love for God (Col 2:2; see 2 Thess 3:5) and for each other (Col 1:4, 8; 3:19; see 2 Thess 1:3), "clothing" themselves with love, which is "the bond of perfection" (*syndesmos tēs teleiotētos*) (Col 3:14). In the Pastoral Letters, love has become one of the characteristic Christian virtues (1 Tim 1:5; 2:15; 4:12; 6:11; 2 Tim 1:7; 2:22; 3:10; Titus 2:2).

In Ephesians, love has become a truly central theme. God has "chosen us in Christ before the foundation of the world to be holy and blameless before him in love" (1:4). "God, who is rich in mercy, out of the great love with which he loved us, even when we were dead through our trespasses, made us alive together with Christ" (2:4–5). Paul's prayer is that Christ should "dwell in your hearts through faith, as you are rooted and grounded in love" (3:17), knowing "the love of Christ that surpasses knowledge, so that you may be filled with all the fullness of God" (3:19). This "chain" of love, which reaches back to the Father's pretemporal design and is made palpable in Christ ("the Beloved" [1:6]), should then find expression in the community's love (4:2), as it grows together into the full stature of Christ, building itself up in love (4:15–16; 5:2). A particular expression is the love that husbands should have for their wives (5:25–33), modeled on the love with which "Christ loved the church and gave himself up for her" (v. 25). The letter closes with an expression of "love, with faith from God the Father and the Lord Jesus Christ" (6:23) and "Grace be to all who have an undying love for... Christ" (v. 24), drawing the entire exhortation together around the theme of love.

CHRIST; CHURCH; DEATH; ETHICS; GOD; LAW; SIN; SPIRIT; SUFFERING

Reading

S. C. Barton, *ECB*, 1342–43; Dunn, *Theology*, 649–61; V. P. Furnish, *The Love Command in the New Testament* (London: SCM, 1973), 91–131; W. Klassen, *ABD* 4:392–93; J. S. Kloppenborg, *NIDB* 3:709–11; Matera, *GSG*, 176–81, 236–40; R. Mohrlang, *DPL*, 575–78; G. Schneider, *EDNT* 1:8–12; Schnelle, *Apostle Paul*, 221–22, 292–96, 356–57; Wolter, *Paul*, 192–96, 325–29; Wright, *PFG*, 429–31, 1115–20.

M

MARRIAGE (*see* Sexuality; Mystery; Woman)

MERCY

"Mercy," normally expressed in Paul through the noun *eleos* and cognate verb *eleō*, although sometimes through *oiktirmoi*, becomes a sustained topic only in the Romans 9—11. This may be because of the large amount of scriptural (Old Testament) texts that Paul cites in this section of the letter, mercy being a characteristic of God's dealing with Israel. In the Septuagint, *eleos* frequently translates *khesed*, which has the basic sense of covenant loyalty, although often with a nuance of kindness and mercy (see, e.g., 1 Sam 20:8, 14). In the postexilic period, *eleos* particularly denotes the mercy of God in maintaining covenant faithfulness in the face of Israel's infidelity and sin (e.g., [LXX] Psalm 50:3, where *eleos* stands in parallel to "the abundance of your mercies" [*to plēthos tōn oiktirmōn sou*]; see also [LXX] Ps 68:17; Isa 54:7; 60:10; [LXX] Jer 49:12; [LXX] Dan 3:35; 9:9), coming close to the Pauline sense of God's grace operative where merit is lacking on the human side.

Mercy in Romans 9—11

In Romans 9—11 Paul confronts the issue of Israel's "No" to the gospel in a series of stages, the first being to assert God's sovereign freedom to deal with human beings without regard to worth or merit on their part. By way of scriptural examples he points to the choice of the (deceitful) Jacob over his brother Esau (9:10–13), then moves to the exodus generation, citing the contrasting ways in which God dealt with Moses and Pharoah. To Moses God said, "I will have mercy [*eleēsō*] on whom I have mercy [*eleō*], and I will have compassion on whom I have compassion" (Rom 9:15, citing [LXX] Exod 33:19). All of this shows that "it depends not on human will or exertion, but on God who exercises mercy" (*tou eleōntos theou* [Rom 9:16]). Pharaoh, on the contrary, God "hardens" (*sklērynei*) in order (in the exodus) to display divine power to the ends of the earth (v. 17). Hence, God "has mercy on whomsoever he chooses, and hardens the heart of whomsoever he chooses" (v. 18). This biblical principle applies to the present state of affairs, where Israel appears in a "Pharaoh" situation of hardening. To display wrath and power God has endured with great patience "vessels of wrath, ripe for destruction" (v. 22), while "to make known the riches of his glory," God has prepared "vessels of mercy" (*skeuē eleous*) for glory (v. 23), the "vessels" in each case to be identified with as yet unbelieving Jews and Gentile believers respectively.

This conception of the free operation of divine mercy returns in the final passage of the section where Paul, disclosing a "mystery," foresees the eventual salvation of "all Israel." This will occur, however, not in the order that might have been expected (Israel first, Gentiles later), but only after the full number of the Gentiles has entered in (11:25–26). Israel's current "No" has facilitated the gospel's going forth to the Gentile world (see 11:11–15). So, addressing Gentile believers, Paul asserts, "Just as you were once disobedient to God but have now received mercy [*ēleēthēte*] because of their disobedience [v. 30; see v. 23], so they have now been disobedient in order that, by the mercy [*eleei*] shown to you [see also 15:9], they may now receive mercy [*eleēthōsin*]" (v. 31). And Paul concludes, "For God has imprisoned all in disobedience so that he may be merciful [*eleēsē*] to all" (v. 32; see Gal 3:22–23). In sum, Paul views the paradoxical situation of Israel's current failure regarding the gospel—a failure exacerbated by contrast with the positive response on the part of Gentiles—within the overall desire of God to be and act as a God of mercy. In regard to all human beings, Jews and Gentiles alike, divine mercy, rather than human success or failure, has the last word (see the echo of this in Titus 3:5). It is perhaps in anticipation of this daring theological vision concerning Israel that Paul concludes his, otherwise highly polemical, letter to the Galatians with the prayer wish of "peace and mercy" (*eirēnē kai eleos*) on "the Israel of God" (6:16), although Paul gives no clue that he is understanding the latter phrase in a Jewish ethnic rather than inclusive Christian sense.

Mercy Elsewhere in Paul

Compared to the theological vision regarding mercy deployed in Romans 9 and 11, Paul's other references to mercy are far more conventional in nature. Continuing perhaps the theme from Romans 11, Paul's paraenesis begins in Romans 12:1 with an appeal "through the mercies of God" (*dia tōn oiktirmōn tou theou*; see 2 Cor 1:3; see also Eph 2:4 ["God, who is rich in mercy"]). Paul speaks of himself as one who has received his ministry through the exercise of divine mercy (1 Cor 7:25; 2 Cor 4:1; see also 1 Tim 1:13, 16). God has displayed mercy in saving Epaphroditus from a near-fatal illness (Phil 2:27). Within the community, the one who exercises mercy (*ho eleōn*)—presumably a ministry of care for the disadvantaged is in view—should do so with cheerfulness (Rom 12:8). Compassion (*oiktirmoi*) should be a particular feature of communal life (Phil 2:1; see also Col 3:12).

COVENANT; FREEDOM; GENTILE; GOD; GRACE; ISRAEL; SIN

Reading

Barclay, *Gift*, 420–21, 520–61; J. M. G. Barclay, "'I Will Have Mercy on Whom I Have Mercy': The Golden Calf and Divine Mercy in Romans 9—11 and Second Temple Judaism," *Early*

Christianity 1 (2010): 82–106; R. Bultmann, *TDNT* 2:482–85; Byrne, *Romans*, 392–93; Dunn, *Theology*, 509–14, 526–32; S. Eastman, "Israel and Divine Mercy in Galatians and Romans," in *Between Gospel and Election: Explorations in the Interpretation of Romans 9—11*, ed. R. Wilk and J. R. Wagner (Tübingen: Mohr Siebeck, 2010), 147–70; "Israel and the Mercy of God: A Re-Reading of Galatians 6:16 and Romans 9–11," *NTS* 56 (2010): 367–95; L. Morris, *DPL*, 601–2; L. Ryliškytė, "God's Mercy: The Key Thematic Undercurrent of Paul's Letter to the Romans," *CBQ* 81 (2019): 95–105; F. Staudinger, *EDNT* 1:429–31.

MESSIAH (*see* Christ)

MIND

Paul's use of "mind" (*nous*) stems from the Hellenistic rather than the biblical background of his anthropology. *Nous* describes the human person as a knowing, reasoning, and judging being. It can also designate the *result* of such processes and so indicate the "understanding" that has been formed (Phil 4:7) or the "will" or "intention," as in the text from (LXX) Isa 40:13 ("Who has known the mind of the Lord" [*noun Kyriou*]), cited in Romans 11:34 and 1 Corinthians 2:16. In this respect "mind" overlaps in Paul with the more biblical concept of "heart" (Hebrew *lēb*; Greek *kardia*; see 2 Cor 3:14–15; Rom 1:21, 28; Phil 4:7). Both "mind" and "heart" express the core of the person, the reasoning, intending, purposing self from which all outward action flows. Paul prays that the Corinthians may be "united in same mind [*en tō autō noi*] and the same purpose" (1 Cor 1:10; see also 2 Thess 2:2).

Paul's Preference for the Intelligible

The high premium Paul places on the rational, the intelligible as opposed to the "mindless," the irrational, is shown in 1 Corinthians 14. Addressing the Corinthians' esteem for gifts of the Spirit of a more ecstatic nature, notably tongues, Paul states his clear preference for gifts where the mind is engaged. When a person prays solely in tongues, although the human spirit (*pneuma*) is engaged, the mind (*nous*) is "unproductive" (*akarpos*) (14:14). There is no scope for an interpretation that may build up the community (see vv. 3–5). Far better to pray with both spirit and mind so that this wider good may be accomplished (vv. 15–17). In the assembly (*ekklēsia*), Paul would rather speak five words with his mind, in order to instruct others, rather than ten thousand in tongues (v. 19).

The intrinsic goodness of mind emerges also in Paul's portrayal in Romans 7:14–25 of the ethical dilemma of the human person ("I") confronted with the requirements of the Mosaic law. The parallelism in verses 22 and 23 shows that "mind" corresponds to what Paul calls the "inner person" (*ho esō anthrōpos*): the true self as distinct from outward manifestation (see 2 Cor 4:16). As regards the "inner man" the "I" agrees with the law of God and wills to fulfill it (see vv. 15–16, 18b–19, 22). But the "I" sees "another regime [*nomon*] operating in my members, fighting against the law of my mind" (v. 23; see v. 25b). Although good of itself and desirous of doing the good, the mind lacks the capacity to prevail against the indwelling regime of sin that holds the "I" captive (vv. 14, 17, 20b, 23). That capacity only returns when, as a result of the sending of the Son, the Spirit replaces sin as the indwelling, determining power (Rom 8:1–11).

The Mind Perverted

The mind can also be perverted. Describing at length the alienation of the Gentile world from God in Romans 1:18–32, Paul maintains that human beings, although able to know God through the revelation of the divine power and glory in the created world (vv. 19–20), did not respond with glorification and thanks (v. 21a). Instead, "they became futile in their thinking [*en tois dialogismois autōn*] and their senseless hearts were darkened" (v. 21b). Since they did not think God worthy of recognition), God "gave them up to a worthless mind [*eis adokimon noun*] that led to improper conduct" (v. 28), examples of which are then listed at length (vv. 29–31).

The Mind Renewed

The perversion of the human mind (see Eph 4:17; Col 2:18; 1 Tim 6:5; 2 Tim 3:8; Titus 1:15) is not, however, the end of the story. "Mind" features significantly in the couplet with which the paraenesis of Romans begins 12:1–2. Exhorting the audience to present their "bodies as a living sacrifice, holy and acceptable to God, the worship owed as rational beings" (*tēn logikēn latreian*), Paul continues:

> Do not be conformed to this world but be transformed by the renewal of your mind [*tē anakainōsei tou noos*], that you may discern [*eis to dokimazein*] what is the will of God: what is good and acceptable and perfect. (v. 2)

Transformed by the renewal that has taken place in Christ, the mind that had become worthless as regards right moral discernment (1:28) now has the capacity to truly discern God's will, enabling believers to offer, in their bodily life, the "worship" that they owe as rational beings. They may no longer look to the Jewish law as moral guide; instead, with their renewed minds (see also Eph 4:23) they discern how the essential values it enshrines are to be lived out in the new creation (see Rom 14:5).

BODY; DISCERN; ETHICS; HEART; LAW; PROPHECY; SIN; SPIRIT

Reading

R. Bultmann, *Theology*, 1:211–16; Byrne, *Romans*, 63–79, 224–34, 362–67; J. K. Chamblin, *DPL*, 765–75; Dunn, *Theology*, 73–75; Fitzmyer, *Romans*, 126–27; Jewett, *Anthropological Terms*, 358–90, 450–51; A. Sand, *EDNT* 2:478–79; Schnelle, *Apostle Paul*, 536; Stacey, *Pauline View of Man*, 198–205; Wells, *Grace and Agency*, 227–31; Wright, *PFG*, 1120–25.

MINISTRY

In Paul, the topic of "ministry" gathers around the word group *diakon–*: *diakoneō* ("serve"); *diakonos* ("minister"/"deacon"); *diakonia* ("ministry"/"administration"). If a basic idea is to be detected in this word group it is that of action undertaken as the agent *of* another or of providing some service *to* another party. Paramount, then, is the sense of mediation. The word group appears in Paul with respect both to the ministering of the gospel to outsiders and to services of various kinds rendered within the believing communities.

Paul employs the noun *diakonos* in the general sense of any agent of another power. The official who exercises civic authority is to be respected, for he is "God's minister [*theou diakonos*] for your good" (Rom 13:4). Just as people can be "ministers of Christ [*diakonoi Christou*]" (2 Cor 11:23; see also 1 Tim 4:6), so too those who are in reality "ministers of (Satan)" can disguise themselves as "ministers of righteousness [*diakonoi dikaiosynēs*]" (2 Cor 11:15). But Paul dismisses with horror the suggestion—possibly an objection thrown at him—that seeking to be justified in Christ could in any way be construed as tantamount to making Christ "a minister of sin [*hamartias diakonos*]" (Gal 2:17).

The Apostolic Ministry of the Gospel

The most important ministry (*diakonia*) that Paul performs is that of evangelization. He and Apollos are "ministers through whom you (the Corinthians) came to faith [*diakonoi di' hōn episteusate*]" (1 Cor 3:5). In proclaiming the gospel to the Gentile world, he makes his fellow Jews aware of the success of this ministry (*tēn diakonian mou doxazō*) in the hope that, by provoking them to jealousy, he might save some (Rom 11:13–14). Responding to the demand in Corinth to present letters of recommendation (2 Cor 3:1), Paul responds that the Corinthians themselves are his letter (v. 2), "a letter of Christ, supplied by us [*diakonētheisa hyph' hēmōn*], written not with ink but with the Spirit of the living God" (v. 3). His apostolic accreditation comes from God, who "has accredited us to be ministers of a new covenant [*diakonous kainēs diathēkēs*]" (v. 6). The accreditation stems from the superior glory that attends the administration (*diakonia*) of the new covenant, which is one of righteousness leading to life, in contrast to the inferior and fading glory that attended Moses's administration (*diakonia*) (of the law), which was one of condemnation, leading to death (vv. 7–11). The *diakonia* in each case refers to the promulgation of a covenant by a divinely appointed minister (Moses and Paul, respectively). Having been "engaged in this ministry [*echontes tēn diakonian tautēn*]" by God's mercy, Paul does not lose heart (4:1). God has reconciled the world to himself through Christ and has given "us (the apostles) the ministry of the reconciliation [*tēn diakonian tēs katallagēs*]" (5:18). The fundamental reconciliation of the world has been achieved by God in Christ. It is Paul's task as *minister* (*diakonos*) to *pass on* (*diakonein*) that gift of reconciliation to others. He and his team strive to put no obstacle in anyone's way "lest fault be found with the ministry [*diakonia*]" (6:3); rather, they "commend themselves as

God's ministers [*theou diakonous*]," with endurance of multiple afflictions (vv. 4–10). This is the essential task and mode of ministry according to Paul (see 11:23–33; see also Eph 3:7; 4:12; Col 1:23, 25; 1 Tim 1:12; 2 Tim 4:11).

Ministry within the Community

Within the believing community there are "various kinds of services [*diaireseis diakoniōn*]" (1 Cor 12:5), which work to the common good (v. 7) because they are all inspired by the same Spirit. In the quasi-parallel listing of charismatic gifts (*charismata*) in Romans 12:3–8 "the (gift) of service (shown) in (the exercise of) serving [*diakonian en tē diakonia*]" (v. 7) would seem to have a more concrete reference, possibly to financial relief provided to the poorer members by specially designated officials. To what extent those who exercised this role were regarded in the time of Paul as "deacons" in the sense of holders of a stable office within the church is disputed. The question arises acutely in regard to the description of Phoebe as a "deacon [*diakonos*] of the church in Cenchreae" (16:1), as also in Paul's singling out "overseers [*episkopoi*] and deacons [*diakonoi*]," along with "all the saints" in the opening address of Philippians (1:1). The description "faithful minister" (*pistos diakonos*) applied in Colossians to Epaphras (Col 1:7) and Tychicus (Col 4:7; see also Eph 6:21) suggests a faithful service of Paul and the community in general rather than a stable office (see Phlm 13). But the latter is certainly the case when deacons are mentioned in the post-Pauline Pastoral Letters (1 Tim 3:8–10, 12–13) and possibly also with reference to the injunction in Colossians 4:17 to Archippus to "fulfill the ministry [*diakonian*]" he has received from the Lord.

The Ministry to the Saints

At the conclusion of his account of a meeting in Jerusalem where he won recognition of his law-free mission to the Gentiles (Gal 2:1–10), Paul mentions a commitment that he was happy to undertake as the quid pro quo for that recognition: to "remember the poor" (v. 10). The concrete form in which this remembrance was to take place, the collection for the "saints" (the mother church in Jerusalem), is a ministry (*diakonia*) that finds constant mention in his letters. No mere measure of financial relief, the collection in Paul's eyes was a symbol of the unity of the communities of believers (Jewish and Gentile) across the Greco-Roman world. Through it the Gentile communities founded by Paul acknowledged their spiritual debt to the community where faith in the Crucified Messiah had its origin and from which it had spread to them. By the same token, in graciously receiving the relief of the Pauline communities the mother church would also acknowledge their rightful presence in the community of the faith. When indicating his travel plans toward the end of Romans, Paul mentions that his hope is to come to Rome after he had completed the task of "ministering to the saints [*diakonōn tois hagiois*]" (15:25) and to this end begs his audience in Rome to pray that the ministry (*diakonia*) will find acceptance in Jerusalem (v. 31). At the end of 1 Corinthians, he gives detailed instructions concerning the gathering of this collection (16:1–4) and mentions how the house of Stephanas in particular had devoted themselves to this service to the saints (*eis diakonian tois hagiois*) (v. 15). A central block of 2 Corinthians (8:1—9:15) is entirely taken up with persuading the Corinthians to contribute to this ministry and with the arrangements Paul sets in place to guarantee its success (see 8:4, 19–20; 9:1, 12, 13) (see RICHES).

The "Ministry" of Christ

Behind all ministry on the part of believers lies a fundamental "service" of Christ. Concluding his exhortation to the believers in Rome for tolerance in matters of diet (Rom 14:1—15:13), Paul urges them to "accept one another as Christ accepted you to the glory of God" (15:7). He continues:

> [8] I declare that Christ has become a minister [*diakonon*] to the circumcision for the sake of God's truthfulness, in order to confirm the promises given to the fathers
> [9] and (he has performed a similar function) in the case of the Gentiles that they might glorify God for his mercy.

Christ is the *diakonos*, the accredited minister of the Father, in conveying to the whole of humanity the fruits of the divine faithfulness (literally, "truth") and mercy. It is tempting to relate this instance of *diakonos* to Christ's description of his mission as not having come "to be served [*diakonēthēnai*] but to serve [*diakonein*]" (Matt 20:28 // Mark 10:45). However, the "servant/slave" note prominent in the gospel pericope (Matt 20:26–27; Mark 10:43–44) stems from the context; it is not intrinsic to the meaning of the *diakon–* word group.

APOSTLE; CHRIST; COVENANT; GENTILES; GIFT(S) OF THE SPIRIT; GLORY; MOSES; RECONCILIATION; RICHES, POVERTY

Reading

Byrne, *Romans*, 428–33 (on Rom 15:7–13), 447–49 (on Rom 16:1–2); J. N. Collins, *Diakonia: Re-interpreting the Ancient Sources* (New York and Oxford: Oxford University Press, 1990); Dunn, *Theology*, 580–93; Holloway, *Philippians*, 66–67 (on Phil 1:1); L. E. Keck, "The Poor among the Saints in the New Testament," *ZNW* 56 (1965): 100–129, esp. 117–29; C. G. Kruse, *DPL*, 602–8; Matera, *GSG*, 142–46; Schnelle, *Apostle Paul*, 570–73; A. Weiser, *EDNT* 1:302–4.

MIRACLES (*see* Signs and Wonders)

MOSES

In Paul's estimate of biblical (Old Testament) figures, Moses takes a decided back seat to Abraham. Whereas God's dealings with Abraham prefigure the outreach of the gospel to the Gentile world, Moses is virtually synomous with the restrictive Sinai covenant and the law. It is perhaps too much to say that Paul depicts Moses as the "fall guy" in the divine scheme of salvation but in some contexts where he appears—notably the extensive midrash on Exodus 34:29–35 in 2 Corinthians 3:4–18—that is not far from the picture. What one can say is that Paul certainly privileges the covenant God made with Abraham over that emanating from Mount Sinai in the person of Moses (Rom 4:1–25; Gal 3:1–29).

Moses and the Sinai Covenant

Moses is mentioned by name only ten times in the Pauline letters as a whole, including an isolated reference to him as the object of rebellion on the part of Jannes and Jambres in 2 Timothy 3:8. He is not mentioned at all in Galatians, although he lurks in the background of Paul's portrayal in Galatians 3:15–29 of the Sinai dispensation as a later and temporary measure, unable to disturb the promise God made to Abraham focused solely and singly on Christ (v. 16). There is indeed an oblique reference to Moses in the passage when Paul, anxious to distance the law from God, speaks of it as "dispensed by angels at the hands of a mediator [*mesitēs*]" (v. 19) and goes on to explain, in a cryptic aside, that a mediator functions to deal with a plurality (here the angels), whereas God is one (v. 20). The portrayal of Moses in a mediatorial role, dealing with angels rather than immediately with God, contrasts with the promise "graciously given [*kecharistai*]" directly to Abraham by God (v. 18b; see v. 8).

In Romans, Moses receives a passing mention indicating the end of the period between Adam and the giving of the law ("from Adam to Moses" [5:14]), when death "reigned" over humankind, despite the absence of the kind of sinning—"transgression" (*parabasis*)—that the law, with its explicit indication of the will of God, facilitated (see 4:15b; 5:20a). Later, 9:15, Paul cites God's words "to Moses" in Exodus 33:19, "I will have mercy on whom I have mercy and I will have compassion on whom I will have compassion," as part of an extended scriptural argument defending the sovereign freedom of God to act without regard to the presence or lack of merit on the human side (v. 16). It is ironical, perhaps not unintentionally so, that Paul should recall God's statement of this principle to Moses, the figure par excellence of righteousness through practice of the law.

It is in fact in connection with such a role that Moses reappears in Romans 10:5–13 as the spokesperson for righteousness by law in so far as he "writes" (*graphei*) the text from Lev 18:5 that specifically links "doing" (*poiēsas* [v. 5b]) with the gaining of (eschatological) life (*zēsetai en autois*) (see Gal 3:12). Paul then sets over against this a further Pentateuchal passage, from Deuteronomy 30:11–14, in support of justification—and ultimately salvation—through a confession proceeding solely from faith (Rom 10:9–10). Based on Moses's authorship of the Pentateuch as a whole, the Deuteronomy passage is of course equally "Mosaic" and, in fact, in its original context, it features Moses pointing out the "ease" of fulfilling the requirements of the law. Paul, however, does not mention Moses in this connection. On the contrary, he disingenuously employs a text supposedly "written" by Moses to trump law-righteousness with the righteousness by faith proclaimed in the gospel. Shortly afterward, 10:19, Paul again simply introduces a further quotation from Deuteronomy (32:21) with "Moses says…."

Moses in 2 Corinthians 3

As previously mentioned, Paul's most sustained mention of Moses appears in the extended midrashic comparison in 2 Corinthians 3:4–18 between the promulgation of the old covenant by Moses and the new covenant proclaimed by the apostles. The old covenant, being one of "letter" was an administration of condemnation (v. 9) and death (vv. 6b, 7a). The new covenant, as one of Spirit, is an administration of (eschatological) life (v. 6c). If, nonetheless, the administration of death was, according to Exodus 34:29–35, attended by glory—the glory that shone on Moses's face to such an extent that the Israelites could not look on it v. 30)—how much more, Paul argues in defense of his apostolic credentials, must the promulgation of the administration of righteousness and life be attended by a surpassing credentialling glory (2 Cor 3:7–11).

Paul goes on, in verses 12–14, to interpret Moses's recourse to a veil to shield the Israelites from the glory radiating from his face (Exod 34:33–35) as an attempt to conceal that it was a fading glory, indicating the temporary nature of the covenant he was promulgating, although whether he sees this as involving an element of deception on Moses's part is not clear. In 2 Corinthians 3:15, the veil moves from Moses's face to rest on the unbelieving hearts of the present generation when "Moses," that is, the law, is read out. Finally, and more positively, he interprets Moses's removal of the veil when he returns to commune with God (v. 16; see Exod 34:34) as a foreshadowing of the removal of the "veil" of unbelief when those who do "turn to the Lord" in faith experience an "unveiled" vision of the glory of the Lord on the face of the risen Christ, who is the image of God (2 Cor 3:17–18; 4:4b, 6).

Nonpolemical References to Moses

In less polemical contexts Paul can simply appeal to what is "written in the law of Moses" concerning not muzzling an ox while it is treading out grain" (1 Cor 9:9a, citing Deut 25:4) as a scriptural warrant for the right of ministers of the gospel to be financially supported by the communities to whom they are sent. But his immediately following exclamation, "Does God care about oxen? (v. 9b). Does he not speak entirely for our sake? (v. 10a)," wrests the prescription into a meaning for the messianic age totally divorced from its original Mosaic context.

Paul's most intriguing reference to Moses appears as part of the extended warning against coming too close to idolatry in 1 Corinthians 10. He portrays the Israelites ("the fathers" [v. 1]) as having undergone a prefiguring of baptism through their being under the cloud and passage through the sea, which brought about their being "baptized into Moses" (v. 2). The concept of "baptism into Moses" is modeled on the Christian idea of baptism "into Christ" (Rom 6:3; 1 Cor 12:13; Gal 3:27), which is the primary analogue. Paul has no independent "theology" of Moses as corporate saving figure.

ABRAHAM; BAPTISM; COVENANT; GLORY; IDOLATRY; LAW; LIFE; RIGHTEOUSNESS

Reading

L. L. Belleville, *DPL*, 620–21; *Reflections of Glory: Paul's Polemical Use of the Moses-Doxa Tradition in 2 Corinthians 3:1–18* (Sheffield: JSOT Press, 1991); N. Bonneau, "Paul and the Biblical Figure of Moses," *TBT* 55 (September–October 2017): 341–47; Byrne, "Glory," 19–26; S. J. Hafemann, *Paul, Moses, and the History of Israel* (Peabody, MA: Henrickson, 1996), 92–110, 255–436; Hays, *Echoes*, 131–53; Wright, *PFG*, 677–80, 871–73, 980–84.

MYSTERY

The Greek word *mystērion*, from which the English *mystery* derives, basically refers to what is secret, especially in regard to knowledge or ritual. In Paul's day, it was widely used in the Greco-Roman world with reference to the mystery cults, such as those of Mithra and Isis. Such cults offered salvation in various forms to their initiates on the basis of secret rituals and esoteric knowledge, which members were forbidden to divulge.

Paul's usage of *mystērion* probably owes more to the late biblical background where the Greek term was used to translate the Semitic word *raz*, as in the Septuagint translations of Daniel (2:18, 19, 27–30, 47; see Wis 2:22; 6:22). *Mystery* is common in this sense in Jewish apocalyptic literature, including that of Qumran.

"Mystery" in the Letters of Paul

Countering the Corinthians' predilection for wisdom—"the wisdom of the world," which God has made "foolish" (1 Cor 1:20)—Paul insists that he did not come to Corinth "proclaiming the mystery of God [*to mystērion tou theou*] in high-sounding language or wisdom" (2:1). On the contrary, he had decided to "know nothing among you except Jesus Christ, and him crucified" (v. 2). What made it appropriate to speak of the content of the gospel as "mystery" was its focus on the Crucified Messiah, "a stumbling block to Jews, folly to Gentiles" (1:23). The plan of God to bring salvation to the world through the paradox of the Crucified Messiah reflected "the wisdom of God hidden in mystery [*theou sophian en mystēriō tēn apokekrymmenēn*]" (2:7) because precisely as "mystery" it eluded the capacity of unaided human understanding. Had the rulers of this world come to know it, "they would not have crucified the 'Lord of glory'" (v. 8) and so brought it to pass. In contrast to them, the mystery has been revealed "to us" through the Spirit (vv. 9–10). And *this* is what Paul speaks about, "not in words taught by human wisdom but taught by the Spirit" (v. 13a). Hence Paul and his fellow ministers should be thought of as "servants of Christ and stewards of the mysteries of God [*oikonomous mystēriōn theou*]" (4:1), accountable as such not to human judgment but solely to the Lord (vv. 2–4) (see WISDOM).

The sense of "mystery" as knowledge of heavenly matters not normally accessible to human understanding reappears later in 1 Corinthians. To "know all mysteries" (see also 2 Cor 12:2–4) is worthless if unaccompanied by love (13:2).

The gift of prophecy is to be preferred over tongues since the person who speaks in tongues, rather than communicating intelligibly to human beings, converses with God, "speak(ing) mysteries in the Spirit [*pneumati...lalei mystēria*]" (14:2). Unlike prophecy, this does not serve to build up and bring encouragement to the community (vv. 3–4).

Aside from reference to the basic gospel, Paul speaks of "mystery" in connection with eschatological events yet to occur. Israel's current "hardening" (*pōrōsis*) in regard to the gospel until the full number of Gentiles has entered in is a "mystery" that will end with her ultimate inclusion within the community of the saved (Rom 11:25–26). Likewise, Paul describes as a "mystery" the transformation of present, corruptible bodily life into the bodily form enlivened by the Spirit that will take place at the resurrection (1 Cor 15:51). At one level this may simply indicate that he is at a loss to explain it further (see v. 35), at another the description may hint at an event long hidden in the plan of God that will surely come to pass at the appropriate time (see 2:9). The phenomenon described as "the mystery of lawlessness [*to mystērion... tēs anomias*]" in 2 Thessalonians 2:7 represents a similar eschatological usage of the term.

"Mystery" in the Later Pauline Letters

"Mystery" emerges as almost a technical term in the deutero-Pauline literature, especially Colossians and Ephesians, perhaps as a conscious Christian attempt to take over the language of the mystery cults. The deutero-Pauline doxology at the end of Romans speaks of "the proclamation [*kerygma*] of Jesus Christ, according to the revelation of the mystery [*kata apokalypsin mystēriou*] kept secret for eternal ages but now disclosed through the prophetic writings" (Rom 16:25b–26a). Although the surrounding language is atypical of Paul, the use of "mystery" itself reflects the way he describes his preaching as "mystery" in 1 Corinthians 2:1, 7.

"Mystery" appears in Colossians to describe the fulfillment in Christ of God's design of salvation, hidden before the ages, but now revealed to "the saints" (Col 1:26). To these God has made known "the riches of the glory of this mystery [*to ploutos tēs doxēs tou mystēriou toutou*] among the Gentiles," which is "Christ among you, the hope of glory" (v. 27). Where in 1 Corinthians 2:1, 7 "mystery" referred to the paradoxical design of God to bring human beings to glory through the *Crucified* Messiah, here it seems to refer to "the riches" of God's glory in the extension of that hope to Gentiles, here represented by the recipients of the letter. As apostle to the Gentiles, "Paul" wants them to know how much he is struggling so that they (the Gentiles) may have "the knowledge of God's mystery, that is, Christ himself, in whom are all the treasures of wisdom and knowledge" (2:2–3). He asks for prayers that God may "open a door for the word," so that he may continue to "declare the mystery of Christ," for which, currently, he is in prison (4:3).

The significance of "mystery" in Ephesians is evident almost from the start. The opening thanksgiving (1:3–14) reviews the saving events that God has wrought in Christ as "making known the mystery of his will [*to mystērion tou thelēmatos autou*]," which is, at the fullness of time, to bring all things together in unity under

Christ as head (vv. 9–10). This divine project of unification has already gotten underway through Christ's overcoming the hostility between Jews and Gentiles when he reconciled both groups to God in one body through the cross (2:13–16). Hence the "mystery" that was not made known to humankind in former generations but has now been revealed is that "the Gentiles have become fellow heirs, members of the same body and sharers in the promise in Christ Jesus through the gospel" (3:4–6). The grace given specifically to "Paul" (see 3:3, 4) is that of "bringing to the Gentiles the news of the boundless riches of Christ and to make everyone see what is the plan of the mystery hidden for ages in God… so that through the church the wisdom of God in its rich variety might now be made known to the rulers and authorities in the heavenly places" (vv. 8–10 NRSV; see also 6:19). Here, as in Colossians (1:27; 2:2–3), the content of the mystery has to do with the inclusion of the Gentiles. The union of Jews and Gentiles "in the one body" (2:16) has rendered the church in its reconciled unity a witness to the power and wisdom of God, and a guarantee of the wider cosmic reconciliation yet to come (see 1:10).

The Pauline author again appeals to mystery when, toward the end of the letter, he encourages love between husband and wife (5:21–33). Citing (v. 31) the account in Genesis 2:24 of the first human couple, male and female, uniting to become "one flesh," he describes this union as a "great mystery [*to mystērion touto mega estin*]" and explains that he is applying it to the relationship between Christ and the church (v. 32).

In 1 Timothy "the mystery" has become identified with "the faith," the content of Christian belief (3:9), spelt out in a hymnic sequence as the "great mystery of our religion" [*mega...to tēs eusebeias mystērion*]" (v. 16).

APOSTLE; CHRIST; CHURCH; CROSS; GENTILES; GOSPEL; RECONCILIATION; WISDOM

Reading

R. E. Brown, *The Semitic Background of the Term "Mystery" in the New Testament* (Philadelphia: Fortress, 1968); A. E. Harvey, "The Use of Mystery Language in the Bible," *JTS* NS 31 (1980): 320–36; H. W. Hoehner, *Ephesians: An Exegetical Commentary* (Grand Rapids: Baker Academic, 2002), 428–34 (Excursus: "Mystery"); H. Krämer, *EDNT* 2:446–49; Lincoln, "Colossians," 614–15; *Ephesians*, liv–lv, 30–31, 174–88, 193–99, 380–84, 453–54; P. T. O'Brien, *DPL*, 621–23; Schnelle, *Apostle Paul*, 201–3; Thiselton, *1 Corinthians*, 210–11, 240–52, 1039–40, 1085–86.

N

NEW

The common adjective *new* (*kainos*; less frequently *neos*) has a more than ordinary resonance in Paul because of his conviction that in the resurrection of Christ the new age has already dawned. In the modification of Jewish apocalyptic expectation required by God's intervention in Christ believers live in an "overlap of the ages" situation. Although still anchored bodily in the present age, they are already part of the new creation, called to live out the hopes and values flowing from the resurrection.

The essential link of "new" to Christ's resurrection is patent in the assertion that "we have been buried with (Christ) through baptism into death, in order that, as Christ has been raised through the glory of the Father, so we too should walk in newness [*en kainotēti*] of life" (Rom 6:4). "Walk" has the biblical sense of how one should live before God. Believers should allow the ethical pattern of their lives to be conformed to the "new" situation in which, through baptism, they find themselves: dead to sin and alive in Christ with the newness of his resurrection (v. 11).

A New Creation

In two places Paul describes this transformation as involving nothing less than a "new creation." Reaching back to the language of (Second) Isaiah (43:18–19), he writes,

> So if anyone is in Christ, there is a new creation [*kainē ktisis*]: everything old [*ta archaia*] has passed away; see, everything has become new [*kaina*]! (2 Cor 5:17 NRSV)

And similarly toward the end of Galatians:

> For neither circumcision nor the lack of it (means) anything; there is simply a new creation [*alla kainē ktisis*]. (6:15)

Through faith and baptism "into" Christ (Rom 6:3; 1 Cor 12:13; Gal 3:27), believers have become part of the new creation, foretold in Isaiah (65:17; 66:22) and made a reality in the resurrection of Christ.

A New Covenant

The second concept to which "new" is particularly attached in Paul is that of "covenant." It is generally recognized that his references to a "new covenant" (*kainē diathekē*) (1 Cor 11:25; 2 Cor 3:6) presuppose the prophetic oracle of Jeremiah 31:31–34 where the Lord pledges to make a new covenant with the house of Israel (v. 31), promising "to put my law within them" and to "write it on their hearts" (v. 33). It is likely that Paul read this prophecy in close connection with the similar promise in Ezekiel 36:22–28: "A new heart I will give you, and a new spirit I will put within you; and I will remove from your body the heart of stone and give you a heart of flesh" (v. 26). The combination allowed Paul to identify the law placed "within" in Jeremiah's new covenant prophecy with the spirit (Spirit) placed within according to Ezekiel. Hence Paul in 2 Corinthians 3:6 can describe himself and his co-workers as "ministers of a new covenant, not of letter but of spirit (Spirit)," an administration of righteousness and life, in place of the "old covenant" (v. 14), which was one of death and condemnation (vv. 6b, 7a, 9a). Although "covenant" is not mentioned, the same distinction between old and new lies behind the reference in Romans 7:6 to the life of believers, set free from the law, as enlisted in a "service" (*douleuein*) of God in "newness of Spirit" (*en kainotēti pneumatos*) and not in "oldness of letter" (*en palaiotēti grammatos*). Finally, in the eucharistic tradition that Paul recalls in 1 Corinthians 11:23–26, the words over the cup attributed to the Lord are, "This cup is the new covenant [*hē kainē diathēkē*] in my blood" (v. 25; see also Luke 22:20). By sharing in the cup believers enter into and share the blessings of the new covenant brought about through the shedding of Christ's blood on the cross.

"New" in the Deutero-Pauline Letters

In the paraenesis of Colossians, the audience are reminded that they have cast off "the old self" (*palaion anthrōpon*) with its (evil) practices and have clothed themselves with "the new self" (*neon*), the one that is "being renewed [*anakainoumenon*] in knowledge according to the image of its Creator" (3:9–10). The old distinctions ("Greek"/"Jew," etc.) no longer apply (3:11).

This theme of unity between Jews and Gentiles is greatly developed in Ephesians. Christ, in his death, has abolished the law with its commandments and ordinances, and out of the two has created in himself one new human being (*kainon anthrōpon*), making peace (2:15). Later, in the paraenesis, the audience are reminded that they were taught to put off the "old self" (*palaion anthrōpon*) that belonged to their "former way of life" (4:22) and "to clothe" themselves with the new self (*kainon anthrōpon*), created according to the likeness of God (4:24). Behind this development stands the Pauline conception of participation in the new creation that God is bringing into being through Christ (see Rom 8:22).

ADAM; BAPTISM; BODY; COVENANT; CREATION; ETHICS; GENTILES; RESURRECTION; SPIRIT

Reading

W. S. Campbell, *DPL*, 179–83 ("Covenant and New Covenant"); Dunn, *Theology*, 146–50, 217–28; Fee, *Pauline Christology*, 513–23; J. C. Gibbs, *Creation and Redemption: A Study in Pauline Theology* (Leiden: Brill, 1971); J. R. Levison, *DPL*, 189–90 (Creation and New Creation); Matera, *GSG*, 118–20; Wolter, *Paul*, 86–87; Wright, *PFG*, 724–27, 980–84, 1091–95.

O

OBEDIENCE, OBEY, OBEDIENT

As a devout Jew, Paul would regularly have recited the summons contained in the Shema: "Hear, O Israel, the Lord is our God, the Lord alone" (Deut 6:4). "Hear" in Hebrew (*shm'*) also has the meaning "obey." The Shema summons Israel to be an "obedient" people, an obedience expressed in performance of the Mosaic law. Introducing himself in Romans, Paul describes the grace and apostleship he has received "to bring about an obedience of faith [*eis hypakoēn pisteōs*] among all the Gentiles" (Rom 1:5; see also 16:26). His role is that of calling from the Gentile world a new people, obedient not through practice of the law but through faith (see

15:18: "what Christ has accomplished through me to win obedience from the Gentiles [*eis hypakoēn ethnōn*]"). The "obedience" in view here is virtually equivalent to responding to the gospel with faith (see 10:16; 16:19; see also 2 Thess 1:8).

The Obedience of Life in Christ

For Paul the way people live out their faith is also an "obedience." In Romans 6:16, he employs a "transfer of slavery" image to describe believers' move from their former way of life to their present life in Christ. When a slave undergoes a transfer from one master to another, there is no cessation of obedience: the slave has to be obedient to the new master as previously to the former. What *can* change is the quality of life in the new situation and the effects produced. In their former situation, believers found themselves in an "obedience to sin," leading to death. Now, set free from sin, they have become "obedient to righteousness," leading to life. Paul seems to apologize for using the "slavery" image (v. 19a), especially, it would seem, for speaking of obedience in the negative as well as the positive case. He thanks God that his audience, having once been slaves of sin (see also 6:12), have now become "obedient from the heart to the pattern of teaching [*typon didachēs*]" to which they have been handed over (v. 17). The reference is obscure, but Paul seems to have in mind a contrast between the purely servile obedience that slaves are forced to render, whether they want to or not, and the new obedience of believers, which, flowing from the free choice of faith, involves a willing engagement of the whole person. And "the pattern of (ethical) teaching" is not something imposed from without but in fact the ethical example and influence of Christ whose risen person they have "entered" through faith and baptism.

Paul speaks of obedience more specifically in regard to his authority as an apostle. In the brief letter to Philemon, he asserts that, while being bold enough to command Philemon to do his duty, he prefers to appeal out of love (vv. 8–9). His confidence in Philemon's obedience (v. 21) suggests that he thinks of Christian obedience as proceeding out of love rather than constraint. Paul exhorts the Philippians to be as obedient to him in his absence as they have always been in his presence (2:12a; see also 2 Cor 2:9; 7:15 [obedience to Paul's emissary, Titus]; see also 2 Thess 3:14). His threat to enforce obedience in the polemical context of 2 Corinthians 10:5–6 appears to rest on the grounds that obedience to him as apostle is ultimately obedience to Christ: "We take every thought captive to obey Christ" (*eis tēn hypakoēn tou Christou*).

The Obedience of Christ

Behind all obedience on the part of believers stands the personal obedience of Christ. In Romans 5:19, Paul sets this obedience, which has opened up righteousness and life for all (v. 17b), over against the disobedience of Adam, which has led to sin and death for all (vv. 12, 17a). Whereas Adam disobeyed a specific prohibition of God (Gen 2:17; 3:1–7, 11b–12), Paul does not specify further the obedience of Christ, save to say, in the words of the Christ-hymn in Philippians that he was "obedient unto death" (*hypēkoos mechri thanaton*) (2:8). Christ was not obedient to a specific command of God. His obedience consisted in total embodiment in his incarnate life of the divine love that lay behind his mission from the Father (Rom 5:8–10, 15c; 8:3–4, 32; 2 Cor 5:14), a commitment that, in the historical context of his earthly life, inevitably brought him into conflict with the forces opposed to life and love. The lordship of the universe conferred on him in response to his obedience is directed "to the glory of the Father" (Phil 2:9–11; see also 1 Cor 15:27–28). As risen Lord, he continues to live out his obedience to the Father in the bodily life of believers, whose obedience he empowers as life-giving Spirit (1 Cor 15:45; see Rom 8:9–11; see also 6:10–13; Gal 2:19–20).

Obedience in the Later Pauline Letters

Obedience in the later Pauline letters is confined to exhortations contained in the Household Codes in Colossians and Ephesians. Children are to obey their parents (Eph 6:1–3; Col 3:20–21) and slaves their masters (Eph 6:5–9; Col 3:22–4:1). The injunction is tempered by an emphasis on reciprocity in the relationship in each case. The specific instruction that slaves should render service to their masters as to Christ reflects a seemingly unquestioning acceptance of slavery as an institution, along with a sense that all unalterable situations of present life are, for believers, relativized by the supreme advantage of belonging to the Lord (see 1 Cor 7:21–23; Col 3:17).

CHRIST; ETHICS; FAITH; GENTILES; HEART; LAW; SLAVERY; SPIRIT

Reading

Byrne, *PES*, 140–48, 159–67, 185–89; *Romans*, 40–41, 45–46, 199–208; G. N. Davies, *Faith and Obedience in Romans: A Study in Romans 1–4* (Sheffield: JSOT, 1990), 25–31; D. G. Garlington, *"The Obedience of Faith": A Pauline Phrase in Historical Context* (Tübingen: Mohr Siebeck, 1991), 11–13, 242–68; A. J. Goddard, "Paul and Obedience," in *One God, One People, One Future: Essays in Honour of N. T. Wright*, ed. J. A. Dunne and E. Lewellen (London: SPCK, 2018), 316–45; Holloway, *Philippians*, 124–25; Moo, *Romans*, 51–53; Rainbow, *Way of Salvation*, 204–9.

P

PEACE

"Peace" (*eirēnē*) most frequently occurs in the Pauline letters in the greeting or salutation that is the second element of the introduction, almost always preceded by "grace," as in Romans 1:7b: "Grace to you and peace from God our Father and the Lord Jesus Christ" (see also 1 Cor 1:3; 2 Cor 1:2; Gal 1:3; Phil 1:2; 1 Thess 1:1; Phlm 3; see also Eph 1:2; Col 1:2; 2 Thess 1:2; 1 Tim 1:2; 2 Tim 1:2; Titus 1:4). Where "grace" (*charis*) may be a Pauline adaptation of the Hellenistic greeting "*Chaire*," "peace" reflects the Septuagint's translation of the Semitic greeting, "peace be with you" (in Hebrew, *shalōm lekhem*). Prayer wishes for the gift of "peace" also appear in the closing stages of Pauline letters, especially in the farewell benedictions (Rom 15:13, 33; 2 Cor 13:11; Gal 6:16; Phil 4:7, 9; 1 Thess 5:23; see also Eph 6:23; 2 Thess 3:16). In this way Paul's letters are "enclosed" at beginning and end by the "bond of peace" (Eph 4:3).

The fact that the greetings qualify "grace and peace" as stemming "from God our Father and the Lord Jesus Christ" suggests that Paul is employing something more than a stereotypical formula. He is reminding his audience from the start that the atmosphere of grace and peace in which they now live stems from the saving work of God in Christ. Paul sends the greeting as the accredited emissary of the divine figures behind it.

Peace with God

The antithesis of "peace" is enmity. What makes it possible for Paul to send a greeting of peace is the fact that God has radically overcome the enmity that prevailed in divine-human relations prior to the divine intervention Christ. "Peace," then, for Paul is first and foremost peace with God. This emerges particularly in Romans 5:1–11. Following the extended statement of the justification God has made available to believers through the sacrificial death of Christ (Rom 3:21–26; 4:25), Paul begins the new section of the letter (5:1—8:39) with the assertion, "Justified then by faith, we have peace with God through our Lord Jesus Christ" (5:1). A few lines further on, elaborating the case for the hope of salvation that stems from the extremity of God's love already displayed in the Christ event (vv. 6–10), he writes, "For if, while we were enemies [*echthroi ontes*] we have been reconciled to God through the death of his Son, how much more surely, now that we have been reconciled, will we be saved through his life" (v. 10). Here, as more extensively in 2 Corinthians 5:18–21, the peace with God that believers enjoy is attributed to the divine work of reconciliation—a reconciliation stemming entirely from the side of God, who, in graciously reaching out to a hostile world, paid the cost of that outreach in the death of the Son (Rom 5:8; 8:32).

Peace in Christian Life

Paul thinks of peace as a defining characteristic of the ongoing life of believers both individually (1 Cor 7:15c; 16:11) and in assembly gathered for worship (14:33). It is particularly the gift of God (Phil 4:7, 9; see also 2 Thess 3:16) and one of the indicative "fruits" of the Spirit (Gal 5:22; see Rom 8:6; 14:17). The letters regularly contain exhortations to the fostering of peace within the community (Rom 14:19; 2 Cor 13:11; 1 Thess 5:13; see also Eph 4:3; Col 3:15; 2 Tim 2:22) and also with the surrounding world (Rom 12:18). In line with the Jewish apocalyptic tradition, in Romans 2:10 "peace" joins "glory and honor" as one of the eschatological benefits to which those practicing good may aspire.

Peace in the Deutero-Pauline Letters

The sense of divine peace-making through the reconciling work of Christ is greatly elaborated in the deutero-Pauline letters: first, in a cosmic sense, in Colossians 1:20–22 and then, more extensively, in Ephesians 2:14–18, a passage actually headed by the statement: "For he himself (Christ) is our peace" (v. 14a). The peace in view presupposes reconciliation with God (2:4–10, 16) but is more specifically peace in the "horizontal" sense as between Jews and Gentiles. Christ "has made the two one," breaking down "the dividing wall that is the hostility between us" (v. 14bc), "in order to create in himself one new humanity, making peace" (v. 15). Hence the gospel, proclaimed in first instance by Christ, may be described, echoing Isaiah 57:19, as "an announcement of peace" to those "far off" and to those "near" (v. 17; see also 6:15).

DEATH; GENTILES; GRACE; HOPE; LOVE; RECONCILIATION

Reading

Byrne, *Romans*, 164–72; W. Foerster, *TDNT* 2:411–20; V. Hasler, *EDNT* 1:394–97; E. M. Keazirian, *Peace and Peacemaking in Paul and in the Greco-Roman World* (New York: Peter Lang, 2014), 83–188; S. E. Porter, *DPL*, 695–99.

PERFECT, MATURE

The Greek word *teleios*, along with its cognate forms, *teleioō* and *teleiōtēs*, has the sense of that which is without blemish, that which has arrived at perfection in either a physical or moral sense, that which is mature (as of an adult in contrast to a child). In the Greco-Roman world of Paul's day, those who had undergone full initiation in the mystery cults were known as *teleioi*. It is unlikely, however, that his usage owes anything to this background. More influential is likely to have been the Septuagint's use of *teleios* to translate the Hebrew *tamim* in regard to those who are blameless in God's sight (Gen 6:9 [Noah]; Deut 18:13; 2 Sam 22:26; see also Wis 9:6; Sir 44:17).

Perfection for Paul: Past and Present

Regarding righteousness according to the law Paul speaks of his pre-conversion life as "blameless" (*amemptos*) rather than "perfect" (*teleios*) (Phil 3:6; see Gal 1:14). The description, however, amounts to much the same thing. In the passage from which it comes (Phil 3:2—4:1), his concern is to warn the community against succumbing to the kind of pressure to take on the practice of the Jewish law, especially circumcision (see 3:2–3, 19), that had been applied to his Gentile converts in Galatia. The Philippians should imitate his own steadfastness in not going back to the past that once had meant so much to him (v. 17). He is not yet "perfect" (*ouch ēdē teteleiōmai*) (v. 12), but, as though involved in a "race," leaving the past (his former impeccable Jewish credentials; see vv. 4–6) behind, he presses on to win the prize, which is the "upward" call of God in Christ Jesus (v. 14). "Perfection" now is to be fully conformed to the death of Jesus in order to gain a share in his resurrection from the dead (vv. 10–11). Paradoxically, although he has described himself as "on the way" to perfection (v. 12), he urges, "Let those of us who are *teleioi*, be of the same mind" (v. 15). The sense seems to be, "Let those of us who *would be* perfect, be of the same mind," that is, be of the same mind as himself: not going back to past ways (see v. 13b) but holding fast to what has been attained (v. 16).

Perfection in Christian Life

No longer reliant on the Jewish law for ethical guidance, believers now have the capacity to discern what living in accordance with the divine will requires. Their "renewed mind" allows them to "discern what is the will of God—what is good and well-pleasing (to God) and perfect" (*teleion*) (Rom 12:2).

In 1 Corinthians 1—4, Paul confronts a divisive aspiration on the part of members of the community in Corinth to receive instruction in terms of wisdom. Dismissing what he calls "the wisdom of the world" as totally incompatible with the gospel of the Crucified (1 Cor 1:18–25; 2:1–5), he then turns around and asserts, "Yet among the mature [*en tois teleiois*] we do speak wisdom, though not a wisdom of this age" (2:6). This is not to suggest that the community as a whole is divided into two groups: the mature and the immature. Rather, he is insisting that, if the community at Corinth were really mature it would, through the revelation of the Spirit (v. 10), be able to understand the message of the Crucified as truly divine wisdom, revealing what is in store for those who love God (vv. 7–16). The factions that exist among members of the community display their immaturity, requiring Paul to treat them as "infants" (*nēpioi* 3:1), rather than as mature in Christ (vv. 2–4; see also 14:20) (see WISDOM).

Christian Maturity in the Deutero-Pauline Letters

The Pauline sense of growth to Christian "maturity" is prominent in the deutero-Pauline letters. In Colossians, the aim is to "present (presumably on the day of the Lord) everyone mature [*panta anthrōpon teleion*] in Christ" (Col 1:28; see also 4:12). Love is "the bond of perfection" (*syndesmos tēs teleiotētos*) (3:14).

Christian growth to maturity finds its most striking expression in the discussion of the gifts given by Christ for the building up of the community in unity and love in Ephesians 4:7–16. The diverse gifts are all designed

> to build up the body of Christ, until we all attain…to full maturity [*eis andra teleion*], to the measure of the full stature of Christ [*eis metron hēlikias tou plērōmatos tou Christou*]. (vv. 12–13)

Christ is the head of the church, which is his body (1:23). The whole purpose of the gifts given to the community is that the body should grow into the full stature of its head, Christ (see 2:15 [*eis kainon anthrōpon*]).

BODY OF CHRIST; CIRCUMCISION; CROSS; ETHICS; LOVE; WISDOM

Reading

A. Asanang, "Perfection of God's Good Work: The Literary and Pastoral Function of the Theme of 'Work' in Philippians," *Conspectus* 23 (2017): 1–56; G. Delling, *TDNT* 8:75–77; H. Hübner, *EDNT* 3:342–48; W. W. Klein, *DPL*, 699–701; R. Schnackenburg, "Christian Adulthood according to the Apostle Paul," *CBQ* 25 (1963): 354–70; Schnelle, *Apostle Paul*, 353–55, 377; Thiselton, *1 Corinthians*, 224–26, 232–33.

POWER

This entry focuses on the word(s) for power in Pauline usage, not on power relations in the early communities in a sociological sense.

Paul speaks of "power" (*dynamis*; less frequently *kratos*, *ischyos*) chiefly in connection with direct manifestations of divine power or the empowerment of human beings by God for particular purposes. In the plural, "powers" (*dynameis*) can refer to miracles worked through divine power or, in a very different usage, to transcendent spiritual beings that impact on human life. For the latter see PRINCIPALITIES AND POWERS.

Manifestations of Divine Power

The divine power is revealed in creation: "Since the creation of the world God's eternal power [*hē...aïdios dynamis*] and deity has been clearly perceived in the things that have been made" (Rom 1:20); it is also revealed in divine saving acts (Rom 9:17, citing Exod 9:16; Rom 9:22). For Paul, however, the divine power has been supremely displayed in the raising of Christ from the dead (Rom 1:4; 1 Cor 6:14; 2 Cor 13:4; see Rom 6:4). The gospel, focused on his death and resurrection, is "the power of God leading to salvation [*dynamis...theou eis sōtērian*] for every believer" (Rom 1:16b), because it communicates to those who respond to it in faith the righteousness required for salvation (v. 17a). Thus, while the gospel announcement of the Crucified Messiah may be sheer folly to those who are being lost, for those who are being saved it is the power of God (*tois sōzomenois... dynamis theou*) (1 Cor 1:18; see v. 24).

Not only is the gospel a power leading to salvation, but its very proclamation is attended by manifestations of divine power, especially in the experience of the Spirit. Paul reminds the Thessalonians how the gospel came to them not just in word but "also in power and in the Holy Spirit [*en dynamei kai en pneumati hagiō*] and with full conviction" (1 Thess 1:5). More sharply, he reminds the Galatians about the circumstances of their hearing of the gospel, when God supplied the Spirit to them and "worked deeds of power" (*energōn dynameis*) among them (Gal 3:5). Paul's proclamation of the gospel from Jerusalem as far around as Illyricum has been attended "by the power of signs and wonders [*en dynamei sēmeiōn kai teratōn*], by the power of the Spirit of God" (Rom 15:19). His initial preaching at Corinth did not rely on persuasive words of wisdom but on demonstration of the Spirit and of power (*en apodeixei pneumatos kai dynameōs*); this was so that the faith of the Corinthians might rely "not on human wisdom but on the power of God" (*en dynamei theou*) (1 Cor 2:4–5; see 4:19–20). The "treasure" of the gospel is contained in fragile human vessels to show that its "overwhelming power" (*hē hyperbolē dynameōs*) stems not from the apostles but from God (2 Cor 4:7). The "signs and wonders and works of power" (*dynameis*) Paul performed at Corinth were the signs of a true apostle (2 Cor 12:12; see 6:7). Such "deeds of power" (*dynameis*) are included among the variety of gifts of the Spirit that should continue to flourish in the community (1 Cor 12:10, 28–29). They would include "miracles" in the sense that that term is usually understood but may go beyond it to include exorcisms (see Mark 6:5). (For a negative sense of such phenomena as worked by Satan, see 2 Thessalonians 2:9.)

At times Paul speaks of power more generally, as when he recounts how he begged the Lord three times that he be relieved of the "thorn in the flesh" but was told that divine grace was sufficient, since "power is made perfect in weakness [*hē...dynamis en astheneia teleitai*]" 2 Cor 12:8–9). Nonetheless, in summoning the Corinthians to call an assembly to expel a member living in open immorality, he assures them that when they do so his spirit will be present there with "the power of the Lord Jesus" (*syn tē dynamei tou kyriou hēmōn Iēsou*) (1 Cor 5:4).

Finally, Paul speaks of divine power in connection with the resurrection of believers. The (mortal) human body may be "sown in weakness, but it will be raised in power" (*egeiretai en dynamei*) (1 Cor 15:43b; see Rom 8:11; 1 Cor 6:14). On a more personal note, he describes how he presses on in his apostolic labor in order to "know Christ and the power of his resurrection [*tēn dynamin tēs anastaseōs autou*]," so that, having been conformed to the pattern of his sufferings and death, he may also attain resurrection from the dead (Phil 3:10–11). In contrast to the impotence of the law to give life (see Gal 3:21), the risen Christ, as "last Adam," has become "life-giving Spirit" (1 Cor 15:45). He will "transform the body of our lowliness so that it may be conformed to his glorious body, according to the power that enables him [*kata tēn energeian tou dynasthai auton*] to subject all things to himself" (Phil 3:21).

"Power" in the Deutero-Pauline Letters

"Paul" prays that the Colossians may be "strengthened with all power [*en pasē dynamei dynamoumenoi*] that comes from (God's) glorious might" (Col 1:11 ESV); he himself "struggles with all the energy that (Christ) powerfully [*en dynamei*] works" in him (1:29; see also Eph 3:7; 2 Tim 1:7, 8, 12). The sense of God's power at work within believers is particularly prominent in Ephesians. "Paul" prays that the audience may "know the immeasurable greatness of (God's) power [*to hyperballon megethos tēs dynameōs*] for us who believe" (1:19), that they may "be strengthened in their inner being with power [*dynamei krataiōthēnai...eis ton esō anthrōpon*] through the Spirit" (3:16). He gives glory to the One who "by the power [*tō dynamenō*] at work within us is able to accomplish far more than we could ask or imagine" (v. 20). In the spiritual "warfare" in which believers are engaged (6:10–17), they are urged to "be strong in the Lord and in the strength of his power" (*endynamousthe en kyriō kai en tō kratei tēs ischyos autou*) (6:10; see vv. 11, 13, 16; see also 2 Thess 1:11).

BODY; CHRIST; CROSS; GOD; RESURRECTION; SPIRIT; STRONG, WEAK; WISDOM

Reading

C. E. Arnold, *DPL*, 723–25; Fee, *God's Empowering Presence*, 35–36, 822–27; G. Friedrich, *EDNT* 1:355–58; P. J. Gräbe, *The Power of God in Paul's Letters* (Tübingen: Mohr Siebeck, 2000); Schnelle, *Apostle Paul*, 151–53, 174–76, 310–12; Thiselton, *1 Corinthians*, 233–39, 952–56; Wolter, *Paul*, 64–69.

PRAYER, PRAY

Paul would have brought to his moment of faith in the Crucified Messiah his regular practice as a pious Pharisee of personal prayer to God. The great difference following that moment would have been the association of the risen Lord with the God to whom he prayed. God was now "the Father of our Lord Jesus Christ" (Rom 15:6), as in the grace formula with which the Pauline letters regularly begin (Rom 1:7; 1 Cor 1:3; 2 Cor 1:2; Gal 1:3; Phil 1:2; 1 Thess 1:1; Phlm 3). The Spirit impels believers to address God with the intimate address, preserving the Aramaic (*Abba*, "Father"), of Jesus himself (Rom 8:15; Gal 4:6; see Mark 14:36).

References to prayer in Paul reflect a considerable range of vocabulary in Greek, the most common terms being the cognate verb *proseuchomai* and the noun *proseuchē*, along with to a lesser extent *deēsis* ("request"). To these can be added the verb *epikaleō*, especially in the phrase "calling on the name of the Lord" as an expression of fundamental Christian identity (Rom 10:12, 13, 14; 1 Cor 1:2; see also 2 Tim 2:22). References to prayer and actual expressions of prayer in Paul, however, are not confined to such vocabulary, as in the case of thanksgiving (see below).

Thanksgiving

All of Paul's undisputed letters, with the exception of Galatians, begin with an extended opening thanksgiving to God (Rom 1:8–15; 1 Cor 1:4–9; 2 Cor 1:3–7 [as a "blessing"]; Phil 1:3–11; 1 Thess 1:2–10; Phlm 4–7; see also Eph 1:15–19; Col 1:3–14; 2 Thess 1:3–10; 2 Tim 1:3–5). In 2 Corinthians 4:15, Paul points to the happy outcome that "grace, as it extends more and more, will multiply thanksgiving [*eucharisteian*] to the glory of God." The suggestion is that what God wants from human beings above all is simply gratitude, reversing the fundamental human sin of refusing to glorify or thank the Creator (Rom 1:21). The extended epistolary thanksgivings include prayer for the communities addressed (Rom

1:9–10; Phil 1:4, 9; 1 Thess 1:2; see also Phlm 4; Col 1:3, 9; 2 Thess 1:11; 2 Tim 1:3). Ephesians 3:14–21 is really an extended prayer of adoration and petition to the Father, concluding with a solemn doxology (vv. 20–21; see Rom 11:33–36; 15:6; see also Col 3:16 ["with gratitude in your hearts sing psalms, hymns, and spiritual songs to God"]).

Prayer as a Feature of Christian Life

Paul simply presumes that prayer, both private and communal, will be a regular expression of Christian life (Rom 12:12; 1 Cor 7:5; 1 Thess 3:10; 5:17; see also Col 4:2; Eph 6:18; 1 Tim 5:5). Granted the eschatological expectation of the time, prayer will often be an expression of hope. Since what is hoped and prayed for is not yet in view, Paul offers the consoling consideration that "when we do not know what to pray for [*to... ti proseuxōmetha*], the Spirit intercedes for us with groans too deep for utterance [*stenagmois alalētois*]" (Rom 8:26). Assuring the Philippians that "the Lord is near," he exhorts them not to worry about anything but "in everything by prayer and supplication [*tē proseuchē kai tē deēsei*], with thanksgiving, let your requests [*ta aitēmata*] be made known to God" (Phil 4:5b–6).

Individual believers and communities as a whole assist each other by prayer (2 Cor 9:14). Faced with the hazardous and delicate business of conveying the collection for the saints to Jerusalem, Paul begs the churches in Rome "to join him in earnest prayer to God" that his mission might meet with acceptance (Rom 15:30–31). In his imprisonment (in Rome?), he is confident that the prayers of the Philippians, with the help of the Spirit of Jesus Christ, will ensure his deliverance (Phil 1:19; see also 2 Cor 1:11; Phlm 22; Col 4:3). Closing 1 Thessalonians, he simply writes, "Beloved, pray for us" (5:25; see also Col 4:12; 2 Thess 3:1). To ensure a quiet and peaceful life for all, the Pauline author of 1 Timothy instructs that prayer and intercessions should extend beyond the community: for everyone, for kings and all who are in high positions (2:1–2).

Prayer is not always answered exactly in accordance with what is requested. Such was Paul's personal experience in regard to "the thorn" in the flesh that he three times begged the Lord to remove (2 Cor 12:7b–8). Instead, he received the precious instruction: "My grace is sufficient for you; for power is made perfect in weakness" (v. 9).

Prayer in the Christian Assembly

Paul speaks of prayer in the assembly of believers in two contexts. In 1 Corinthians 11:2–16, he accepts the right of women to pray and prophesy in the assembly but insists that in so doing they should not obscure gender distinction by having their hair bobbed up rather than hanging down (see WOMAN). In a subsequent passage resuming his lengthy instruction on the gifts of the Spirit (1 Cor 14), he expresses a clear preference for the gift of prophecy over that of tongues. A person who prays in tongues speaks to God, not to human beings (14:2). Such prayer may build up the individual (v. 4a) but, in contrast to the gift of prophecy, does nothing for the community (v. 4b). A person who speaks in tongues should pray for the power to interpret, since (otherwise), their spirit may pray but their mind is "unfruitful" (*akarpos*) (vv. 13–14). Although the value of tongues is not set aside (v. 18), Paul prefers prayer that leads to a revelation intelligible to all.

GLORY; GOD; GRACE; HOPE; PROPHECY; SPIRIT; THANKSGIVING; WOMAN

Reading

H. Balz, *EDNT* 3:164–69; O. Cullmann, *Prayer in the New Testament* (Minneapolis: Fortress, 1995), 69–88; Dunn, *Theology*, 46–49, 192–93, 437–39; W. B. Hunter, *DPL*, 725–34; Hurtado, *Lord Jesus Christ*, 138–43; R. N. Longenecker, "Prayer in the Pauline Letters," in *Studies in Paul: Exegetical and Theological* (Sheffield: Phoenix, 2004, 2006), 28–52; K. Stendahl, "Paul at Prayer," *Int* 34 (1980): 240–49; Thiselton, *1 Corinthians*, 1098–1102; G. P. Wiles, *Paul's Intercessory Prayers: The Significance of the Intercessory Prayer Passages in the Letters of Paul* (Cambridge: Cambridge University Press, 1974); Wright, *PFG*, 1348–50, 1516–19.

PREDESTINATION (*see* Election)

PRINCIPALITIES AND POWERS

"Principalities and powers" is a traditional translation of the Greek phrase *archai kai exousiai*, which appears (in the singular) in 1 Corinthians 15:24 (*pasan archēn kai pasan exousian*) and then, with some frequency, in the deutero–Pauline Colossians and Ephesians. While these terms can refer to human rulers (as clearly in Titus 3:1), in Pauline usage the reference is mainly to transcendent spiritual forces, personal or personified, that impact on human life in a punitive and threatening way. Belief in the existence and threat of such powers was a significant aspect of the apocalyptic worldview that Paul shared with much of the Judaism of his time. Their prominence in the later Pauline letters (see below) suggests that fear of control by them had grown in some circles of Gentile Christianity in the latter half of the first century, requiring renewed stress on the efficacy of Christ's redemptive work.

Paul's Usage

In Romans 8:38, "rulers" (*archai*) appears in a long list of factors (vv. 38–39a) that will not separate believers from the love of God revealed in Christ (v. 39b). The suffering of the present time (v. 18) might suggest that such forces are gaining the upper hand and preparing accusation for believers at the judgment. Evoking the great assize itself (vv. 33–34), Paul defiantly dismisses such a prospect. Suffering in union with Christ (v. 17) and in his cause (v. 36), believers are enveloped in God's love, already sharing his victory (v. 37).

In 1 Corinthians 2:6–8, Paul refers to "the rulers of this age" (*archontes tou aiōnos toutou*), who, ignorant of the saving wisdom of God, crucified "the Lord of glory" (v. 8). In mind may be earthly rulers such as Pilate and Caiaphas, but more likely the reference is to malignant spiritual powers who manipulate such authorities to their own ends. In the description of Christ's final triumph in 1 Corinthians 15:24–28, "the end" will come when he will have "removed" (*katargēsē*) "every ruler and every authority and power" (*pasan archēn kai pasan exousian kai dynamin*) (v. 24). It is not entirely clear whether the "removal" means the annihilation of such powers or simply their subjection (see vv. 25, 27). In the case of death, "the last enemy" (v. 26), destruction is certainly in view as a prelude to the general resurrection (see Phil 3:21).

Colossians

The letter to the Colossians reassures its recipients of the all-sufficiency of the redemption effected by Christ (1:13–14). It does so in the face of what would appear to be continuing belief that day-to-day existence is threatened and controlled by spiritual forces ("the elemental spirits of the universe" [*stoicheia tou kosmou* (2:8, 20; see also Gal 4:3, 9)]) that need to be placated by various ascetical practices and observances (Col 2:16–23), including the veneration of angels (v. 18). A hymnic passage (1:15–20) establishes from the start the supremacy of Christ, asserting that "all things in heaven and on earth," including "thrones, dominations, rulers, and authorities [*thronoi, kyriotētes, archai, exousiai*] were created through him and for him" (v. 16). Although created "for him" (*eis auton*), these powers seem to have become hostile. Hence the reference in the closing lines to his reconciling all things to himself, "having made peace through the blood of his cross" (v. 20). Later (2:10b) Christ is described as "the head of every rule and authority" (*hē kephalē pasēs archēs kai exousias*). This relatively benign reference sits in some tension, however, with the assurance a few lines later that, through the cross, God has stripped the rulers and authorities (*apekdysamenos tas archas kai tas exousias*) of any accusing power they might have had and made a public spectacle of them in the triumphal procession of Christ (2:14–15; see Rom 8:33–34, 38–39).

Ephesians

The author of Ephesians stresses the power of God in raising Christ from the dead and setting him at his right hand in the heavenly places, "far above all rule and authority [*hyperanō pasēs archēs kai exousias*] and power and dominion,…not only in this age but also in the one to come" (1: 21). The subjection of the powers that is still a work in process according to 1 Corinthians 15:24–28 is described here as set in place for all time. Moreover, God has given Christ as "head" to the church, which then, as his "body," shares his exaltation over all things (Eph 1: 22–23; 4:8–10). The inclusion of Gentiles within the same body through the reconciling work of Christ (2:11–18) is the mystery that Paul has been called to serve (3:1–3), in order that, through the church, that is, through the unity of Jew and Gentile established in the church, "the manifold wisdom of God may be made known to the rulers and authorities in the heavenly places" (*tais archais kai tais exousiais en tois epouraniois*) (v. 10). The age-old division of humankind over which these powers presided has been overcome in Christ. That their influence has not been entirely removed, however, is suggested by the concluding exhortation (6:10–17) to believers to put on the full armor (*panoplia*) of God (v. 11), since the battle is not against human foes but "against the rulers...the authorities...the cosmic powers..., against the spiritual forces of evil in the heavenly places" (v. 12). Thus the letter concludes with the sense that the divine victory won by Christ is still running its course in the present lives of believers.

CHRIST; JUDGE, LAST JUDGMENT; KINGDOM OF GOD; POWER; RESURRECTION; SUFFERING

Reading

C. E. Arnold, *Powers of Darkness: Principalities and Powers in Paul's Letters* (Downers Grove, IL: Intervarsity, 1992), 87–165; Dunn, *Theology*, 104–10; Matera, *GSG*, 93–96, 203–7, 241–44; P. T. O'Brien, "Principalities and Powers: Opponents of the Church," in *Biblical Interpretation and the Church*, ed. D. A. Carson (Nashville, TN: Thomas Nelson, 1984), 110–50; D. G. Reid, *DPL*, 746–52; Thiselton, *1 Corinthians*, 233–39; W. Wink, *Naming the Powers: The Language of Power in the New Testament* (Philadelphia: Fortress, 1984).

PROMISE

The motif of "promise" (in Greek, *epangelia*; *epangelomai*), specifically in regard to the promises God made to Abraham, plays a significant role in Romans and Galatians. Behind Paul's references to the promises, including their listing among the privileges of Israel in Romans 9:4, lies a developed biblical and postbiblical Jewish tradition in which Abraham's ancestral role continues in a truly representative sense in that the promises he received remain determinative for his descendants, including from an eschatological perspective the gaining or loss of salvation (see ABRAHAM).

The promises that God made to Abraham fall into three categories, more than one of which can feature in the same context:

1. The *Blessing* promise: that all the nations (LXX *ethnē*, "Gentiles") will be *blessed* in him (Gen 12:3; 18:18; 22:18 ["blessed in your descendant" (LXX *sperma*)]) (see BLESSING).
2. The *Son* promise: that he will have a son and heir and a vast progeny (Gen 15:4–5; 17:5; 18:10; 22:17).
3. The *Land* promise: that God will give "this land" to him and to his descendants (Gen 12:7; 13:15; 15:18; 17:8). This promise, which in the narrative of Genesis refers to the land of Canaan, had by Paul's day undergone significant "expansion" in the Jewish tradition to include, first, the whole world and then, in an eschatological sense, all the blessings of salvation, including the "world to come" (for references, see Byrne, *Romans*, 157).

The Blessing Promise

The Blessing promise features in the central argument of Galatians, where Paul points to the community's experience of the Spirit (3:2–5) as the fulfillment of God's promise to Abraham (Gen 12:3; 18:18) that "all the nations" ("Gentiles") would be blessed in him, understanding the latter phrase "in him" as meaning on the same basis as him, that is, as justified by faith (Gal 3:6–9). The saving work of Christ on the cross has removed the law's curse (v. 13), so that the blessing promised to Abraham might flow to all believers (Gentile and Jewish) in the shape of justification as attested by the Spirit (v. 14).

The Land Promise

In Galatians 3:15–23, Paul sorts out the relationship between the promise to Abraham and the Sinai dispensation of the law very much in favor of the former. Portraying the promise as a will or testament (*diathēkē* [v. 15]) that the Mosaic law, a latecomer on the scene, cannot set aside (v. 17), he exploits the singular sense of "offspring" (*sperma*) in the Greek of Genesis 13:15; 15:18; 17:8) so as to interpret the promise, now the *Land* promise, as focused solely and singly on Christ (v. 16; see vv. 18–22). The only way, then, to come under the scope of the promise is through "entry into" Christ through faith and baptism. Since the Galatians have in fact made that entry (Gal 3:25–28a), they are now all "one person" in Christ Jesus (v. 28b). One in and with Christ in this way, they are then "offspring of Abraham [*tou Abraam sperma*], heirs according to the promise" (v. 29). In a subsequent short passage (4:1–7), Paul points again to the experience of the Spirit as guaranteeing their filial status in relation to God and hence their destiny, as heirs, to inherit the promise, and with it all the blessings (of salvation) that it contains.

The Son Promise

In Romans 4, Paul provides scriptural validation for the case that he has been making (1:16—3:31) that God has graciously made available in Christ the righteousness required for salvation solely on the basis of faith. According to Genesis 15:6, cited by Paul in Romans 4:3 (see Gal 3:6), it was on the basis of Abraham's faith in the *Son* promise (Gen 15:4–5) that he was "reckoned" righteous in God's sight and in this way became, as specified in the promise, the "father" of a vast progeny of believers who follow him in his faith (Rom 4:11b–12).

The Son and the Land Promise

In Romans 4:13–25, with the sequence of Genesis 15 in mind, Paul goes on to argue that it was on the basis of his being found righteous through his faith in the *Son* promise that Abraham received a second promise, this time the *Land* promise (Gen 15:18–19), understood, according to Paul's formulation, in its expanded, eschatological sense, as "the inheritance of the world" (*klēronomon...kosmou*) (Rom 4:13). Had the promise been given on the basis of law, faith would have been "emptied out" and the promise destroyed (vv. 14–15). Whereas, operating on a principle of grace (*kata charin* [v. 16]), faith ensured that it would be secure to all Abraham's offspring, not only to those who proceed from law (Jews) but to all who follow his way of faith, in accordance with the divine promise of Genesis 17:5, "I have made you the father of many nations" (*ethnē* ["Gentiles"], cited in verse 17a).

Paul then takes a step backward, so to speak, to explore more deeply the nature of Abraham's faith in the *Son* promise (Gen 15:4–5). Granted the "deadness" of his bodily capacity for procreation and that of his wife Sarah (Rom 4:19), believing that he would have a son and heir meant believing in a God "who raises the dead" (Rom 4:17b). Granted also the time gap between the initial promise and the actual birth of his son, his faith was not a one-off matter but required perseverance and hope in the space of time between promise and fulfillment, an enduring confidence that God was capable of bringing about what had been promised (vv. 20–21). This enables Paul to bring out the parity between Abraham's faith and that of his believing progeny. Abraham had to believe in a God who had the power to raise the dead. The focus of Christian faith lies on God's raising of Christ from the dead (see Rom 10:9; 1 Cor 15:2–5). Hence the scriptural note of "reckoning righteousness" applies to "us" as well as to our father in faith (vv. 22–24). Moreover, our faith too, not only looks back to that past event but also, like that of Abraham, to the future as well. As Paul will assert later, the God who raised Jesus from the dead will also raise our mortal bodies through the power of the indwelling Spirit (Rom 8:11). In this way Paul's intricate scriptural analysis shows how all subsequent believers are drawn under the scope of the promise(s) made to Abraham.

Children of the Promise (Rom 9:6–9; Gal 4:21–31)

Paul further exploits the gap between promise and fulfillment in regard to the birth of Isaac when beginning to address the issue of Israel's failure to respond to the gospel in Romans 9—11. He questions the makeup of "Israel," asserting that not all the descendants of Abraham are "children"—that is, children of God, destined to inherit the eschatological blessings (9:6b–9; see 8:14–17)—but only those "in the line of Isaac" (v. 7, citing [LXX] Gen 21:12). They, and not the "fleshly" descendants of Abraham, are reckoned as "true offspring" (*sperma*) (v. 8), because they are "children of the promise" (*tekna tēs epangelias* [see also Gal 4:28]), the promise in question being the "Son" promise in the form made to Abraham at Mamre (Gen 18:10, 14, cited by Paul in Rom 9:9). The time gap between promise and fulfillment allows for the sovereign freedom of God to act independently of merely human connections or deserts, which is the main "thesis" of the first stage (9:6–29) of Paul's exploration of the fate of Israel. In the end of course (11:25–29), Paul foresees the salvation of "all Israel" as resting on the truth that "the gifts and calling" of God are "irrevocable" (v. 29).

Employing a highly allegorical interpretation in Galatians 4:21–31 of the traditions concerning Abraham's two wives, Hagar and Sarah (Gen 16:1–15; 21:1–21),

Paul presents the two women as mothers, respectively, of Abraham's two sons: one (Ishmael), born into slavery, and one (Isaac), born into freedom on the basis of a divine promise (Gen 21:1–3). He argues that the Galatians, as "in the line of Isaac children of the promise" (*kata Isaak epangelias tekna*, v. 28), should stand firm in their freedom and not submit to the yoke of slavery that is being aggressively imposed on them (4:29—5:1) (see COVENANT; JERUSALEM).

More General References to Promises

In Romans 15:8, Paul writes that "Christ became a servant of the circumcised on behalf of the truth of God that he might confirm the promises made to the fathers" (*eis to bebaiōsai tas epangelias tōn patrōn*); he then adds, "and that the Gentiles might glorify God for (their receiving of) mercy" (v. 9a; see 11:29). The highly cryptic formulation does not make clear whether "promises" in verse 8 refers to all the promises God made to Israel or has the more specific sense of the promises bearing on the inclusion of the Gentiles, as verse 9a and the following quotations (vv. 9b–12), might suggest. In an attractive aside early in 2 Corinthians, Paul describes Christ, the model he strives to emulate, as the "'Yes' to all the promises of God" (1:20; see also 2 Cor 6:16—7:1).

Later Pauline Literature

The recipients of the letter to the Ephesians, on the basis of their faith, have been "sealed with the promised Holy Spirit" (*pneumati tēs epangelias tō hagiō*) (1:13; see Gal 3:14). In their former life, precisely as Gentiles, they were "strangers to the covenants of promise [*xenoi tōn diathēkōn tēs epangelias*], having no hope and without God in the world" (2:12). Now, however, they have become "fellow heirs,...and sharers in the promise [*symmetocha tēs epangelias*] in Christ Jesus" (3:6; see 2 Tim 1:1; Titus 1:2). Elsewhere in the Pauline literature "promise" has the ordinary, day to day sense of what is likely to happen or what one pledges or professes (Eph 6:2; 1 Tim 2:10; 4:8; 6:21).

ABRAHAM; BLESSING; COVENANT; FAITH; GENTILES; HOPE; ISRAEL; SPIRIT

Reading

Byrne, "Jerusalems," 215–31; *PES*, 83–86, 103–4, 178–81; *Romans*, 141–62, 289–95, 428–33; N. L. Calvert, *DPL*, 1–9; Dunn, *Theology*, 376–79, 503–9; Hays, *Echoes*, 105–21; Moo, *Romans*, 271–90, 568–78, 875–78; A. Sand, *EDNT* 2:13–16; Schnelle, *Apostle Paul*, 323–27; S. K. Williams, "Promise in Galatians: A Reading of Paul's Reading of Scripture," *JBL* 107 (1988): 709–20.

PROPHET, PROPHESY, PROPHECY

The motif of "prophet" (*prophētēs*) and "prophecy" (*prophēteia*) appears in Paul in three ways: in reference to the biblical prophets of Israel, with reference to "the prophets" in the sense of the prophetic books of the Bible, and finally and most extensively with reference to a particular gift of the Spirit.

Biblical Prophets

To rebut the suggestion that God has rejected Israel (Rom 11:1), Paul points to the complaint made by the biblical prophet Elijah according to 1 Kings 19:10, 14 and to the response the prophet received from God concerning a remnant that had remained faithful (v. 18). Paul finds in the "remnant" a foreshadowing of the Christian Jewish minority that, on the basis of election and grace, had come to faith, rebutting any suggestion that God had abandoned Israel (Rom 11:2–6). Paul may be identifying his own situation with that of Elijah and that of the prophets of Israel generally (see Rom 1:1; Gal 1:15 in light of Isa 49:1, 5; Jer 1:5). The biblical prophets are presumably in mind in the negative—and possibly un-Pauline—reference to "killing the prophets" in 1 Thessalonians 2:15.

Prophetic Books of the Bible

In Paul's introduction of himself as "apostle, set apart for the gospel of God" in Romans 1:1, he characterizes the gospel as "announced beforehand through his prophets in the holy Scriptures" (*ho proepēngeilato dia tōn prophētōn en graphais hagiais*) (v. 2). He does not specify the prophetic books in mind. Granted, however, the biblical origins of the motif of "gospel" in Isaiah, it is not unlikely that in view are texts such as Isaiah 40:9; 52:7; 61:1–2. Later, proclaiming the revelation of the righteousness of God to all believers through God's act in Christ (Rom 3:21–26), Paul maintains that the revelation has occurred "apart from the law, but with the law and the prophets bearing witness to it" (*martyroumenē hypo tou nomou kai tōn prophētōn*) (v. 21b). In the following chapter (4:1–12), he expands on this scriptural witness to righteousness by faith. He cites first (v. 3) a text from "the law" (the Pentateuch), namely, Genesis 15:6, and supports this (Rom 4:6–8) with a text from "the prophets," Psalm 32 (LXX 31):1–2, the Psalms being reckoned among "the prophets" on the basis of their attribution to David.

The post-Pauline doxology appearing in most manuscripts at the close of the letter (16:26–27) refers to the mystery, which has been wrapped in silence for long ages but has "now been made known through the prophetic writings" (*dia...graphōn prophētikōn*) (v. 26). Rather than referring to the scriptural (Old Testament) prophetical books, "prophetic writings" here more likely means writings composed in the New Testament period and considered "prophetic" in the sense of being filled with revelatory power (see 2 Pet 3:15b–16). An allusion to Paul's letters in this sense would form a fitting concluding comment on his letter to Rome.

Prophecy as a Gift of the Spirit

Apart from a brief mention as the first of the gifts listed in Romans 12:3–8 (see v. 6) and a similar isolated reference in 1 Thessalonians 5:20 ("Do not despise the words of the prophets" [*prophēteias mē exoutheneite*]), mention of "prophecy" (*prophēteia*) in Paul is confined to 1 Corinthians 12–14. The precise nature of the gift of the Spirit in question remains a matter of some controversy. An earlier tendency to look to the phenomenon of prophecy in the contemporary Greek world as model for Christian usage has now been largely abandoned. Greek prophecy involved interpreting the will of the gods or giving an oracular response in an ecstatic state, whereas the evidence for Christian usage points away from ecstasy to communication in a conscious state, albeit through the influence of the Spirit. Paul's clearly expressed preference for the gift of prophecy over that of tongues derives from the fact that prophecy involves communication that serves to build up the community, whereas the more ecstatic phenomenon of tongues, while it may build up the faith of individuals, contributes nothing to the community (1 Cor 14:1–5, 6). Prophecy, although amounting to nothing without love (13:2), involving merely partial knowledge (v. 9), and ultimately destined to cease (v. 8), is nonetheless the first of the gifts that, after love, is to be sought (14:1). A stranger (nonbeliever) entering the assembly where all are speaking in tongues would be inclined to say, "You are mad" (v. 23). But the same person encountering prophesying would undergo a conversion: the secrets of the heart would be disclosed, leading to worship of the true God (vv. 24–25). Prophecy, then, has a "missionary" effect besides building up the community. Hence Paul's detailed instructions in the matter of prophecy and tongues: all should proceed with the aim of building up (v. 26) and in due order (vv. 27–31), so that everyone may learn and be encouraged (v. 31).

It is clear, then, that prophecy involved conscious communication. Distinct from and secondary to the initial proclamation of the gospel, it presumably involved the application of the gospel to the present situation of the community. The fact that it came as a gift of the Spirit did not mean that it was necessarily spontaneous—any more than gifts of the Spirit such as "assistance" (*antilēpseis*) or "leadership" (*kybernēseis*) (1 Cor 12:28) had to be spontaneous, which, of course, they could not have been. It is likely that prophecy involved an interpretation of the Scriptures (Old Testament) in the light of God's action in Christ. When Paul writes, "For whatever was written in former days was written for our instruction, so that by steadfastness and by the encouragement of the Scriptures [*dia tēs paraklēseōs tōn graphōn*], we might have hope" (Rom 15:4), he would appear to be describing both the operation and the desired effect of the prophetic gift.

The instruction in 1 Corinthians 11:2–16 concerning what women should wear when praying or prophesying in the assembly—whatever be the precise issue (hairstyle or veil)—may not represent Paul at his best either as pastor or theologian. It does, however, provide evidence that women were allowed, through the gift of prophecy, to offer leadership in this public way. The sharp injunction appearing later in the letter (14:33b–36), imposing silence on women in the assembly in clear contradiction of the practice emerging from 11:2–16, is plausibly regarded as an addition to the original, reflecting concerns for order more characteristic of the post-Pauline letters (see WOMAN).

ENCOURAGE, EXHORT, CONSOLE; GIFT(S) OF THE SPIRIT; LAW; SCRIPTURE; SPIRIT; WOMAN

Reading

D. E. Aune, *Prophecy in Early Christianity and the Ancient Mediterranean World* (Grand Rapids: Eerdmans, 1983, repr. 1991), 189–205, 219–22, 247–62; M. E. Boring, *The Continuing Voice of Jesus: Christian Prophecy and the Gospel Tradition* (Louisville: Westminster John Knox, 1991), 35–186; Dunn, *Theology*, 552–61, 580–82; Fee, *1 Corinthians*, 780–92 (on 1 Cor 14:33b–36); *God's Empowering Presence*, 888–92; W. A. Grudem, *The Gift of Prophecy in 1 Corinthians* (Lanham, MD; University Press of America, 1982); C. M. Robeck Jr., *DPL*, 755–62; Schnelle, *Apostle Paul*, 570–73; Thiselton, *1 Corinthians*, 970–88, 1087–94; A. C. Wire, *The Corinthian Women Prophets: A Reconstruction through Paul's Rhetoric* (Minneapolis: Fortress, 1990).

PROPITIATION, EXPIATION

Propitiation arises in Paul in connection with the singular description in Romans 3:25 of God's putting forward Christ as a *hilastērion* in the shedding of his blood. Before discussing the Greek term itself, it is advisable to consider the meaning of *propitiation* in English, especially in its distinction from the closely related term *expiation*. Both terms have to do with the removal of an offense caused to some other party and the consequent disfavor on the part of that other party toward the party responsible for the offending behavior. *Propitiation* looks more to the subjective disposition of the offended party (God, a god, or a superior human being), and seeks to appease the anger or disaffection caused by the offensive behavior. "Expiation" looks more to the objective act itself and seeks, usually through some painful exercise, to remove or overcome its offensive nature or effects. Thus one "propitiates" a person but "expiates" a crime.

The Greek term *hilastērion*, along with cognates such as the verb *hilaskomai* and the noun *hilasmos*, in wider usage beyond the New Testament, has the sense of "make gracious," usually with respect to placating an angry god or offended human being. The wider context of Romans 3:25, notably the reference to the revelation of the divine wrath in 1:18 and the continuing prospect of looming divine judgment across 1:18—3:20 as a whole, together with subsequent references to divine wrath in the letter (4:15; 5:9; 9:22; 12:19; see also 1 Thess 1:10; 2:16; 5:9), make it reasonable to take the reference to Christ's death in terms of *hilastērion* in 3:25 as having this propitiatory sense with respect to the divine offense at human sin.

On the other hand, *hilastērion* occurs in the Septuagint's translation of the Hebrew *kapporet* with reference to the cover placed over the ark of the covenant in the inmost recesses of the temple, the holy of holies (Exod 25:17–22). It was on this cover that, on the yearly Day of Atonement, the high priest sprinkled the blood of an animal as an enactment of the divine "wiping away" or "expiating" of the pollution of the sanctuary due to the accumulated offenses of the people (Lev 16:15–16). If, as is widely argued, the description of Christ's obedient death in Romans 3:25 as a *hilastērion* alludes to this yearly ritual (as explicitly in Hebrews 9:3–7), then it is possible to find in the use of the term here an expiatory rather than a propitiatory sense. Elsewhere (Rom 5:10–11; 2 Cor 5:18–21) Paul speaks of God's action in the death of Christ in terms of "reconciliation" (*katallagē*), which would be open to either a propitiatory or an expiatory understanding, although the latter might be more appropriate. In any case, it is important to note that in all of Paul's references to the redemptive act of Christ, the divine initiative is paramount (see also Rom 8:3–4; 8:32; Gal 4:4–5), with absolute continuity between the action of the Father and the obedience of the Son. There is no sense of Christ acting independently to induce a reluctant Father to move from a disposition of anger to one of favor.

CHRIST; COVENANT; CROSS; DEATH; GRACE; RECONCILIATION; REDEMPTION; SALVATION; SIN

Reading

Byrne, *PES*, 97–102, 204–9; *Romans*, 122–35; Campbell, *Deliverance*, 640–56, 1107–8; A. Y. Collins, "The Metaphorical Use of *hilastērion* in Rom 3:25," in *Sōtēria: Salvation in Early Christianity and Antiquity*, ed. D. S. du Toit et al. (Leiden; Boston: Brill, 2019), 273–86; Dunn, *Theology*, 213–16; J. M. Gundry-Volf, *DPL*, 279–84; B. J. Ribbens, "Forensic-Retributive Justification in Romans 3:21–26: Paul's Doctrine of Justification in Dialogue with Hebrews," *CBQ* 72 (2012): 548–67; J. Roloff, *EDNT* 2:185–87; Schnelle, *Apostle Paul*, 447–51; Wolter, *Paul*, 95–107.

R

RECONCILIATION, RECONCILE

"Reconciliation" (noun: *katallagē*; verbs: *katallassō*; *apokatallasō*) is one of the key images Paul employs to describe God's action in Christ. In itself the language of reconciliation has no religious resonance. In secular Greek it appears in the sphere of interpersonal relations and diplomacy to indicate the restoration of friendly relations between parties hitherto hostile and estranged. In 2 Maccabees 1:5; 5:20; 7:32–33; 8:29, it is employed with reference to the reconciliation of the Jewish nation with God, but in this case the impetus or motive for the assuaging of the divine wrath stems from the human side. When Paul employs the language of reconciliation, in 2 Corinthians 5:18–21 and Romans 5:10–11, the initiative is entirely with God.

One may think of reconciliation occurring in two circumstances. In one case, a mediator may intervene or be employed to assist two estranged parties to achieve a reconciliation that neither of them itself sought to initiate. In a second case, without the intervention of a mediator, one party may unilaterally reach out to the estranged party seeking reconciliation. In the latter case the party seeking reconciliation runs the risk of rejection; even if successful, overcoming the hostility of the other party is likely to involve a cost.

The Reconciliation Offered in the Gospel

It is this latter situation that applies in Paul's view of the reconciliation brought about by God in Christ. Christ is not a mediator between God and the estranged human world (but see 1 Tim 2:5). Christ is entirely "on the side of" God, in total continuity with the divine outreach in love to an alienated, hostile world. Paul expresses this in a double statement in 2 Corinthians 5:18–19:

> [18] All this is from God, who reconciled us [*tou katallaxantos hēmas*] to himself through Christ, and has given us the ministry of reconciliation; [19] to put it in another way: in Christ God was reconciling [*katallassōn*] the world to himself, not reckoning their trespasses against them, and entrusting to us the message of reconciliation [*ton logon tēs katallagēs*].

Both formulations (vv. 18 and 19) locate the apostolic ministry as the extension of the divine outreach of reconciliation, offering the "word of reconciliation" to the world. The reconciliation has already been achieved in a fundamental sense by God's act in Christ; human sin is no longer being "reckoned." The summons contained in the gospel is for human beings to align themselves, through faith, with the reconciliation already achieved and on offer: "We are ambassadors on behalf of Christ [*hyper Christou presbeuomen*], with God appealing (to you) through us. We entreat you, 'Be reconciled to God' [*katallagēte tō theō*]" (v. 20)."

The Corinthians to whom Paul is describing the divine action in these terms have, of course, already responded to the gospel and in this sense are already reconciled to God. However, Paul recalls the initial proclamation of the gospel as part of his own running plea for reconciliation with the community (2 Cor 2:14—7:4). Reconciliation is not a one-off event. The God to whose appeal the community responded when they first came to faith continues to appeal to them now to live out the reconciliation that they have received in their relations with Paul.

Reconciliation in Romans

The language of "reconciliation" reappears in Romans 5:10–11, where Paul points to the extremity of divine love already displayed in the Christ event as a guarantee of the hope for final salvation. In the second of two a fortiori arguments, Paul argues, "For if, while we were enemies [*echthroi ontes*] we have been reconciled to God through the death of his Son, how much more surely, now that we have been reconciled, will we be saved through his life" (v. 10). Prior to the divine intervention in Christ the human world was in a state of "enmity" with God. In the sacrificial death of the Son God reached out into that enmity (vv. 6, 8–9), offering justification and reconciliation. Those who have responded in faith and found justification, no longer have enmity but "peace" with God (5:1). They can "boast now in God through our Lord Jesus Christ, through whom we have received the reconciliation" (*tēn katallagēn*) (v. 11).

Later in the letter, in connection with a hope for the final salvation of unbelieving Israel, Paul briefly employs a similar a priori argument in rather cryptic terms. If the present (temporary) rejection of Israel on the part of God has led to the reconciliation (*katallagē*) of the world (i.e., the extension of the gospel to the Gentiles), what will their (Israel's) eventual acceptance mean? Surely, resurrection from the dead, that is, the general resurrection (11:15).

In these passages "reconciliation" has the "vertical" sense of reconciliation between human beings and God. The only remaining reference to reconciliation, aside from the deutero–Pauline letters, has the "horizontal" sense of the reconciliation of an estranged wife to her husband (1 Cor 7:11).

"Reconciliation" in the Deutero-Pauline Letters

In the cosmic scope of the christological hymn in Colossians 1:15–20, Christ is not only the agent of creation but the one "*for* whom" (*eis auton*) all things have been brought into being (v. 16). Included are the spiritual forces ("rulers or powers" [*archai eite exousiai*]), whom the author is concerned to put in their place in view of the audience's inclination to accord them worship (2:8–23). At some stage, in a way that is not explained, the created order has been put out of joint, so that it has been necessary for Christ to reconcile to himself all things (*apokatallaxai ta panta eis auton*), including these powers, making peace by the blood of his cross (1:20). The author reminds the audience of how they have been drawn into God's work of cosmic reconciliation in Christ: "And you who were once estranged and hostile in mind, doing evil deeds, he has now reconciled [*apokatēllaxen* (var. *apokatēllagēte* = "have been reconciled")] in the body of his flesh through death" (1:21–22).

Reconciliation in Ephesians has a "horizontal" as well as a "vertical" dimension in that central to the letter's portrayal of the redemptive work of Christ is the overcoming of the division and hostility between Jews and Gentiles (2:11–18). Both dimensions of reconciliation are present in that Christ "has made the two one," breaking down "the dividing wall" of hostility (v. 14bc), in order "to create in himself one new humanity, making peace" (v. 15) and "to reconcile [*apokatallaxē*] both groups in one body to God through the cross, destroying the enmity through it" (or "in himself") (v. 16).

CROSS; DEATH; GENTILES; JEW, JUDAISM; MINISTRY; PEACE; PRINCIPALITIES AND POWERS

Reading

Byrne, *PES*, 204–9; *Romans*, 168–69, 172; C. Constantineanu, *The Social Significance of Reconciliation in Paul's Theology: Narrative Readings in Romans* (London: T & T Clark, 2010); Dunn, *Theology*, 228–33, 387–88; Fee, *Pauline Christology*, 197–98, 308–16; J. A. Fitzmyer, "Reconciliation in Pauline Theology," in *To Advance the Gospel*, 2nd ed. (Grand Rapids: Eerdmans, Dove, 1998), 162–85; Harris, *2 Corinthians*, 434–49; R. P. Martin, *Reconciliation: A Study of Paul's Theology*, 2nd ed. (Grand Rapids: Academie Books, 1989; repr. Eugene, OR: Wipf & Stock, 1997); Matera, *GSG*, 103–117, 152; H. Merkel, *EDNT* 2:261–63; Schnelle, *Apostle Paul*, 451–54; Wright, *PFG*, 879–89, 1487–1516.

REDEMPTION, REDEEM

The concept of "redemption" in Paul is mostly carried by two Greek terms: the noun *apolytrōsis* and the verb (*ex*)*agorazō*. Outside the New Testament, the comparatively rare noun *apolytrōsis* occurs with reference to the gaining of freedom from an unpleasant constraint of some kind, especially that of slavery incurred as a consequence of being taken prisoner in war. As this process usually involves the payment of money *apolytrōsis* has the connotation of freedom obtained at a cost. Whether the note of cost or price (ransom) being paid is intrinsic to the meaning of the *apolytrōsis* or has to be inferred from the context is disputed. The term has the simple sense of "freedom" in New Testament passages such as Luke 21:28; Romans 8:23; Hebrews 11:35. The Septuagint's regular usage of the shorter cognate form *lytrōsis* with reference to the liberation of the Israelites from Egypt without any implication of a cost might support the more general meaning of the longer form. However, it is not clear that the two forms simply overlap in meaning in this way. *Lytrōsis* does have the implication of a cost in some places (e.g., LXX Lev 25:29, 48; Num 18:16; Judg 1:15) and, in its sole appearance in the Septuagint (Dan 4:34), *apolytrōsis* has this sense also. It is doubtful whether the implication of a cost is ever entirely absent.

Redemption in Romans

The centrality of the notion of "redemption" in Christian theology stems from Paul's reference to God's action in Christ as an *apolytrōsis* in the statement recapitulating the theme of the Letter to the Romans in 3:21–26, specifically in verses 23–25:

> [23] For all had sinned and stand deprived of the glory of God. [24] They are being justified freely as a gift through the redemption [*dia tēs apolytrōseōs*] that is in Christ Jesus, [25] whom God put forward as an expiatory sacrifice in (the shedding of) his blood.

The liberation in question is the freedom from the captivity to sin affecting the entire human race (v. 23; see 3:9b; see also 5:12d; 6:16–23; 7:14b, 23, 25c), along with the alienation from God concomitant with sin. Through the self-sacrificial death of Christ, God has freely made available a divine righteousness ("righteousness of God" [3:21, 22; see 1:17]) accessible through faith. Those who respond to the gospel in faith access this righteousness "in Christ Jesus" and so find freedom from sin and right relationship with God (justification).

There is of course a cost involved in this liberation, a cost paid by Christ in the shedding of his blood. There is, however, no sense that this cost is paid *to* God (the Father) as distinct from the Son. There is total continuity between the action of God in "putting forth" Christ as an expiatory sacrifice (v. 25) and the disposition of Christ himself. In the person of the Son, God pays the cost in a continuity of divine love (5:6–10 [especially v. 8]; see also 4:25; 8:32; Gal 2:20). This (metaphorical) sense of a "cost" paid by Christ to effect liberation emerges also in two references in 1 Corinthians: "For you were bought with a price [*ēgorasthēte...timēs*]; therefore glorify God in your body" (6:20); "You were bought with a price [*timēs ēgorasthēte*]; do not become slaves of human masters" (7:23). Although Paul employs here the alternative verb (*agorazō*), there is the same sense of believers having been redeemed from slavery to sin for a new "service" to Christ as Lord (see Rom 6:16–23).

"Redemption" in the fundamental sense of right relationship with God (justification) is something that God brings about for believers as they respond to the gospel in faith (Rom 3:24–26; 5:1). *Bodily*, however, they are still in the old creation, awaiting "the redemption of the body [*tēn apolytrōsin tou sōmatos*]" (8:23), which will occur when they fully share the risen life of Christ (see 8:9–11; Phil 3:21). Hence redemption itself is part of the "already/not yet" pattern of believers' current existence in Paul's eschatology. It may be on this account that, in a formula listing all that Christ means for believers in virtue of existence "in" him, Paul sets "redemption" (*apolytrōsis*) as the final item in a sequence that begins with "our wisdom from God," then follows with "righteousness" and "sanctification" (1 Cor 1:30). A stricter sense of the *ordo salutis* might have suggested placing redemption second.

Redemption in Galatians

References to Christ's redeeming work in Galatians are expressed through the alternative verb *exagorazein*, which, with its primary commercial meaning (see 1 Cor 7:30), also connotes the sense of "cost." In Galatians 3:13, Paul describes Christ as having redeemed us (*hēmas exēgorasen*) from the curse of the law, having himself become a curse for us. Granted the universal prevalence of sin, the law could only rain down on human beings its Deuteronomic curse (Deut 27:26, cited in Gal 3:10). Christ, who, as sinless in himself (see 2 Cor 5:21), was the only one immune to the curse of the law, representatively and in our place, in his costly death took on himself the curse incumbent on the human race, so transforming the situation from one of curse to one of blessing (3:14). The later statement in 4:4–5 describes the redemptive work of Christ as the outcome of his being sent by the Father, thereby, in a way parallel to Romans 3:21–26 (see also 8:3–4), bringing out the total continuity of the divine redemptive action. The outcome is that from being in a situation of or akin to slavery (4:1–3) believers receive the status of sons (and daughters) (*huiothesia*), attested by the Spirit (v. 6).

Redemption in the Deutero-Pauline Letters

In Colossians 1:14, in an echo of Romans 3:24, redemption (*apolytrōsis*) is simply summed up as "the forgiveness of sins" (*tēn aphesin tōn hamartiōn*). The summary appears again in the hymnic thanksgiving with which Ephesians begins (1:3–14): "in whom (Christ) we have the redemption [*apolytrōsin*] through his blood, the forgiveness of (our) trespasses" (v. 7). At the close of the thanksgiving, a more eschatological note attaches to redemption with the description of the Spirit as, literally, "the pledge of our inheritance towards the redemption of the possession" (*ho estin arrabōn tēs klēronomias hēmōn, eis apolytrōsin tēs peripoiēseōs*) (v. 14). The cryptic final phrase is best understood as having the same future reference as in Romans 8:23, that is, to the liberation from bodily bondage to death that will attend the general resurrection. "Possession" (*peripoiēsis*) could then refer either to *believers'* gaining possession of the "inheritance" at that point or to their attaining the final stage of *God's* possession of them as a people (NRSV). The latter interpretation seems to push the phrases beyond any meaning they can bear. In favor of the former is the description of the Spirit later in the letter (4:30) as that with which the audience have been sealed "towards the day of redemption" (*eis hēmeran apolytrōseōs*), the moment of release from all the bonds of the present time (see Luke 21:28).

In the paraenetical sections of Colossians and Ephesians there appears the curious phrase "redeeming the time" (*ton kairon exagorazomenoi* [Col 4:5b]; *exagorazomenoi ton kairon* [Eph 5:16a]). The basic sense of the verb *exagorazō* here is that of "make the most of," as, in a commercial sense, diligent traders miss no opportunity to promote their wares. The context in Colossians 4:2–6 is that of relations with outsiders, who by gracious speech can be induced to think well of the faith and those who live it. Although the verb has the same meaning in Ephesians 5:16a, the context is more pessimistic ("for the days are evil" [5:16b]). Beyond "making most of the time," there may be the nuance that the space of time itself needs to be redeemed from its prevailing evil and won, at least in the lives of believers, for the service of Christ.

BODY; DEATH; FREEDOM; JUSTIFICATION; PROPITIATION, EXPIATION; RESURRECTION; RIGHTEOUSNESS; SIN; SLAVERY; SPIRIT

Reading

F. Büchsel, *TDNT* 4:351–56; Byrne, *PES*, 96–97, 191–96; Campbell, *Deliverance*, 656–57, 1106–7; R. Dabelstein, *EDNT* 2:1; Dunn, *Theology*, 227–28, 461–72; K. Kertelge, *EDNT* 1:138–40; S. Lyonnet and L. Sabourin, *Sin, Redemption, and Sacrifice* (Rome: Biblical Institute, 1970), 61–184; L. Morris, *DPL*, 784–86; B. J. Ribbens, "Forensic-Retributive Justification in Romans 3:21–26: Paul's Doctrine of Justification in Dialogue with Hebrews," *CBQ* 72 (2012): 548–67.

RESURRECTION, RAISE, RISE

As a committed Pharisee, Paul undoubtedly had a firm belief in the resurrection of the dead, a distinctive tenet of the Pharisaic movement (see Acts 23:8; see also 24:15; 26:6–8). His encounter with the risen Lord on the Damascus road did not, then, originate his belief that God raises the dead. Rather, the experience radically transformed that belief and brought it into the center of all he believed and lived by. As a Pharisee, his belief would have focused on a general resurrection of the dead at the close of the epoch, along the lines of Daniel 12:1–2. Now he was confronted with the resurrection of a single individual prior to the general resurrection. To believe that the individual in question, one who had died on a Roman cross, was Israel's Messiah and indeed Son of God (Gal 1:16) involved for Paul a transformation akin to the act of creation itself, if, as seems to be the case, it was in reference to his call that he later wrote, "For it is the God who said, 'Let light shine out of darkness,' who has shone in our hearts to give the light of the glory of God in the face of Jesus Christ" (2 Cor 4:6 NRSV). God's raising of the crucified Nazarene meant that the new age was already breaking in before the present had run its course.

Paul uses a variety of language in reference to resurrection, whether of Christ or of believers. In both cases, however, the verb *egeirō* predominates (almost forty instances) and, to a much lesser extent, *anistēmi* (1 Thess 4:14, 16; see Eph 5:14), while the noun *anastasis* serves for "resurrection" (Rom 1:4; 6:5; 1 Cor 15:12, 13, 21, 42; Phil 3:10, 11 [*exanastasis*]; see also 2 Tim 2:18). Paul also uses various cognate forms of "live"/"life" (*zaō/zōopoieō/zōē* [sometimes qualified as "eternal" (*aiōnios*)]) with reference to resurrection (Rom 1:17; 4:17; 5:10, 21; 6:10, 22-23; 8:10, 11; 14:9; 1 Cor 15:22, 45; 2 Cor 2:16; 3:6; 4:10, 11; 13:4; Gal 3:21; Phil 2:16; 4:3; 1 Thess 5:10).

The Resurrection of Christ

Paul's brief reference to his encounter with the risen Lord in Galatians 1:15–16, "When God…was pleased to reveal his Son to me," shows that central to his discovery at this point was the revelation of Christ as Son of God. This also emerges from the two-stage summary of the gospel appearing in the introduction to Romans (1:3–4):

> [3] The gospel concerning his Son, who was descended from the seed of David according to the flesh, and [4] was designated Son of God in power according to the Spirit of holiness by resurrection from the dead, Jesus Christ, our Lord.

While the first line of this creedal fragment asserts Jesus's messianic credentials, according to the second his resurrection reveals him to be Son of God. The phrase "in power" likely represents a Pauline insertion into the formula in order to safeguard the sense that all along—in his preexistent state—Christ was Son of God (see Phil 2:6–7; Rom 8:3; Gal 4:4); his resurrection unveiled a status that was already there.

Other creedal fragments preserved in Paul reveal the centrality of the resurrection in the basic proclamation of the gospel. Most notable is that cited by Paul in 1 Corinthians 15:3–5, followed by a list of the key witnesses down to himself (v. 8). The fundamental requirement for salvation is to "confess with your lips that Jesus is Lord and believe in your heart that God raised him from the dead" (Rom 10:9). For believers, God is predominantly "the One who raised Christ from the dead" (Rom 4:24; 8:11; 10:9; 1 Cor 6:14; 15:15; 2 Cor 4:14; Gal 1:1; 1 Thess 1:10; see also Eph 1:20; Col 2:12). Paul sees Abraham's faith in "a God who raises the dead [*tou zōopoiountos tous nekrous*]" (Rom 4:17b) to be paradigmatic of the faith of believers, which is focused on God's raising of the dead Christ (*ton egeiranta Iēsoun*) (v. 24). The added relative clause, "who was given up for our transgressions and raised for our justification" (v. 25)—again, likely a creedal fragment—implies that Paul understood the resurrection as God's vindication or justification of the obedient Christ (Phil 2:8–9; see Rom 5:19), a justification "into" which believers may "enter" through faith and baptism, and so find justification in him (see 5:1).

Paul defends the fragility and vulnerability of his own apostolic ministry in light of the death and resurrection of Christ. At all times, he and his apostolic team are "carrying in the body the death of Jesus, so that the life of Jesus [*hē zōē tou Iēsou*] may be made visible in our bodies" (2 Cor 4:10; see v. 11). They do so confident that "the One who raised the Lord Jesus will raise us also with Jesus, and bring us with you into his presence" (v. 14; see also 1 Cor 4:9; 15:30–34; 2 Cor 13:4). Speaking even more personally in the same vein, Paul tells the Philippians that he wants "to know Christ and the power of his resurrection and the sharing of his sufferings...if somehow I may attain the resurrection from the dead" (3:10–11).

The Resurrection of Believers

The major issue that Paul had to address in regard to resurrection was not so much the resurrection of Christ but that of believers. He initially addressed this question in response to reports from Thessalonica about excessive grieving for loved ones who had died. He assures the community (1 Thess 4:13–18) that such grief is misplaced: "For if we believe that Jesus died and rose again, even so through Jesus God will bring with him those who have died" (v. 14). In the following brief outline of the events of the *parousia* (vv. 16–17), resurrection is solely for the dead; there is no suggestion that those who have remained alive will need to undergo change of some kind in order to join Christ in his risen life.

Paul addresses the issue at far greater length in 1 Corinthians 15, countering denial on the part of some that believers who had already died would be raised (v. 12). The essence of the argument in 15:1–19 is the necessary connection between the resurrection of Christ and that of believers. Denying the latter means denying the former, with all the ill consequences for the truth of the gospel and ultimate salvation that depends on it. Hence Paul recites the basic creed in verses 3–5, adding the list of witnesses down to himself (vv. 6–11). His intent is not to defend belief in the resurrection of Christ but to remind the community that this tenet was central to the gospel to which they had assented and to which they must adhere in order to be saved (vv. 1–2). He deploys at some length (vv. 12–19) a *reductio ad absurdum* argument reiterating the consequences of denying Christ's resurrection. Faith would be rendered in vain, they would be "back in their sins" (v. 17), and those who had died in Christ would indeed be lost (v. 18). If it was for this life only that they had placed their hope in Christ, they would of all people, be most to be pitied (v. 19).

The linkage between the resurrection of Christ and that of believers stems from Paul's conviction that, through faith and baptism, believers enter "into" Christ, henceforth to live "in him" as in a personal corporate sphere of salvation; they constitute his "body" in this sense (1 Cor 12:13). This entrance into Christ and the ensuing union with him is not static but dynamic; believers enter not only into his person but into his total "career": death, burial, and resurrection (Rom 6:3–5, 8). In baptism they have died and been buried with Christ. As regards sharing Christ's risen life, Paul is careful to cast this in the future (Rom 6:5 [*kai tēs anastaseōs esometha*]; v. 8 [*syzēsomen autō*]; see also Rom 8:11; 1 Cor 6:14). However, despite the time gap between the resurrection of Christ and that of believers, the connection remains secure.

Paul addresses the time gap in 1 Corinthians 15:20–28. Christ has been raised as the "firstfruits" (*aparchē*) of those who have "fallen asleep" (v. 20), an image from the "harvest" ritual where the offering of a small initial part of the harvest is a guarantee of the remainder to follow. Paul continues (v. 22), "if in Adam all die (see Rom 5:12), all in Christ will be made alive" (*zōopoiēthēsontai*). Adam and Christ are representative figures, for ill and for good, respectively. If believers die because of their connection, simply as human, with the sin and consequent mortality stemming from Adam, their incorporation, through faith and baptism, in Christ means that they will share his risen life. But—and here (v. 23) Paul reaches the nub of his argument—each will do so in their own "rank" (*tagma*): (first) Christ as "first fruits," and (only) "then those who belong to Christ, at his coming [*parousia*]." In the meantime there intervenes the messianic "reign" of Christ (vv. 24–27) involving the removal of every hostile power and authority. Only when death, the "last" of these, is done away with will the way be open for the general resurrection and Christ's handing over "the kingdom" to the God and Father (v. 28).

The Risen Body

After throwing in a couple of side arguments for the resurrection (the [for us totally obscure] practice of "baptism for the dead" [v. 29] (see BAPTISM); the pointlessness of the risks of his apostolic life [vv. 30–34; see above on 2 Cor 4:7–15]), Paul takes up the very real difficulty in regard to how risen *bodily* life may be conceived (1 Cor 15:35–49) (see BODY, *"Resurrection" Body* above). Paul argues from the capacity of God to create a variety of ways in which bodily life may present itself (vv. 36–44a), concluding (vv. 44b–49) that, if there can be a body vivified by a soul (*sōma psychikon*), there can be a body vivified by the Spirit (*sōma pneumatikon*). To reinforce the point, he has recourse to Scripture (Gen 2:7): the first man Adam became a living being (*eis psychēn zōsan*), the "last Adam" (Christ) became a life-giving Spirit" (*eis pneuma zōopoioun*). As we have born the image (*eikona*) of the first Adam, who was of dust (*choïkos*), so we shall bear the image of the last Adam, who is "of heaven" (*epouranios*) (v. 29). Ultimately, then, Paul conceives of risen bodily existence as heavenly existence, replete with the "glory" (*doxa*) that pertains to God and the divine realm. As such, it means arriving at the status intended by the Creator for human beings from the start (Gen 1:26–28; Ps 8:3–5; Rom 2:10; 3:23; 5:2; 8:17, 18, 21, 29–30; 9:23; 2 Cor 3:18; 4:17; 5:1).

In the description of the end-time scenario in 1 Thessalonians 4:13–18, there is no suggestion that those who had remained alive at the *parousia* of Christ would have to undergo a change before entering into heavenly existence. In the later account (1 Cor 15:50–58), such is the case, since "flesh and blood" (present human existence) cannot "inherit the kingdom of God" (v. 50). Paul shares with the Corinthians what he describes as a "mystery" (v. 51): "We will not all die, but we will all be changed." The present corruptible (body) will have to put on "incorruption" (*aphtharsia*); this mortal (body) immortality (*athanasia*) (v. 53; see 2 Cor 5:1–4). This is as far as Paul is prepared to go in describing the final state of the elect.

Wisely (in contrast to later Christian theology), he refrains from further speculation concerning "what God has prepared for those who love him" (1 Cor 2:9).

Resurrection in the Later Pauline Literature

Resurrection is one area where the later Pauline literature shows significant development beyond the eschatology of Paul. Where Romans 6 speaks of the baptized as buried with Christ and participating in his resurrection only in so far as they must "walk (i.e., live in an ethical sense) in newness of life" (v. 4), Colossians speaks of their "being raised with him" (*synēgerthēte*) (2:12), of God's having "made them alive with him" (*synezōopoiēsen*) (2:13), so that, raised with him, they now share his heavenly life at God's right hand (3:1). The same realized eschatology is even more explicit in Ephesians: "God has raised us up with him and seated us with him in the heavenly places" (2:6). Whereas Colossians does still speak of a hope yet to come (1:5), in Ephesians the future perspective has more or less entirely collapsed into the present. Christ's own resurrection has become merely a stage to his exaltation at the right hand of God, "far above all rule and authority" (1:20–22; 4:8–10). Later, in 2 Timothy 2:18, we find a warning against the extension of the tendency in the direction of claiming that the resurrection has already taken place.

ADAM; BAPTISM; BODY; DEATH; ESCHATOLOGY; GLORY; GOSPEL; HOPE; "IN CHRIST"; LIFE; MYSTERY; SON OF GOD; SPIRIT

Reading

P. J. Brown, *Bodily Resurrection and Ethics in 1 Corinthians 15: Connecting Faith and Morality in the Context of Greco-Roman Mythology* (Tübingen: Mohr Siebeck, 2014); Byrne, *PES*, 105–6, 180–85, 217–27; M. E. Dahl, *The Resurrection of the Body: A Study of 1 Corinthians 15* (London: SCM, 1962); Dunn, *Theology*, 235–40, 487–93; J. Gillman, "Transformation in 1 Cor 15, 50–53," *ETL* 58 (1982): 309–33; L. J. Kreitzer, *DPL*, 805–12; Matera, *GSG*, 75–81, 194–98, 235–36; G. W. E. Nickelsburg, *Resurrection, Immortality and Eternal Life in Intertestamental Judaism* (Cambridge, MA: Harvard University Press, 1972); Sanders, *Paul*, 375–432; Schnelle, *Apostle Paul*, 412–29; 577–97; Wolter, *Paul*, 201–10; N. T. Wright, *The Resurrection of the Son of God* (Minneapolis: Fortress, 2003), 207–374.

REVELATION, REVEAL

Revelation as such is not a theological topic in Paul, as it is in later Christian theology, although the language of revelation (*apokalypsis*; *apokalyptō*; sometimes *phaneroō*) appears in the letters with some frequency. The heavenly world, the abode of God, and God's designs remain hidden from ordinary human knowledge. As such, they can be made known solely through divine revelation. In particular, Paul shared the belief, common to the apocalyptic thought of his day, that God had plans for the final age that had long remained hidden, but which were being disclosed to a privileged few in anticipation of an imminent divine intervention. For Paul, of course that intervention and the revelation attending it was already decisively under way in the sending, death, raising, and exaltation of God's Son. However, it remains to be completed with his second coming and revealing on "the day of the Lord" (1 Cor 1:8; 5:5; 2 Cor 1:14; Phil 1:6, 10; 2:16; 1 Thess 5:2). Thus revelation regularly has an eschatological reference in Paul.

Revelation of the Creator in the Natural World

Paul shares the belief of Hellenistic Judaism, seen especially in the Book of Wisdom (see Wis 13), that human refusal to acknowledge God and the resultant lapse into idolatry are "inexcusable" because God has revealed (*ephanerōsen*) "God's invisible nature, namely his eternal power and deity" in the created world (Rom 1:19–20). Acts presents Paul making a similar appeal to what has traditionally been called "natural theology" when speaking before the Areopagus in Athens (Acts 17:24–28; see also 14:15–17; 1 Thess 1:9–10).

The Revelation of God's Son

Paul describes his encounter with the risen Lord as "when it pleased God…to reveal his Son to me [*apokalypsai ton huion autou en emoi*] in order that I might proclaim him among the Gentiles" (Gal 1:15–16; see also Eph 3:3; Col 4:4). In an act akin to that of creation itself God revealed the crucified Nazarene to be in fact Messiah and Son of God—in short, the very "image" (*eikōn*) of God (2 Cor 4:4, 6). All Paul's subsequent career as apostle and founder of churches goes back to that moment of revelation and apostolic commissioning on the Damascus road.

The gospel that Paul has been commissioned to preach is "the power of God leading to salvation for every believer" (Rom 1:16), because "in it (or "through it") a righteousness of God is being revealed" (*dikaiosynē gar tou theou en autō apokalyptetai*) (v. 17). This "revelation" goes well beyond mere information in a cognitive sense. For those who receive it in faith it is a gracious divine communication of the righteousness required for salvation at the last judgment. The urgency of the summons contained in the gospel stems from the quasi-parallel revelation of the divine wrath (*apokalyptetai gar orgē tou theou*) (v. 18) already patent in the depravity of the idolatrous Gentile world (Rom 1:19–32); a similar threat, Paul goes on to argue, also looms over the Jewish world (2:1–29). In the face of this threat and the universal human lack of righteousness that occasions it (3:19–20, 23), Paul resumes the thematic statement of the gospel (1:16–17) to announce, now with reference to Christ, "But now, apart from the law, a righteousness of God stands revealed [*nuni de chōris nomou dikaiosynē theou pephanerōtai*], …a righteousness of God through faith in Jesus Christ (3:21–22; see Gal 3:23 [*eis tēn mellousan pistin apokalyphthēnai*]). God has graciously intervened in Christ to communicate the righteousness required for justification (Rom 3:24–26) at the judgment. What is required of human beings is a response in faith to this saving revelation (3:27–30).

Revelation in the Ongoing Life of Believers

Besides the fundamental revelation contained in the gospel, believers continue to receive indications of God's will described as "revelation(s)." Stressing his apostolic independence, Paul describes how it was "in response to a revelation" (*kata apokalypsin*) (Gal 2:2) that he went up to the meeting at Jerusalem, along with Barnabas and Titus. It is likely that the charismatic gift of prophecy, which Paul so strongly favors over that of speaking in tongues because of its capacity for communal rather than individual edification (1 Cor 14:1–5), has to do with the revelation of God's will to the community: "...how will I be of benefit to you if I do not speak to you with some revelation [*en apokalypsei*] or knowledge or prophecy or teaching" (1 Cor 14:6; see vv. 25, 26, 30; see Phil 3:15). In contrast to human wisdom (1 Cor 1:20; 2:5), the Spirit has revealed to believers the good things in store for those who love God (2:9–10). More personally, defending his status as an apostle, Paul dares to boast of his mystical experiences, "the visions and revelations of the Lord" (*optasias kai apokalypseis kyriou*) (2 Cor 12:1), the "revelations of exceptional character" (*tē hyperbolē tōn apokalypseōn*) that he received when rapt to the third heaven (v. 7).

Eschatological Revelation

Some things remain to be revealed. The impenitent and hard of heart are storing up for themselves a day of wrath and revelation of the strict justice of God (*en hēmera orgēs kai apokalypseōs dikaiokrisias tou theou*) (Rom 2:5). Above all, believers await the "the revelation [*tēn apokalypsin*] of our Lord Jesus Christ" on "the day" of the Lord (1 Cor 1:7–8; see also 2 Thess 1:7). That same day will reveal how well or otherwise ministers such as Paul and Apollos have "built" the communities they have served (1 Cor 3:13). Such assessment must be left to Christ, who will bring to light things now hidden in darkness and disclose the purposes of the heart (*phanerōsei tas boulas tōn kardiōn*) (4:5).

The glory to be revealed in believers themselves (*tēn mellousan doxan apokalypthēnai eis hēmas*) (Rom 8:18), for which creation has been eagerly longing (v. 19; see v. 22), will be their "revelation" (*tēn apokalypsin*) as sons (and daughters) of God (v. 19). As Christ's resurrection revealed his status, hitherto hidden, as Son of God (Rom 1:4), so the filial relationship with God that believers already enjoy (Rom 8:14–17; Gal 3:26; 4:4–7) will be publicly revealed when they share his bodily risen life (Rom 8:23; see also Col 3:4).

Revelation in the Deutero-Pauline Letters

The sense of a divine plan long hidden but now revealed is prominent in the deutero-Pauline letters. In Colossians the extension of the riches of salvation to the Gentiles is a "mystery" hidden before the ages but now made known to (God's) "holy ones" (*nyn de ephanerōthē tois hagiois autou*) (1:26). This is the mystery that Paul proclaims and teaches in all wisdom (v. 28). Ephesians develops this theme in the description of Paul's calling and mission in 3:1–13. The "mystery" that the Gentiles have become "co-heirs…and sharers in the promise in Christ Jesus through the gospel" (3:6), a mystery not made known to humankind in previous generations (v. 5a), has been made known to Paul "by revelation" (*kata apokalypsin*) (v. 3; see Gal 1:16); it has now been "revealed [*nyn apokalyphthē*] to (Christ's) holy apostles and prophets through the Spirit" (v. 5b). The post-Pauline doxology with which most manuscripts of Romans conclude contains an echo of this, referring to "the proclamation of Jesus Christ, according to the revelation of a mystery [*kat'apokalypsin mystēriou*] wrapped in silence for long ages but now revealed [*phanerōthentos de nyn*] through the prophetic writings" (Rom 16:25–26).

Revelation in the Post-Pauline Letters

The post-Pauline letters speak of Christ's incarnation as his "revelation" in the flesh" (1 Tim 3:16), according to a previously hidden, now revealed design of God (2 Tim 1:10; Titus 1:3). In 2 Thessalonians, on the other hand, the language of revelation is used with reference to "the lawless one," the "revelation" of whom must occur before the *parousia* of Christ (2:3, 6, 8).

ADOPTION; CREATION; GLORY; MYSTERY; PROPHET; RIGHTEOUSNESS; SON OF GOD; WRATH

Reading

M. Barth, *Ephesians 1–3* (New York: Doubleday, 1974), 350–56; Byrne, *Romans*, 64–65, 247–65, 461–64; T. Holtz, *EDNT* 1:130–32; Lincoln, "Colossians," 571–72, 614–15; M. A. Mininger, *Uncovering the Theme of Revelation in Romans 1:16–3:26: Discovering a New Approach to Paul's Argument* (Tübingen: Mohr Siebeck, 2017); G. O'Collins, *Theology and Revelation* (Cork: Mercier, 1968), 51–55; A. Oepke, *TDNT* 3:582–87; Schnelle, *Apostle Paul*, 88–91, 311, 319; Wolter, *Paul*, 55–61.

RICHES, POVERTY

The antithetical themes of "rich" and "poor" appear in both a literal and a spiritualized sense in Paul's letters, although the latter is more prevalent.

Material Wealth and Poverty

In contrast to other New Testament documents, for example, the Synoptic gospels and the Letter of James, neither the danger of riches nor the plight of the materially poor emerge as significant concerns in Paul's letters. His personal indifference in the matter is clear from his stated policy in regard to receiving financial support from the churches. He has the right, as apostle, to receive such support (1 Cor 9:4–12a, 13–14), but has chosen to forgo it so as not to impose a burden on the churches and possibly hinder the gospel (vv. 12b, 15; see also 2 Thess 3:7–9). This meant working with his hands to support himself (1 Cor 4:12), thereby in the eyes of some placing his apostolic status in question (2 Cor 11:7). The hardships of the apostolic life included going hungry, thirsty, and naked (1 Cor 4:11; 2 Cor 6:5; 11:27). While very grateful for the gifts that the Philippians have sent him (Phil 4:10, 14–19), Paul is indifferent to having little or having plenty, of being well-fed or hungry (vv. 11–13). Although poor, he and his fellow workers, are "making many rich"; although "having nothing," they "possess everything" (2 Cor 6:10; see 1 Cor 3:21–23). Here we see the linkage in his mind between material poverty and spiritual riches that was later to flourish in the ascetical tradition of the Christian church.

If not a significant theme, concern for the poor does emerge from occasional references in Paul's letters. "Contribute to the needs of the saints" (v. 13a) appears among the pithy injunctions listed in Romans 12:9–13. More significant is the nub of Paul's complaint about the way in which the Corinthians are celebrating the Lord's supper (1 Cor 11:17–34). When the community failed to wait for everyone to arrive (v. 33), when each one went ahead with his or her own meal (v. 21), they not only deprived the poorer members of food. Much worse, they "shamed" them (*kateischynete tous mē echontas*) (v. 22b); they made them feel their social inferiority in a way that cut right across the meaning imprinted on the supper by the Lord (vv. 23–26) (see EUCHARIST).

Generosity in Contributing to the Collection for the Saints

Most references to wealth occur in 2 Corinthians 8—9, where Paul is urging the community to generosity in regard to the collection for the saints (see MINISTRY). He cites the example of the churches in Macedonia, where the gift of God's grace has meant that their "abundant joy and extreme poverty, during a time of severe affliction, overflowed in a wealth of generosity" (8:2; see also Rom 15:26). Later he points out to the Corinthians that God "who supplies seed to the sower and bread for food will supply and multiply your seed for sowing and increase the harvest of your righteousness" (9:10); they will be "enriched in every way" (v. 11), "for the rendering of this ministry not only supplies the needs of the saints but also overflows with many thanksgivings to God" (v. 12).

Here we see the theological vision that underpins Paul's appeal for generosity in material relief. It begins with the grace of God (8:2) and ends with stimulating thanksgiving to God (9:12), which in fact is the goal of Paul's ministry as a whole (4:15). The core consideration is christological:

> For you know the generous gift [*tēn charin*] of our Lord Jesus Christ, who, though he was rich [*plousios ōn*], became poor for your sake [*di' hymas eptōcheusen*], in order that you might be enriched by his poverty [*tē ekeinou ptōcheia ploutēsēte*]. (2 Cor 8:9)

The "richness" of Christ and the "poverty" that he embraced hardly refer to the material circumstances of his earthly life. Most are agreed that his preexistent state as described in Philippians 2:6 and his self-emptying embrace of the enslaved human condition (Phil 2:7–8) are, respectively, in view here, while the resultant "enrichment" of human beings would be the righteousness that leads to salvation (2 Cor 5:21). It is this supreme act of divine generosity that, for Paul, lies behind and should motivate the generosity of believers toward those less materially fortunate than themselves.

Warnings about the danger of riches are more frequent in the post-Pauline literature (1 Tim 3:8; 6:9, 17; Titus 1:7), although Paul himself lists the "greedy" among the kinds of unregenerate persons with whom believers should not have dealings (1 Cor 5:11).

The "Riches" of God's Grace

Aside from the connection between material generosity and spiritual enrichment mentioned above, Paul speaks frequently of the "riches" lavished on human beings by God: Romans 2:4 ("the riches of God's kindness and patience and mercy"); 9:23 ("the riches of his glory [*ton plouton tēs doxēs autou*] for the vessels of his mercy, which he has prepared beforehand for glory"); 10:12 ("bestowing his riches on all who call on him" [*ploutōn eis pantas tous epikaloumenous auton*]); 11:12, 33; 1 Corinthians 1:5; Philippians 4:19. The "riches" in question would for the most part be the eschatological glory in store for believers according to age-old design of God (Rom 5:2; 8:17, 18, 30; 1 Cor 2:8–10; 2 Cor 4:16–18; Phil 3:21; see Eph 1:18; Titus 3:6).

The "Riches" of God's Grace in the Later Pauline Letters

The hymnic nature of so much of the content of Ephesians lends itself to repeated celebratory expressions of the riches of God's grace (Eph 1:7), mercy (2:4), and glory (3:16). Paul's prayer is that the recipients "may know…what are the riches of (God's) glorious inheritance amongst the saints" (1:18). We have been raised up with Christ so that in the ages to come God might show "the surpassing richness [*to hyperballon ploutos*] of his grace in kindness to us in Christ Jesus" (2:7). To Paul, "the very least of all the saints," has been given "the grace of proclaiming to the Gentiles the inexhaustible richness [*to anexichniaston ploutos*] of Christ" (3:8). This last formulation would seem to build on the similar christological expression in Colossians concerning God's making known to the saints "how great among the Gentiles are the riches of the glory of this mystery [*to ploutos tēs doxēs tou mystēriou toutou*], which is Christ in you, the hope of glory" (Col 1:27; see also 2:2–3).

APOSTLE; CHRIST; GLORY; GRACE; SLAVERY

Reading

Byrne, *PES*, 190, 196; Dunn, *Theology*, 707–11; Harris, *2 Corinthians*, 577–81, 588–93, 631–46; S. Joubert, *Paul as Benefactor: Reciprocity, Strategy and Theological Reflection in Paul's Collection* (Tübingen: Mohr Siebeck, 2000); B. W. Longenecker, *Remembering the Poor: Paul, Poverty, and the Greco-Roman World* (Grand Rapids: Eerdmans, 2010), 135–316; H. Merklein, *EDNT* 3:114–17; T. E. Schmidt, *DPL*, 826–27; Schnelle, *Apostle Paul*, 62–63; Wolter, *Paul*, 40–42.

RIGHTEOUSNESS

It is generally agreed that Paul's usage in regard to righteousness reflects the Septuagint's employment of *dikaiosynē* to translate the Hebrew terms *sedeq* and *sedaqa* (see JUSTIFICATION). This Hebrew word group, however, is currently understood in two rather different ways: as indicating either "behavior according to a norm or standard" or "faithfulness within a relationship." The former aligns with an understanding of *dikaiosynē* going back to ancient Greece, especially Aristotle, and continues in the sense of "justice" in the Western philosophical and legal tradition ("conformity [of an action or thing] to moral right or to reason, truth, or fact" [*OED* 1:1466]). When understood in regard to the deity, God's righteousness in this sense would refer to the divine commitment to act always in accord with the norm of God's being. In a biblical (Old Testament) frame of reference, then, God would display righteousness in ever seeking as Creator, ruler, and judge of the universe to preserve and restore its order.

The alternative view of righteousness as indicating faithfulness within a relationship became prominent in biblical studies at the turn of the twentieth century and has remained strong ever since. In regard to Israel, the relationship in question is the covenant relationship whereby God displays righteousness by consistently coming to the rescue of Israel, while, on the human side, Israel discharges its covenant obligations by faithful observance of the Mosaic law. With respect to God, this relational understanding lends a salvific note to God's righteousness, seen particularly in the Psalms and (Second) Isaiah—salvific for Israel, while often destructive for Israel's enemies and oppressors.

These two understandings of the divine righteousness—conformity to the norm of divine being in the sense of distributive justice and saving fidelity to the covenant relationship—are not necessarily at odds with each other. It has been plausibly argued (Irons) that the comparatively frequent references to the exercise of God's righteousness in a salvific sense should be seen as a subset of the divine distributive justice whereby God is faithful to the covenant relationship, seeking to rescue, purify, and restore Israel. Faithfulness to the covenant relationship, then, is not the essence of divine righteousness but rather a significant particular *instance* of it. By the same token, the righteousness required of Israel to observe the law retains the sense of conformity to a norm, the Mosaic law being the norm in question.

Justification enters into this understanding of righteousness when one party forms an assessment of how another party has acted in light of a norm or obligation incumbent on that other party. One "justifies" the other party, when one recognizes or declares that they have acted in conformity with that obligation, that they have acted "righteously" in this sense, and so are righteous. Thus in the matter of righteousness and justification a "triangular" pattern is operative: required is (1) a law or norm or principle, which may remain implicit rather than something consciously appealed to; (2) a person or behavior that is the subject of assessment on the part of another; and (3) another party, divine or human, who assesses and declares whether the person or conduct is righteous (or unrighteous) in light of the accepted norm. Furthermore, it is to be noted that such an assessment does not "make" the person righteous; it is the behavior that makes the person righteous and so apt to be declared such—just as, in a negative case, the negative assessment does not make a person unrighteous; what "makes" a person unrighteous is the bad behavior that renders the person liable to be declared unrighteous. Where justification is likely to have a forensic nuance because of its obvious relevance in a legal or law court context, righteousness, on the other hand, has a more wide-ranging reference, tending to feature wherever there is question of behavior in light of an explicit or implicit norm.

"Righteousness" in Paul

The forensic aspect of "righteousness"/"justification" explains the prominence of these related concepts in the letters of Paul. A key feature of the apocalyptic cast of thought that he shared with the Judaism of his time was the expectation of a more or less imminent divine intervention in which God would institute a day of judgment to deal once and for all with the evil of the present age, vindicate the righteous, punish or eliminate the wicked, and bring in a new age that would truly fulfill the Creator's original design for Israel and the world. Axiomatic in the biblical and postbiblical tradition is the intrinsic link between righteousness and the gaining of (eternal) life. In the eschatological scenario just outlined the most pressing question then was whether one would be found righteous at the judgment and so apt to be saved from the divine wrath destined to be unleashed on the world. For the devout in Israel the hope was that practice of the Mosaic law would render one righteous and that such righteousness—law-righteousness—would be the "passport" to life in the new age. Such is exactly the righteousness on which Paul the devout Pharisee placed his hopes according to his own report, "as to righteousness in the law becoming blameless" (Phil 3:6b; see Gal 1:13–14).

The revelation to Paul of the Crucified as Messiah and Son of God (Gal 1:16) was at the same time a revelation of total unrighteousness on the human side, not only in the unbelieving Gentile world but also in Israel as well (Rom 3:19–20, 23; 5:12d; Gal 3:22). Observance of the Mosaic law was not a path to obtaining the righteousness required for justification (see Phil 3:7–9). But equally, and this came to be the heart of the gospel that Paul was to preach, God in Christ was offering, not just to Israel but to the world at large, a righteousness that would avail at the judgment, "a righteousness of God," accessible to human beings solely on the basis of faith.

Righteousness in Galatians

The prominence of the issue of "justification"/"righteousness" in Galatians stems from the aim of the letter, which is to deter Paul's Gentile converts in Galatia from yielding to pressure from intrusive Christian-Jewish teachers to complete their Christian formation and ensure their justification by taking on precepts of the Jewish law, specifically circumcision. Paul vigorously recalls (Gal 2:11–21) a riposte he made to Cephas and others at Antioch in the face of a similar attempt to reinstate, in the name of righteousness, the division between Jews and Gentiles at communal meals (separate tables). The nub of Paul's protest is that if righteousness were to be gained through observance of the law that would have the—unthinkable—effect of rendering null the costly death of Christ (Gal 2:21).

As Paul argues (Gal 3:1–4:7), the Galatians' experience of the Spirit when coming to faith in the gospel of the Crucified (see 3:2–5) shows that they already enjoy the eschatological justification, in line with the scriptural promise to Abraham that God would justify the Gentiles and do so on the same pattern as shown in him: that is, by faith (Gen 15:6, cited in Gal 3:6; see Rom 4:3). The law, coming centuries later could not set aside the operation of this promise focused entirely on Christ and his saving work (3:13–18). Had it been able to give life, righteousness might have been found in the law (3:21), but the law was given not to provide life but "for the sake of transgressions" (3:19), that is, to expose and condemn sin (see Rom 7:13). As the Spirit attests, through faith and baptism, the Galatians are already "sons (and daughters) of God, heirs (of Abraham) according to the promise" (3:26–29; see 4:6–7); they have no need to seek righteousness by any route other than through faith. To do so would cut them off from Christ (5:4), whereas, "We through the Spirit have by faith the hope that righteousness holds out" (5:5). Alternatively, and more commonly, the genitive in the last phrase (*elpida dikaiosynēs*) can be translated in an objective sense: "the hope of righteousness." But this throws "righteousness" into the future, whereas the whole thrust of Paul's argument in the letter has been that, as attested by the Spirit, faith has *already* allowed the Galatians to have the status of righteousness (see also Phil 1:11: "fruit [*karpon*] of righteousness").

Righteousness in Romans

In contrast to the sparse references in Galatians, righteousness occurs frequently in Paul's letter to Rome. Writing to a community he had not himself founded, he sets out explicitly and at length the gospel message of salvation with righteousness at its heart (Rom 1:16–17):

> [16] For I am not ashamed of the gospel. It is the power of God leading to salvation for all who come to faith, the Jew first, but also the Greek. [17] For in it a righteousness of God is being revealed, from faith to faith, as it is written, "*The person righteous by faith will live*" (Hab 2:4).

As will soon be made clear (v. 18), the salvation in question is salvation from the "wrath" destined to be unleashed at the judgment. The gospel is "the power of God leading to salvation" because it makes available the righteousness required for being justified at the judgment and so escaping the wrath. At this point Paul does not further specify the meaning of "a righteousness of God." (There is no definite article before the Greek phrase *dikaiosynē tou theou*.) He simply states that the gospel makes such righteousness universally available through the human response of faith. He bolsters this with a quotation from the prophet Habakkuk that forges a link between being righteous through faith and the gaining of (eternal) life. The quoted text is open to alternative translation (e.g., "The one who is righteous will live by faith," NRSV). The translation favored above (NRSV alternative) stems from the consideration that what is at issue here is not how the righteous person lives but by what kind of righteousness a person must be clad in order to "live" in the sense of gaining (eschatological) life at the judgment. To which Paul's answer is: "a righteousness attained through faith," the implicit exclusion being: "not by law" (see 3:19–20).

The thematic statement (1:16–17), is followed by a lengthy prophetic declamation (1:18—3:20) designed to exclude the possibility of gaining righteousness on any basis other than through faith. Specifically excluded is the possibility of doing so on the basis of the law (2:1—3:20). The law gives Jews no advantage, because all—Jews and Gentiles alike—are "under sin" (3:9). Lumping Israel, however, along with the sinful Gentile world in this way, puts in question God's faithfulness to Israel. Paul allows a series of objections to rise (3:1–8), one of which (v. 5) asks in this connection about "God's righteousness," clearly meaning the phrase to be understood in the subjective sense of God's personal righteousness.

In the face of the sustained assertion of universal sinfulness (1:18—3:20) and the issue it has raised in regard to God's own righteousness (3:5), Paul restates the theme of the letter at some length (3:21–26). The passage is so central to the understanding of righteousness in Paul that it needs to be set out in full:

> [22] But now, apart from the law, a righteousness of God [*dikaiosynē theou*] stands revealed, with the law and the prophets bearing witness, a righteousness of God [*dikaiosynē theou*] through faith in Jesus Christ for all who believe. For there is no distinction— [23] for all have sinned and lack the glory of God. [24] They are being justified [*dikaioumenoi*] freely by his grace through the redemption which has come about in Christ Jesus. [25] God put him forward as a means of expiation, (operative) through faith, in (the shedding of) his blood. This was to display God's righteousness [*tēs dikaiosynēs autou*] because of the passing over of sins previously committed [26] in (the time of) God's patience; it was (also) to show God's righteousness [*tēs dikaiosynēs autou*] at the present time: that God is righteous [*dikaion*] and (that God) justifies [*dikaiounta*] the one who has faith in Jesus.

As can be seen, the passage is "enclosed" at beginning and end by double statements of the revelation (or display) of the divine righteousness. Moreover, the final statement of this in verse 26 ("that God is righteous...") makes clear that God's own personal righteousness is in question. From one angle, as previously noted, the issue arises out of the series of objections formulated in 3:1–8: if Israel is bound up with the sinfulness of the entire world (3:9), how has God been faithful to the promises (*ta logia tou theou* [v. 2]) made specifically to this people? How has God been righteous in this (salvific) respect? On the other hand, how can the all-holy God simply be true to Godself if sin is left unpunished, "un-dealt with" in some way? Would not this impugn the divine righteousness in a more judicial or forensic sense (see v. 25b)?

Taken as a whole, Romans 3:21–26 responds to this tension in regard to the divine righteousness. God has found a way to resolve it by making a gift of divine righteousness accessible to human beings simply on the basis of faith (vv. 21–22). Through faith in God's action in Christ human beings can access an outreach of divine righteousness that expiates sin and leads to their being justified (*dikaioumenoi* [v. 24a]). As such they are liberated from the threat of the wrath (1:18) and set on the path to salvation. In this God, as covenant partner, has been faithful to Israel. But God has also been faithful, as Creator, to the entire world, since justification by faith, aside from the law, makes salvation available to all (3:29–30).

Hence "righteousness," specifically the righteousness specified as "a righteousness of God," emerges from this passage in a range of reference. In origin it is God's own righteousness in a subjective sense (as in 3:5). But in Christ believers access this divine righteousness as a gift so that, while never ceasing to be God's righteousness, it serves to render *them* righteous. The second half of verse 26 holds together these dual aspects of the divine righteousness. One can even add a third, mediating aspect of righteousness in a christological sense. Paul in 1 Corinthians 1:30 speaks of Christ as having become "our righteousness from God" (*apo theou dikaiosynē*). Believers access the divine righteousness in that, through faith and baptism, they participate in Christ, who personally embodies the divine righteousness in the world. This christological sense of the divine righteousness can be seen also in the striking statement Paul formulates toward the end of his appeal for reconciliation in 2 Corinthians 5: "God made him who knew no sin into sin so that we might become righteousness of God in him" (*dikaiosynē theou en autō*) (v. 21).

In Romans 4 Paul provides scriptural validation focused on the experience of Abraham for the principle that the righteousness required for salvation is by faith and not performance of the law. He cites (LXX) Genesis 15:6, the "gold mine" text for him in this connection: "Abraham believed God and it was reckoned to him as righteousness" (*logisthē autō eis dikaiosynēn*). Read entirely through the lens of the gospel, the patriarch's experience is more than a scriptural example of righteousness by faith. It sets a paradigm in that his "progeny" who follow him in his faith will have righteousness "reckoned" to them in their believing exactly as in the case of their "father" Abraham (4:11b, 23–24).

The second main section of Romans (chapters 5—8) asserts the hope of salvation for those justified by faith (5:1). It addresses the time gap between justification already granted to believers (5:1) and final salvation at the judgment (8:31–39). The hope of salvation rests primarily on the faithfulness of God, whose love, already shown in such extreme degree in the Christ event, will surely not fail to see the justified through to full salvation (5:6–11; 8:31–39). At the same time believers also have a role in the attaining of salvation in that the task before them is to preserve and live out the righteousness that has been gifted to them in Christ. In Romans 5:12–21, Paul pursues the case for hope by setting up a reiterated comparison/contrast between Christ and Adam. There is hope for eternal life because God's gift in Christ of the righteousness that leads to (eternal) life is so "much more" powerful than the legacy of sin leading to death stemming from Adam (5:17, 21).

Paul personifies sin and death, on the one hand, and grace, righteousness, and life, on the other hand, as "powers" that affect human life for ill and good respectively. The personification, for rhetorical effect, does not notably alter the sense of righteousness operative up to this point. From the beginning of chapter 6, however, and continuing through to 8:13, the stress is on the necessity and possibility of *living out* the gift of righteousness in order to preserve the destiny to eternal life. So Paul exhorts his readers to offer all aspects of their bodily life (*ta melē*) as "instruments of righteousness to God" (*hopla dikaiosynēs tō theō*) (6:13). Employing a "slavery" image (for which he apologizes [v. 19a]), on the positive as well as on the negative side of the equation he speaks of them as "enslaved" to righteousness as once they were enslaved to sin. Where the outcome in the previous case was eternal death, the outcome in the new situation is, first, sanctification (the transformation of their moral life), and ultimately eternal life (vv. 18–23). The capacity for living out the gift of righteousness stems from the fact that for those, in Christ, the "impossibility" of living righteously under the regime of the law (7:5, 7–25) has been replaced by the possibility of so living because, following the divine intervention in Christ (8:1–4), the Spirit has replaced sin as the controlling indwelling power (8:4–11). In Paul's succinct formulation, "If Christ is in you, while the body may be mortal because of sin, the Spirit means (eternal) life, because of righteousness" (*to de pneuma zōē dia dikaiosynēn*) (8:10).

"Righteousness" reappears in Romans where Paul confronts the issue presented by the continuing refusal of the bulk of Israel to respond to the gospel (Romans 9—11). The issue has been exacerbated by the positive response on the part of Gentiles, so that Gentiles, who did not originally pursue righteousness at all, have obtained it through faith, whereas "they" (the Jews), pursuing a righteousness through practice of the law, did not "arrive" at it (9:30–31). They failed to do so because, proceeding by works of the law and not from faith, they "stumbled at the rock of offense," the Crucified Messiah placed in their path by God (vv. 32–33; see 1 Cor 1:23; Gal 3:1). They clung to their own pursuit of righteousness (*tēn idian dikaiosynēn*), failing to recognize and submit to the righteousness of God (*tēn tou theou dikaiosynēn*) (10:3). For Christ is "the end (or "goal") of the law as far as righteousness is concerned (*eis dikaiosynēn*) for every believer" (v. 4; see 1:16–17; 3:21–26; 2 Cor 3:9; 5:21).

Paul supports (Rom 10:5–13) his analysis of Israel's failure with an appeal to Scripture in the shape of Deuteronomy 30:11–14. Going against the original thrust of the text, where Moses was speaking of the ease of practicing the law, Paul invokes the final verse of this passage (v. 14), "The word is near you, on your lips and in your heart" (cited in Rom 10:8) in favor of righteousness by faith: "For one believes with the heart (leading) to righteousness" (*pisteuetai eis dikaiosynēn* [v. 10a]).

Righteousness aside from Galatians and Romans

In Philippians 3:4–11, Paul sharply contrasts the righteousness he had been seeking through blameless practice of the law with "the surpassing value of knowing Christ Jesus" (v. 8) and being "found in him, not having a righteousness of my own [*emēn dikaiosynēn*] stemming from the law but, the (righteousness) that comes from faith in Christ, the righteousness from God based on faith [*tēn ek theou dikaiosynēn epi tē pistei*]" (v. 9). We might have expected the statement in 2 Corinthians 5:21 cited above, to conclude, "that we might become righteous" (*dikaioi*). Instead it reads, "so that we might become righteousness of God in him" (*genōmetha dikaiosynē theou en autō*). Paul's formulation preserves the sense of a righteous status attained totally through participation in the One who embodies the righteousness graciously gifted by God (Rom 5:17b; 1 Cor 1:30).

Elsewhere in Paul "righteousness" appears without strict connection to response to the gospel, having become more or less synonymous with appropriate apostolic or general Christian living (Rom 14:17; 2 Cor 6:7, 14; 9:10; 11:15; Phil 1:11). This is certainly the case where the term appears in Ephesians (4:24; 5:9; 6:14) and the post-Pauline literature (1 Tim 6:11; 2 Tim 2:22; 3:16; 4:8), although a relic of the more polemical contrast with law-righteousness makes an appearance in Titus 3:5.

ABRAHAM; ADAM; DEATH; FAITH; HOLINESS, SANCTIFICATION, GRACE; JUDGE, LAST JUDGMENT; JUSTIFICATION; LAW; LIFE; MOSES; SALVATION; SPIRIT; WRATH

Reading (Select):

Barclay, *Gift*, 375–76, 461–79, 536–44; Beker, *Paul the Apostle*, 260–69; Bultmann, *Theology*, 1:270–85; Byrne, "Living Out," 560–81; *PES*, 35–41, 71–76, 92–103, 113–16, 132–33, 140–45, 229–38; *Romans*, 52–60, 122–34, 234–47, 307–23; Dunn, *Theology*, 334–85; C. L. Irons, *The Righteousness of God: A Lexical Examination of the Covenant-Faithfulness Interpretation* (Tübingen: Mohr Siebeck, 2015); E. Käsemann, "'The Righteousness of God' in Paul," in *New Testament Questions of Today* (London: SCM, 1969), 168–82; K. Kertelge, *DPL*, 325–30; Moo, *Romans*, 71–90; K. L. Onesti and M. T. Brauch, *DPL*, 827–37; Schnelle, *Apostle Paul*, 317–23; M. A. Seifrid, *Christ, Our Righteousness: Paul's Theology of Justification* (Downers Grove, IL: Intervarsity, 2000); Westerholm, *Perspectives*, 273–96; "The Righteousness of the Law and the Righteousness of Faith in Romans," *Int* 58 (2004): 253–64; J. A. Ziesler, *The Meaning of Righteousness in Paul* (Cambridge: Cambridge University Press, 1972).

S

SALVATION, SAVE, SAVIOR

"Salvation" is a concept that has been greatly broadened in the theological tradition beyond its meaning in the Pauline letters. When considering Paul's usage of "salvation" (*sōtēria*) and related terms (*sōzō* ["save"]; *sōtēr* ["savior"]) it is necessary to keep in mind the apocalyptic cast of his thought and expectation. The word group has the general sense of rescue from any necessity or danger, especially from disease or death (see Phil 1:19). In various forms of religious expression in the Greco-Roman milieu it had already acquired the transcendental sense (divine rescue from eternal death or ruin) that mainly pertains to it in the New Testament. Within the apocalyptic schema presupposed in the undisputed Pauline letters salvation almost always indicates rescue from the wrath (*orgē*) destined to fall on the unbelieving world at the imminent judgment. The rescue in every case is that achieved by God in Christ—though only once in these letters is Christ described as "Savior" (*sōtēr*) (Phil 3:20).

Salvation from the Wrath

In Romans, Paul's characteristic reference of salvation is clear from the start. The opening thematic assertion that the gospel is "the power of God leading to salvation [*eis sōtērian*]" for every believer because a righteousness of God is revealed in it (1:16–17) is followed immediately by a statement concerning the revelation of God's wrath (v. 18). This in turn introduces a long sequence (1:19—3:20) indicating the perilous situation of all humanity because all, being "under sin" (Rom 3:9), lack the righteousness required for salvation. Thus the pressing need for salvation from the wrath is the essential background to the proclamation of the gospel.

The same future reference of salvation to the wrath is explicit in 5:9–10 when Paul expresses the sure hope that, "having been justified in (Christ's) blood, we shall be saved through him from the wrath" (*sōthēsometha...apo tēs orgēs*), and that "having been reconciled [*katallagentes*], we shall be saved through his life" (*sōthēsometha en tē zōē autou*). In his earliest letter, Paul reminds the Thessalonians that, having turned from idolatry to the worship of a living and true God, they now "await his Son from heaven... Jesus, who will rescue us from the coming wrath" (*ton rhyomenon hēmas ek tēs orgēs tēs erchomenēs*) (1 Thess 1:10). Later he assures them that "God has destined us not for wrath but for obtaining salvation [*eis peripoiēsin sōtērias*] through our Lord Jesus Christ" (5:9).

Thus for Paul the present life of believers is situated between justification already received through their faith in Christ (see Rom 5:1) and salvation, which remains outstanding though radically in process because of justification and the gift of divine righteousness consequent on it (5:9). While Paul normally speaks of salvation as something yet to come (besides the references above, see Rom 10:9–10, 13 [quotation from Joel 3:5]; 11:26 ["all Israel"]; 13:11; 1 Cor 3:15; 5:5; 7:16; 9:22; 10:33; Phil 1:28; 3:20 [expectation of a "savior (*sōtēra*) from heaven"]), he can also speak of it as a work currently in progress: "The cross is foolishness to those who are perishing [*tois apollymenois*], but to us who are being saved [*tois sōzomenois*] it is the power of God" (1 Cor 1:18; see the same dichotomy in 2 Cor 2:15); the Corinthians "are being saved" (*sōzesthe*) through the gospel (1 Cor 15:2). In this sense the Philippians are exhorted to "work out their salvation [*sōtērian katergazesthe*] in fear and trembling" (2:12). In one case only (Rom 8:24a) is salvation expressed in the past tense when Paul writes, "we have been saved in hope" (*tē...elpidi esōthēmen* [Rom 8:24a]) but the qualification "in hope" immediately directs the perspective to the future. The past (aorist) tense of the verb expresses the decisiveness of the transformation already under way, while the qualification preserves the sense that it will only be complete with the "redemption [*apolytrōsis*] of the body" (v. 23c) in resurrection. Believers are thus "on the way" to salvation though they already enjoy its essence in the new relationship with God already effected in justification.

Paul frequently speaks of salvation as the goal of the divine intervention in Christ and his own apostolic efforts without strict indication of time (Rom 11:11, 14; 1 Cor 1:21; 9:22; 10:33; 2 Cor 1:6; 6:2; 7:10; 1 Thess 2:16). One may ask whether the goal in question refers strictly to rescue from the wrath or extends more positively to embrace entrance into the transformed, glorious existence of the new creation (see Rom 5:2; 8:17, 30; 1 Cor 15:49, 54; 2 Cor 4:17)—as in the later theological tradition. However, the sense of rescue from the present evil age and negative destiny (*apōleia*) awaiting the unredeemed world in Paul's apocalyptic perspective always seems to be present, a rescue that can also be expressed by the verb *ruomai* (1 Thess 1:10; Rom 11:26 [quotation from LXX Isa 59:20–21]; see also Col 1:13).

Salvation in the Later Pauline Literature

If salvation in the undisputed Pauline letters primarily refers to future rescue from the wrath, in Ephesians the eschatological reference is played down in favor of a sense of salvation already present because of what God has brought about in Christ. In an echo of Romans 1:16–17, the gospel is "the gospel of salvation" (*to euangelion tēs sōtērias* [Eph 1:13]), but elsewhere salvation is set (in the perfect tense) as something the audience has already experienced, the effect of which lingers on: hence the reiterated expression, "by grace you have been saved" (*chariti...sesōsmenoi* [2:5, 8]; see also 2 Tim 1:9). In 5:23, Christ is described as "the head of the church, of which he is the Savior" (*sōtēr*).

In the post-Pauline letters, the title "Savior" is applied to God (1 Tim 1:1; 2:3; 4:10; 2 Tim 1:9; Titus 1:3; 2:10; 3:4) and Christ (2 Tim 1:10; Titus 1:4; 2:13; 3:6) alike, without any suggestion of a distinction in the work of salvation. "Salvation," though vaguely referred to the future (see, however, 1 Tim 2:15; 4:16), has really become the standard general description of all that God willed and has begun to achieve for the world through Christ (2 Thess 2:10, 13; 1 Tim 1:15; 2:4; 2 Tim 2:10; 3:15; Titus 3:4), thus preparing the way for the furtherance of this tendency in the later theological tradition.

ADAM; APOCALYPTIC; CHRIST; DEATH; ESCHATOLOGY; FAITH; HOPE; JUSTIFICATION; LIFE; RIGHTEOUSNESS; WRATH

Reading

G. W. Burnett, *Paul and the Salvation of the Individual* (Leiden; Boston: Brill, 2001); Byrne, *PES*, 73–75, 109–21, 125, 132–35, 175–76, 178–79, 212–13, 224; Dunn, *Theology*, 317–33, 460–72, 487–98; Fee, *Pauline Christology*, 481–88; W. Foerster, *TDNT* 7:965–69, 992–95;

Matera, *GSG*, 120–23; L. Morris, *DPL*, 858–62; Schnelle, *Apostle Paul*, 577–92; J. L. Sumney, "'For Our Sins': Understandings of Salvation," in *Steward of God's Mysteries: Paul and Early Church Tradition* (Grand Rapids: Eerdmans, 2017), 70–95.

SAVIOR (*see* Salvation)

SANCTIFICATION (*see* Holiness)

SATAN

In the Hebrew Bible, "satan" (*satan*) refers in first instance to an adversary that stands in one's way (e.g., Num 22:22, 32; 1 Kgs 11:14, 23). In Job 1—2 and Zechariah 3:1–2, "the Satan" is a name applied to a member of the angelic heavenly court ("the sons of God" [see Job 1:6]) who acts as a prosecutor or accuser. Hence the Septuagint's translation *ho diabolos*, which in due course becomes "the devil." In later Jewish literature, "Satan" appears as the head and principal agent of an array of spiritual beings hostile to God and bent on frustrating God's designs for human beings. Ongoing contest with this adversary was a significant feature of the apocalyptic background to Paul's theology and that of the New Testament as a whole. Paul in the undisputed letters refers to this being as "Satan," whereas "the devil" is more frequent in the later Pauline letters, as also in the gospels. Paul himself also refers to Satan under other titles and descriptions: "Beliar" (2 Cor 6:15); "the god of this age" (2 Cor 4:4); "the serpent" (2 Cor 11:3); "the tempter" (1 Thess 3:5; see also "the evil one" in Eph 6:16; 2 Thess 3:3).

Although ultimately destined to be destroyed, Satan's rule is permitted by God to endure while the present, evil age runs its course. This offers an explanation for the continuance of evil and sin despite the saving intervention of God in Christ. In principle, believers, through faith and baptism, have been "rescued from the power of darkness and transferred to the kingdom of God's beloved Son" (Col 1:13). But outside the community of salvation Satan's rule still runs and, in subtle ways, still exerts destructive influence on individuals and the community at large.

God's Permissive "Use" of Satan

In an instruction that remains largely mysterious, Paul insists that the community in Corinth expel a member living in an openly immoral situation (1 Cor 5:1–5). They are "to hand this man over to Satan [*paradounai ton toiauton tō satana*] for the destruction of the flesh, so that (his) spirit may be saved [*hina to pneuma sōthē*] on the day of the Lord" (v. 5). Assignment to Satan appears here to have an ultimately salvific purpose, to be realized on the day of judgment.

God's permissive "use" of Satan seems to apply in Paul's case when, as he reports, lest he become too elated by the revelations he received (2 Cor 12:1–4) "a thorn in the flesh, an angel of Satan" (*angelos satana*) has been given to "buffet" (*kolaphizē*) him (v. 7). God allows this satanic onslaught for his spiritual benefit. By contrast, the simply adversarial role of Satan is apparent when Paul attributes his failure to revisit the Thessalonians as due to "blocking" (*enekopsen*) on the part of Satan (1 Thess 2:18).

Satan as Subtle Tempter

In 1 Corinthians 7, Paul responds to questions the Corinthians had raised concerning whether, with the end of the age at hand (see 7:29–31), those who were married should continue to have sexual relations. Paul shares the keen eschatological expectation but, in view of the danger of recourse to prostitution (*dia tas porneias*) (v. 2; see 6:12–20), advises that each man should have his own wife and each wife her husband. If they choose to abstain from sexual relations to devote themselves to prayer, it should be only by mutual agreement and for a time (v. 5a), lest Satan tempt them through want of self-control (v. 5b). Satan may subtly employ a good thing (abstaining in order to have leisure for prayer) to bring about a bad end (recourse to sexual comfort outside marriage).

In 2 Corinthians 2:5–11, Paul is concerned that the Corinthians treat with forgiveness and console a person who has seriously offended lest he be overcome with excessive grief (v. 7). Otherwise, Satan might make use of their continuing anger, righteous though it may be, to cause deep spiritual harm to the man himself and to the community as a whole (v. 11).

Later in the letter, when attempting to counter the influence of intrusive teachers ("super-apostles" in 2 Cor 11:5), Paul expresses the fear that "as the serpent deceived Eve by its cunning, your minds may be led astray from the sincerity and purity of your devotion to Christ" (v. 3). It is not clear whether Paul is here identifying the serpent with Satan or simply pointing to the parallel in deception between the serpent's trickery of Eve and the intruders tricking the Corinthians into a false understanding of Christ (v. 4). Later, he characterizes these adversaries as "false apostles (*pseudapostoloi*), workers of deceit" (*ergatai dolioi*) (v. 13). He points out that, since "Satan himself disguises himself as an angel of light" (v. 14), it is not surprising that "his ministers" (*diakonoi autou*) should disguise themselves as "ministers of righteousness" (v. 15). The invective in Philippians 3:2 ("dogs") and 3:18–19 seems close to this demonizing of opponents. Paul and all believers are continuously engaged in a war with Satan, and nothing is more to be feared than a deceptive working of the adversary *within* the community, perverting the gospel that is leading it to salvation (see also 1 Thess 3:5). On a more positive note, the (likely post-Pauline) warning appearing in Romans 16:17–20 concludes with the assurance that "the God of peace will swiftly crush Satan under your feet" (v. 20a).

Satan/the Devil in the Later Pauline Letters

Along with its more realized eschatology, the letter to the Ephesians retains a strong sense of engagement in spiritual warfare, most apparent in the extended image of putting on the armor required for battle (6:10–17). The whole armor of

God is needed to withstand "the wiles of the devil" (*tas methodeias tou diabolou*) (v. 11). Anger should not be bottled up from one day to the next but discharged before sundown; retaining it may give "opportunity" (*topos*) to the devil (*tō diabolō*) (4:26–27).

In the distinctive eschatological scenario of 2 Thessalonians, the day of the Lord cannot arrive before the appearance of "the lawless one" (*ho anthropos tes anomias*) (2:3). This figure is not clearly identified but he represents an instrument of Satan, his works betraying in every way the characteristics of the one driving him, especially by "deceptive signs and wonders" (vv. 9–10). Although not with the same sense of a fixed eschatological process, the risk of yielding to the wiles of Satan remains a significant concern in other post-Pauline letters (1 Tim 3:6–7; 5:15; 2 Tim 2:26).

APOSTLE, DISCERN, ESCHATOLOGY; SALVATION; SIGNS AND WONDERS; SIN

Reading

M. Becker, "Paul and the Evil One," in *Evil and the Devil*, ed. I. Fröhlick and E. Koskenniemi (London: Bloomsbury, 2013), 127–41; O. Böcher, *EDNT* 1:297–98; 3:234; D. R. Brown, *The God of This Age: Satan in the Churches and Letters of the Apostle Paul* (Tübingen: Mohr Siebeck, 2015), 61–202; Fitzmyer, *1 Corinthians*, 237–40 (on 1 Cor 5:5); V. P. Hamilton, *ABD* 5:985–89; D. G. Reid, *DPL*, 862–67; D. R. Smith, *"Hand This Man Over to Satan": Curse, Exclusion and Salvation in 1 Corinthians 5* (London: T&T Clark, 2008); Thiselton, *1 Corinthians*, 395–400 (on 1 Cor 5:5); W. Wink, *Unmasking the Powers: The Invisible Forces That Determine Human Existence* (Philadelphia: Fortress, 1986), 9–40.

SCRIPTURE

Paul directly quotes from Scripture around a hundred times and makes many other allusions that can be identified as taken from Scripture though not specifically introduced as such. His Bible was the Greek translation of the Hebrew Scriptures known as the Septuagint (LXX), although not all his quotations cohere exactly with that version as it has been preserved. Some of the quotations are composite and, to suit his purpose, Paul changes tense, person, and word order, omits phrases, and makes additions. He employs typology (see Rom 5:14; 1 Cor 10:1–11) and allegory (1 Cor 9:9–10; Gal 4:21–31) with considerable freedom.

Introducing Scriptural Quotations

Paul's scriptural quotations are taken mainly from the Pentateuch, the Psalms, and Isaiah. They appear in Romans, the Corinthian correspondence, and Galatians, but are absent from 1 Thessalonians, Philippians, and Philemon. For the most part, they are introduced with the passive perfect construction, "as it is written" (*hōs gegraptai*). A less frequent alternative amounting to a personification of Scripture, giving it a "voice," appears in various forms of the phrase "as Scripture says" (*hōs hē graphē legei*) (Rom 10:11; 11:2; Gal 4:30; see also 3:8; 3:22, where Scripture acts on God's behalf). Elsewhere quotations are introduced by the scriptural agents who originally voiced or wrote them: Moses (Rom 10:5,19); Hosea (Rom 9:25); Isaiah (Rom 9:27, 29; 10:20, 21; 15:12); David (Rom 4:6; 11:9); the law (*nomos*), as Scripture rather than legal code (Rom 3:19 [with reference to the preceding chain of quotations in vv. 10–18]; 1 Cor 9:8–10); God speaks directly to Moses in Romans 9:15. In all cases the quotation is introduced in the present tense (usually "says" [*legei*]), an actualizing feature also preserved in the more frequent perfect passive "as it is written." The scriptural story is not tied to the past; it is a living commentary on what is taking place in the present messianic age.

Scripture as Pointing to the Messianic Age

As a devout Jew, Paul would have treasured the writings acknowledged as the word of God, especially the Pentateuch containing the torah and attributed to Moses. The prophetic writings, including the Psalms, attributed to David, he would have regarded as indicating God's will for the messianic age, providing "the script" for the Messiah. The revelation of the Crucified One as Messiah and Son of God (Gal 1:16) doubtless required considerable adjustment on his part to see the scriptural promises focused on Jesus—an interpretive task already under way among those who had come to Easter faith before him. Their reinterpretations of key texts in creedal summaries such as 1 Corinthians 8:6; 15:3b–5 (see also Rom 10:9, 11, 12) were there for him to inherit and shape according to his own call and mission. Henceforth Christ—crucified, risen, and established as universal Lord—was the lens through which all Scripture would be read. It was not about "back there" in its original context; it spoke of the most recent past—the death and resurrection of Jesus; it spoke of the present and the future in the sense of what God was doing and would do for the community through the power of the Spirit. A sentence early in 2 Corinthians sums it all up very attractively: "For however many the promises of God the 'Yes' to them all is in him (Christ)" (1:20); and, in similar vein, "whatever was written beforehand, was written for our instruction, so that by steadfastness and the encouragement of the Scriptures, we might have hope" (Rom 15:4 NRSV; see the string of quotations in vv. 9–12).

The freedom with which Paul cites and alludes to Scripture stems from this intense christological focus. God's interaction with biblical figures not only illustrates but genuinely foreshadows God's action in the messianic age now dawned. Paul "reads" Christ's story in Scripture—even at one point to the extent of identifying the rock from which Israelites of the Sinai generation drank as "Christ" (1 Cor 10:4c). He introduces his account of the gospel in Romans by stating that "it was preannounced [*proepēngeilato*] through the prophets in the holy scriptures" [*en tais graphais hosiais*] (1:2). "Scripture" (*hē graphē*), foreseeing (*proïdousa*) that God would justify the Gentiles from faith, "preannounced the gospel" (*proeuēngelisato*) to Abraham (Gal 3:8).

Reclaiming the Scriptural Story for Christ

While occasionally Paul employs a scriptural text in an isolated, simply illustrative way (e.g., Rom 8:36; 1 Cor 2:9; 5:13; 9:9; 14:21; 2 Cor 6:2; 9:9), for the most part, especially in Romans and Galatians, and in the extended midrashic comparison between Moses's promulgation of the torah and the apostolic proclamation of the gospel in 2 Corinthians 2:14—4:6, he engages at length with a running scriptural story that he is reclaiming for Christ.

The argument of Romans is thrust into life at the end of the thematic statement (1:16–17) by the quotation from Habakkuk 2:4 linking the gaining of eschatological life with righteousness by faith (v. 17d). The all-important restatement of the theme in 3:21–26, now with explicit reference to Christ, is introduced as something to which "the law and the prophets bear witness" (v. 21b). The promise implicit in this phrase finds fulfillment in the following chapter, Romans 4. Employing a standard Jewish exegetical technique (*gezerah shawah*) linking two texts via a common term (here *reckon*), Paul quotes (v. 3) a text from "the law" (Pentateuch), Genesis 15:6, and then (vv. 6–8) one from "the prophets" (Psalms, attributed to David as prophet), (LXX) Psalm 31:1–2. The combined witness of these texts allows him to claim Abraham as primarily a figure found righteous in God's eyes by faith, rather than works, and instigator solely on that basis of an inclusive lineage of believers (4:11b–12). The revelation of God's saving righteousness on the basis of faith is not simply revealed in the gospel (1:16–17; 3:21–22); it is revealed as the fulfillment—or, better, the true eschatological enactment—of the great scriptural story of Abraham recaptured for Christ. Paul returns to this story in Romans 9—11 (see 9:6b–9) to find hope for "all Israel's" ultimate salvation (11:26) on the basis that God's word cannot "fail" (9:6a; see 11:29).

Paul engages in similar fashion with the story of Abraham in Galatians 3:1–4:7 to interpret the community's reception of the Spirit (3:2–3, 5; 4:6) as fulfillment of Scripture's pledge to Abraham that all the Gentiles would be "blessed in him," that is, find justification on the basis of faith (Gal 3:6–9). So certain is Paul, on the basis of texts such as Genesis 15:6 (cited in Gal 3:6, as well as Rom 4:3), that the experience of Abraham validates righteousness by faith that he presents texts such as Habakkuk 2:4 (cited in Gal 3:11; as well as Rom 1:17) that encapsulate such validation as prevailing against texts such as Leviticus 18:5 (cited in Rom 10:5 and Gal 3:12) that insist on practice of the law. In Romans 10:5–13, he takes a passage (Deut 30:11–13), where Moses speaks of the ease of such practice, and turns it around to make it serve the principle of righteousness by faith. He finds hints in the text that anything other than this would be to go against what God has already done: drag Christ down from heaven or seek to raise him (again?) from the dead (vv. 6–7).

Such radical reinterpretations of texts, involving significant tensions within Scripture itself, seemingly caused no difficulty for Paul—as also for Jewish interpretation (the rabbis; Qumran) generally. In scriptural interpretation the "newness of Spirit" (*en kainotēti pneumatos*) in the community of the new creation prevails against the "oldness of letter" (*palaiotēti grammatos*) (Rom 7:6; see 2:29) that attended the dispensation of the law (2 Cor 3:3, 6). As one imbued par excellence with the prophetic Spirit (Rom 15:19; 1 Cor 2:4, 13), Paul doubtless saw himself equipped to make such interpretations without hesitation.

Scripture in the Later Pauline Letters

Explicit citation of Scripture is rare in the later Pauline literature. There is a somewhat intrusive citation and application of (LXX) Psalm 67:19 in Ephesians 4:8–10 in connection with the distribution of offices in the community; there are appeals later in the letter to Genesis 2:24 (Eph 5:31) and Exodus 20:12 (Eph 6:2–3) to support the exhortations dealing with relations within the household. First Timothy 5:18 echoes the appeal to Deuteronomy 25:4 in 1 Corinthians 9:9 and a little later (v. 19) the requirement of two witnesses to sustain an accusation from Deuteronomy 19:15. In 2 Timothy, there is a singular reflection on Scripture (*hē graphē*) as such: it is "inspired by God" and "useful for teaching, for reproof, for correction, and for training in righteousness" (3:16). Scripture has become a pastoral resource. Its radical witness to the gospel as argued by Paul has been absorbed into the nascent theological tradition.

ABRAHAM; BLESSING; CHRIST; FAITH; LAW; MOSES; PROMISE; RIGHTEOUSNESS; SPIRIT

Reading

Dunn, *Theology*, 169–73, 235–40, 725–26; Hays, *Echoes*, ix–xiii, 1–33; Horrell, *Introduction*, 80–83; H. Hübner, *EDNT* 1:262–63; R. C. Olson, *The Gospel as the Revelation of God's Righteousness: Paul's Use of Isaiah in Romans 1:1—3:26* (Tübingen: Mohr Siebeck, 2016); S. E. Porter and C. D. Land, eds., *Paul and Scripture* (Leiden: Brill, 2019); S. E. Porter and C. D. Stanley, eds., *As It Is Written: Studying Paul's Use of Scripture* (Atlanta: SBL, 2008); Schnelle, *Apostle Paul*, 108–11; C. D. Stanley, ed., *Paul and Scripture: Extending the Conversation* (Atlanta: SBL, 2012); J. R. Wagner, "Paul and Scripture," in Westerholm, *Paul*, 154–71; R. D. Witherup, *Scripture and Tradition in the Letters of Paul* (Mahwah, NJ: Paulist Press, 2021).

SEXUALITY

As a devout Jew, Paul shared the abhorrence of the lax sexual mores of the Hellenistic culture with which Jews had been in contact following the conquests of Alexander the Great. As apostle to the Gentiles he faced the task of ensuring that new converts from that world understood the demands made on them in this area by their new life in Christ. Hence the greater frequency of reference to sexual behavior in his letters compared to the gospels. Most of such references bear on the avoidance of *porneia*, commonly translated "fornication" and understood as including all sexual behavior outside the bond of heterosexual marriage.

The Call to Holiness: 1 Thessalonians 4:3–8

In his earliest letter, Paul puts before the Thessalonians the ideal of "sanctification/holiness" (*hagiasmos*) as God's will for them (1 Thess 4:3–8) and immediately suggests its primary quality to be that of abstaining from "fornication" (*apechesthai apo tēs porneias*) (v. 3). Each one should know how "to control their own body [*to heautou skeuos ktasthai*] in holiness and honor (v. 4), not with lustful passions [*mē en pathei epithymias*], like the Gentiles who do not know God" (v. 5). The term *skeuos* here, although it has been understood as referring to a man's wife, more likely refers to the body, particularly in its sexual function. "Holiness," then, describes the positive ideal of confining one's sexual activity to lust-free and honorable relations with one's spouse, not exploiting a brother or sister (presumably through infidelity) in this matter (v. 6). Paul places upright conduct in this area in the context of vocation: "For God did not call us to uncleanness [*epi akatharsia*] but to holiness [*en hagiasmō*]" (v. 7). Although often couched in negative terms—the avoidance of *porneia*—Paul's view of the sexual relationship is primarily positive: it stems from the holiness the all-holy God requires of Israel (Lev 19:2), into which the believers from the Gentile world are now being drawn.

Sexual Morality in 1 Corinthians 5—7

Sexual morality emerges as a significant topic in Paul's correspondence with the community in Corinth. He is appalled at their tolerance of one of their members living with his father's wife. Such sexual immorality (*porneia*) is not known even among pagans (1 Cor 5:1). He had told the Corinthians in an earlier letter not to associate with sexually immoral persons (*pornoi*) in general (v. 9). But those outside the community are not the issue. What he is concerned about is association with a brother or sister who is sexually immoral (v. 11).

Paul sharply contrasts the Corinthians' present way of life as "washed (in baptism), …sanctified,…justified" (6:11), with their former existence in a world of "wrongdoers" (*adikoi*) who will not inherit the kingdom of God (v. 9a). The sexually immoral, headed by *pornoi* (to be understood broadly, as in 5:10), feature prominently among those listed as such (vv. 9b–10; see also Gal 5:19, where *porneia* heads the list of the "works of the flesh"). Some Corinthians, it seems, understand the freedom they enjoy as believers (v. 12a) to mean that what they do with their bodies is morally irrelevant. Paul counters with a strong theology of present bodily existence: the body is meant "not for fornication [*porneia*] but for the Lord" (v. 13), destined to share his risen life (v. 14). Believers' bodies are members of Christ. It is unthinkable that believers should take the members of Christ and make them members of a prostitute (v. 15). Paul cites (LXX) Genesis 2:24c ("and the two will become one flesh") to indicate that the sexual act brings about the deepest personal union. The union forged with a prostitute is totally incompatible with the union that each believer has with Christ, having become "one spirit" (*hen pneuma*) with him (vv. 16–17). Every (other) sin that a person commits is "outside" (*ektos*) the body. But the one who commits fornication (*ho porneuōn*) sins in a particular way against the body itself (v. 18bc), which is a temple of the Holy Spirit and really belongs to God (vv. 19–20a; see v. 13c). Hence believers should at all costs "shun fornication" (v. 18a) and glorify God in their bodies (v. 20b; see, by contrast, Rom 1:24). While Paul's primary intent in this passage may be to warn against sexual immorality (*porneia*), a positive theology of sexual relations—within the marital relationship—also emerges.

The passage just discussed serves as a foundation for Paul's response to questions the Corinthians have put to him in the area of sexuality and marriage (1 Cor 7:1–40). The questions appear to have been prompted by keen eschatological expectation among the Corinthians. Some believed that, because the end of the age is fast approaching, existing marriages ought to be dissolved or at least not expressed sexually, while young unmarried people should not be allowed to go ahead and marry. Paul shares the eschatological expectation (7:29–31) and is sympathetic to the ascetical impulse arising out of it (see v. 1). Pastoral realism, however, urges him to caution lest the forbidding of marriage or the denial of relations leads to instances of sexual immorality (*porneia*—probably in the sense of recourse to prostitutes) (v. 2). Hence each one should have their own wife or husband respectively and not refuse conjugal rights (v. 3), since they no longer dispose entirely over their bodies but share them (v. 4). They should not deprive one another in this matter save by mutual agreement and for a distinct period of time in order to devote themselves to prayer, after which they should come together again lest Satan tempt them because of lack of self-control (*dia tēn akrasian*) (v. 5). By the same token, Paul agrees that it is well for the unmarried and widows to remain as they are. However, this presupposes that, like him, they have the gift (*charisma*) for this way of life that he himself has (vv. 7–8). If that is not the case, better to marry rather than be consumed with passion (v. 9).

Although Paul has been taken to task for presenting marriage simply as an outlet for sexual passion, his instruction here—couched not as an order but as a concession (v. 6)—should not be taken in isolation from the unitive sense of the conjugal act in the previous passage (6:16–18). Nor should the sense of mutuality—remarkable for its time—emerging from the agreement stipulated in regard to abstinence be overlooked. In any case, Paul was counseling a community living in a milieu (Corinth) notorious for its sexual excess. He seems to have retained a fear that some may revert to their old ways in this regard (see 1 Cor 10:8; see also 2 Cor 12:21).

The Later Pauline Literature

Warnings against sexual immorality remain prominent in the later letters. The Colossians should put aside whatever is purely earthly: "fornication, impurity, passion, evil desire and greed [*porneian akatharsian pathos epithymian kakēn*], and the greed which amounts to an idolatry" (Col 3:5). Such sexual vices should not even find mention among the saints (Eph 5:3); those who practice them will not inherit the kingdom of Christ and God (5:5). For the reference to *pornoi* in the vice list of 1 Timothy 1:9–11, see the discussion of homosexuality below.

BODY; DESIRE; ESCHATOLOGY; ETHICS; HOLINESS; SATAN

Reading

B. Byrne, "Sinning against One's Own Body: Paul's Understanding of the Sexual Relationship in 1 Corinthians 6:18," *CBQ* 45 (1983): 608–16; J. E. Ellis, *Paul and Ancient Views of Sexual Desire: Paul's Sexual Ethics in 1 Thessalonians 4, 1 Corinthians 7 and Romans 1* (London and New York: T&T Clark, 2007); V. P. Furnish, *Theology and Ethics in Paul*, with new introduction by R. B. Hays (Louisville: Westminster John Knox, 2009); W. R. G. Loader, *Sexuality in the New Testament: Understanding the Key Texts* (London: SPCK, 2010); E. H. Lovering and J. L. Sumney, eds., *Theology and Ethics in Paul and His Interpreters* (Nashville: Abingdon, 1996); R. H. von Thaden, *Sex, Christ and Embodied Cognition: Paul's Wisdom for Corinth* (Blandford Forum: Deo Publishing, 2012); F. Watson, *Agape, Eros, Gender: Towards a Pauline Sexual Ethic* (Cambridge: Cambridge University Press, 2000); D. F. Wright, *DPL*, 871–75.

Homosexuality

Jewish abhorrence of the sexual mores of the Hellenistic world was particularly focused on same-sex relations, which for Jews, at least as regards men, was the subject of severe condemnation arising out of Leviticus 18:22; 20:13. This highly negative attitude is evident in representative texts of Hellenistic Judaism such as the works of Philo (*Abr.* 135–37; *Spec.* 2:50) and the writer known as Pseudo–Phocylides (190–91, 210–14), and the Book of Wisdom (14:26). It is not surprising, then, that the three clear references to such behavior in the New Testament all stem from the Greek-speaking Jew Paul of Tarsus.

In two cases (1 Cor 6:9 and 1 Tim 1:10), the references occur in vice lists that appear to be preformed and conventional rather than something directly composed at the time of writing. In 1 Corinthians 6:9–10, Paul lists ten kinds of "wrongdoers" (*adikoi*) who will not inherit the kingdom of God: fourth and fifth on the list are, in literal translation, "the effeminate" (*malakoi*) and "males who lie with males" (*arsenokoitai*), the reference being to those who engage in homosexual acts passively (male prostitutes) and actively, respectively. In 1 Timothy 1:9–10, the writer is listing those for whom the law is laid down: not for the righteous but for all classes of wrongdoers, fourteen of which are mentioned, the ninth (v. 10) being "the sexually immoral" (*pornoi*—probably to be translated here as "adulterers"), followed by "males who lie with males" (*arsenokoitai*—as in 1 Cor 9:10). The references to same-sex behavior in such lengthy lists give the impression of being included without intent to target this kind of conduct in particular.

The same cannot be said of the references in Romans 1:26–27, where same-sex behavior—on the part of females as well as males—is singled out as a manifestation of the "base passions" (*pathē atimias*) to which God "gave them up" (*paredōken*) in reaction to human exchange of the truth about God for a lie, whereby, in idolatry, "they worshipped and served the creature rather than the Creator" (v. 25). The "base passions" found expression in an exchange of "the natural form of (sexual) relations" (*tēn physikēn chrēsin*) for that which Paul dubs "contrary to nature" (*para physin*) (vv. 26–27), "nature" being understood in the Stoic sense as the established order of things. What is striking is that Paul lists female attraction for female—something rarely attested in ancient literature—before male for male, perhaps to highlight what he believes to be the distortion of the natural order in both cases. Only, however, in the case of male-to-male relations does he mention their "burning with passion for one another" (v. 27a), under the force of which they committed "shameful acts" and received in their persons "the due penalty for their error" (*tēn antimisthian...tēs planēs*) (v. 27b). The "error" refers to the primal sin of refusing to recognize God (vv. 19–20), with resultant lapse into idolatry (vv. 21–23, 25); the "penalty" would be the consequent enslavement to the "shameful passion" itself (see v. 26a).

This passage provides undeniable evidence that Paul, in line with his Jewish tradition, condemned same-sex activity, whether on the part of males or females, as not only immoral but as a particularly characteristic manifestation of the shameful immorality of the Gentile world. While in recent decades attempts have been made to get around this seemingly absolute judgment (for a survey and critique of such see the works of W. R. G. Loader, cited below), the reference to such behavior in this case is hardly incidental.

That said, it is important for valid interpretation to take account of the context in which such reference occurs here in Romans. The entire passage (Rom 1:19–32) is probably based on a Hellenistic Jewish apologetic tract against idolatry (see Wis 13—14), which reflects the well-documented Jewish abhorrence of homosexuality as typical of the worst aspects of Hellenic degeneracy. Paul's purpose at this stage of the letter is not one of ethical instruction. His concern is rhetorical: to lull his (at this point Jewish) reader into a complacent, conventional judgment on the degenerate behavior of the Gentile world in order all the more powerfully in due course to spring a trap: "You who judge do the same" (2:1–3). The passage should not, then, be extrapolated from its context and given an independent ethical weight that it does not, in fact, possess.

Moreover, what both the ancient literature in general and Romans 1:26–27 in particular have in mind is homosexual behavior on the part of those who have deliberately chosen to abandon what was considered to be the universal norm: heterosexual relations. The ancient world in general, and early Christian writers such as Paul in particular, made no distinction between being of homosexual disposition as an *abiding* personal orientation, the cause of which remains mysterious, and free choice on the part of heterosexual persons to engage in homosexual activity. Any modern moral assessment of the issue in which Scripture plays a part must clearly take this gap between ancient and modern thinking into consideration.

Reading

B. J. Brooten, *Love Between Women: Early Christian Responses to Female Homoeroticism* (Chicago: University of Chicago, 1996), 195–302; R. A. J. Gagnon, *The Bible and Homosexual Practice: Text and Hermeneutics* (Nashville: Abingdon, 2001), 229–339; R. B. Hays, "Relations Natural and Unnatural: A Response to John Boswell's Exegesis of Romans 1," *JRE* 14 (1986):

184–215 (full bibliography); W. R. G. Loader, "Reading Romans 1 on Homosexuality in the Light of Biblical/Jewish and Greco-Roman Perspectives of Its Time," *ZNW* 108 (2017): 119–49; "Paul on Same-Sex Relations in Romans 1," *Int* 74 (2020): 242–52; Sanders, *Paul*, 727–47; R. Scroggs, *The New Testament and Homosexuality* (Philadelphia: Fortress, 1983), 99–122.

SIGNS AND WONDERS

The phrase "signs and wonders" (*sēmeia kai terata*) appears in the biblical tradition in connection especially with the miracles that attended the liberation of Israel from Egypt (Exod 7:3; Deut 4:34; 6:22; 7:19; 26:8; 29:3; Deut 34:11; Neh 9:10; Ps 135:9; Jer 32:20; Bar 2:11; see also Acts 7:36). It is taken up very strongly in the Acts of the Apostles, with reference to the miracles of Jesus (Acts 2:22) and those of the apostles (2:43; 4:30; 5:12), of Stephen (6:8), and of Barnabas and Paul (14:3; 15:12; see also Heb 2:4). Where *sēmeion* has the sense of an event that points beyond itself to a transcendent power at work, *teras* adds to this the note of wonder, even terror, at what is taking place.

Defending his apostleship in 2 Corinthians 10—13, Paul has to counter adversaries who were claiming on various grounds that he had not displayed the credentials of an apostle, included among which, it seems, was the working of miracles (see 12:12). His main response to the charge was to point to the labors and sufferings he had endured as the true indication of an apostle conformed to the gospel of the Crucified (11:23–33; see also 4:7–15; 6:4–10). Adopting a necessary "foolishness" (11:16, 23), however, he goes on not only to "boast" of the visions and revelations he received (12:1–4) but also to remind the Corinthians that "the signs of an apostle [*ta... sēmeia tou apostolou*] were performed among you with utmost patience, signs and wonders and mighty works [*sēmeiois te kai terasin kai dynameis*]" (12:12). The Corinthians were at no disadvantage compared to other churches in that regard (v. 13), seen also in his earlier claim that his initial preaching to them did not rely on persuasive words of wisdom but on "a demonstration of the Spirit and of power [*en apodeixei pneumatos kai dynameōs*]" (1 Cor 2:4). Paul speaks of his proclamation of the gospel as attended by manifestations of the Spirit in other letters as well (1 Thess 1:5; Gal 3:2, 5). In Romans 15:15–33, summarizing his apostolic ministry up to the present, Paul tells of what Christ has worked through him in word and deed "by the power of signs and wonders, by the power of the Holy Spirit [*en dynamei sēmeiōn kai teratōn en dynamei pneumatos*]" (v. 19a). The conviction that led to faith in the gospel was, at least to some degree, brought about through the power of the Spirit displayed in miracle working—exorcisms, healings—of various kinds (see also Acts 13:6–12; 14:8–18; 16:16–18; 20:7–12; 28:7–9).

Paul, then, does not minimize the significance of miracle working in the proclamation of the gospel, provided that its true source—Christ working through the power of the Spirit—is acknowledged. Beyond the initial proclamation, "workings of power" (*energēmata dynameōn*) appears among the gifts distributed by the Spirit to members of the community (1 Cor 12:10; see also vv. 28, 29) and this is likely to include the working of miracles, perhaps exorcism. But Satan can also make use of "all power, signs, lying wonders" (*en pasē dynamei kai sēmeiois kai terasin pseudous*) to deceive those on the way to perdition (2 Thess 2:9).

APOSTLE; GIFT(S) OF THE SPIRIT; GOSPEL; MINISTRY; POWER; SATAN; SPIRIT

Reading

O. Betz, *EDNT* 3:238–41; Dunn, *Romans 9—16*, 862–63; P. J. Gräbe, *The Power of God in Paul's Letters* (Tübingen: Mohr Siebeck, 2000); K. H. Rengstorf, *TDNT* 7:258–60; Schnelle, *Apostle Paul*, 151–53, 258–64, 310–12; G. H. Twelftree, *DPL*, 875–77; *Paul and the Miraculous: A Historical Reconstruction* (Grand Rapids: Baker Academic, 2013).

SIN

Paul refers to sin predominantly through the Greek word *hamartia* (see also the cognate forms *hamartēma*, *hamartanein*; *hamartōlos*). Of the sixty-four appearances of *hamartia* in Pauline literature as a whole, fifty-two are in the singular ("sin"), twelve in the plural ("sins"). Of the fifty-nine appearances in the seven undisputed letters, fifty-two are in the singular, seven in the plural. The plural references for the most part stem either from scriptural quotations or inclusion of early creedal material, as in 1 Corinthians 15:3 ("Christ died for our sins"; see 15:17; see also Gal 1:4). Most striking of all is that forty-eight of these fifty-nine appearances are in the letter to the Romans, with forty-five in the singular and only three in the plural, two of which are in quotations from the Scriptures (LXX Ps 31:1, cited 4:7; Isa 27:9, cited in 11:27) and one as part of the odd phrase "the passions of sins" in 7:5. No less than forty of the occurrences of *hamartia* in the singular occur in Romans 5:12—8:13, where Paul for rhetorical purposes personifies sin as an enslaving power dominating unredeemed human life. To bring out this distinctive understanding of sin it is best to consider his use of *hamartia* in the plural and singular separately.

"Sins" (*Hamartiai*)

The plural usage "sins," along with other passing references to sinning (e.g., Rom 1:29–31; 14:23; 1 Cor 6:18; 7:28, 36; 8:12; 15:34; 2 Cor 11:7), reflects a view of sins and sinning against God in a conventional sense shared with Judaism as a whole. Following his coming to Christian faith, Paul accepted and presupposed in his letters the soteriological conviction that God's work of reconciliation in Christ had freed believers from the guilt of such sin, certainly as regards the past (see Rom 3:25b; 1 Cor 15:3, 17; 2 Cor 5:18–21). That such sins have been forgiven is simply presumed; forgiveness, in fact, is remarkably unmentioned in Paul, appearing only in the quotation from (LXX) Psalm 32:1 in Romans 4:7.

Of course, Paul knew that sinning continued in the communities he had founded and addressed it in his letters (see 1 Cor 5:1–2; 8:12; see also the warnings in Gal 5:15, 19–21), but his theology struggles to account for postbaptismal sin. It is the "impossible possibility" (see 1 Cor 6:9–11). His emphasis on the grace (graciousness) of God and freedom from the constraints of the law led, it seems, to the charge that his teaching in this area might induce some to sin all the more in order to draw forth even greater measures of divine grace (see Rom 6:1). The scorn with which he dismisses such a charge in Romans 3:8 testifies to the vulnerability of his theology in this area and the need to work out a satisfactory account of the necessity and possibility of living righteously in the epoch of grace that God has brought about in Christ. It is this necessity, presumably, that led him to evolve the distinctive theology of sin as enslaving power that appears in Romans 5:12—8:13 (with some anticipation in 3:9; see also Gal 3:22).

"Sin" (*Hamartia*) as Enslaving Power

In Romans, especially 5:12—8:13, Paul presents the human condition, aside from the redemption in Christ, as an enslavement to "sin," personified as a tyrannical enslaving power over against the power, equally personified, of divine grace. The sequence begins in Romans 5:12–21 with a sustained comparison/contrast between Adam, as instigator of a universal legacy of sin and death in the human race, and Christ, as the facilitator of an equally universal possibility of righteousness, leading to (eternal) life. Adam let the "beast" of sin, so to speak, "into the garden" and death has followed for all. However, while presupposing this legacy of sin and death stemming from Adam, Paul is careful to add the qualification in the final clause of 5:12d, "in that all sinned" (*eph' hō pantes hēmarton*), to indicate that all subsequent human beings have ratified the legacy from the ancestor in their personal sinning and so have come under the slavery that Adam set in motion. This is not an empirical judgment on Paul's part, resting on observation. It is a retrospective assessment of the human situation based on faith's perception of the "remedy"—the expiatory death of the Son—that God put in place to rescue the human race. The reason that there is hope, as Paul formulates over and over in verses 15–21, is that the force of divine grace, leading to righteousness and (eternal) life, is so much more powerful than the force of sin, leading to (eternal) death: "Where sin abounded, grace superabounded" (v. 20b).

Having died with Christ in baptism, believers are—or ought to be—free from enslavement to sin (6:1–14). Normally, as especially in Galatians, Paul speaks of "slavery" solely with reference to the past from which believers have been set free. In Romans 6:15–23, however—though not without a hint of apology (v. 19)—he images the transfer that believers have undergone as a transition from one slave master to another. In both cases an obedience is required: in the former an obedience to sin, resulting in "lawlessness" (*anomia*) leading to (eternal) death (vv. 19b, 20–21, 23a; see also 7:5); in the new case, an obedience to righteousness, leading to sanctification and (eternal) life (vv. 19c, 22, 23b). Enslaved to sin (see 7:14), human beings have no option other than to obey its dictates—and the Mosaic law, for all its essential goodness (7:12), is no help in this situation. Impotent against sin's ally the "flesh" (Rom 8:3a), the law serves only to provoke the desire to sin

(7:6, 7–25). But God, sending the Son right into the flesh situation of human beings dominated by sin, has condemned sin, broken its grip and released the Spirit to replace sin as empowering force in human life (8:3b–4), leading to righteousness and eternal life (v. 10): "The 'law' of the Spirit of life in Christ Jesus has set you free from the 'law' of sin and death" (8:2; see 2 Cor 3:17b).

It should be noted that in this depiction of sin as "power" Paul is not concerned with various species of "sins" (murder, adultery, lying, etc.). Such for him would simply be manifestations or "symptoms" of a more deep-seated tendency, which is the essence of sin. Here Paul's radical sense of sin adheres closely to that emerging from the second creation story in Genesis 2—3, namely a refusal of creaturehood (enacted in disobedience to the prohibition against eating from one particular tree), a "desire" on the part of human beings for complete autonomy, refusing to acknowledge dependence on God, and give glory and thanks in response (see Rom 1:18–23). In the wake of Augustine, Martin Luther provided the most apt "definition" of sin in this radical Pauline sense as "*homo inclinatus in se*" (literally, "man turned in on himself"), a radical selfishness that poisons relations in all directions (to God, to one's fellow human beings, to one's body, to the wider human world).

Sin and the Law

It is impossible to consider Paul's distinctive sense of sin in this radical sense without reference to the Mosaic law. Although in itself "holy...and righteous and good" (Rom 7:12), the law was impotent in the face of the sin (8:3a). Far from acting as a source of restraint and correction, in Paul's view it actually provokes the human tendency to rebel, thereby "increasing the trespass" (Rom 5:20a). It converts wrongdoing in general into deliberate defiance of God ("transgression"), and reckons sin up for punishment (5:13b; see 1 Cor 15:56). Paul describes this process whereby the law became the death-dealing accomplice of sin in a retelling of the "Fall" story (Genesis 3) in Romans 7:7–11, with "sin" cast in the role of the serpent. He brings the conflict into the present in the dramatic sequence 7:14–25, where the "I," albeit desirous of fulfilling the requirements of the law, finds itself helplessly controlled by the indwelling, death-dealing power of sin. All this, however, is a negative foil to the liberation expressed in 8:1–4 consequent on God's sending of the Son and the "condemnation" of sin in the flesh (v. 4). The ensuing replacement of sin as indwelling power by the Spirit (8:2, 4, 9–11) means that those "in Christ" *can* live righteously and so be set in line for eternal life. It is still *possible* to live according to the flesh and so forfeit that destiny (v. 13a), but, in contrast to the previous regime under the law, it is not *necessary* to do so.

The Antidote to Sin: Divine Love

If sin in the radical sense personified in Romans 5:12—8:13 is basically human captivity to selfishness (human beings "turned in on themselves"; see above), the divine antidote is the grace of Christ, the embodiment of the divine "self-emptying" love displayed in his obedience unto death on the cross (Phil 2:7–8; Rom 5:19; see also 15:3 ["Christ did not please himself"]). Sin for Paul is much more than the sum total of individual human acts of sinning. There is a communal aspect, a prior human solidarity in sin that precedes every human life. Paul does not explain how this situation (later dubbed "Original Sin") came about other than to assign it to Adam. Over against this is the solidarity in love established by Christ and continuing through the power of the Spirit. All the commandments and prohibitions of the law are "summed up" in love of the neighbor; love is the "fulfillment [*plērōma*] of the law" (Rom 13:9–10; see Gal 5:14).

Sin in the Later Pauline Letters

The plural references to sin in Colossians (1:14) and Ephesians (2:1) indicate the past situation from which believers have found release through the redemptive act of Christ. The copious references in the Pastoral Letters occur mainly in warnings against ongoing sinful behavior. Paul's sense of sin as "the impossible possibility" has fallen from view.

ADAM; CHRIST; DEATH; FLESH; GRACE; LAW; LIFE; OBEDIENCE; RIGHTEOUSNESS; SLAVERY; SPIRIT

Reading

Beker, *Paul the Apostle*, 215–24; Byrne, *PES*, 76–89, 135–67, 242–44; T. L. Carter, *Paul and the Power of Sin: Redefining "Beyond the Pale"* (Cambridge: Cambridge University Press, 2002); M. C. de Boer, "Paul's Mythologizing Program in Romans 5–8," in Gaventa, *Apocalyptic Paul*, 1–20; Dunn, *Theology*, 79–101, 111–14; P. Fiedler, *EDNT* 1:69–72; Matera, *GSG*, 89–102; L. Morris, *DPL*, 877–81; Schnelle, *Apostle Paul*, 499–505.

SLAVE, SLAVERY, ENSLAVE

In Paul, there are occasional references to slaves and to slavery as a social institution. More prominent is his use of slavery as an image of the human situation from a theological point of view.

References to Slaves in the Pauline Letters

It has been estimated that slaves made up around a third of the population of large cities in the Greco-Roman world. Slavery was an essential factor in the economy. Although there were calls for improvement in the treatment of slaves, the institution itself was simply taken for granted as a necessary part of life. Paul's apparent acceptance of what is now regarded as a thoroughly evil social institution has long been a cause of dismay to interpreters. It is fanciful, however, to think that the tiny communities of believers in his day could bring about wholesale social change in this area, especially, as, with him, they believed the present setup of the world was rapidly hastening to its end (1 Cor 7:31b).

In the context of this conviction that the time was short, Paul interrupts his response to questions about marriage in 1 Corinthians 7 to formulate a more general principle to the effect that "each one" (each believer) should remain in the state they were in when they "were called" (vv. 17, 24). One such state is slavery (vv. 21–23). Paul acknowledges the possibility of a slave gaining his or her freedom (v. 21c). Unfortunately it is not clear whether his cryptic subsequent recommendation (v. 21d) to take advantage of the opportunity (*mallon chrēsai*) means "go ahead and get your freedom" or rather "make the most of the situation you're are in." In favor of the latter is the transformation in regard to slavery and freedom that Paul goes on to outline for those who have become believers: "Whoever was called in the Lord as a slave is a freed person belonging to Christ, just as whoever was free when called is a slave of Christ" (v. 22 NRSV; see Rom 6:19–23; 14:7–12). The sense would then be that the radical freedom that one has been gifted in Christ enables one not only to endure but make the most of the service one has to perform. The reason is that slaves who have become believers have, along with free believers, acquired at tremendous cost (the death of Christ in v. 23a) a new master, to whom they are precious.

Likewise, it is not clear from the brief letter to Philemon whether Paul is subtly asking Philemon to set free Onesimus, the slave who has come to him in prison. What is clear is that Paul wants to transform Philemon's attitude toward his slave, urging him to take him back, "no longer as a slave, but more than a slave, a beloved brother…in the Lord" (Phlm 16). Even if Onesimus's social situation is not changed, the way he ought to be regarded in the household has been radically altered.

This alteration reflects the fact that the pair of opposites "slave" / "free" appears alongside "Jew" / "Greeks," "male" / "female" as expressions of the ethnic, social, and gender differences that have been rendered insignificant for believers through their existence "in Christ," whereby they have become one body in him (Gal 3:27–28; see also 1 Cor 12:13, lacking "male" / "female"; Col 3:11). In the present time these differences are, of course, not erased. The point is, however, that in the community of the new creation they should not count because all are one in the Lord.

Slaves in the Deutero-Pauline Letters

In Colossians and Ephesians, slaves are the third category (after husbands/wives; parents/children) in the household codes that are a feature of the paraenetical portion of these letters (Col 3:18–4:1; Eph 5:21–6:9). There is no suggestion that freedom is something to be hoped for or aspired to. Paul's instruction in 1 Corinthians 7:22–23 appears to have been developed into a kind of "spirituality" of slavery whereby the service of the earthly master becomes in some sense identified with the service of Christ, from whom in the end the slave will receive a heavenly reward (Col 3:23–24; Eph 6:7–8; 1 Tim 6:1–2; see Titus 2:9), while masters are reminded that they have a Master in heaven to whom they will be accountable for the way they have treated their slaves (Col 4:1; Eph 6:9)

"Slavery" as Image in the Letters of Paul

1. Negative

Whatever Paul's attitude toward the institution of slavery in practice, there is no doubt that he shared the general view of the status of the slave as the lowest and least desirable in society, the polar opposite of "lord." This polarity is central to the Christ hymn in Philippians 2:6–11. Christ, who existed in a way of being (*morphē*) proper to God (v. 6a), in becoming human "emptied himself" to take on the way of being (*morphē*) of a slave (v. 7), even to the extent of dying a slave's death, the death of a cross (v. 8). Responding to his obedience God "hyper-exalted him" (v. 9) and gave him "the name [*kyrios*] above all names," so that the entire universe would acknowledge him as "Lord" to the glory of God the Father (vv. 10–11). The presupposition of the hymn's first two stanzas is that the human situation Christ entered into was one of slavery.

Paul speaks of this slavery in a variety of ways. For the Gentiles, it is the slavery involved in the worship of idols (1 Thess 1:9). Paul castigates the Galatians for wanting to return to their enslavement to "the weak and beggarly elemental spirits" (*ta stoicheia*) (Gal 4:8), which is what their taking on the yoke of the law would mean. The argument inevitably implies a parallel between Jewish existence under the regime of the law with the kind of slavery to the elemental spirits endured by the Galatians before their conversion to Christ (see 4:1–3). The same view emerges from the allegorical interpretation of Abraham's two sons, one from a free woman (Sarah), one from a slave (Hagar) in 4:21–31. The central message of the letter is, "For freedom Christ has set us free. Stand firm, therefore, and do not submit again to a yoke of slavery" (5:1 NRSV) (see COVENANT; JERUSALEM). For Paul's imaging of sin as enslaving power throughout Romans 5:12—8:13, especially 6:16–23, see SIN.

2. Positive

Although Paul appears to apologize for employing the image of slavery with reference to present Christian life (Rom 6:19; see SIN), he speaks of himself as "the slave [*doulos*] of Christ" (Rom 1:1; Gal 1:10; see Phil 1:1; Col 4:12; Titus 1:1). Although *doulos* in Greek means "slave" rather than "servant," when directed to a transcendent being, the "slavery" in question is entirely positive, expressing total belonging and dedication to the deity in question, here Christ as "Lord" (*kyrios*). Paul's self-description in this positive sense also reflects the Septuagint's use of *doulos* with regard to key Old Testament figures (patriarchs, kings, prophets, etc.) as "servants of the Lord" (translating the Hebrew *ebed*). He also employs the verbal forms *douleuō* and *douloō* in this same positive sense to indicate service of God or righteousness (Rom 6:18, 22; 7:6; 12:11; 14:18; 16:18; 1 Thess 1:9; see Col 3:24) or the gospel (Phil 2:22 [Timothy]) or fellow believers (1 Cor 9:19; see also 2 Cor 4:5).

The sense of service involved in such expressions in no wise reflects the "slavery" (*douleia*) of the old existence (Rom

8:15a: "a spirit of slavery leading to fear"; see also 8:21). On the contrary, it involves a joyful service "in newness of the Spirit" (7:6) of the Lord (*kyrios*), who in his costly death has brought about the "redemption" (*apolytrōsis*) of believers from enslavement to sin (Rom 3:24; Gal 3:13; 4:5) and led them to the "freedom associated with the glory of the children of God" (Rom 8:21; see Gal 4:6–7; 5:1).

DEATH; FLESH; FREEDOM; LORD; MINISTRY; RIGHTEOUSNESS; SIN; SPIRIT

Reading

S. S. Bartchy, *ABD* 6:65–73; M. J. Brown, "Paul's Use of ΔΟΥΛΟΣ ΧΡΙΣΤΟΥ in Romans 1:1," *JBL* 120 (2001): 123–37; G. W. Dawes, "'But If You Can Gain Your Freedom' (1 Cor 7:17–24)," *CBQ* 52 (1990): 681–97; Dunn, *Theology*, 698–701; J. A. Glancy, *Slavery in Early Christianity* (Oxford, New York: Oxford University Press, 2002), 39–70; J. A. Harrill, "Paul and Slavery," in Sampley, *Paul*, 2:301–45; D. B. Martin, *Slavery as Salvation: The Metaphor of Slavery in Pauline Christianity* (New Haven: Yale University Press, 1990); Schnelle, *Apostle Paul*, 540–43; A. Weiser, *EDNT* 1:349–52.

SON OF GOD (JESUS)

"Son of God" is one of the three main titles, along with "Christ" and "Lord," that Paul accords to Jesus. It is also, of course, implicit in references to God as "the Father of our Lord Jesus Christ" (Rom 15:6; 2 Cor 1:3; see also Eph 1:3).

Earlier views that the designation stemmed from the secular Greco-Roman background have now largely been abandoned in favor of a Jewish origin. In the Old Testament, divine sonship in an adoptive sense was accorded to the Davidic ruler (see the throne oracle in 2 Sam 7:14; Pss 2:7; 89:26–27), as also to the people as a whole (see ADOPTION). In the messianic expectation that arose around a successor to the throne of David in the centuries leading up to the time of Jesus, it is highly likely, especially in light of evidence from the Dead Sea Scrolls, that the title "son of God" was accorded to the expected Davidic Messiah, without, however, any implication of divinity.

"Son of God" as Content of the Christian Gospel

The link between "Messiah" and "Son of God" with reference to the person of Jesus Christ is clear in the letters of Paul. Writing to a community that he has not himself founded Paul begins with a lengthy statement of his apostolic credentials. He describes himself as "set apart for the gospel of God (Rom 1:1), …(the gospel) concerning his Son" and continues:

> [3] who was descended from the seed of David [*tou genomenou ex spermatos Dauid*] according to the flesh, and [4] was designated Son of God in power [*tou horisthentos huiou theou en dynamei*], according to the Spirit of holiness by resurrection from the dead, Jesus Christ, our Lord.

The formal and parallel structure of this couplet (clearer in the Greek original than in translation) points to its origin as an early Christian creed. Paul cites the creed, with some embellishments of his own, in order to highlight the faith he shares with the believers in Rome. The first line asserts Jesus's credentials for the role of Davidic Messiah according to his human origin. The second line associates his divine sonship with resurrection. The link between the title and resurrection might suggest that Jesus became Son of God, in an adoptive sense, at his resurrection. While this may have indeed been the meaning in the original formulation of the creed, it is likely that Paul himself is responsible for the addition of the—formally intrusive—phrase "in power" to safeguard a distinction central to his own view of Jesus as Son of God. As several other texts make clear (see below), Paul believed him to be the divine Son in a transcendent sense throughout his existence. What the resurrection did was *reveal* ("in power") the filial status that he had enjoyed, albeit in a hidden way, all along. This means that in the opening description of the gospel as "concerning his Son" (v. 3) and in the reference a few lines later (v. 9) to Paul's service of "the gospel of his Son" (*en tō euangeliō tou huiou autou*), "Son" has a transcendent sense beyond the "merely messianic."

What emerges here early in Romans is the link between "Son of God" and the gospel. The content of the gospel is that Jesus, raised from the dead, is the Son of God, active in power through the Spirit for the salvation of the world. The same link between title and gospel appears in Paul's own description of his call: "when it pleased God (Gal 1:15),...to reveal his Son to me [*apokalypsai ton huion autou en emoi*], in order that I might proclaim [*hina euangelizōmai*] him among the Gentiles" (v. 16). Although the title itself does not appear, it is also likely that Paul is describing his revelatory encounter with Jesus as God's Son when he writes to the Corinthians: "The God who said, 'Out of darkness let light shine,' has shone in our hearts to light up knowledge of the glory of God on the face of Jesus Christ" (2 Cor 4:6). In an action akin to that of creation itself, God had revealed the face of the Crucified as replete with divine glory, as, in fact, "the image of God" (v. 4). A passing reference earlier in the letter had already pointed to the divine sonship of Jesus as the content of the gospel: "For the Son of God, Jesus Christ, whom we proclaimed among you" (1:19).

Jesus as "Son of God" in Continuity with the Father

Paul refers to Jesus as God's Son particularly in contexts where the continuity between Father and Son in the work of redemption is strongly in play. This is notably the case in the "sending" statements of Galatians 4:4 and Romans 8:3. Christ is not "sent" as, in an inner-worldly sense, God raises up and sends a prophet. God sends the Son from a "prior" existence in the divine realm to make an "entrance" into the human situation from "outside," as it were (see Phil 2:6–7; 2 Cor 8:9). In Galatians 4:4–5, God sends the Son into the human situation of "slavery" under the law, to redeem those under the law, so that "we" might be redeemed from being under the law and receive by adoption (*huiothesia*) the divine sonship that is his by nature. In Romans 5:6–10, arguing from the extremity of divine love already shown in Christ's death to the sure hope of salvation on the basis of the same love, Paul speaks interchangeably about the love of God and the love Christ displayed in his self-sacrificial death for the ungodly (v. 8). He concludes, "For if, while we were enemies we were reconciled to God through the death of his Son, much more now that we are reconciled, shall we be saved by his life" (v. 10). The same thought returns toward the end of this section of the letter (chapters 5—8): "(God), who did not spare his own Son but gave him up for us all, will he not with him give us everything else?" (8:32). The "giving up" here refers not only to the passion and death of the Son but to his whole entrance into the alienated human situation that, inevitably, climaxed in his redemptive suffering and death (see also Rom 4:25a). In similar terms but on a more personal note Paul describes his present existence as living totally "in the faith in the Son of God, who loved me and delivered himself up for me" (Gal 2:20).

These texts bring out the close association of the "Son" title with the suffering and self-sacrificial death of Christ. The association, however, does not stem from an intrinsic prior link between suffering and the title itself. The association between suffering and the Son title, in fact, serves to bring out the paradox in that one who, precisely as God's Son, should have had heavenly immunity to suffering and death, in an extremity of divine love, voluntarily underwent such a fate in order to bring salvation to an alienated world (see Heb 5:8).

The Eschatological Son of God

Paul also refers to Christ as divine Son in contexts that look to the future. He reminds the Thessalonians that, following their turn from idols to the service of a living and true God, they are "awaiting from heaven his Son, whom he raised from the dead" (1:9–10). Expressing the hope that the Corinthians will be found "blameless on the day of our Lord Jesus Christ" (1 Cor 1:8), he rests this hope on the faithfulness of God through whom they "have been called into the fellowship of his Son [*eis koinōnian tou huiou autou*], Jesus Christ our Lord" (v. 9). For believers, the "fellowship" (*koinōnia*) with Christ has already begun in baptism; it will be complete when they fully share the risen existence that displays his divine sonship. Paul's defense of the resurrection of believers toward the end of the letter (1 Cor 15) reaches a climax in a sequence (vv. 24–27) where he describes death as the "last enemy" that Christ, as risen Lord, has to subdue and remove before his messianic reign is complete. That universal subjection accomplished, he will hand over the kingdom to the God and Father (see v. 24) and "the Son himself will be subjected" to the Father so that God may be all in all (v. 28). Here, within an eschatological "program" still to run its course, we see the complete unity between Father and Son in reclaiming the universe for divine rule that is described in more realized terms in Philippians 2:9–11. The eschatological destiny of the elect according to the pretemporal design of God is that they be conformed to the way of being (image) that is his as divine Son (*symmorphous tēs eikonos tou huiou autou* [Rom 8:29b]). He will be "the firstborn" (*prōtotokos*) among *many* brothers (and sisters) (v. 29c) when they join him in his risen existence. At present, as justified, they are "children of God" (8:14–17; see Gal 3:26), but in a hidden way, as Christ was before his resurrection. Impelled by his Spirit, like him in his earthly life (see Mark 14:36), they cry out, "*Abba*, Father" (Rom 8:15–16; Gal 4:6). Their filial status will be publicly revealed, as was his, when they join him in resurrection. Hence the "eager longing" of creation for the full "revelation" of the sons (and daughters) of God (see Rom 8:19).

Jesus as Son of God in the Later Pauline Letters

In the very exalted Christology of Colossians Christ is the "beloved Son" (literally, "the Son of his love" [*tou huiou tēs agapēs autou*]) into whose "kingdom" God has transferred believers, having "rescued them from the dominion of darkness" (1:13). The "kingdom" or "rule" (*basileia*) in question would presumably be that which Christ is exercising until the full reconciliation of the universe to God, as in 1 Corinthians 15:24–28. The sole reference to Christ as divine Son in Ephesians appears where "knowledge of the Son of God" (4:13) is indicated as one goal of the growth to perfect maturity ("adulthood") that is required of the church as body of Christ. The title does not appear in the remaining Pauline letters.

ADOPTION; CHRIST; COMMUNION; DEATH; GOD; GOSPEL; IMAGE; LORD; LOVE; RESURRECTION

Reading

B. Byrne, "Christ's Pre-existence in Pauline Soteriology," *TS* 58 (1997): 308–30; *PES*, 154–58, 184–85, 194–96; *"Sons of God,"* 197–211, 213–16; A. Y. Collins and J. J. Collins, *King and Messiah as Son of God: Divine, Human, and Angelic Figures in Biblical and Related Literature* (Grand Rapids: Eerdmans, 2008), 101–22; Dunn, *Theology*, 224–25, 242–44, 266–88; Fee, *Pauline Christology*, 530–57; M. Hengel, *The Son of God: The Origin of Christology and the History of Jewish-Hellenistic Religion* (London: SCM, 1976), 7–15, 57–83; Hurtado, *Lord Jesus Christ*, 101–8; Matera, *GSG*, 52–56; Schnelle, *Apostle Paul*, 437–43; Wright, *PFG*, 690–701.

SONS (AND DAUGHTERS) OF GOD, CHILDREN OF GOD (*see* Adoption)

SOUL

"Soul" (*psychē*) is a comparatively rare and unimportant term in the Pauline letters. Paul does not use *psychē* in the Greek (Platonist) sense of a constituent part of the human person, the element that vivifies the body and can survive the latter's death. His usage stems from the Hebrew term *nephesh*, which the Septuagint regularly translates as *psychē*. *Nephesh* is used in the Hebrew Bible of the whole human person under the aspect of a living being, as in the creation of the first man: "God breathed into his nostrils the breath of life; and the man became a living being" (*lenephesh khayah*; LXX: *eis psychēn zōsan*) (Gen 2:7).

Paul uses "soul" simply to designate an individual member of the human race, particularly under the aspect of being a creature responsible to God (Rom 2:9 [*epi pasan psychēn anthrōpou*]; 13:1). In this sense, Paul in 1 Corinthians 15:45 quotes the creation account of Genesis 2:7 to distinguish the ordinary human existence that human beings inherit from the first Adam from the risen life that believers derive from the "last Adam" (Christ). Where the first man became simply a living human being (*eis psychēn zōsan*), the last Adam (has become) a life-giving Spirit (*eis pneuma zōopoioun*).

Paul also uses *psychē* in the sense of "life" in contexts where reference is made to one's life being in danger, as in Romans 11:3 quoting the words of Elijah (1 Kgs 19:10, 14) and in the commendation of Prisca and Aquila as having risked their necks to save his life (*hyper tēs psychēs mou*) in Romans 16:4. Epaphroditus also put his life at risk (*paraboleusamenos tē psychē*) for the sake of the work of Christ (Phil 2:30). Paul is prepared to put his life on the line (*epikaloumai epi tēn emēn psychēn*), invoking God as witness that his account of his reasons for not coming to Corinth is true (2 Cor 1:23). Even where life is not at risk, the sense of human beings as precious may be present in Paul's protestation of his love for the Corinthians when he writes "I will gladly…be spent for you"—literally, "for the sake of your souls" (*hyper tōn psychōn hymōn*) (2 Cor 12:15). So dear had the Thessalonians become to Paul that he was prepared to share with them not only the gospel but also his very life (literally, "our very lives" [*kai tas heautōn psychas*]) (1 Thess 2:8).

Paul occasionally uses "soul" as part of a series of phrases expressing unity or total commitment. He hopes to find the Philippians "striving together with one mind [*mia psychē synathlountes*] for the faith of the gospel" (1:27). His hope for the Thessalonians is that their "whole spirit and soul and body [*to pneuma kai hē psychē kai to sōma*] be kept blameless at the coming of our Lord Jesus Christ" (5:23). The triad does not refer to separate elements of the human person but rather serves to express the commitment of the entire person.

The same sense of commitment of the entire person seems to continue in the deutero-Pauline letters. In Colossians 3:23, slaves are encouraged to do what they have to do "from their soul" (*ek psychēs*) as to the Lord and not to human masters, an injunction largely repeated in Ephesians 6:6. "Soul" comes close to "heart" (*kardia*) in such usage.

The Adjective *Psychikos*

The cognate adjective *psychikos* appears in 1 Corinthians 2:14, where Paul speaks of the *psychikos* person who cannot "accept" the wisdom of God in contrast to the *pneumatikos* who can. Translating *psychikos* here is difficult, but the reference is clearly to the person operating through the natural human faculties, including the intellect, as contrasted with the person given over to the Spirit. *Psychikos* and *pneumatikos* are again contrasted in Paul's discussion of the possibility of risen human existence in 1 Corinthians 15:44, 46, this time with respect to "body" (*sōma*). The distinction appears again to be between "body alive with ordinary human life" (*sōma psychikon*) derived from Adam (v. 45b; see discussion of Gen 2:7 above) and "body vivified by the Spirit" (*sōma pneuma-*

tikon), that is, by the "last Adam" (Christ) as *pneuma zōopoioun* (v. 45c).

ADAM; BODY; LIFE; MIND; RESURRECTION; SPIRIT; WISDOM

Reading

Bultmann, *Theology*, 1:203–5; J. K. Chamblin, *DPL*, 765–75; Dunn, *Theology*, 76–78; Jewett, *Anthropological Terms*, 334–57, 448–49; Schnelle, *Apostle Paul*, 535; Stacey, *Pauline View of Man*, 121–27.

SPIRIT (HOLY SPIRIT)

With respect to "spirit" Paul inherits the Septuagint's translation of the Hebrew *ruakh* by *pneuma*. *Ruakh* has the basic sense of air in motion: hence "wind," "breath." In the biblical worldview it also has the sense of "life-giving force." The first human being came alive when God "breathed" into the preformed clay (Gen 2:7, although *neshamah* rather than *ruakh* is used here for "breath"). When God takes away the divine breath from creatures, they die (Ps 104:29; Job 34:14–15; Eccl 12:7); when God restores breath or spirit, they revive (Ezek 37:1–10). The spirit is not a "part" of human makeup. It is always God's gift, able to be given or removed at will. More generally in the Old Testament the spirit is the dynamic life-giving force by which God gets things done, achieves the divine purpose; it rests on chosen persons as a charismatic and prophetic power.

In postbiblical Judaism, both angels and demons, as forces that act on human beings, for good and for ill, are called "spirits." "Spirit" becomes that aspect of the human person that is particularly open to such nonhuman influence, especially that of God. In some works, perhaps under Greek influence, "spirit" approaches the notion of "soul," an element of human makeup that can survive the death of the body, awaiting resurrection.

In the Jewish tradition leading up to the time of Jesus, especially under the influence of Ezekiel, an outpouring of the divine Spirit was expected to be a feature of the messianic age (Joel 2:28–29 [LXX 3:1–2] and Isa 11:2; 42:1; 61:1–2; Ezek 36:26–27 [interpreted messianically]). But the phrase "holy spirit" is rare in the Old Testament (Ps 51:11; Isa 63:10, 11; see also Wis 9:17), and while "spirit" indicates the presence and power of God, it is not in itself a personal entity distinct from God.

The Holy Spirit in Paul

The comparative frequency of references to the Holy Spirit in the New Testament, beginning with the letters of Paul, reflects the early disciples' sense of themselves as the community of the Messiah. As such, they were gathered around not only the memory but also the continuing influence of Jesus, whom God had raised from the dead, attesting his messianic status (Rom 1:3–4). For the early community this experience of divine power, which they recognized as the promised outpouring of the divine Spirit (see Acts 2:17–21), was inevitably tied to the person of Jesus. In the gift of the Spirit they felt the force of the new creation (2 Cor 5:17) while still bodily tied to the old.

The Spirit as Attending the Preaching of the Gospel

In the letters of Paul, we find multiple roles and aspects of Christian life attributed to the Spirit. The Spirit accompanies the preaching of the gospel, working powers and wonders (Rom 15:19; 1 Thess 1:5–6), bringing about a response in faith to the "folly" of the Crucified Messiah (1 Cor 1:18–25; 2:1–5; Gal 3:2–5; 2 Cor 11:4; see Eph 1:13). It is only through the Spirit that the apostles can teach and believers can grasp the divine wisdom whereby, unknown to the "rulers of this world," through the crucified "Lord of glory" God "has prepared for those who love Him" things that "the eye has not seen, nor the ear heard" (1 Cor 2:6–10a). Only the person operating on the level of the Spirit (*pneumatikos*), rather than on human reason (*psychikos*), can discern and understand such things (2:10b–16). Defending the credibility of his apostolic ministry, despite the fragility that attends it from a worldly point of view (see 2 Cor 4:7–18), Paul insists that if glory attended the administration of the old covenant, which was one of "letter," leading to condemnation and death, how much more must glory attend the administration of the new covenant, which is one of the Spirit, leading to righteousness and eternal life (3:6–8).

The Spirit as Assurance of Right Standing with God and Hope of the Inheritance to Come

A key role of the Spirit for Paul is to give those who have responded to the gospel with faith assurance of their right standing (justification) with God. For the Galatians the experience of the Spirit is—or ought to be—the assurance that, in accordance with God's promise to Abraham and on the same basis as him (faith), they have received the blessing of justification (Gal 3:1–9, 14). To show that believers enjoy a filial status, God has sent the Spirit of the Son into their hearts, crying out (as he cried out in his earthly life [see Mark 14:36]) "*Abba*, Father" (Gal 4:6; see Rom 8:15–16). With their filial status guaranteed in this way, believers are also "heirs of God, "co-heirs with Christ," (Rom 8:17; see Gal 4:7), destined to inherit all the blessings of the final age. Hence the Spirit can be described as the "first fruits" (*aparchē* [Rom 8:23]) or "down payment" (*arrabōn* [2 Cor 1:22; 5:5; see Eph 1:14]) of the fullness of life (resurrection) to come (see Gal 5:5: "For we, through the Spirit by faith, await the hope that righteousness holds out"). When in regard to this hope believers do not know what to pray for, the Spirit comes to their aid "with groans too deep for utterance " (Rom 8:26–27). In the midst of suffering, the hope that believers have will not be disappointed "because the love of God has been poured out into our hearts through the Spirit that has been given us" (Rom 5:5). Simply put, the experience of the Spirit is the experience of knowing that one is loved by God.

The Spirit as Indwelling, Transformative Power

Paul's most sustained presentation of the role of the Spirit appears in Romans 8:1–13. In the wider context (6:1—8:13), Paul has been asserting the necessity and possibility of living out the gift of righteousness in order to sustain the hope of salvation that is the main theme of the section Romans 5—8 as a whole. Over against the "impossibility" of living righteously under the law because of law's impotence to counter the regime of "sin" (personified) in the flesh (7:7–25), Paul asserts the possibility of living righteously because God, in sending the Son, has condemned sin in the flesh (8:3), enabling believers to "walk, not according to the flesh, but according to the Spirit" (8:4). "The law (in the shape) of the Spirit of life" has set believers free from "the law (in the shape) of (the regime of) sin and death" (v. 2; see the thematic anticipation of this in the couplet 7:5–6). By speaking of the Spirit here as "law" (*nomos*), Paul likely has in mind the fulfillment of Jeremiah 31:33 and Ezekiel 36:26–27, taken together as expressing the divine intent and promise for the messianic age: the placing *within* human beings of "the law" (Jeremiah)/"the Spirit" (Ezekiel), giving the capacity to live the obedience required for the gaining of eternal life. For similar echoes of these prophetic texts, see Romans 2:29; 2 Corinthians 3:6a.

It is important to note that Paul expresses this Spirit-given capacity on the part of believers in the passive. The goal of the divine action in sending the Son is that "the righteous requirement of the law *might be fulfilled in us* [*plērōthē en hēmin*], who walk not according to the flesh but according to the Spirit" (Rom 8:4). The passive indicates the action of God at work through the Spirit in continuity with the sending of the Son (v. 3). The new obedience, although expressed in believers' bodily life (see 6:12–13), is not their own achievement; it is the work of God within them through the Spirit.

In the following passage (8:5–11), as earlier in Galatians 5:13–26, Paul sets up an extended contrast between the two ways of living that are now possible and the outcomes that will flow from each: "according to the flesh" (still possible though no longer inevitable, as formerly under the law), and leading to (eternal) death; "according to the Spirit" (now possible and necessary). Whereas "the mindset" (*phronēma*) of the flesh is "death" (v. 6a), that of the Spirit is "(eternal) life and peace" (*zōē kai eirēnē*) (v. 6b; see "the fruit [*karpos*] of the Spirit" [Gal 5:22]). In the final sentences (vv. 9–11), Paul rings the changes with remarkable freedom in regard to the indwelling power: "the Spirit of God" (v. 9b); "Spirit of Christ" (v. 9c); "Christ" (v. 10a); "the Spirit of the One who raised Jesus from the dead" (v. 11a); "the indwelling Spirit" (v. 11b)—all demonstrating the fluidity with which Paul can describe the divine power at work within believers following the resurrection of Christ. One can point here, as elsewhere in Paul (8:3–4; 1 Cor 12:4–6; 2 Cor 13:13), to a "trinitarian" pattern, although hardly a distinction of persons as in the later theological tradition. It is not easy to see much difference between the Spirit and the continuing impact of the risen Lord (see 2 Cor 3:17a: "The Lord is the Spirit"). The terse phrases of verse 10bc sum up the new possibility created by the Spirit: "Though the body be mortal because of sin, the Spirit (means) life because of righteousness" (*to de pneuma zōē dia dikaiosynēn*). Believers have a hope of eternal life ("the raising of their mortal bodies" [v. 11b]) because the Spirit is creating/preserving within them the righteousness that leads thereto (see Gal 6:8). For the same reason, Paul can describe Christ, "the last Adam," as "life-giving Spirit" (*pneuma zōopoioun* [1 Cor 15:45b; see Rom 5:17b]). See also "the transformation" described as coming about "through the Lord qua Spirit" in 2 Corinthians 3:18; "the offering consisting of the Gentiles... sanctified through the holy Spirit" (Rom 15:16c) as the fruit of Paul's worldwide proclamation of the gospel.

The Spirit as Empowering Presence in the Community

Beside the influence of the Spirit in the "ethical" sense just discussed, Paul speaks of its empowering agency more generally. Possibly with reference to the beginning of life as a believer, he insists that "no one can say, 'Jesus is Lord' except by the Holy Spirit" (1 Cor 12:3; see Rom 10:9a; 1 Cor 6:11; 2 Cor 11:4). Baptized "in the one Spirit into the one body," all "have been made to drink of the one Spirit" (1 Cor 12:13; see Phil 1:27; 2:1). This "oneness" of the Spirit common to all is the foundation for the unity toward which the gifts of the Spirit (*pneumatika*, *charismata*) in all their variety tend. Whereas the Corinthians are inclined to rate highly the more ecstatic manifestations of the Spirit, as in the gift of tongues, Paul stresses the variety of the Spirit's gifts. He places tongues last on the list of offices and gifts in 1 Corinthians 12:28; in the parallel list in Romans 12:4–8, tongues do not rate a mention at all. The gifts that are most to be valued are those that serve to build up the church (1 Cor 14:12) (see GIFT[S] OF THE SPIRIT). Speaking more personally as apostle, Paul claims "to have the Spirit of Christ" and as such to be qualified to give authoritative rulings (1 Cor 7:40b; see also 1 Cor 5:3–5).

The Spirit as "Atmosphere" of Christian Life

Although Paul can speak of the Spirit in personal terms, there are places in the letters where references to "spirit" indicate it more as the "atmosphere" in which the life of believers is—or ought to be—lived, determining the quality of their interaction with one another (Rom 12:11; 14:17; 15:13, 30; 2 Cor 6:6; 12:18; 13:13; Gal 5:16, 22, 25; 6:1; Phil 1:27; 2:1; 1 Thess 4:8). God's Spirit dwells in the community as in a temple (1 Cor 3:16; see 6:19). Anyone united to the Lord becomes "one spirit" with him (1 Cor 6:17). Fundamentally, the Spirit is how in the present time Christ, as risen Lord, exerts on believers the transformative influence that the original disciples experienced from him in his earthly life. The Spirit is the "bridge" between these two stages of Christ's existence.

The Holy Spirit in the Later Pauline Letters

The rarity of mention of the Spirit in Colossians (only the vague passing reference to "your love in the Spirit" in 1:8) is one of the differences that set it apart from the undisputed letters. This is not the case, however, in Ephesians. Toward the end of the opening thanksgiving (1:3–14), the author reminds his audience—believers of Gentile origin of how, having responded in faith to the gospel of salvation, they were "marked with the seal" (*esphragisthēte*) of the promised Spirit (1:13; see also 4:30), an elaboration of Galatians 3:2–5 in the direction of indicating ownership. The audience should know that they belong to God through the experience of the Spirit, which is immediately described, following 2 Corinthians 1:22, as the "down payment [*arrabōn*] of the inheritance" (Eph 1:14). Later, speaking of the unity between Jew and Gentile that God has created in Christ (see also 4:3), the author speaks of the "access" (*prosagōgē*) to the Father that both parties have in the one Spirit (2:18), possibly an allusion to the fact that both are impelled by the Spirit to make Christ's "*Abba*" cry their own (see Rom 8:15; Gal 4:6). As members now of the "household of God" (*oikeioi tou theou* [2:19]), the Gentiles are being "built into a dwelling place for God through the Spirit" (*eis katoikētērion tou theou en pneumati*) (v. 22). The "mystery," unknown to former generations, that Gentiles were to be made co-heirs and sharers in the promise held out by the gospel has been made known to Paul, and the other apostles and prophets (of the New Testament era) through the Spirit" (3:3–6). "Paul" prays that the audience "may be strengthened with power in their inner being through the Spirit" (3:16) and the paraenetical sections of the letter frequently invoke the Spirit as a central feature of Christian life (4:23; 5:18; 6:17, 18). The curious warning not to "grieve the Holy Spirit" (4:30; see Isa 63:10) suggests a step on the way to recognizing the personal nature of the divine Spirit. As the bond of the community's corporate life, the Spirit would find divisive talk (see v. 29) especially grievous.

The Spirit hardly appears in the Pastoral Letters aside from traditional formulations (e.g., the christological hymn in 1 Tim 3:16, which speaks of Christ as "justified in the Spirit" [*edikaiōthē en pneumati*]; see also Titus 3:5) and stereotypical echoes of Paul (2 Tim 1:7, 14). In 1 Timothy 4:1, the author appeals to an utterance of the Spirit, presumably speaking through a prophet, warning of apostasy as a feature of the last times.

ADOPTION; BLESSING; CHRIST; COVENANT; CREATION; CROSS; ESCHATOLOGY; FLESH; GIFT(S) OF THE SPIRIT; GLORY; HOPE; RESURRECTION; RIGHTEOUSNESS

Reading

Beker, *Paul the Apostle*, 278–87; Byrne, *PES*, 49–53, 145–68, 190–96; Dunn, *Theology*, 413–41, 469–77; Fee, *God's Empowering Presence*, 803–95; Matera, *GSG*, 142–44; 162–70; Moo, *Romans*, 471–506; T. Paige, *DPL*, 404–13, 417–81; Schnelle, *Apostle Paul*, 486–93; E. Schweizer, *TDNT* 6:415–34; T. Wiarda, *Spirit and Word: Dual Testimony in Paul, John, and Luke* (London and New York: Bloomsbury/T&T Clark, 2017), 9–103; Wolter, *Paul*, 147–75; J. W. Yates, *The Spirit and Creation in Paul* (Tübingen: Mohr Siebeck, 2008).

SPIRIT (HUMAN)

When speaking of "spirit" (*pneuma*) Paul is referring for the most part to the Spirit of God or of Christ (see SPIRIT [HOLY]). However, he does use *pneuma* in an anthropological sense to refer to human beings under various aspects. The distinction between the Spirit of God and the human spirit is clear in Romans 8:16 ("the Spirit bearing witness to [or "along with"] our spirit") and 1 Corinthians 2:11 ("For what human being knows what belongs to the human except the human spirit that is within him [*to de pneuma tou anthrōpou ho en autō*]"). In other contexts, it is not always clear whether the human or divine spirit is meant (e.g., 1 Cor 5:5; 14:2; 2 Cor 4:13; Phil 1:27).

As in the case of other anthropological terms, Paul does not use *pneuma* to refer to a part or element of human makeup, but to describe the whole person acting in a particular way or regarded from a particular point of view. At times, *pneuma* seems to overlap with "soul" (*psychē*) but, whereas "soul" refers basically to the principle of vitality in a natural sense, *pneuma* represents the human being operating at the highest level of aspiration or from self-awareness at notable inner depth, thereby designating the reflective, integrative aspect of a person (1 Cor 7:34; 1 Thess 5:23).

Thus Paul uses *pneuma* especially in contexts where communion with God or where service of or openness to God or God's Spirit is especially in view (Rom 1:9 ["God whom I serve with my spirit"]; 1 Cor 14:2). This may also be the sense of "spirit" in the concluding farewells of letters that run, as in Galatians 6:18: "The grace of our Lord Jesus Christ be with your spirit" (see also Phil 4:23; Phlm 25). The Holy Spirit has particular access to the human person *qua* "spirit" (Rom 8:15–16), even where, perhaps, the person cannot perceive this process because it is internally operative at a depth below normal awareness (see Rom 8:26–27). In the context of ecstatic prayer (1 Cor 14:14–16), the person is praying to God "with the spirit," in a prayer not accessible to the mind (*nous*) and therefore not communicable to others (see also Rom 8:26–27). The Holy Spirit does not create the spirit in persons but brings this aspect to dominance, so that they live not "according to the flesh but according to the spirit" (or "Spirit") (Rom 8:4–5; see Gal 5:16–17). As "spirit" human beings are everything that as "flesh" they are not: open to God, receptive of (eternal) life (not merely natural life), living in companionship with God, being transformed into the divine likeness (2 Cor 3:17–18). Joined to Christ, the believer becomes "one spirit" (*hen pneuma*) with him (1 Cor 6:17).

In a less theological direction, Paul refers to "spirit" when indicating the inner core of a person that needs "refreshment" (1 Cor 16:18) or reassurance (2 Cor 2:13; 7:13). Paul also refers to his spirit when speaking of his presence as transcending locale and so able to make authoritative judgments and rulings despite physical absence (1 Cor 5:3; see also Col 2:5). Thus, although not set over against "body" as indicating the immaterial element of a person's makeup, "spirit" does seem to refer to the impact of a person beyond spatial, tangible limits.

BODY; FLESH; PRAYER; SOUL; SPIRIT (HOLY)

Reading

J. K. Chamblin, *DPL*, 770–71; Dunn, *Theology*, 76–78; Fee, *God's Empowering Presence*, 22–28, 63–66, 124–27; Jewett, *Anthropological Terms*, 167–200, 451–53; E. Schweizer, *TDNT* 6:434–37; Stacey, *Pauline View of Man*, 128–45.

STRONG, WEAK

The complementary antinomy "strong" (*ischyros*)/"weak" (*asthenēs*) appears with some frequency in Paul, although in fact "weakness" (*astheneia*) is a significant motif by itself.

The Weakness of the Human Condition

"Weakness" for Paul characterizes the human condition as such aside from the grace and assistance of God (Rom 6:19a; 8:26). It can simply consist in poor health, as in the "weakness of the flesh" that occasioned Paul's preaching of the gospel in Galatia (Gal 4:13) or in the serious ill-health that brought Epaphroditus close to death (Phil 2:26–27; see 1 Cor 11:30; see also 1 Tim 5:23; 2 Tim 4:20). But Paul also speaks of human weakness in an ethical sense. It was while we were "weak" (*eti...ontōn hēmōn asthenōn*) that Christ died for us (Rom 5:6a), a description filled out by parallel statements in the same context—"godless" (*asebōn*) (v. 6b); "sinful" (*hamartōlōn*) (v. 8); "enemies" (*echthroi*) (v. 10). As portrayed so forcefully in Romans 7:14–25, the law is "weak" (*ēsthenei*), that is, powerless "because of the flesh" (8:3b).

Strength and Weakness: Paul's Relationship with the Church in Corinth

The antinomy between strength and weakness features prominently in Paul's accounts of his interaction with the community in Corinth. At some stage after his initial evangelization, factions began to develop around other teachers whose teaching ("wisdom") and rhetoric were regarded as impressive compared to that of Paul (see WISDOM). The apostle tackles this head on by appeal to the very nature of the message that he had to preach: "a crucified Messiah, to Jews a stumbling block, to Gentiles sheer folly, but to the called...Christ, the power of God and the wisdom of God" (1 Cor 1:23–24), "because the foolishness of God is wiser than human wisdom, and the weakness of God [*to asthenes tou theou*] is stronger than human strength" (*ischyroteron tōn anthrōpōn*) (v. 25). This divine way of dealing is reflected in the composition of the community: not many "wise...powerful...or wellborn" (v. 26); God chose "what is weak (*ta asthenē*) in the world to shame the strong" (*ta ischyra*) (v. 27b). Accordingly, Paul came to Corinth not with persuasive words of wisdom but "in weakness [*en astheneia*] and fear and much trembling" (2:3), "with demonstration of the Spirit and (divine) power" (v. 4). This was so that their faith might rest "not on human wisdom but on the power of God" (v. 5). Later (4:10), he mocks their pretensions: "We are fools for Christ's sake, but you are wise in Christ. We are weak [*hēmeis astheneis*], but you are strong [*hymeis de ischyroi*]."

The "strong/weak" antinomy returns in the "letter in tears" (2 Cor 10–13; see 2:4) occasioned by further deterioration in Paul's relationship with Corinth. The arrival of fresh adversaries had led to renewed criticism of Paul. His letters may be "weighty and strong" (*bareiai kai ischyrai*), but his bodily presence is weak" (*hē de parousia tou sōmatos asthenēs*) (10:10). Sarcastically, Paul exclaims that he was "too weak" (*ēsthenēkamen*) to "enslave" the Corinthians as others have attempted to do (11:20–21). At the same time, one of the trials of the apostolic life is taking on himself the weakness seen in some members of his churches: "Who is not weak and I am not weak" (*tis asthenei kai ouk asthenō*) (11:29). If he must boast, it is of his weaknesses (*ta tēs astheneias*) that he will do so (v. 30; 12:5). When he prayed to God for relief from the "thorn in the flesh" given to prevent him from being too elated by visions and revelations (v. 7), he received the response: "My grace is enough for you, for power is made perfect in weakness" (*hē gar dynamis en astheneia teleitai*) (v. 9a NRSV). Hence his reflection on this paradox:

> 9b ...I will boast all the more gladly of my weaknesses [*en tais astheneiais mou*], so that the power of Christ [*hē dynamis tou Christou*] may dwell in me. 10 I am content with weaknesses,...for when I am weak, then I am strong [*hotan gar asthenō, tote dynatos eimi*]. (NRSV)

The literal paradox here is eased perhaps by thinking of "strong" (*dynatos*) as having the sense of "effective": Christ's power, working through Paul's weakness, is of benefit for those he serves (see 2 Cor 4:12).

The Corinthians desire proof that Christ is speaking in him (2 Cor 13:3). Well then Paul will base his option for weakness on a christological foundation. Christ was crucified in weakness (*estaurōthē ex astheneias*)—that is, the "poverty" that he embraced in taking on the human condition (see 8:9; Phil 2:6–8)—"but he lives by the power of God" (*alla zē ek dynameōs theou*) (v. 4a). Hence, for the sake of the community, Paul may now be weak in him (*hēmeis asthenoumen en autō*) but "will live with him by the power of God" (*zēsomen syn autō ek dynameōs theou*) (v. 4b). "Live," expressed here in the future tense, presumably has reference to the risen life of the age to come, where the body that has been "sown in weakness" (*speiretai en astheneia*) will be "raised in power" (*egeiretai en dynamei*) (1 Cor 15:43b). Paul is content to live with the "weaknesses" of the apostolic life (see 2 Cor 11:23–33) because he knows that, should his apostolic service involve death, he will share the risen life of the Lord (see 2 Cor 4:7–15; Phil 3:10–11). In this ultimate way, his weakness gives scope to the power of God (see 1 Cor 2:3–5; Phil 4:13). He rejoices when he is weak and the Corinthians are strong (2 Cor 13:9a), presumably because his apostolic weakness, in union with Christ, serves their strength.

Strength and Weakness in Matters of Food

A less positive understanding of "weakness" emerges when Paul has to respond to a question from the Corinthians arising out of the weak conscience of some believers in regard to the legitimacy of eating food that has been sacrificed to idols (1 Cor 8:1–13; 10:23–30). On this passage see CONSCIENCE.

Paul addresses a similar issue in Romans 14:1—15:13, this time concerning differences that appear to arise from very strict observance of the Jewish food laws (no meat, no wine [14:2, 21]) and calendar rituals (14:5–6). Those of strict observance in such matters he describes as "the weak in faith" (*ton asthenounta tē pistei*) (14:1, 2). Those who eat all food he eventually describes as "the strong" (*hoi dynatoi*). The main burden of the instruction is directed at the "strong," whose position on the matter he himself shares (15:1). They should accept the weak and, on the same principle as enunciated in 1 Corinthians 8:1–13, be prepared to refrain from eating meat and drinking wine so as not to place a stumbling block in the way of the weak brother (or sister) for whom Christ died (14:15, 20, 21). At the same time, all—the weak included—should refrain from judging one another because the only account that each will have to render is that which will take place before the judgment seat of God, the one Lord of all (14:3–12).

Earlier, and with more general reference, Paul had counseled the Thessalonians "to encourage the fainthearted and to help the weak" (*antechesthe tōn asthenōn*, 5:14; see Gal 6:2).

CONSCIENCE; CROSS; FLESH; FREEDOM; IDOLATRY; SPIRIT; SUFFERING; WISDOM

Reading

M. L. Barré, "Qumran and the Weakness of Paul," *CBQ* 42 (1980): 500–526; D. A. Black, *Paul, Apostle of Weakness: Astheneia and Its Cognates in the Pauline Literature* (New York: Lang, 1984); Fee, *God's Empowering Presence*, 822–26; Harris, *2 Corinthians*, 827–69; G. G. O'Colllins, "Power Made Perfect in Weakness: 2 Cor 12:9–10," *CBQ* 33 (1971): 528–37; reviewed and updated as "Power in Weakness: The Fate of a First Love (2 Cor 12:9–10)," in G. O'Collins, *Illuminating the New Testament* (Mahwah, NJ: Paulist Press, 2022), 191–201, 255–58 (Notes); Schnelle, *Apostle Paul*, 245–47, 258–64; M. B. Thompson, *DPL*, 916–18.

SUFFERING

Several Greek terms give expression to the subject of suffering in Paul: *paschō*, *sympaschō*, *pathēma*, *thlibō*, *thlipsis*. The topic itself may conveniently be addressed according to the three categories of persons who are the subject of suffering: Christ, Paul himself, fellow believers, although, of course, in Paul's view an intimate connection exists between all three.

The Sufferings of Christ

Paul is acutely aware of the sufferings endured by Christ. The cross stands at the center of his gospel (1 Cor 1:18–25; Gal 3:1). When, in all likelihood, he himself added the phrase "death on a cross" to the description of Christ's slave-like abasement in Philippians 2:8, he would have done so in full consciousness of what that horrific form of Roman execution involved. Hence his sense of the "cost" of the redemption won by Christ (1 Cor 6:20; 7:23), his patent outrage at any suggestion that Christ might have died "to no purpose" (Gal 2:21c), his sense of the extremity of love that brought Christ to his death (2:20d), an expression, ultimately, of the love of God (Rom 5:6–8; 8:32, 37–39).

The Sufferings of Paul the Apostle

Paul describes the suffering his apostolic life and travels involved in the "afflictions lists" appearing in his letters to Corinth: first in 1 Corinthians (4:9–13) and then in ever greater detail in 2 Corinthians (4:7–12; 6:3–10; 11:23–29, 32–33; see also Gal 6:17b; Eph 3:13). The theme of the sufferings and trials besetting his life as an apostle are notably prominent in this letter (beginning already in 1:3–7; see also 7:5) because his own status as apostle is *the* issue that runs through its otherwise rather disparate content. The Corinthians, it seems, considered the vulnerability and fragility of his ministry (4:7), his physical weakness (e.g., "the thorn in the flesh" [12:7; see also 11:6]), his deliberate choice to work with his hands rather than rely on their support (11:7–9; see 1 Cor 4:12; 1 Thess 2:9), as putting in question his apostolic status. For Paul it was precisely his suffering and weakness in all these respects that guaranteed apostleship because it conformed him to the pattern of Christ, who "was crucified in weakness and lives by the power of God" (2 Cor 13:4). As Christ's suffering and death brought life, so it is through "always carrying in the body the death of Jesus" (4:10) that, while "death may be at work in our mortal flesh, life (may) be (at work) in you" (v. 12). The same attitude shows through even more personally in Philippians 3:10–11: "I want to know (Christ) and the power of his resurrection and the sharing of his sufferings, becoming conformed to the pattern of his death, if somehow I may attain the resurrection from the dead" (NRSV; see also 2 Cor 4:13–14).

The Sufferings of Believers

Paul considered a life of persecution to be the lot of believers (2 Cor 8:2; Phil 1:29; 1 Thess 3:3–4 [see 1:6; 2:14; 2 Thess 1:4–5]). They are called to live through the power of the Spirit the life of the new creation, while still vulnerable in their mortal bodies, as was Christ, to the powers of the present, unredeemed age.

Paul addresses this situation most explicitly in Romans 5—8, the section of the letter (1:16–17) that, in the context of the sufferings of the present time (5:2c–4; 8:18), asserts the hope of salvation for those justified by faith (5:1–2). The sufferings that believers endure could be interpreted as divine punishment, as indications of the wrath to come, as putting in question the justification already received. Paul counters this by arguing that the extremity of divine love already displayed in the Christ event (5:6–10) renders it unthinkable that "we" will not be "saved from the wrath" (v. 9). As in his own case (see above), the sufferings of believers are an expression of their "conformity" to the death and resurrection of Christ (see 6:5–8). They are "heirs of God, co–heirs of Christ" but this means sharing his suffering in order to share his glorification (8:17). At present, along with creation as a whole, they "groan" awaiting resurrection, the redemption of the body (v. 23), but "the sufferings of the present time are a small price to pay (literally, 'are not worth comparing') with the glory destined to be revealed in us" (v. 18).

At the close of Romans 5—8 as a whole (8:31–39), Paul sets out what would appear to be an evocation of the last judgment in order to counter any interpretation of suffering as indicating that spiritual powers might succeed in indicting believers before the judgment seat of God (vv. 31–34). He asks, "Who (if any) will separate us from the love of Christ?" (v. 35a) and then lists (v. 35b) a series of earthly trials commonly endured by believers, not excluding execution itself ("the sword"). In a rare appeal to Scripture in this section of the letter, he confirms the description with a quotation from LXX Psalm 43:23: "For your sake we are being done to death the whole day long. We are reckoned as sheep ready for the slaughter" (v. 36). The crucial phrase in the text comes at the very start: "For your sake" (*heneken sou*): believers suffer *because of* their allegiance to Christ; they suffer "with" him (v. 17); in their suffering they are "super-conquerors [*hypernikōmen*] through him (Christ), who has loved us" (v. 37). Hence it is inconceivable that any of the spiritual forces that Paul goes on to list (vv. 38–39a) could separate them from the love of God that comes to them in Christ Jesus (v. 39b). Thus, as in so many other areas, Paul views suffering through a totally christological lens.

In a curious statement early in Colossians, "Paul" states that he rejoices in his sufferings "on behalf of you" and then continues, "I am completing what is lacking in Christ's afflictions in my flesh for the sake of his body, that is, the church" (1:24). Nowhere else in the New Testament does any similar challenge appear to the all-sufficiency in soteriological terms of Christ's death. Although many explanations have been made, it seems best to refrain from understanding "complete" in the causal sense that such a challenge would require. The meaning is simply that the sufferings Paul endures in his apostolic ministry continue the pattern set by Christ. As Christ's suffering brought great benefit to all, so, albeit on a much smaller scale, the sufferings that Paul endures in his ministry benefit the church, and this is for him a source of joy.

APOSTLE; CHRIST; CROSS; DEATH; FLESH; HOPE; JUDGE, LAST JUDGMENT; LOVE; STRONG, WEAK

Reading

Byrne, *PES*, 168–72, 213–14; *Romans*, 164–72; 274–81; Dunn, *Theology*, 482–87; D. E. Fredrickson, "Paul, Hardships, and Suffering," in Sampley, *Paul*, 2:1–25; A. Gieniusz, *Romans 8:18–30: "Suffering Does Not Thwart the Future Glory"* (Atlanta: Scholars, 1999); S. J. Hafemann, *DPL*, 919–21; K. Y. Lim, *"The Sufferings of Christ Are Abundant in Us": (2 Corinthians 1.5); A Narrative Dynamics Investigation of Paul's Sufferings in 2 Corinthians* (London: T&T Clark, 2009); Lincoln, "Colossians," 613–14 (on Col 1:24); Siu Fung Wu, *Suffering in Paul: Perspectives and Implications* (Eugene, OR: Pickwick, 2019).

T

TEMPLE

The temple in Jerusalem was still standing in Paul's day. It played no part in his theology, however, save for a brief appeal to the right that its officials enjoyed to receive sustenance for their service (1 Cor 9:13). Paul shared the early Christian belief that the atoning function of the temple in Jerusalem had been replaced by Christ's sacrificial death on the cross (Rom 3:24–26). However, the biblical sense of the temple as the dwelling place of God (1 Kgs 8:10, 12–13; 2 Kgs 19:14; Pss 27:4; 84:1–4; Isa 2:2–3; 6:1–4; Ezek 8:6; 11:22–25; 43:4–9) does play a role in his imaging of the community as the temple of God. The Qumran community, alienated from priestly service at the Jerusalem temple, had already adopted this view of themselves as constituting a "holy house" or temple in which perfect observance of the law atoned for sin (1QS VIII, 4–10; CD III, 19).

The Local Community and Individual Believers as Temple

Dealing with the factions in the community at Corinth that have formed around preferences for particular ministers, Paul calls for a correct evaluation of the role and responsibility of those who have ministered to them (1 Cor 3:5–23). Stressing the accountability that will be required of each minister at the judgment, he images the community first as a plantation (vv. 6–9ab), then as a building (vv. 9c–15), and finally as a holy building or temple (*naos*) (vv. 16–17):

> [16] Do you not know that you are the temple of God [*naos theou*] and that the Spirit of God dwells in you? [17] If anyone destroys the temple of God, God will destroy that person. For the temple of God is holy, as are you yourselves.

The community as a whole, rather than its individual members, makes up the temple in which the Holy Spirit dwells. The image and especially the threat uttered in verse 17, underscores the extreme responsibility that ministers bear in view of the holiness of the community as the dwelling place of God's Spirit.

The understanding of the community as a temple reappears in 2 Corinthians 6:14—7:1, a passage so obtrusive in its context as to suggest that it may be a fragment, possibly non-Pauline, inserted from some other source; it would certainly be at home in the literature from Qumran. Nevertheless, its strong assertion, "we are the temple of the living God" (*hēmeis*...*vaos theou esmen zōntos*) (v. 16b), followed by a collage of scriptural texts (Lev 26:11–12; Ezek 37:27) indicating God's intention to dwell within the people, goes along with Paul's image of the community as God's temple in 1 Corinthians 3:16–17.

In 1 Corinthians 6:19, Paul bolsters his case for sexual purity, including a complete rejection of recourse to prostitutes, by reminding the Corinthians, "Are you unaware that your body is a temple of the

Holy Spirit [*naos tou en hymin hagiou pneumatos*], which you have from God?" Here it is the body of the individual member of the community that is the temple in which God's spirit dwells.

Finally, it is possible that Paul's frequent use of the language of "building" (*oikodomē, oikodomeō*) in the sense of both founding (Rom 15:20) and building up (Rom 14:19; 15:2; 1 Cor 8:1; 10:23; 14:3, 4, 5, 12, 17, 26; 2 Cor 10:8; 12:19; 13:10; 1 Thess 5:11) the local community is consciously connected with his sense of the community as a holy building in which dwells the Spirit of God. One could add that his description of himself as "serving the gospel of God as a priest [*hierougounta to euangelion tou theou*], in order that the offering (consisting) of the Gentiles may be acceptable (to God), sanctified by the Holy Spirit" (Rom 15:16), albeit metaphorical, owes something to his sense of believers as continually engaged in a worship of God in the holy temple that they themselves constitute (see Rom 12:1): "present your bodies as a living sacrifice [*thysian zōsan*], holy and acceptable to God, the worship you owe as rational beings [*tēn logikēn latreian hymōn*]."

"Temple" Imagery in Ephesians

The motif of the community as a "building" is prominent in Ephesians. Believers from the Gentile world are assured that they are "no longer strangers and aliens, but fellow citizens of the saints and members of the household of God" (2:19). As such they "have been built [*oikodomēthentes*] on the foundation of the apostles and prophets, with Christ Jesus himself as cornerstone" (v. 20). In him, "the whole building [*pasa oikodomē*], joined together, is growing into a holy temple in the Lord" (*auxei eis naon hagion en kyriō*) (v. 21), in whom "you are being built together, through the Spirit, into a dwelling place for God" (*synoikodomeisthe eis katoikētērion tou theou*) (v. 22; see also 1 Tim 3:15). In the overladen style typical of Ephesians, the idea of growth, more suitable for the description of the church as Christ's body (see 1:23; 2:16; 3:6; 4:4, 12, 16; 5:23, 29), is here continued into the temple imagery. The images of "body" and "building" are brought together to express the "growth" of the church into the full stature of Christ (4:13) as the whole body builds itself up in love (*poieitai eis oikodomēn heautou en agapē*) (v. 16). Strictly speaking, the phrase *pasa oikodomē* could refer to each and every separate local church, with the variant reading *pasa hē oikodomē* being a later expansion to safeguard the reference to the worldwide church. However, the usage of the article in Koine Greek is sufficiently loose to accommodate the universal reference as elsewhere in Ephesians.

APOSTLE; BODY; CHURCH; MINISTRY; SPIRIT

Reading

B. Byrne, "Sinning against One's Own Body: Paul's Understanding of the Sexual Relationship in 1 Corinthians 6:18," *CBQ* 45 (1983): 608–16; P. W. Comfort, *DPL*, 923–25; B. Gärtner, *The Temple and the Community in Qumran and the New Testament* (Cambridge: Cambridge University Press, 1965), 47–71; J. R. Lanci, *A New Temple for Corinth: Rhetorical and Archaeological Approaches to Pauline Imagery* (New York and Bern: Lang, 1997); Lincoln, *Ephesians*, 156–59, 162; Thiselton, *1 Corinthians*, 307–18; Wolter, *Paul*, 290–94.

THANKSGIVING

For Paul, "thanksgiving" (expressed through the verb *eucharisteō*, the noun *eucharistia* and occasionally in the short expression "Thanks be to God" [*charis tō theō*]) represents perhaps the most basic and necessary disposition of human beings toward God. Two passages in particular—one negative, the other positive—make this clear. In Romans 1:19–23, Paul maintains that human beings should have been able to "know" the eternal power and deity of the unseen Creator through the revelation patent in the created world. They failed, however, to respond with glorification (i.e., acknowledgment) and thanks (*ouch... edoxasen ē ēucharistēsan*) (v. 21); they "exchanged the glory of the immortal God" for all kinds of idolatrous images (v. 23). Over against this account of fundamental human alienation from God may be set the positive statement of the goal of the apostolic ministry in 2 Cor 4:15: "Yes, everything is for your sake, so that grace, as it extends to more and more people, may increase thanksgiving [*tēn ēucharistian perisseusē*] to the glory of God." In the wake of God's gracious intervention in Christ, Paul's apostolic task is to be the instrument of bringing about as widely as possible the gratitude that is, fundamentally, all God wants to receive from human beings: human "grace" (*charis*) in response to overwhelming divine grace (see 2 Cor 1:11; 9:11, 12; see also 1 Tim 4:3, 4).

The Introductory Thanksgivings

Within this basic aura of thanksgiving, all Paul's letters, with the exception of Galatians, begin with an extended thanksgiving (Rom 1:8–15; 1 Cor 1:4–9; Phil 1:3–11; 1 Thess 1:2–10; Phlm 4–7; see also Col 1:3–14; 2 Thess 1:3–12; 2 Tim 1:3–5). (In 2 Corinthians 1:3–7, the note of thanksgiving is present in the "blessing" of God that Paul expresses for the consolation he has received in the midst of so many afflictions.) The epistolary thanksgivings, an adaptation of the prayer wish for the recipients' health customary in ancient letters, allow Paul to rehearse the "grace" history of the community and set the right tone from the start, even if, as in the case of the Corinthian correspondence, passages of caution and reprimand will follow. The same sense of gratitude to God as a characteristic of Christian life appears regularly throughout the letters (Rom 14:6 [over food]; 1 Cor 10:30 [also over food]; 14:16, 17; Phil 4:6; 1 Thess 5:18), as also for particular favors granted (Rom 16:4; 1 Cor 1:14; 14:18; 1 Thess 3:9). Thanksgiving, along with praise and petition, is to be a regular element of communal prayer (Phil 4:6; 1 Thess 5:18; see Eph 5:4, 20; Col 2:7; 3:17; 4:2; 1 Tim 2:1).

Paul employs the short expression "Thanks be to God" (*charis tō theō*), sometimes to wind up a section (e.g., Rom 7:25a, although this could be a gloss; 1 Cor 15:57), sometimes to indicate a transition or new situation (Rom 6:17; 2 Cor 2:14), and sometimes simply as an expression of overwhelming gratitude for a favor received (2 Cor 8:16; 9:15 ["Thanks be to God for (God's) indescribable gift"]; see also 2 Tim 1:3).

The Eucharistic Thanksgiving

In Paul's appeal to the tradition concerning the Lord's Supper in 1 Corinthians 11:23–25, Jesus's words over the bread begin with thanksgiving (*eucharistēsas* [v. 24]). In the Matthean and Markan parallels (Matt 26:26–28; Mark 14:22–24), the corresponding word over the bread is *eulogēsas*, with *eucharistēsas* over the cup (as in both cases in Luke 22:17, 19). The parallels suggest little difference between the two verbal forms. Both introduce Jesus's words of institution as a development of the regular Jewish table blessing, albeit here in a Passover context. The Pauline version, the earliest record of the tradition, has led to the naming of the Christian sacrament derived from it as "Eucharist": a happy development, granted the overriding significance of thanksgiving in Paul's sense of the Christian attitude to God.

BLESSING; EUCHARIST; GLORY; GRACE; IDOLATRY; PRAYER

Reading

P. T. O'Brien, *DPL*, 69–71; *Introductory Thanksgivings in the Letters of Paul* (Leiden: Brill, 1977); H. Patsch, *EDNT* 2:87–88; S. E. Porter and S. A. Adams, *Paul and the Ancient Letter Form* (Leiden; Boston: Brill, 2010), 101–84 (chapters by D. W. Pao, 101–27; P. Arzt-Grabner, 129–58; R. F. Collins, 159–84); J. T. Reed, "Are Paul's Thanksgivings 'Epistolary'?" *JSNT* 61 (1996): 87–99.

TONGUES (*see* Gift[s] of the Spirit)

W

WEAK (*see* Strong)

WISDOM

The motif of "wisdom" features in Pauline literature in two ways. First are actual references to "wisdom" (*sophia*) or "wise" (*sophos*), almost all of which are confined to the first four chapters of 1 Corinthians. Second are passages reflecting the wisdom speculation of the biblical and postbiblical tradition of Israel, even if the language of "wisdom"/"wise" does not itself appear.

Wisdom, True and False, in Corinth

The presenting issue in 1 Corinthians stems from the report that factions have developed in the community around allegiances to particular teachers such as Paul, Apollos, or Cephas (1:10–16). Behind these allegiances lies a deeper issue. One or other of the teachers is presenting the faith as a form of wisdom in a way that, by contrast, makes Paul's stark proclamation of the gospel seem elementary, inappropriate for those who consider themselves "mature" (*teleioi*). Defending his initial proclamation, Paul seizes on the language of "wisdom," relating it to God's action in the Crucified Messiah over against the wisdom favored in Corinth, which he dubs "the wisdom of the world" (v. 20).

Initially (v. 17b), Paul insists that he has been sent to preach the gospel, "not with wisdom of word, lest the cross of Christ be emptied (of its power)." Later he claims that his "word" and his "preaching" did not rest on "persuasive words of wisdom but with a demonstration of the Spirit and of power," so that the faith of the Corinthians "might rest not on human wisdom [*en sophia anthrōpōn*] but on the power of God" (2:4–5). These statements suggest that the problematic aspect of the wisdom teaching in view had to do with its employing persuasive rhetorical techniques as practiced and taught by the Sophists (see v. 20). For Paul, a persuasiveness intrinsic to the message erodes the role of the Spirit in bringing about the conviction of faith.

However, besides persuasive rhetorical technique, purveyors of wisdom in the Greek milieu had a *doctrine* to teach. This wisdom took the form of knowledge, derived either from observation of nature and human affairs or communicated from a higher power, showing how to live in accordance with reality. The appropriation of wisdom in such terms by Hellenistic Judaism can be seen in the Book of Wisdom. It is feasible that wisdom, as commended in that work (6:12—11:1) and possibly promoted in Corinth by the Alexandrian convert Apollos (Acts 18:24; 19:1; 1 Cor 1:12; 3:4–6, 22; 4:6; 16:12), is also the target of Paul's polemic in 1 Corinthians 1—4.

Paul appropriates the language of wisdom—"the wisdom of God" (1 Cor 1:24)—for the gospel of the Crucified. The "word of the cross" may be "foolishness" (*mōria*) for those who are on the way to perdition but for those on the way to salvation it is the power of God (v. 18; see Rom 1:16). When "the world" (human beings in their fallen state) did not know God through (worldly) wisdom, it pleased God with divine wisdom (*en tē sophia tou theou*) to bring about the salvation of believers through the very opposite of (worldly) wisdom: the "foolishness" displayed in the cross (v. 21). Thus, where the Jews seek signs and "Greeks" wisdom (v. 22), Paul preaches the antithesis of a sign: the stumbling block (*skandalon*) of a Crucified Messiah (see Rom 9:32–33) and the antithesis of wisdom: foolishness (v. 23). What may be a stumbling block and foolishness to unbelievers is, for those who have been called, the power and wisdom of God (v. 24). The very makeup of the community at Corinth, where not many are wise in human terms, influential or of high station, illustrates the intention of God to act in this way (vv. 26–28). In their present existence "in Christ Jesus," *he* (Christ) has become for them "wisdom from God" (*sophia apo theou*) (v. 30).

Paul's initial preaching at Corinth proceeded in total conformity with this mode of divine action (2:1–5). He came not with an excess of argument or persuasive words of wisdom (vv. 1, 4) but, in fear and trembling, having decided to "know among them" only Jesus Christ and him crucified (vv. 2–3). This was so that their coming to faith might rest not on human wisdom but on the power of God (v. 5).

At this point (2:6), Paul proceeds as if to say, "If it is wisdom that you want, well, there *is* a wisdom that we speak about among the perfect" (v. 6). It is a wisdom of God, hidden in mystery and predetermined before the ages, involving a plan to bring believers ("us" [v. 7]) to glory. Ignorant of this divine design, the rulers of this world actually implemented it by carrying out the act, crucifying "the Lord of glory," destined to bring it about (v. 8). Knowledge of such divine wisdom and of what has been prepared for those who love God (v. 9) is imparted only through the Spirit (v. 10). It cannot be spoken about in words framed by human wisdom but in discourse taught by the Spirit (v. 13). Those who proceed by natural understanding alone (*psychikos anthrōpos* [v. 14]) cannot grasp these matters of the Spirit and think them foolishness, but those who are "spiritual" (*pneumatikoi*) discern all such things (v. 15).

Paul is not proposing here two classes of believers. Rather, having dismissed the false wisdom of the world, he is responding to the Corinthians' desire for wisdom by maintaining that, if they were truly open to the Spirit given to them, they would perceive the divine plan to bring them to glory through the "foolishness" of the cross as the saving wisdom of God. The very fact that they are divided into factions shows their immaturity and explains why Paul in his preaching had to treat them not as spiritual people but as "infants" (3:1–4). Those who think they are wise in (the wisdom of) the present age should become "foolish" (*mōros*) in order that they might become truly wise (v. 18). For the wisdom of this world is foolishness with God (v. 19a), as two further scriptural texts (Job 5:12a, 13b and LXX Ps 93:11) attest (vv. 19b–20).

The entire sequence, 1 Corinthians 1:10–3:23, in which "wisdom" (*sophia*) or its cognate "wise" (*sophos*) appears no less than twenty-six times as against only three times elsewhere in the undisputed letters (1 Cor 6:5; 12:8; 2 Cor 1:12), shows Paul's skill in taking a term or concept used by others and, in light of God's action in Christ, discerning where its usage is appropriate and where it reflects the "foolishness" of a fallen world. In so doing he has both defended his initial preaching and endeavored to persuade the community that if they want to be truly wise, with the wisdom of mature believers, they have to grow in openness to the Spirit.

Pauline Passages Reflecting the Wisdom Tradition of Israel

Passages in Paul that appear indebted to speculations about wisdom in biblical and postbiblical Jewish literature include, first of all, the creedal fragment in 1 Corinthians 8:6: "For us there is one God, the Father, from whom all things are and from whom we exist, and one Lord, Jesus Christ, through whom are all things and for whom we all exist." The text presents Christ as instrumental in both creation and the destiny of believers in ways reminiscent of wisdom in passages such as Proverbs 8:22–31; Sirach 24:1–12; and Wisdom 7:22–27; 8:1–4; 9:9–11. Likewise based on Jewish wisdom speculation would be the identification of Christ with the rock that followed the Israelites and supplied them with "spiritual drink"

(1 Cor 10:4c). In Romans 10:6–8, Paul co-opts Deuteronomy 30:11–14, a text where Moses commends the ease of observing the law, for the alternative that he himself is proposing: righteousness through faith (v. 6a). His procedure closely parallels the quest for wisdom described with reference to the same Deuteronomic passage in Bar 3:29—4:1. It is also generally agreed that the wisdom tradition lies behind the "sending of the Son" motif seen in Romans 8:3 and Galatians 4:4 (see Wis 9:9–10). The wider appearance of such statements in the New Testament (John 3:17; 1 John 4:9), suggests that this was something Paul inherited rather than developed himself.

Wisdom in the Deutero-Pauline Letters

It is in the letter to the Colossians that wisdom comes into its own in Pauline literature. The letter counteracts an "apparent wisdom" (2:23) involving worship of/with angels (2:16–18) and exaggerated ascetical practices (2:20–22) by insisting on the unique role of Christ in creation and redemption. A hymnic passage early in the letter (1:15–20) portrays him as Wisdom is portrayed in texts such as Proverbs 8:22–31 and Wisdom 7:22–27. In him (Christ) "are hidden all the treasures of wisdom [*hoi thesauroi tēs sophias*] and knowledge" (2:3). "Paul" speaks of himself ("we") as instructing humanity (literally, "every human being") "in all wisdom" (1:28). His opening prayer is that the recipients of the letter will be "filled with the knowledge of God's will in all wisdom and spiritual understanding [*en pasē sophia kai synesei pneumatikē*]" (1:9; see 1 Cor 2:10–16). They are "to teach and admonish one another in all wisdom" (Col 3:16) and to "conduct themselves wisely [*en sophia*] towards outsiders" (4:5). So wisdom permeates the letter on all levels.

The opening thanksgiving hymn in Ephesians (1:3–14) speaks of the riches of God's grace "that overflowed to us in all wisdom and insight [*en pasē sophia kai phronēsei*], making known to us the mystery of his will" (vv. 8–9). Rather than divine qualities, "wisdom and insight" appear here to be gifts bestowed on believers as an effect of grace (see v. 17). Later, however (3:10), there is reference to the "manifold wisdom of God" (*hē polypoikilos sophia tou theou*) made known to the heavenly powers through the church, the qualification "manifold" referring presumably to the divinely achieved union of Jews and Gentiles in the one body of the church, a major thesis of the letter (2:11–22). As beneficiaries of divine wisdom, believers should take care to live not as unwise (*asophoi*) people but as wise (*sophoi*) (5:15).

BODY; CHURCH; CROSS; RICHES, POVERTY; SON OF GOD; SPIRIT; THANKSGIVING

Reading

S. C. Barton, *ECB*, 1318–23; W. D. Davies, *Paul and Rabbinic Judaism: Some Rabbinic Elements in Pauline Theology*, 3rd ed. (London: SPCK, 1970), 147–76; Fee, *1 Corinthians*, 66–129; Gorman, *Apostle*, 286–93; R. B. Hays, "Wisdom according to Paul," in *Where Shall Wisdom Be Found? Wisdom in the Bible, the Church and the Contemporary World*, ed. S. C.

Barton (Edinburgh: T&T Clark, 1999), 111–23; Hurtado, *Lord Jesus Christ*, 123–26; Lincoln, "Colossians," 571, 575–76, 598–607; E. J. Schnabel, *DPL*, 967–73; Schnelle, *Apostle Paul*, 197–205; E. Schweizer, *TDNT* 8:374–75; Thiselton, *1 Corinthians*, 196–204.

WOMAN, WIFE

No area of Paul has been more injurious to his reputation than the instructions and remarks in writings attributed to him that concern women. While we cannot extradite him from his own time and culture in this area, it is important to distinguish what emerges from writings indisputably attributed to him from what emerges from those written later in his name.

Greek has the term *anthrōpos* to refer to human beings, male and female, generically. The term can also mean a male person and, at times, the reference is simply indefinite, corresponding to "one," "someone," and so on. For more specific usage, especially in regard to marriage, Greek has *anēr* for "man" or "husband," *gynē* for "woman" or "wife." Paul's usage reflects this specification, avoiding the problem in English, where—aside from recent efforts to be inclusive—"man" has a generic as well as a gender specific reference. In two cases, where the distinction between male and female is stressed, Paul employs (as substantives) the adjectives *arsen* and *thēly* (Rom 1:26–27; Gal 3:28).

No Longer Male and Female in Christ (Gal 3:28)

In Galatians 3, Paul is insisting upon the exclusive focus of the Abrahamic promise on Christ without any interference from the Mosaic law (vv. 15–18). Those destined to "inherit" the promise and the eschatological blessings that it holds out (see BLESSING) do so by "entering," through faith and baptism "into" the person of Christ, who is the "last Adam" of the new creation (6:15; see 1 Cor 15:45). In the "oneness" of his person understood in a corporate sense (see "IN CHRIST"), the distinctions—ethnic, social, gender—that mean so much in the present, passing age fall away:

> (There is) no longer Jew or Greek, slave or free, male and female [*arsen kai thēly*]. For you are all one (person) [*heis*] in Christ Jesus. (v. 28)

The change to the copula "and" in the third pair echoes the formula in the first creation story, Genesis 1:27 ("male and female he created them"). Although the change signals that believers are already part of the new creation, Paul hardly means that these distinctions are simply abolished; he certainly wants Gentiles to retain their identity and to praise God alongside Israel precisely as such (Rom 15:9–12). The point is that in the present passing age the distinctions shouldn't count as regards status and value.

Woman in 1 Corinthians

In light of the keen expectation in Corinth of a more or less imminent end of the present age, some members of the community appear to hold that those who are married should not express their relationship sexually and that the unmarried should not be allowed to marry. Because they are living or are soon to live the life of angels, sexual expression, belonging to present (evil) age, is not appropriate. Paul sympathizes with this aspiration (1 Cor 7:8, 26, 29–35) but points out that it is only for those, such as himself, who have the gift of celibacy (v. 7). His pastoral concern is that those who do not have such a gift, unable to resist their sexual appetites, may have recourse to sex outside the married bond (*porneia* [6:12–20; 7:2]). Thus he counsels that existing marriages should not be dissolved (7:10–11) and the married should not deprive one another of sexual relations, save by mutual agreement and only for a set period to allow for prayer, after which they should come together again, lest Satan take advantage of the situation (v. 5) (see SATAN). What is remarkable about this passage is the mutuality in the relationship between husband and wife. Each has "authority" (*exousia*) over the body of the other (v. 4). The wife's wishes have equal weight with those of her spouse. The respect for the woman in the relationship established at the start permeates the remaining aspects of the instruction right to the end.

Far more controversial and hardly Paul at his theological best is the subsequent instruction concerning how women should appear when praying and prophesying in the assembly (*ekklēsia*) (11:2–16). Although often taken as a passage instructing women to be *veiled* in the assembly, the word "veil" (Greek *kalymma*) is lacking here (contrast 2 Cor 3:12–18). It is now widely agreed that the issue is not whether women should or should not be veiled but how they are to wear their hair—a matter of widespread discussion at the time. Paul's main concern here is that when praying or prophesying in the assembly men should appear as men and women as women, and for him at least, hairstyle is central to that display of identity.

Exploiting the capacity of the Greek word *kephalē* to mean either "head" or "source," Paul sets up (vv. 3–6) a chain-like sequence to the effect that as Christ is the "head" (or "source") of every man, man is the "head" (or "source") of woman, while God is the source of Christ. Thus when a man or woman prays in a way that is shameful, they bring disgrace upon their "source": Christ or the man (presumably a husband is meant) respectively. The shame would consist in the man's praying with long locks hanging down, while in the case of the woman, it would consist in her having her hair up, thereby uncovering her head and making it appear shorn.

Paul bolsters the grounds for regarding the covered head of a man as shameful and vice versa in the case of the woman, by arguing that the man is "the image and glory [*eikōn kai doxa*] of God, while the woman is the "glory of the man" (v.7). The "image" language is taken from the first creation account (Gen 1:26), yet illegitimately, since that account specifically refers creation in the divine image to "male *and* female" (v. 27). Perhaps aware of this, Paul reinforces the derivative sense of woman's creation by reference to the second creation story (Gen 2:21–23) where the woman is created from the man and for his sake (1 Cor 11:8–9). In the most perplexing statement in the whole sequence, Paul then draws a conclusion: "Therefore the woman should have authority on her head [*exousia epi tēs kephalēs*] because of the angels" (*dia tou angelous*) (v. 10). The "authority" in question has been seen as meaning the man's (the husband's) authority *over* the woman. But the Greek word *exousia* never has the passive sense of an authority *to* which one is subject; it always means the active authority, right, or capacity to do something (see AUTHORITY). The best explanation appears to be that, when praying and prophesying in the assembly the woman must not compromise her new right (*exousia*) in Christ to do so by appearing other than she is, that is, appearing through her hairstyle as a man. The latter would dangerously affront the angels, the guardians of the created order, who are participants, albeit unseen, in the worship taking place.

At this point, Paul resiles to some extent from the subordinationist argument. Focused more upon the new creation ("in the Lord") than the old, he points out the mutual dependence and indeed equality between man and woman, and concludes "All this is from God" (vv. 11–12). Feeling, perhaps, that his theological argument is slipping away, he makes a plea (vv. 13–15) for what is and is not appropriate according to "nature" (*physis*), meaning by this term little more than what is conventional according to the prevailing culture. Finally, almost it seems in desperation, he appeals simply to authority and what is customary in "the churches of God" (v. 16).

All in all, the passage is hardly Paul at his best. The tension it displays—the back and forth between the old creation and the new—is very much part of his wider struggle to lead the Corinthians to live out the freedom that they have gained in Christ in a discerning way. (It is significant that the echo of the Galatians 3:28 formula that appears in the instruction of 1 Corinthians 12:12–13 lacks the final "no longer…male and female" duality [see also Col 3:11].) What the instruction in 11:2–16 does at least show is that women in the Pauline communities had the right to take an active and fully equal role in the praying and prophesying that was the gift of the Spirit.

The latter is one consideration, among several, that has led interpreters to regard the passage later in the same letter, 1 Corinthians 14:33b–36, commanding that women be silent in the churches as an interpolation inserted clumsily into Paul's discussion of the gift of prophecy (14:1–40). The passage should not be attributed to Paul but associated with the similar restrictive observations about women in the post-Pauline letters.

Women as Coworkers

Paul's letters contain highly commendatory references to a number of women who exercise leadership in the churches and share his apostolic mission. In Philippians 4:2–3, he calls on an unnamed colleague ("true comrade") to help two women, Euodia and Syntyche, currently at odds with each other, to be of the same mind in the Lord. He adds that they "have labored side by side with me in the gospel" (*en tō euangeliō synēthlēsan moi*). Above all, rich evidence in this connection is found in the final chapter of Romans (16), notably in the unstinting commendation of Phoebe, deacon of the church at Cenchreae and likely bearer of the letter (vv. 1–2), and the women singled out for greeting—

Prisca (vv. 3–5a), Mary (v. 6), Junia (v. 7; see APOSTLE), and the sisters, Tryphaena and Tryphosa (v. 12). It is noteworthy that, in regard to the contribution of all these women, Paul employs the same language of "working" (*kopiaō*) that applies to his own apostolic service of the gospel (1 Cor 15:10).

Women in the Later Pauline Letters

A genuinely subordinationist view of women emerges in the "household codes" of Colossians (3:18—4:1) and Ephesians (5:21—6:9). Wives are urged "to be subject" to their husbands, "as is fitting in the Lord" (Col 3:18), while husbands are commanded to love their wives and not to be harsh to them (v. 19). Ephesians considerably expands the element of the code dealing with husband and wife, intensifying the subordination of the woman theologically by comparing the husband/wife relationship to that existing between Christ and the church, which is his body (5:22–32; see BODY; CHURCH). In both letters, a "love-patriarchalism" has replaced the basic equality seen in 1 Corinthians 7:3–5; 11:11–12.

In the Pastoral Letters, the household code that earlier regulated relationships between specific groups has become the model for the church itself, "the household of God" (1 Tim 3:15). Women are not to teach or have authority over men (1 Tim 2:11–15); any teaching role must be directed to other women only (Titus 2:3–5; see 1 Cor 14:33b–36). Their chief responsibilities are childbearing (1 Tim 2:15) and management of their households (5:14). In a considerable measure of conformity to the surrounding culture, the church will, in this way, appear before the world as a well-governed household.

APOSTLE; AUTHORITY; BLESSING; BODY; CHURCH; GLORY; IMAGE; "IN CHRIST"; SATAN

Reading

B. Byrne, *Paul and the Christian Woman* (Homebush, NSW: St Paul Publications, 1988); R. F. Collins, *PBC*, 1321–23; M. D. Hooker, "Authority on Her Head: An Examination of 1 Corinthians 11.10," *NTS* 10 (1964): 410–16, repr. *From Adam to Christ: Essays on Paul* (Eugene, OR: Wipf and Stock, 1990), 113–20; Horrell, *Introduction*, 161–69; C. S. Keener, *Paul, Women, and Wives: Marriage and Women's Ministry in the Letters of Paul*, 2nd ed. (Grand Rapids: Baker Academic, 2004); D. A. Lee, *The Ministry of Women in the New Testament: Reclaiming the Biblical Vision for Church Leadership* (Grand Rapids: Baker Academic, 2021), 97–135; A.-J. Levine, ed., *A Feminist Companion to Paul* (London and New York: T&T Clark, 2004); E. Schüssler Fiorenza, *In Memory of Her: A Feminist Theological Reconstruction of Christian Origins*, 2nd ed. (London: SCM, 1995), 205–41, 251–59, 266–70, 285–91; E. Schüssler Fiorenza, ed., *Searching the Scriptures, Volume Two: A Feminist Commentary* (New York: Crossroad, 1994), 153–345, 361–80; C. N. Westfall, *Paul and Gender: Reclaiming the Apostle's Vision for Men and Women in Christ* (Grand Rapids: Baker Academic, 2016).

"WORKS OF THE LAW" (*see* Law)

WORD

The Greek word *logos* has a wide range of meaning, enhanced in Paul's case by its LXX background as the translation of the Hebrew *dabar*, which can mean "thing" or "event" as well as "word," and which has, of course, a rich theological background in the sense of the "word of the Lord" (e.g., Gen 15:1; Deut 30:14; 1 Sam 3:1; 2 Sam 7:4; 1 Kgs 17:8; Ps 33:6; Isa 2:1; 38:4; 45:23; 55:11; Jer 1:4; Ezek 1:3).

"Word" (*logos*) in Pauline literature can have its very basic meaning of a vocal or written expression as distinct from action (2 Cor 10:10, 11; 11:6; 1 Thess 4:18; see also Col 3:17; 2 Thess 2:2; 2:15, 17; 3:14) but usually it refers to discourse that is qualified in some way, either positively (see Col 4:6) or negatively (see Eph 4:29; 5:6). In their difficult ministry, the apostles strive to commend themselves in every way by "truthful speech" (*en logō alētheias*) (2 Cor 6:7). When Paul gives thanks that the Corinthians "have been enriched in (Christ) in every way, in word [*en panti logō*] and knowledge of every kind" (1 Cor 1:5), the "word" in question presumably refers to the gift of prophecy communicated by the Spirit (see also 12:8: "word of wisdom" [*logos sophias*]; "word of knowledge" [*logos gnōseōs*]; 14:9, 19; 2 Cor 8:7; 1 Thess 4:15).

The "Word" of the Gospel

"Word" appears frequently in Paul in connection with both the content and mode of proclamation of the gospel. The gospel is "the word" (1 Thess 1:6; see also Col 4:3); "the word of the Lord" (1 Thess 1:8; see also 2 Thess 3:1); "the word of God," as distinct from "a purely human word" (1 Thess 2:13; see 1 Cor 14:36; 2 Cor 4:2; Phil 1:14; see also Col 1:25; 3:16); "the message of reconciliation" (2 Cor 5:19); "the word of life" (Phil 2:16); "the word of truth" (Col 1:5; Eph 1:13). It has a content—see 1 Cor 15:2: "with what form of words [*tini logō*] I preached the gospel to you"—but it is not "wordy" in the sense of relying on rhetorical persuasion. Paul gives thanks that the gospel came to the Thessalonians, "not in word only [*ouk...en logō monon*], but also in power and in the Holy Spirit and with full conviction" (1 Thess 1:5). In Corinth, Paul's proclamation of the gospel of the Crucified Messiah ("the word of the cross" [*ho logos...ho tou staurou*] [1 Cor 1:18; see Gal 3:1]) was not accompanied "with an excess of rhetoric [*kath' hyperochēn logou*] or wisdom" (2:1). Nor was his "message" (*logos*) and proclamation supported by "persuasive words of wisdom [*en peithois sophias logois*] but by demonstrations of the Spirit and power" (v. 4; see 1 Thess 1:5). Had he relied on the persuasive force of rhetoric the faith of the Corinthians would have rested on human wisdom rather than on the power of God (v. 5) (see WISDOM). Likewise, summarizing his ministry for the benefit of the community in Rome, Paul will not speak of anything except what Christ has accomplished through him "to win obedience from the Gentiles, by word and deed [*logō kai ergō*], by the power of signs and wonders, by the power of the Spirit of God" (Rom 15:18–19). The gospel, then, is more than a message. It wins a response of faith and conviction through being accompanied by "signs and wonders" wrought by the Spirit.

Although Paul almost always uses *logos* to express the content of the proclamation, in adducing the witness of Deuteronomy 30:12, 14 to righteousness by faith in Romans 10:6–8, he picks up the word *rhēma* from the Deuteronomic text to express that content (see also Eph 6:17). It is the "word of faith that we preach" (*to rhēma tēs pisteōs ho kēryssomen*) (Rom 10:8); faith come through hearing, and hearing comes "through the word (the preaching) about Christ" (*dia rhēmatos Christou*) (v. 17).

Scripture as God's Word

Introducing the issue of the current failure of Israel to believe in the gospel, Paul asserts, "It is not as if the word (promise) of God [*ho logos tou theou*] has fallen through" (Rom 9:6a). He cites the exact words of God's promise to Abraham (*epangelias...ho logos houtos*) (v. 9; see Gen 18:10, 14) to show that the patriarch would have a son (Isaac) as a fulfillment of a divine promise. In the loose quotation of Isa 28:22 in 9:28, *logos* seems to have the sense of the divine plan or purpose, which God is accomplishing—for the time being at least—by diminishing Israel. Occasionally, Paul introduces scriptural quotations as "the word" (Rom 13:9; 1 Cor 15:54; Gal 5:14; see also Rom 3:4).

Logos has the sense of a human promise in 2 Corinthians 1:18. It features as the "account" that everyone will have to render to God at the judgment (Rom 14:12). It has the commercial sense of an account of giving and receiving (*eis logon doseōs kai lēmpseōs*) in Philippians 4:15, which Paul "spiritualizes" in seeing the generosity of the Philippians as increasing "the credit" that accrues to their account (*eis logon hymōn*) in the divine reckoning (v. 17).

Logos in the Post-Pauline Letters

"Word" (*logos*) appears across all three Pastoral Letters in the formulation "Trustworthy is the saying" (*pistos ho logos*), which serves to introduce a creedal or hymnic formula of the faith on which instruction can be built (1 Tim 1:15; 3:1; 4:9; 2 Tim 2:11; Titus 3:8). Everything created by God is good and can be sanctified by prayer ("God's word" [1 Tim 4:5]). Although there is still mention of "gospel" (1 Tim 1:11; 2 Tim 1:8, 10, 11; 2:8), "word" now appears more frequently with reference to a body of truths into which the content of the gospel has been distilled for the purpose of preaching and teaching (1 Tim 5:17; 4:6; 6:3; 2 Tim 1:13; 2:9, 15; 4:2, 15; Titus 1:3, 9; 2:5,8; see also Gal 6:6). In 1 Timothy 4:12; 2 Thessalonians 2:17; and Titus 2:8, "word" simply means "speech."

GOSPEL; POWER; SCRIPTURE; SPIRIT; WISDOM

Reading

Bultmann, *Theology* 1:306–14; H. Ritt, *EDNT* 2:356–59; T. Wiarda, *Spirit and Word: Dual Testimony in Paul, John, and Luke* (London and New York: Bloomsbury/T&T Clark, 2017), 9–103; Wolter, *Paul*, 64–69; Wright, *PFG*, 1173–74 (on Rom 10:6–8).

WORLD

Although Paul can occasionally use the Greek term *kosmos* in reference to creation as a whole (Rom 1:20; 1 Cor 8:4; 14:10; Phil 2:15; see also Eph 1:4), predominantly in his letters the reference is to the world's human population. Thus his acknowledgment that the faith of the community in Rome is proclaimed "throughout the whole world" (Rom 1:8; see also Col 1:6) has reputation among human beings in view rather than geographical extent. "World" designating the whole of humanity in this neutral sense corresponds to "all the earth" (*gē*) and to "the ends of the world" (*oikoumenē*) in the quotation from (LXX) Psalm 18:5 in Romans 10:18b.

The Fallen World

For Paul, however, as also for the author of the Fourth Gospel, the human world is a fallen world, alienated from God since its very beginnings. Sin entered the world through "one man," the primal ancestor Adam, and in sin's train came death (Rom 5:12). Paul does not explicitly say, as does the author of the Fourth Gospel, that God "so loved the world that he gave up his only Son" to rescue it for eternal life (John 3:16). But the recall of the divine salvific action in Romans 5:6–10 makes clear that love for the world lay behind the costly mission and death of the Son, sent (Rom 8:3–4; Gal 4:4) and given up (Rom 8:32; see 4:25) by the Father. "God was in Christ reconciling the world to himself, not counting their trespasses against them" (2 Cor 5:19). Paul saw this reconciliation brought about through the costly death of the Son (Rom 5:10; see also Col 1:20, 22) as a unilateral outreach of divine grace to a universally (Jews as well as Gentiles) alienated human world (Rom 3:9; 5:12d; Gal 3:22). *Fundamentally*, God has reconciled the world in Christ. The task of Paul and his fellow apostles is to spread the good news (gospel) of this reconciliation to the world, urging human beings to align themselves with it by responding with faith (2 Cor 5:20; 6:1–2).

Outside the sphere of those who have responded in faith, the world remains untouched by the divine reconciliation, its values and way of thinking continuing to reflect alienation from God. Hence it is for the most part with a negative tone that *kosmos* appears in Paul (Rom 3:6, 19; 1 Cor 7:31; 11:32). In this sense *kosmos* overlaps with *aiōn* ("period of time," "age"), as especially in the phrase "this age" (1 Cor 1:20; 2:6, 8; 3:18; see also Eph 1:21; 2:2; Titus 2:12), that is, the present (evil [see Gal 1:4]) epoch, which, according to the apocalyptic worldview, was destined soon to be condemned at the judgment and replaced by a new creation of righteousness and life. For Paul, of course, the divine intervention in Christ had overthrown that simple linear "program." Those who have responded to the gospel and been reconciled to God have, through faith and baptism, become part of the new creation in Christ (2 Cor 5:17; Gal 6:15). Like Paul (Gal 6:14), they have become "crucified to the world" and "the world to them" (see Rom 6:6; Gal 2:19). They are, however, in an "overlap of the ages" situation. While already part of the new creation, as attested by Spirit (Rom

8:23), bodily they are still in the present world and have to deal with it. But radically they have been set apart from the world not yet won to the gospel and must not conform to its values (Rom 12:2).

Relating to the World

In many respects, the issue of how to relate to the unredeemed world in this sense runs through 1 Corinthians. The body of the letter begins with a remonstration on Paul's part against factions in the community that appear to have arisen around allegiances to preferred teachers, one at least or some of whom are presenting the faith as an eloquent wisdom of the world rather than the gospel of the Crucified as proclaimed by Paul (1:17–25) (see WISDOM). In an earlier letter, Paul had instructed the Corinthians not to associate with sexually immoral persons (5:9). He now needs to correct their understanding. He did not mean that they were not to associate with the immoral of this world in general, that is, with the general population in its present unconverted state. That would have meant going out of the world entirely, which is impossible (v. 10). What he meant was that they were not to continue to associate with *brothers or sisters* who had begun to live immoral lives (v. 11), as in the particular case in question (5:1). A further source of concern for Paul is that some are taking cases against fellow believers before courts outside the community (6:1). He protests, "If the world is to be judged by you, are you incompetent to try trivial cases?" (v. 2). A list of malefactors (vv. 9–10) in the world to which the Corinthians once belonged (see also Eph 2:2, 12) brings out the stark distinction between what they then were and what they are now: "washed, sanctified, justified in the name of the Lord Jesus Christ and in the Spirit of our God" (v. 11).

The hesitations Paul expresses (7:25–35) about encouraging young believers to marry stems from an eschatological sense that the present world, to which marriage belongs, is soon to pass away (vv. 29a, 31b). Those who have wives should live as though they had none (v. 29b); those who have to deal with the world (should live) as not having to deal with it (v. 31a). Here the problem is not so much the evil of the world, but the fact that it represents a setup (the present age) destined very soon to pass away. The present world has to be dealt with and, when hostile, responded to with graciousness (1 Cor 4:13; 2 Cor 1:12; see also Rom 12:14–21). It remains the field for mission (Phil 2:15–16, taking *epechontes* as "holding out" [so NIV] rather than "holding fast to," as the NRSV), its ultimate reconciliation continuing to be a matter of hope (Rom 11:12, 15).

Inheriting the World

In Romans 4:13, Paul insists that the promise God made to Abraham and to his descendants that he should "inherit the earth"—literally, "be heir of the world" (*to klēronomon auton einai kosmou*)—was given on the basis not of practice of the law but of faith. "World" here has an entirely positive sense, referring initially to the land of Canaan, that God promised to Abraham (Gen 12:7; 13:15; 15:18; 17:8), but then extended in the Jewish postbiblical tradition, first to embrace the entire world and ultimately, in an eschatological sense, "the world to come," that is, all the blessings of salvation (see PROMISE).

The Elemental Spirits of the World (*ta stoicheia tou kosmou*)

The meaning of the phrase *ta stoicheia tou kosmou*, appearing in Galatians 4:3, 9 and Colossians 2:8, 20 is much disputed. The term *stoicheion* basically means a component part or element of something, hence rudimentary knowledge. In both Galatians and Colossians, however, the context suggests subjection to entities of a spiritual nature, possibly to the constituent elements of the universe (earth, fire, air, water) held to be under the control of spiritual powers and hence determinative of the fate of human beings. In Galatians, Paul seems to identify Jewish subjection under the angels who guarded the law (4:3; see 3:19d, 23) with the former "enslavement" of the Galatian Gentiles to such entities, who were "not gods" (4:8–9). The teaching against which the letter to the Colossians is directed appears to view entities of a similar nature as needing to be placated by various observances, thereby challenging the all-sufficiency of the saving work of Christ (2:8–9, 16–19).

ABRAHAM; ADAM; CREATION; CROSS; ESCHATOLOGY; GOD; LAW; RECONCILIATION; SIN

Reading

E. Adams, *Constructing the World: A Study in Paul's Cosmological Language* (Edinburgh: T&T Clark, 2000); H. Balz, *EDNT* 2:309–13; Bultmann, *Theology* 1:254–59; Byrne, *PES*, 173–78; 225–31; *Romans*, 152, 157–58; *"Sons of God,"* 174–78; Lincoln, "Colossians," 565–67; J. Painter, *DPL*, 979–82.

WRATH

In the apocalyptic cast of Paul's theology, the threat of the looming divine wrath (*orgē*) is the continuing backdrop to his proclamation of the gospel. The salvation offered in the gospel is salvation from the wrath destined to be unleashed on a sinful world following the great judgment. This is why Paul's thematic announcement of the gospel in Romans as "the power of God leading to salvation for all who have faith because in it a righteousness of God is revealed" (1:16–17) is followed immediately and indeed grounded by the statement that "the wrath of God is revealed from heaven against all human impiety and wickedness" (v. 18). It is the pressing prospect of the wrath that underwrites the urgency of Paul's worldwide mission and the heavy responsibility that it presses on him (Rom 1:14; 15:15–21; 1 Cor 9:16; 2 Cor 6:1–10). The essential connection between wrath and gospel explains why references to the divine wrath in Paul, at least as regards the undisputed letters, are confined to Romans, which is basically an exposition of the gospel, and 1 Thessalonians, which is a recollection of Paul's initial evangelization of the community in Thessalonica and an encouragement to continue living by the hope it holds out.

The Wrath to Come

For the most part, Paul portrays the wrath as something yet to come. For the present God is providing a space of time—a time of divine "patience" (*anochē* [Rom 2:4; 3:26])—during which, as proclaimed in the gospel, the mission of the Son has made available to believers redemption from sin and the righteousness ("righteousness of God" [Rom 1:17; 3:21, 22; 10:3; 2 Cor 5:21; Phil 3:9]) required for salvation from the wrath (Rom 5:9; 1 Thess 1:10; 5:9) that is soon to be unleashed on evildoers (Rom 2:5, 8; 12:19; see Col 3:6).

Present Manifestation of the Wrath

In Romans 1:18–31, however, Paul speaks of the *present* revelation "from heaven" of God's wrath in response to the—inexcusable (vv. 19–20)—human failure to acknowledge (literally, "glorify") and thank the Creator, lapsing instead into idolatry (vv. 21–23, 25, 28a). The actual revelation of the wrath is to be seen in the various kinds of moral degradation, listed in three "waves" of increasing severity (vv. 24b, 26b–27, 28c–31), into which "God gave them up" (vv. 24a, 26a, 28b) in response.

It is generally held that the moral degradation that Paul portrays here as a revelation of the divine wrath is that which Jews believed to be characteristic of the Gentile world. However, establishing the alienation of the Gentile world from God is not the main intent of the passage; within a Jewish frame of discourse it is simply presumed. In Romans 2:1–11, Paul springs a trap on what would appear to be a fictive Jewish dialogue partner, inveighing against the complacency that would see possession of the law as insurance against experiencing the wrath. Hence the severe warnings against the "hardness of heart" that leads to the "storing up" (*thēsaurizeis*) against oneself of "the wrath on the day of wrath" (v. 5), for "wrath and fury [*thymos*]" await "those who disobey the truth" (v. 8), whether Jew or Gentile (v. 9). The divine wrath already manifest in the Gentile world may be for Jews a threat rather than a reality. Nonetheless, failure to practice rather than merely possess the law (2:12–13, 17–29) places Jews in the same situation, "under sin" (3:9), as Gentiles (see also Eph 2:3). Hence the universal need for a divine intervention (3:21–26) if exposure to the wrath is to be averted.

Dealing with the theological issue thrown up by the ongoing failure of Israel to respond positively to the gospel (Romans 9—11), Paul speaks (9:22) of "vessels of wrath, ripe for destruction" (*skeuē orgēs*), which, God, "desiring to show his wrath and his power," "has endured with much patience" (*makrothymia*). The sentence is incomplete and cryptic but the parallel with the subsequent mention (v. 23) of "vessels of mercy," clearly identifiable as believers (vv. 24–26), requires identifying the "vessels of wrath" with Israelites resistant to the gospel. It is to be noted, however, that the "vessels of wrath" so identified, although "ripe for destruction" (*katērtismena eis apōleian*), are not yet consigned to it. Moreover, the parallel with the situation of Pharaoh as described earlier (9:17–18) suggests that, as indicated earlier (1:24a, 26a, 28b), God has had a hand in the situation. Israel's current refusal to respond to the gospel represents an exercise of both divine sovereignty and human freedom that Paul's theology, although recognizing its difficulty (9:19–21), could hold together. Moreover, as Paul will later maintain, the current refusal of Israel (destined eventually to be reversed [11:25–27]), has, in the inscrutable wisdom of God (11:33–36), led to the "enrichment" (through the gospel) of the Gentiles (11:11c–12, 15)—just as the hardening of Pharaoh's heart led (through the exodus) to the wider proclamation of God's power (9:17). Hence Israel's current involvement in the divine wrath, however it is to be conceived in this obscure passage, will have, in Paul's eyes, an ultimately salvific outcome.

Another possible reference to the divine wrath presently lying on Jews appears in the (possibly not original) paragraph in 1 Thessalonians 2:14–16, where Paul compares the hostility the Thessalonians have had to endure from their fellow citizens with what the churches in Judea have experienced from fellow Jews. The comparison concludes with the remark, "But the wrath has come on them at last" (*ephthasen de ep'autous hē orgē eis telos* [v. 16c]). It is not entirely clear, however, whether the verb *ephthasen* has the sense of "draw near," in which case the wrath would be an imminent threat rather than an actuality, or whether the meaning is "overtaken," in which case the wrath would be presently manifest in some form.

The Wrath: Willed by God?

The sense of divine involvement in the infliction of the wrath that emerges from Romans 1:18–32 and 9:22 (see also Rom 3:5) does seem to exclude the proposal that Paul understands the wrath as something of an impersonal consequence of sin more or less detached from God (C. H. Dodd) and hence less problematic for contemporary theological sensibility. Likewise, when Paul remarks that "the law works wrath [*orgēn katergazetai*]; where there is no law there is no transgression" (Rom 4:15), he appears to be saying that the law specifies sin as a conscious infringement of the divine will and hence as apt to bring about wrath as a willed rather than automatic divine reaction. That said, it is important to remain aware that wrath serves as backdrop to the gospel that proclaims the sending of the Son to effect the costly rescue of human beings from the plight in which their sin had placed them. The divine wrath in Paul should never be considered aside from that overwhelmingly gracious invasion of divine love (see Rom 5:20–21). As Paul assures the Thessalonians, "God has not destined us for wrath but for obtaining salvation through our Lord Jesus Christ" (1 Thess 5:9).

Wrath in Other Contexts

In Paul's warning about paying due deference to civil authorities in Romans 13:1–17, although the authority is described as God's minister (vv. 4a, 4d), the "wrath" executed on wrongdoers (vv. 4e, 5b) most likely refers to civic rather than eschatological punishment. Elsewhere, "wrath" occurs in Pauline literature in warnings about behavior that believers must at all costs set aside (Eph 4:31; Col 3:8), although in regard to human anger *thymos* rather than *orgē* is more usual (2 Cor 12:20; Gal 5:20).

APOCALYPTIC; GOSPEL; IDOLATRY; JUDGE, LAST JUDGMENT; LAW; PROPITIATION, EXPIATION; RIGHTEOUSNESS; SALVATION; SIN

Reading

G. L. Borchert, *DPL*, 991–93; Byrne, *PES*, 14–16, 77–80, 97–102, 110–12, 133–35, 231–33; *Romans*, 62–87, 164–72, 300–308; C. E. B. Cranfield, *The Epistle to the Romans: I–VIII* (Edinburgh: T&T Clark, 1957), 106–11; C. H. Dodd, *The Epistle of Paul to the Romans* (London: Hodder & Stoughton, 1932; repr. Fontana, 1959), 46–50; Dunn, *Romans 1–8*, 54–55, 84–85; *Theology*, 41–42; Moo, *Romans*, 99–102, 134–39, 234–36, 276–77, 606–9; W. Pesch, *EDNT* 2:529–30; Westerholm, *Justification*, 4–11.

Z

ZEAL, JEALOUSY

The word group *zēloō*, *zēlos*, *zēlōtēs* expresses an intensity of feeling and commitment that has a wide range of application in Paul, from the expression of commendable religious zeal to the vice of jealousy.

Zeal for God

Recalling his persecuting activity before coming to faith in Christ, Paul describes himself as "zealous without equal" (*perissoterōs zēlōtēs*) among his contemporaries for the traditions of his ancestors (Gal 1:14). He clearly belonged to a strain of Second Temple Judaism that took with intense seriousness the claim of Israel's God to be a jealous God, utterly intolerant of any turning aside on Israel's part to the worship of alien deities (Exod 20:5; 34:14; Deut 4:24; 5:9; 6:15) and which saw itself as continuing the line of exceedingly zealous—and violent—biblical figures such as Phineas (Num 25:6–13) and the prophet Elijah (see 1 Kgs 18:17–40; 19:10). It was this zeal that led him to persecute with prophetic violence the early community of believers: "as to zeal [*kata zēlos*], a persecutor of the church" (Phil 3:6a; see 1 Cor 15:9b; Gal 1:13). Paul acknowledges the continuance of zeal for God among his Jewish contemporaries (*zēlon theou echousin*) but asserts that it is "without knowledge" (*ou kat'epignōsin*) because, clinging to its own righteousness, it has failed to recognize and submit to the righteousness of God revealed, as he had himself discovered, in the Crucified Christ (Rom 10:2–3; see 9:31–33).

Paul attributes to himself something of a prophetic "jealousy" when he begs the Corinthians to put up with a little foolishness on his behalf (2 Cor 11:1). The reason is that, having betrothed them as a pure virgin to one man, namely, Christ, he is "jealous" for them "with God's own jealousy" (*zēlō gar hymas theou zēlō*) (v. 2).

Less sympathetically, Paul plays on

the multiple meanings of the verb *zēloō* to portray the intrusive teachers in Galatia as "courting you to no good purpose" (*zēlousin hymas ou kalōs*) (Gal 4:17a). They want to make the Galatians feel excluded, presumably through separation from table fellowship (see 2:11–14), in order that "you (the Galatians) may court them" (*hina autous zēloute*) (v. 17b). Paul concedes that it is a good thing to be courted in a good cause (*kalon... zēlousthai en kalō*) and he has no objection in principle to other Christian teachers doing so when he is absent (v. 18), but his play on the verb *zēloō* conveys his unhappiness when those such as the intrusive teachers with their pretended zeal for God do so for no good purpose.

Commendable Eagerness

In the matter of gifts of the Spirit (1 Cor 12–14), Paul encourages the community to "be eager for (*zēloute*) the higher gifts" (12:31). He gives preference to prophecy (14:1, 39), for it is one of those that build up the church (see v. 12). In the midst of his afflictions in Macedonia Paul found comfort on learning from Titus about the Corinthians' "zeal" on his behalf (*to hymōn zēlon hyper emou*) (2 Cor 7:7). The hurt that they had suffered as a result of Paul's hard letter (see v. 8) has had a salutary effect, leading, among other things, to repentance and their zeal (*zēlon*) for him (v. 11). Their eagerness (*to hymōn zēlos*) to contribute to the collection for the saints has stirred up the Macedonian communities to emulation (9:2).

Jealousy and Strife

In a totally negative usage, Paul deplores the existence of "jealousy" (*zēlos*) and "quarreling" (*eris*) in the Corinthian community (1 Cor 3:3; see also Rom 13:13; 2 Cor 12:20); both are manifestations ("works") of the flesh (Gal 5:20), whereas one of the qualities of love (*agapē*) is that it is not jealous (*ou zēloi*) (1 Cor 13:4).

FLESH; GIFT(S) OF THE SPIRIT; IDOLATRY; JEW, JUDAISM; PROPHECY

Reading

Dunn, *Theology*, 350–54; R. B. Hays, *NIB* 11:295 (on Gal 4:17–18); A. B. Luter Jr., *DPL*, 461–63; H. Merkel, *EDNT* 2:101; D. C. Ortlund, *Zeal Without Knowledge: The Concept of Zeal in Romans 10, Galatians 1, and Philippians 3* (London: T&T Clark, 2012); W. Popkes, *EDNT* 2:100–101; Schnelle, *Apostle Paul*, 64–69; Wolter, *Paul*, 15–23.

SELECT INDEX OF PAULINE TEXTS DISCUSSED UNDER PARTICULAR TOPICS

(Topic entries that have more than one word are referred to by the initial word only.)

1 Corinthians

2 Corinthians

Galatians

INDEX OF AUTHORS